ITALIAN RENAISSANCE MAIOLICA

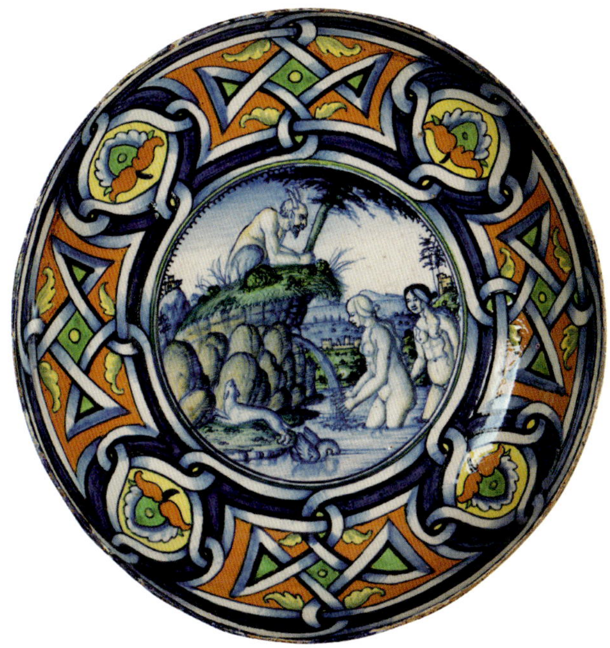

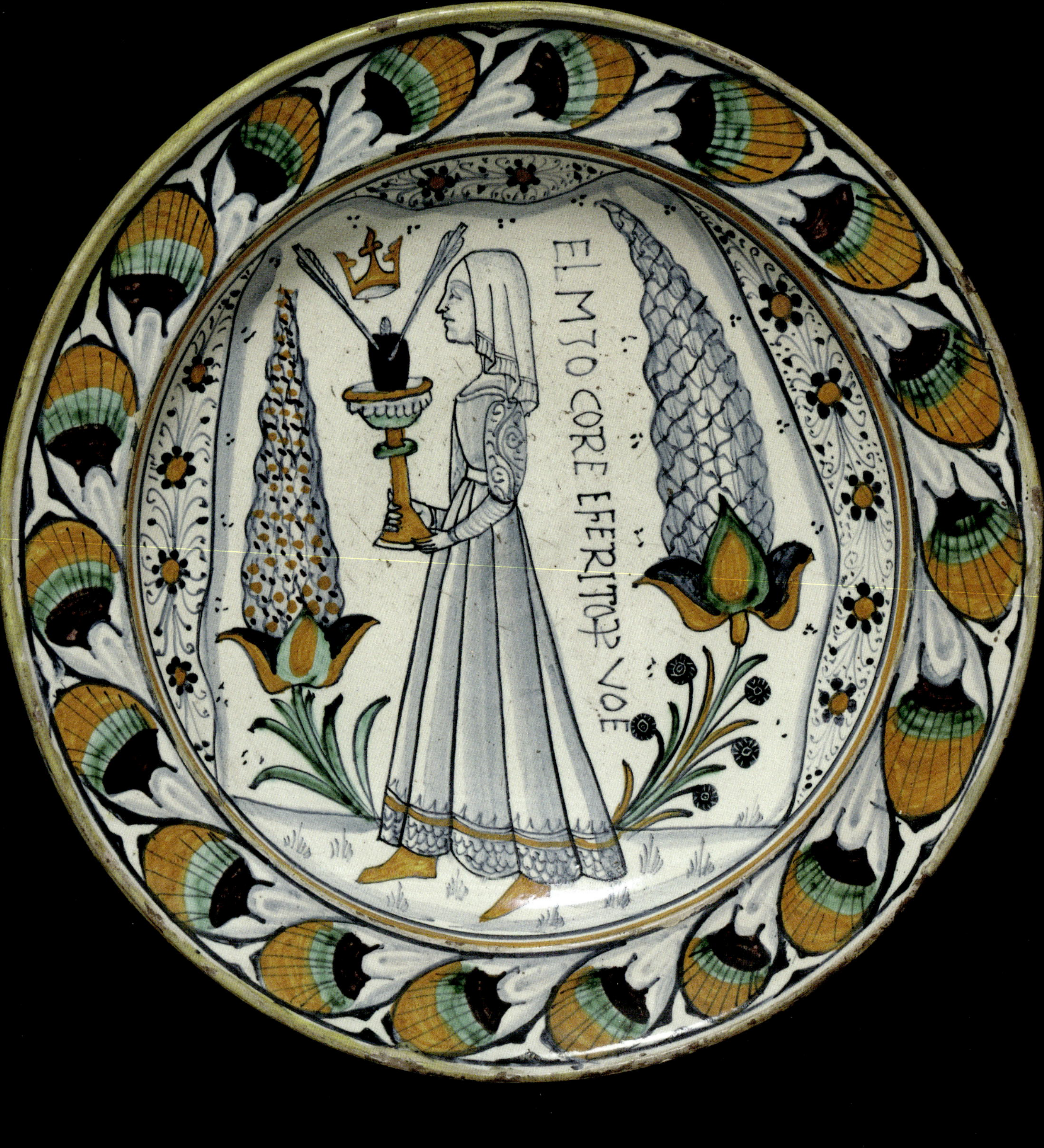
EL MIO CORE E FERITO P VOE

ITALIAN RENAISSANCE MAIOLICA

ELISA P. SANI

with a preface by J.V.G. Mallet and
contributions from Reino Liefkes

V&A Publishing

First published by V&A Publishing, 2012
Victoria and Albert Museum
South Kensington
London SW7 2RL
www.vandabooks.com

Distributed in North America by Harry N. Abrams Inc., New York

Hardback edition
ISBN 978 1 85177 706 8

Library of Congress Control Number 2012936007

10 9 8 7 6 5 4 3 2 1
2016 2015 2014 2013 2012

A catalogue record for this book is available from the British Library.

Front Jacket illustration: Bowl with bust of young woman, V&A: 8923–1863 (pl.172).
Spine and frontispiece illustration: Dish with woman holding cup with a pierced heart, V&A: 2558–1856 (pl.164).
Back jacket illustration: Inkstand with man playing an organ, Patanazzi family workshop, V&A: 8400–1863 (pl.180).
Back jacket flap illustration: Roundel with the Three Graces, Workshop of Maestro Giorgio, V&A: 175–1885 (pl.116).
Half title page: Bowl with satyr looking at nymphs bathing, V&A: 36–1989 (pl.108)

Section openers: pp.14–15 *The Three Books of the Potter's Art*, Cipriano Piccolpasso, fol. 38
pp.38–9 *The Three Books of the Potter's Art*, Cipriano Piccolpasso, fol. 69
pp.112–3 *The Three Books of the Potter's Art*, Cipriano Piccolpasso, fol.13

Designer: Heather Bowen
Copy-editor and indexer: Perilla Kinchin

New photography by Sara Hodges, V&A Photographic Studio
Printed in Hong Kong

V&A Publishing

Supporting the world's leading museum of art and design, the Victoria and Albert Museum, London

Acknowledgements

Writing a book on maiolica based on the collection of the Victoria and Albert Museum is a dream come true if you are passionate about the subject. I started work on the book while an Assistant Curator in the V&A Ceramics section and I would like to heartily thank my colleagues there: Reino Liefkes, Judith Crouch, Hilary Young, Sonia Solicari (now at the Guildhall Art Gallery) and Terry Bloxham. Former V&A Director Mark Jones, Paul Williamson and Tessa Murdoch all encouraged me to take up this enterprise. Liz Miller and Reino Liefkes have been of seminal help to the shaping of the book.

Special thanks are due to Frances Ambler, Clare Davis and Mark Eastment in V&A Publishing for being extremely competent and pleasant colleagues through the hazardous stages of book production. I am also grateful to Richard Davis and Sara Hodges from the V&A Photo studio for the dazzling new photography in the book. Seeing key pieces from the museum skilfully restored was particularly rewarding and I would like to thank Victoria Oakley, Fiona Jordan and Hanneke Raemekers for their wonderful work.

Since I started working in the field of maiolica studies I have been privileged to have the advice and friendship of John Mallet and Timothy Wilson, both of who I would like to thank for having read chapters of the book and making invaluable suggestions.
I am also grateful to many colleagues in Italy, among them Carmen Ravanelli Guidotti, Giulio Busti, Mario Luccarelli, Marino Marini, Claudio Paolinelli, Marco Spallanzani and Richard Goldthwaithe. My sincere thanks go to John Mallet and Reino Liefkes for their wonderful contributions to the book. Lastly, I would like to thank my husband Mark Nicholson for being so supportive in many ways, and my family in Perugia.

The book is dedicated to the memory of Bernard Rackham.

THE BOOK HAS BEEN GENEROUSLY SUPPORTED BY THE CERAMICA-STIFTUNG BASEL

Contents

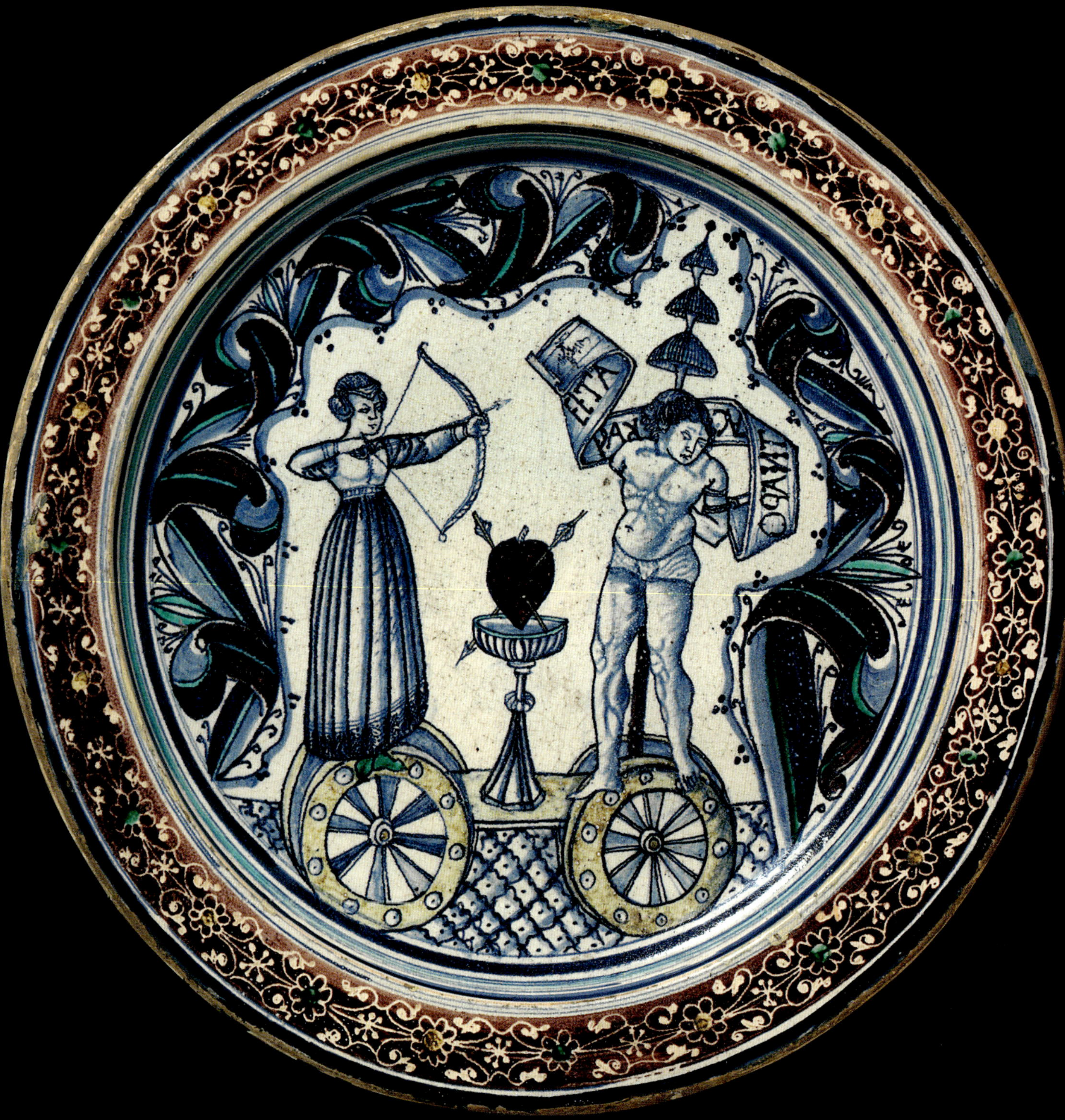

The Formation of the V&A's Maiolica Collection

J.V.G. MALLET

1 Dish with Allegory of Love
Inscribed 'O QUANTA CRUDELTÀ'
('Oh what cruelty')
Probably Deruta, c.1475
Diam: 41.5 cm
Bernal Collection V&A: 1806–1855

How did the Victoria and Albert Museum become the best place in the world for the enjoyment and study of fifteenth- and sixteenth-century Italian maiolica? There are older collections, such as those in the Bargello at Florence or the Herzog Anton Ulrich-Museum in Brunswick; there are collections, like that of the Metropolitan Museum in New York, with astonishing masterpieces; the maiolica at the Louvre and the British Museum was assembled at much the same time as the V&A's, largely in the mid-nineteenth century, and both of these, in point of quality, can hold their own with the collection at South Kensington. But for sheer depth and completeness none of these great collections can quite compare with that of the V&A.

Sir Henry Cole (1808–82), a key figure in the founding of what is now the Victoria and Albert Museum, held wide responsibilities in heading the Department of Science and Art, of which the nascent museum formed only a sub-section. Accordingly in 1853 he appointed a young curator of art, John Charles Robinson (1834–1913), to oversee the Museum. The objectives of that Museum were to instil the principles of good taste into pupils at the Government's School of Design (now the Royal College of Art) and the manufacturers for whom it was hoped that those pupils would work. Instruction in taste was also to be dispensed to the public at large.

Robinson's experience of teaching at Hanley School of Design in the Staffordshire Potteries must have seemed an excellent qualification for running a museum on these didactic lines, but his earlier training as an artist in Paris, where he familiarized himself with the museums and collections, was an even more formative experience for him. In particular the Musée de Cluny, a treasure-house of medieval and Renaissance sculpture and applied arts, seems to have influenced his view of how the South Kensington Museum should develop. It is curious that by the time Robinson fell out with Cole and left the Museum in 1867, the senior man had become more open to buying works for their aesthetic quality, not just their instructiveness. Cole had noticed that beauty was more of a draw to his public than instruction.

2 Lustred dish with horsemen in armour
Deruta, c.1510
Diam: 38 cm
Soulages Collection V&A: 7682–1861

In 1857, when the collections formed at Marlborough House were transferred to temporary buildings at South Kensington, the applied arts and sculpture with which Robinson was concerned shared the new spaces with natural products and machinery. However Italian maiolica was from the first seen as one of the categories of art most desirable for the Museum not just on grounds of its colourful attractiveness, but also as a potential design resource for manufacturers. We tend to think of the mid-nineteenth century as the heyday of the Gothic Revival in architecture but, along with classical and Tudor revivals, the older parts of the Museum's own building bear witness to an Italian Renaissance revival in the historicizing age that gave birth to the V&A's maiolica collection.

The first great opportunity for Cole and Robinson to acquire maiolica came in 1855 when the collection of Ralph Bernal was auctioned in London. Though Government funding was comparatively generous, on this occasion Robinson acted under instructions to allow first pick to Franks of the British Museum. Nevertheless the South Kensington Museum bought for £120 the most expensive piece of maiolica in the sale, a Cafaggiolo dish showing a maiolica painter at work watched by well-dressed clients, optimistically catalogued by Christie's as Raphael painting his mistress, *La Fornarina* (pl. 8). Until the end of the nineteenth century Victorian taste in maiolica leaned heavily towards the narrative or *istoriato* wares of the sixteenth century, but Robinson was ahead of his time in also acquiring from the Bernal sale some magnificent examples of fifteenth-century ware (pl. 1).

The collection of Jules Soulages of Toulouse, which was shipped to Marlborough House with a view to purchase in 1856, contained a considerable quantity of first-rate maiolica, notably lustred Deruta dishes (pl. 2), but hopes of purchase with Government funds were at first disappointed, and Cole resorted to buying by instalment.

Robinson continued to acquire important maiolica for the Museum, both while travelling in continental Europe, and at home. The extent and importance of private collections in Great Britain, which included remarkable riches of maiolica, were demonstrated by the great Loan Exhibition assembled by Robinson and shown in 1862 in the Museum's South Court, and it was Robinson who wrote the catalogue. However relations between Cole and Robinson soured, and in 1863 the latter was in effect demoted to 'Art Referee' with diminished powers. In 1867, Robinson left.

The state of the collection at this time can be gauged from the catalogue published in 1871 by Charles Edward Drury Fortnum (1820–99) who, on an unpaid, informal basis, did much to make good the loss of Robinson's expertise. From then onwards the rate of acquisition slowed. Fortnum may have lacked Robinson's flair, but his earlier experience of collecting beetles in South Australia had left him with a taxonomic mindset that he applied to the enrichment of the Museum's maiolica collection. His influence on the growth of the collection tended to reinforce an already existing drive towards the complete representation of each category of ware.

The year 1884 presented two unrepeatable opportunities for acquisition: the auction in Rome of the more important part of the great collection formed by Alessandro Castellani of Rome and Naples, and the auction in London by Christie's of the collection owned by the Fountaine family of Narford Hall in Norfolk. Rising prices and tight Treasury control over funds somewhat limited what Fortnum and the Museum's 'Director of Art', were able to buy in Rome, whereas even with the aid of a syndicate of private well-wishers of our great museums, South Kensington failed to purchase more than two pieces of maiolica at the Fountaine sale (pl. 3); however a famous Gubbio-lustred roundel was bought soon afterwards from a dealer (pl. 116).

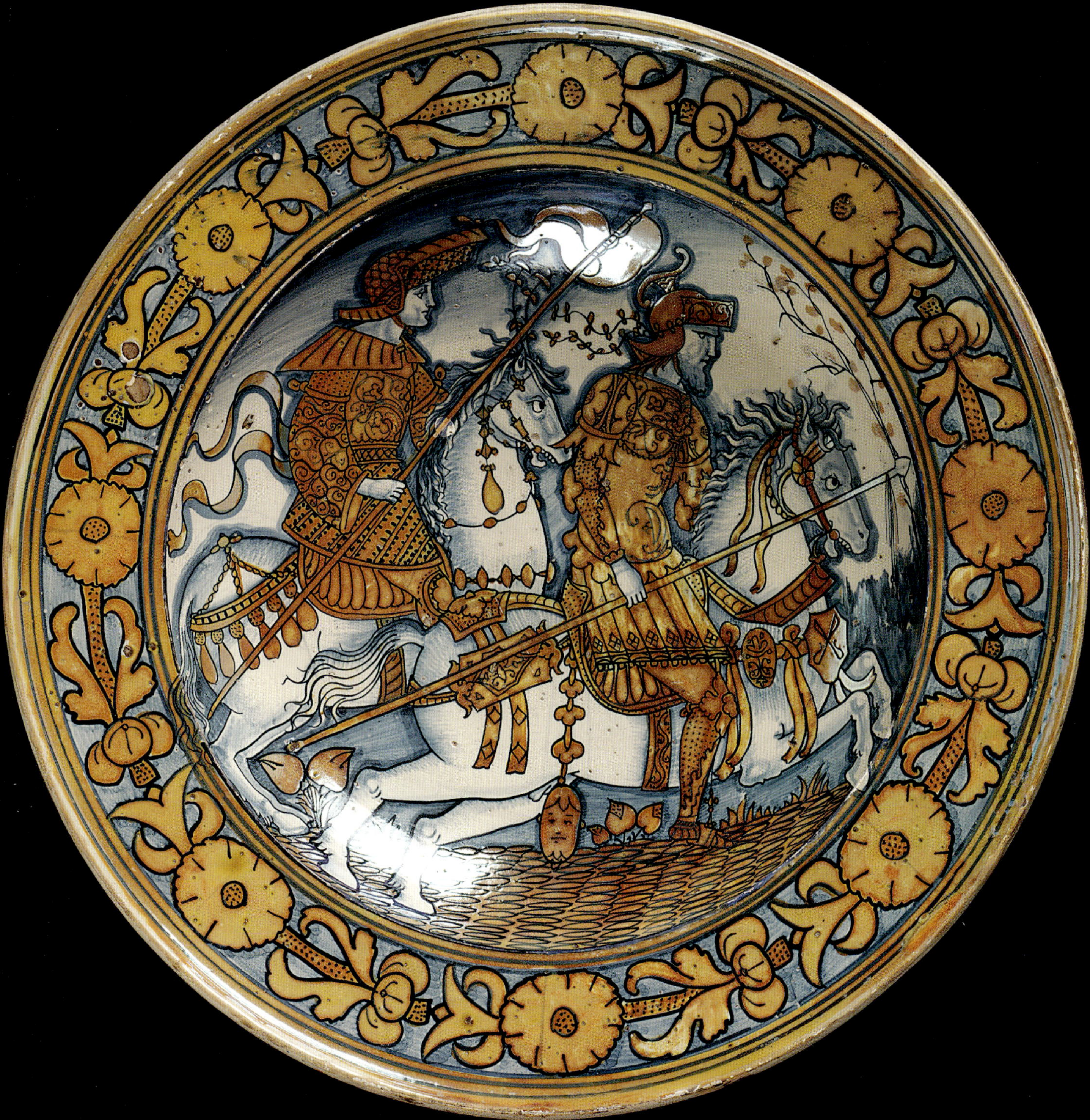

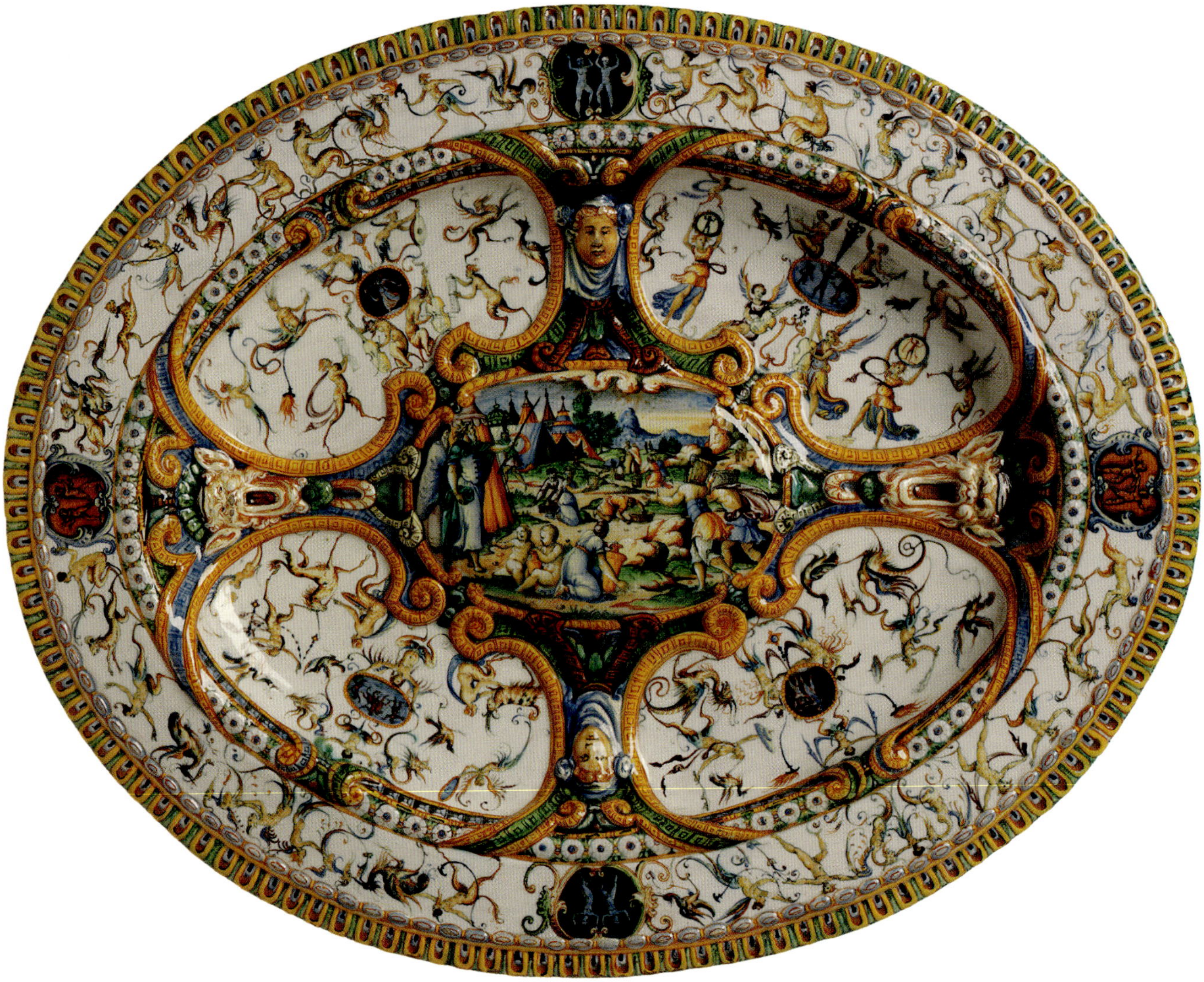

3 Oval dish with the Gathering of the Manna and grotesque ornament on a white ground
Urbino, probably Fontana Workshops, c.1560–70
L: 67 cm
Fountaine Collection V&A: 78–1885

As luck would have it many pieces of maiolica that the Museum might have liked to purchase at the Fountaine sale were included in what was surely the greatest of all the bequests the Museum ever received: that of George Salting, in 1910. Salting's 243 pieces of maiolica, nearly all of the highest quality and many of the *istoriato* category (pl. 4), transformed the collection in ways that become apparent when one compares Fortnum's catalogue of 1871 with the one published in 1940 by Bernard Rackham (1876–1964).

Apart from the essentially nineteenth-century character of the influx from Salting's bequest, through the influence of such men as the painters Henry Wallis (1830–1916) and Charles Fairfax Murray (1849–1919) the Museum had been adding to its holdings of fifteenth-century wares, including such things as the so-called 'oak-leaf jars' of the Florentine region to which the great German museum director, Wilhelm Bode, was also directing attention.

Appointed in 1898, Rackham was one of the first generation of specialist curators assigned to materials-based departments, in his case the Department of Ceramics

4 Plate with The Rape of Ganymede
Duchy of Urbino, c.1525
Diam: 22 cm
George Salting Bequest V&A: C.2077–1910

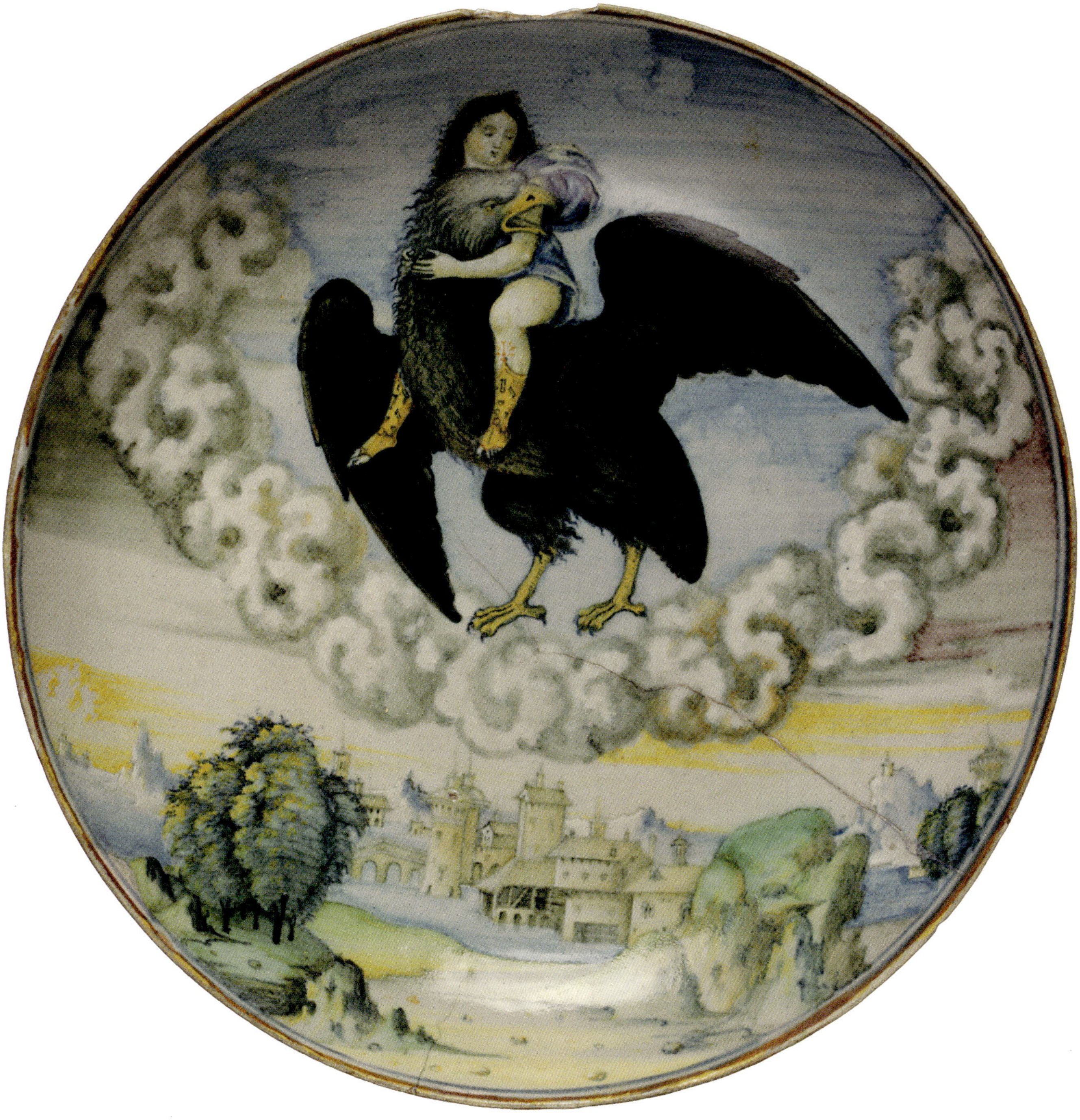

and Glass, of which he served as keeper from 1914 to 1938. Maiolica was not the only ceramic subject Rackham mastered but he and Gaetano Ballardini of Faenza were the internationally acknowledged experts on it. Rackham's *Guide to Italian Maiolica* of 1933, and his *Catalogue* of 1940 sum up advances in knowledge but, after the accession of the Salting maiolica, additions were comparatively modest, with the exception of a few outstanding pieces he was able to buy from the Trust Fund set up with money from the Victorian dealer, John Webb (pl. 5). High prices and competition from across the Atlantic prevented Rackham from buying as many things he might have wished. However excavated examples of archaic wares, especially those from Orvieto, were acquired, and the holdings of relatively cheap seventeenth- and eighteenth-century wares were increased by gift and purchase.

5 Devotional panel with the Annunciation to the Virgin Mary
Probably Pesaro, c.1490
H: 46 cm, W: 46 cm
V&A: C.623–1925
Sir Francis and Wyndham Cook Collections, bought in 1925 with funds from the John Webb Trust by Rackham, who had earlier catalogued the Cooks' maiolica.

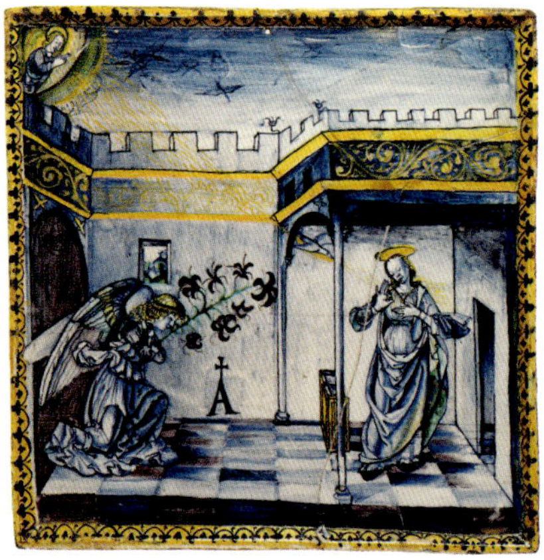

When the collections returned from safe storage at the end of the Second World War, a new generation of curators took over. For a time Renaissance maiolica was, in real terms, cheaper than it had been since early Victorian times, but other priorities for purchase seemed more pressing if the overall representativeness of the collection of ceramics was to be enhanced. Until the advent of Trustees in 1982 purchases were decided between a keeper and the Museum's director without waiting on the decision of a board, and the V&A's consequent speed of decision and payment often gave it, with dealers, an edge over the British Museum or foreign competitors. Robert Charleston, the keeper under whom I served happily from 1963 to 1976, was readily persuaded to propose for purchase a documentary *istoriato* dish from Pesaro after which the 'Zenobia Painter' has been named (pl. 7), as well as a dish that Sir Timothy Clifford and I published as having been painted after a drawing by Battista Franco (pl. 105).

Between 1976 and 1989 I was myself Keeper of Ceramics, the last, as it turned out, to hold that proud title. I did my best, while trying to buy masterpieces like a 1503 dish with a satyr spying on two bathing women (pl. 108), also to enhance the department's taxonomic completeness. However much overlaid by thematic and other arrangements, it is in the completeness of whole series of ware that the V&A's collection is supreme. It is to be hoped that the present publication will introduce a new public to the richness and quality of the Museum's holdings of Italian maiolica.

6 Reverse of pl.7
Inscribed 'Zenobia subjugated before the Emperor Aurelian with her sons. Made in Pesaro, 1552'

7 Dish with Queen Zenobia led captive before the Emperor Aurelian
'The Zenobia Painter'
Pesaro, 1552
Diam: 42.6 cm
V&A: C.47–1970
Work ascribed to this painter has been named after this dish.

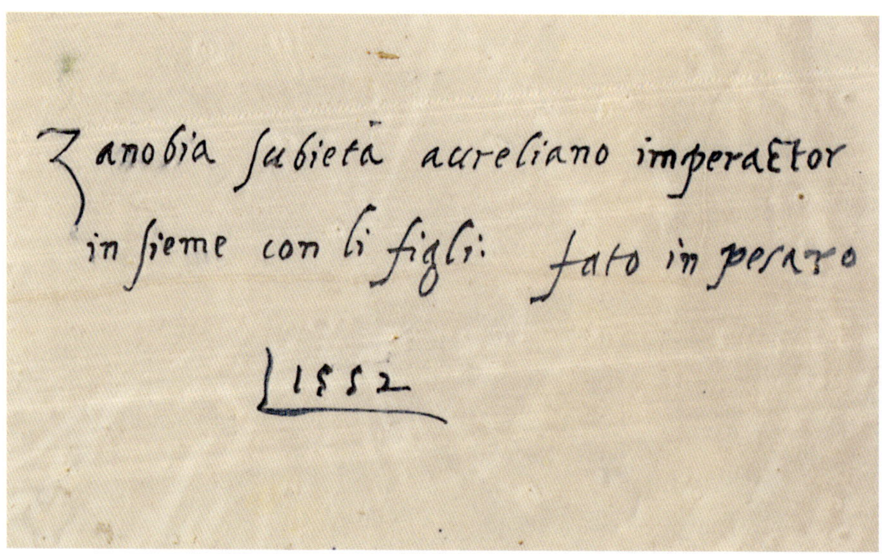

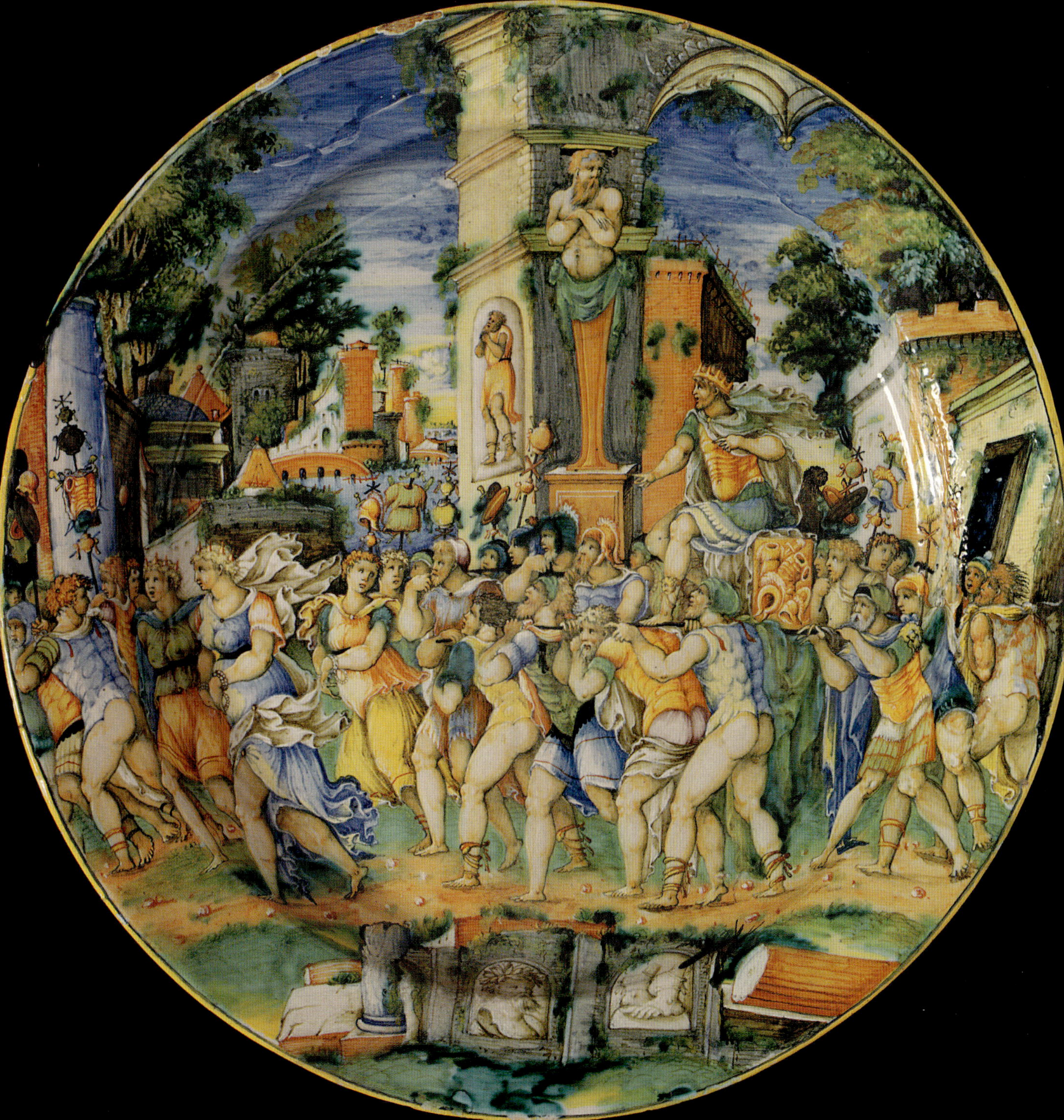

qua la Vedetta il Cacciabragie la forcina e il Trainello

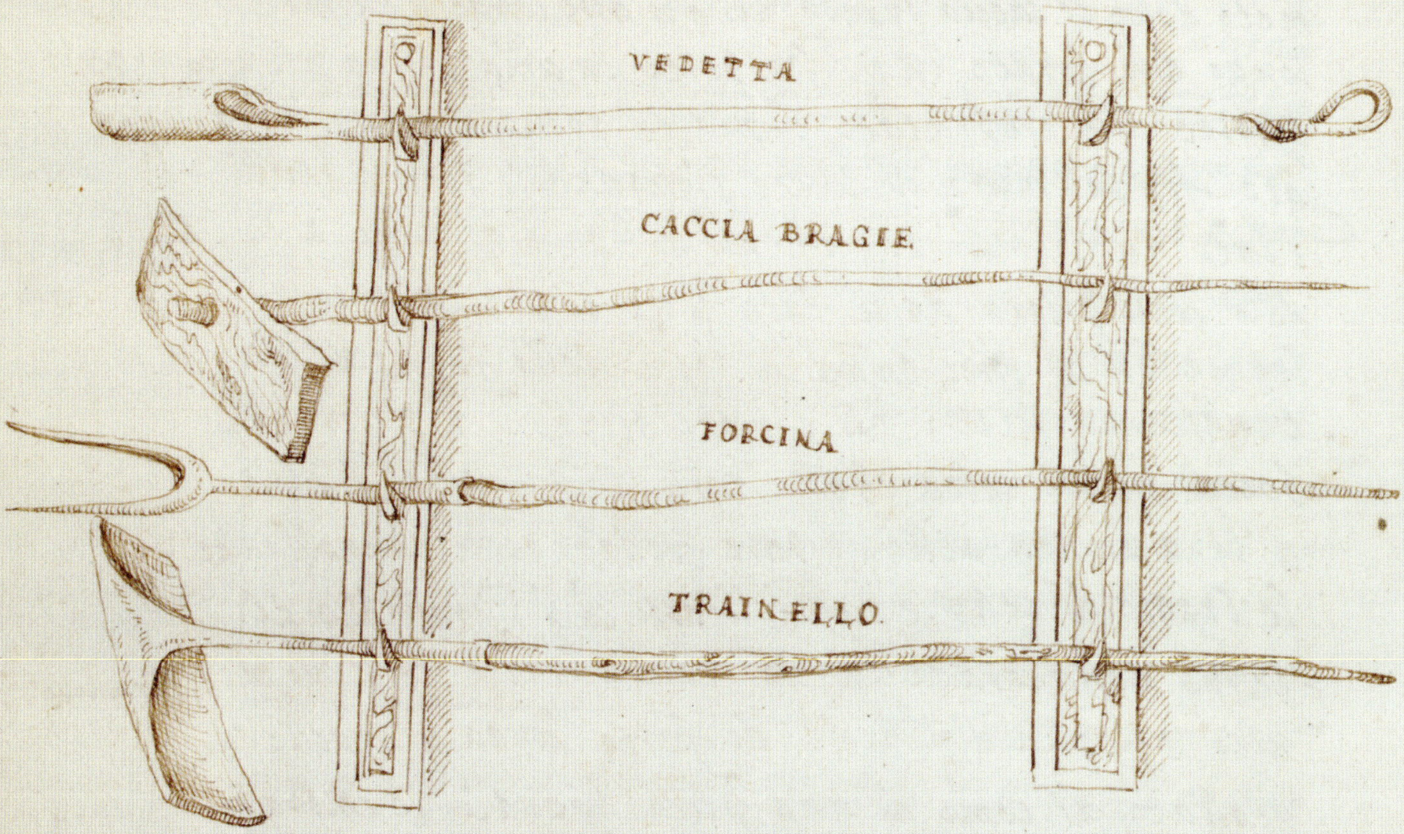

La fornace Disegna mi però cō il fuoco cō la sua murata di vasi acciò più facilmēte se intēda il mio parlare. fatto questo mi piante ro di più sorti mulini. accordaremo alla Pila ragionarassi de pistori il mordacolto. finiremo gli Colore e diremo bre uē mēt alcune cose della maiolica di Oro del mōdo del cogliare li Colori macinati alcuni remedii alli bianchetti si riscaldano

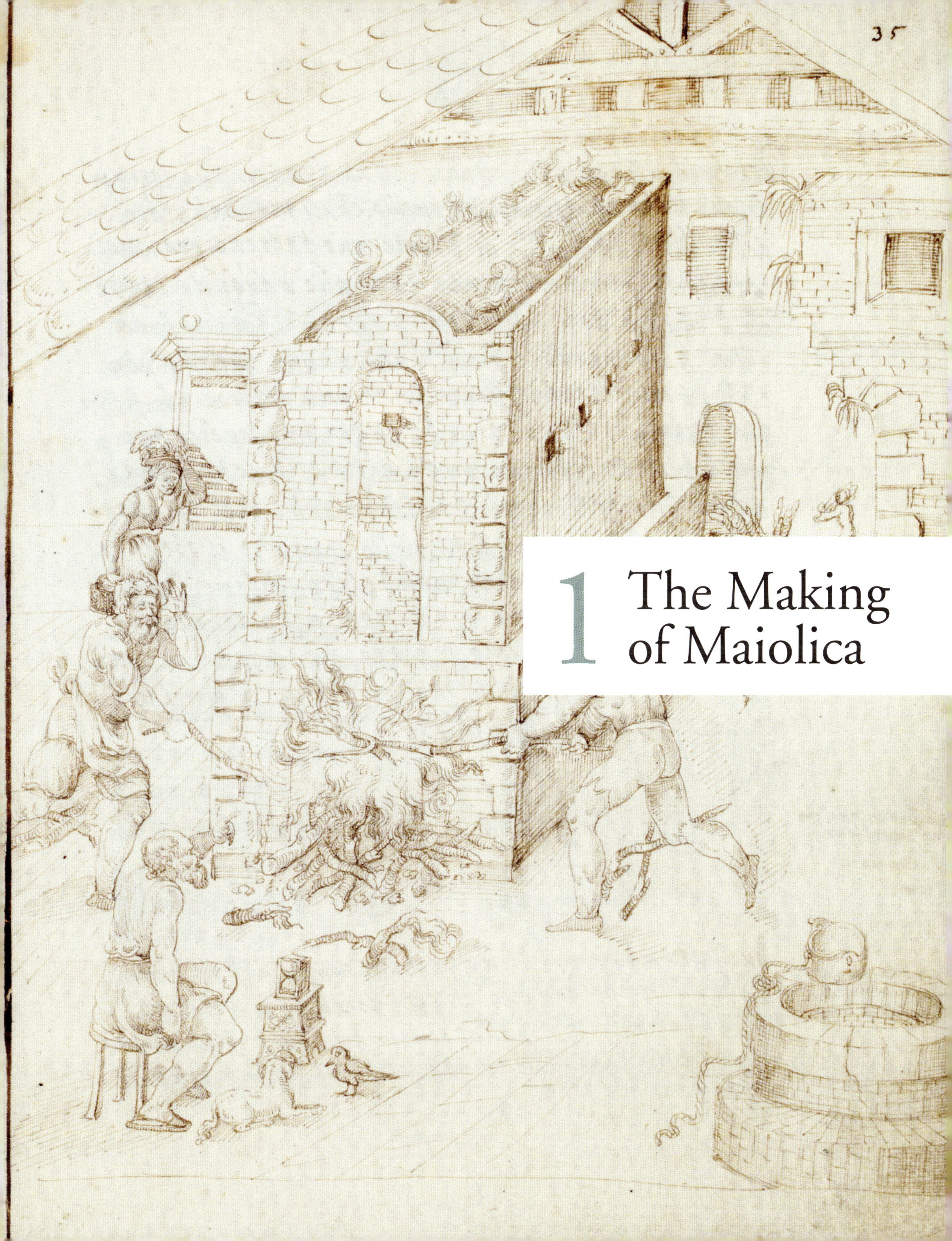

1 The Making of Maiolica

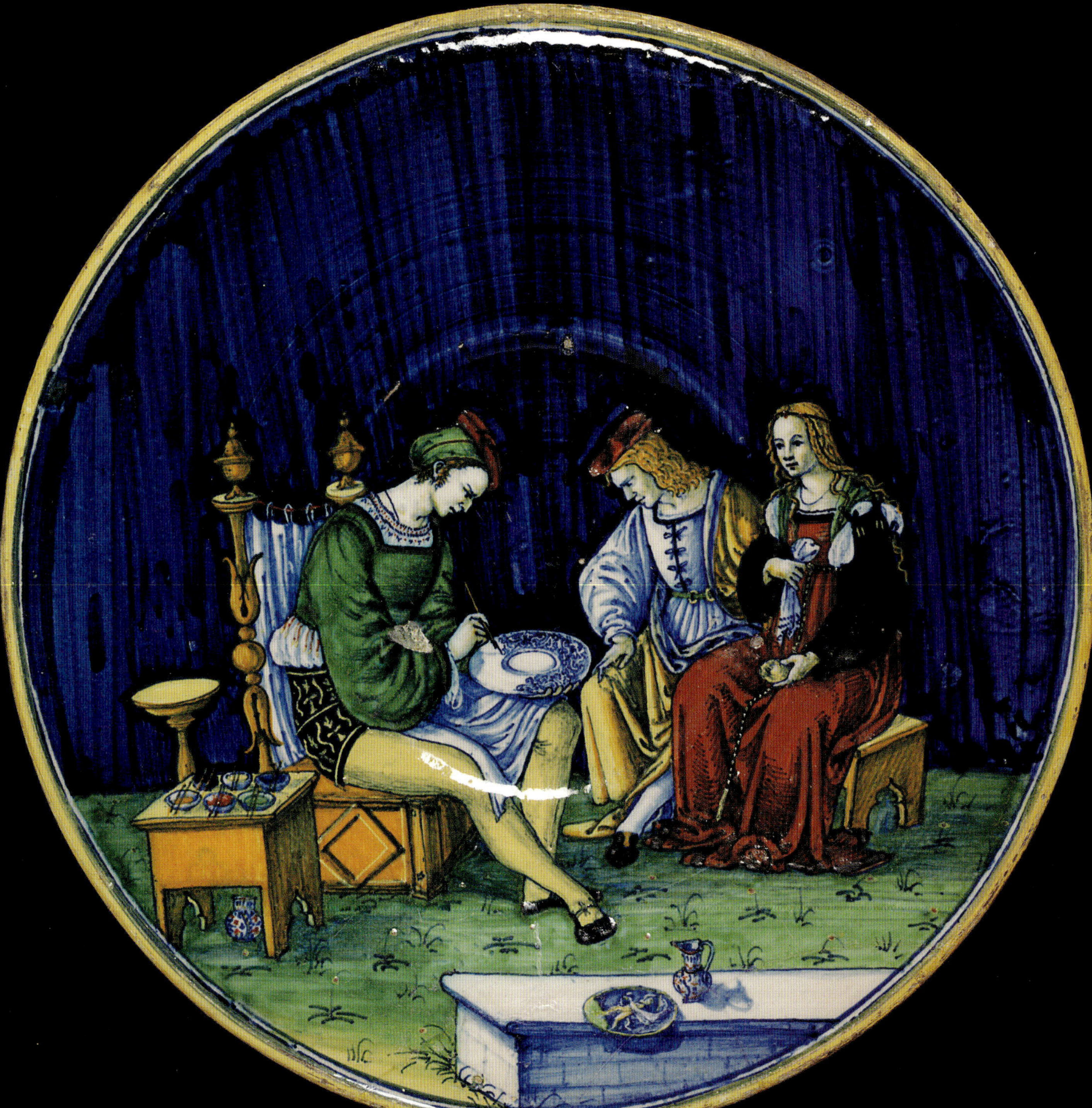

The Making of Maiolica

REINO LIEFKES

8 Dish showing a maiolica painter at work
Jacopo
Cafaggiolo, c.1510–15
Diam: 23.9 cm
V&A: 1717–1855

Italian potters of the Renaissance period developed a new kind of painted earthenware that was more sophisticated than any ceramics made in Europe. In its most extreme form, the entire surface of these wares was covered with elaborate narrative scenes, painted in bright, life-like colours, which surpassed, according to contemporary critics, even the pottery of ancient Greece and Rome.[1] The surviving examples of Italian maiolica, as this pottery is now known, are as bright and colourful today as they were some five hundred years ago on the day that they emerged from the potter's kiln. Made both for use at table and for display, such wares give us a clear picture of the aesthetic values, patterns of consumption, customs and intellectual preoccupations of their original creators and owners.

Maiolica retains the brilliance of its original colours because the fired pigments are stable. Key to the technique is the application of a layer of opaque white glaze to the once-fired vessel. The potter paints his pigments directly onto this unfired layer of glaze. A second firing ensures that the colours and glaze fuse together to form a smooth, permanent surface on which the colours become bright and luminous. The opacity and whiteness of the glaze was the result of the addition of tin oxide to a traditional colourless lead glaze.

Tin oxide was first used in this way in what is now modern day Iraq by eighth-century potters to cover their earthernwares, which they painted in blue. The technique spread throughout the Islamic empire and into southern Europe. In Muslim Spain, the town of Murcia in the east of the country became an important centre for the production of ceramics during the twelfth century. When Murcia fell to the Christian armies in 1243, many of its craftsmen fled and the focus of ceramics production shifted to Malaga and the province of Granada, and later still to Valencia.[2] One of the specialities of the Spanish potters was tin-glazed pottery decorated with metallic lustres. They developed a distinctive style characterized by bold overall patterns in cobalt-blue and golden lustres on a creamy white ground, combining geometric with floral and calligraphic motifs. Superior to any other type of ceramics made in Europe at that time, Spanish lustre pottery was a luxury product exported across Europe and the Middle East (pl. 9).

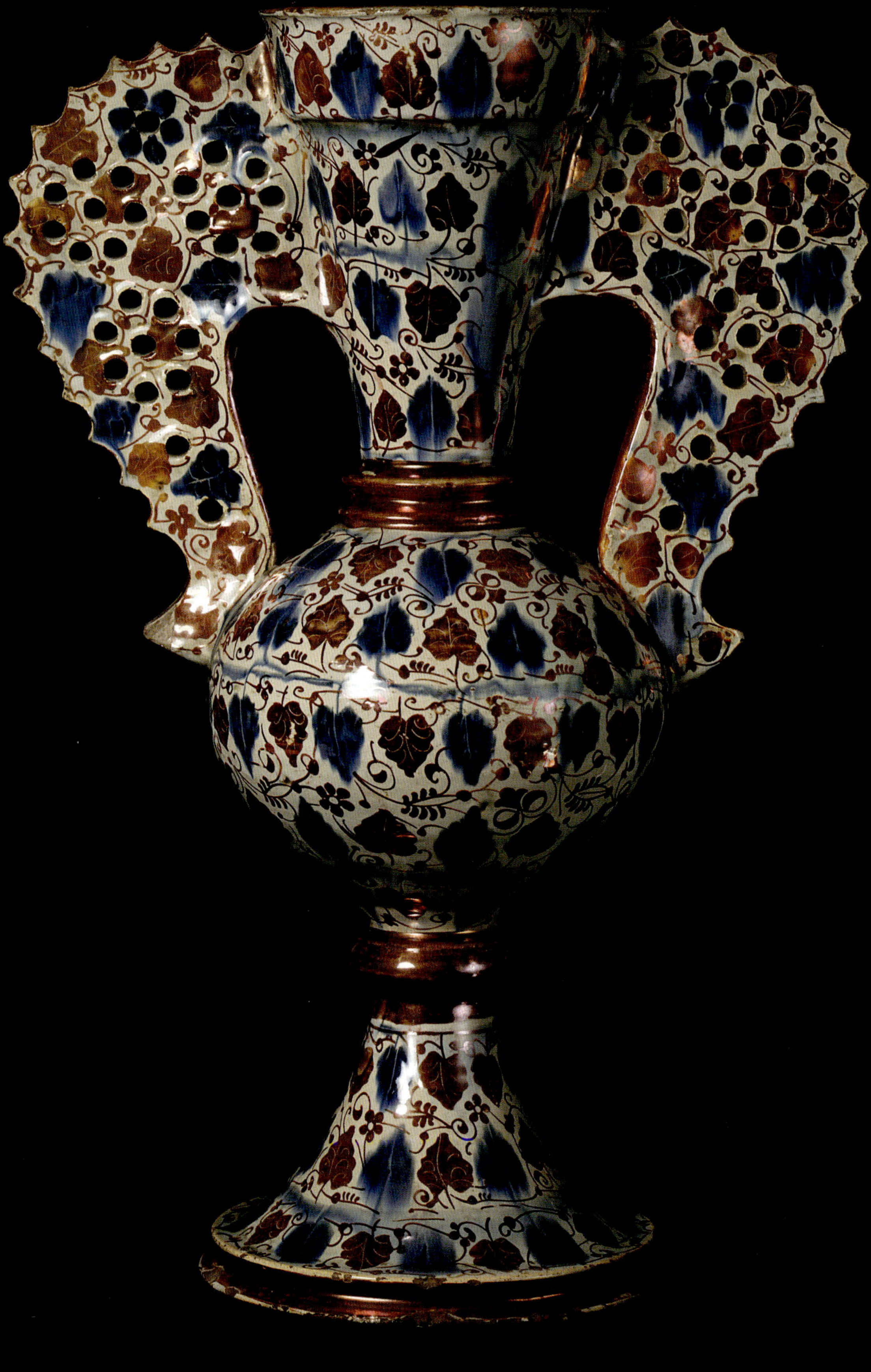

9 Flower vase
Valencia (probably Manises), Spain, 1435–75
Tin-glazed earthenware with lustre decoration
H: 52.8 cm
V&A: 8968–1863

The potters of Valencia supplied Italian merchants with bowls, dishes and vases, which were often embellished with the coats of arms of the intended customer.

The technique of tin-glazing had arrived in Italy by about 1200. But until well into the fourteenth century the potters of northern and central Italy used relatively small amounts of tin in their glazes and decorated their wares only with green or purple-brown pigments, based on the oxides of copper and manganese. The imported Spanish lustrewares were superior in many ways. They were more finely potted and more ambitious in size and shape, their glaze was whiter and smoother, and their decoration more colourful and splendid. It is easy to imagine the visual impact of Spanish lustre wares on contemporary consumers. There must have been something particularly magical about these objects. Formed of earth dug out of the ground, they were made to shine like gold through the transformation of fire. These imports had a strong influence on Italian ceramic production. Potters in the area around Florence were among the first to improve the quality of their wares, during the fifteenth century, but other centres were soon to follow.

The decorative language of imported Spanish pottery was imitated more or less directly. Italian potters initially lacked knowledge of the difficult lustre technique and used orange or purple pigments instead (pls 38, 39). By the time the lustre technology was fully mastered by a few specialized workshops in Deruta and Gubbio around 1500, the Spanish style of ornamentation had become rather old fashioned.

The term used in fifteenth-century inventories to describe imported Spanish lustre wares is *'lavori di maiolicha'* or *'di terra … fatti a Maiolica'*. *'L'isola di majolica'* was the medieval Italian name for the island of Majorca, used by Dante in his *Inferno*.[3] Although the island probably did not produce any lustred ceramics at that time, it was a major trading port on the way to Spain, and contemporaries such as the writer Alberti seemed to believe that Spanish lustre pottery was made in Majorca.[4] The term maiolica was soon also adopted for lustre-decorated pottery made in Italy, and during the course of the sixteenth century it came to describe all tin-glazed pottery. Now, the term maiolica is used for all Italian tin-glazed earthenware.

Most of what we know about the making techniques and technology of Renaissance maiolica comes from a single written source, a manuscript written about 1557 by Cipriano Piccolpasso of Castel Durante (Urbania). *Li tre libri dell arte del vasaio* (*The Three Books of the Potter's Art*) are a detailed treatise on the art of pottery, almost certainly intended to be published. With its many recipes for glazes, detailed descriptions of processes and equipment, and clear illustrations, the manuscript is a complete manual for the potter. It was written at a time when maiolica techniques were well established in Italy, and Italian potters had started to take their skills abroad and establish maiolica workshops in France and the Netherlands. Piccolpasso himself stated that the *Three Books* were commissioned by the French cardinal François de Tournon, to whom he dedicated the manuscript.[5] Tournon, archbishop of Lyons and a French diplomat, stayed in Castel Durante for several months during 1556 and 1557. He had a keen interest in literature and the arts and sciences and it is likely that he intended to use the treatise in his native Lyons, where the manufacture of maiolica had been introduced only a few years before.

The manuscript deals with all aspects of the making of pottery, from the gathering and preparation of clay to the design and the firing of its painted decorations. The author states that he obtained his knowledge mostly from firsthand observation and discussions with potters, mainly in Castel Durante itself. In some instances he describes how the potters of Urbino, Venice or sometimes other centres use different methods for some processes or recipes, but these differences are slight and in general the processes seem more or less the same for all Italian maiolica of the Renaissance period. Piccolpasso himself mentions how trade secrets were traditionally passed from father to son, and one has to admire him for the amount of sound information he managed to gather. It is possible of course that he did not get to the bottom of all the processes he tried to describe, but most of the technical descriptions and recipes have been tried and tested by potters over the last few decades and found to be reasonably accurate and workable.[6] We will describe the processes of maiolica making here, broadly following Piccolpasso.

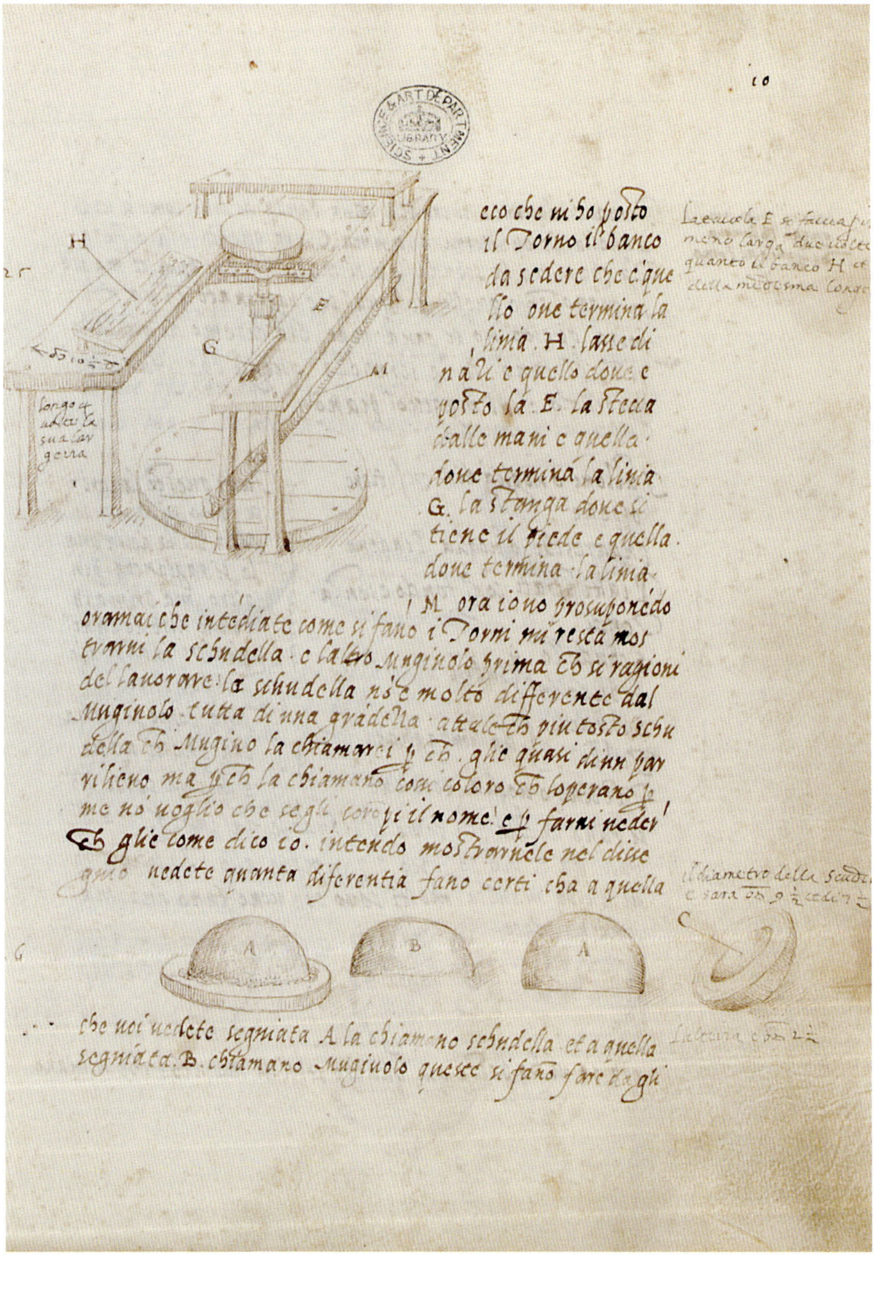

10 Potter's wheel and hump moulds
***The Three Books of the Potter's Art*, fol.10r**
Cipriano Piccolpasso
Pen and ink
Castel Durante, 1557
NAL: MSL/1861/7446

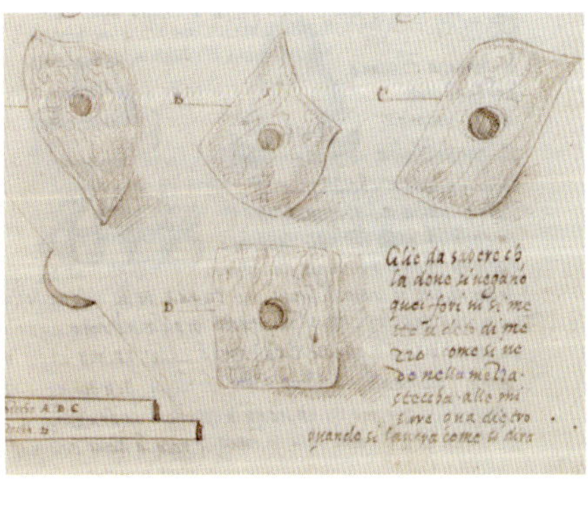

11 Wooden templates
***The Three Books of the Potter's Art*, fol.13v (detail)**
Cipriano Piccolpasso
Pen and ink
Castel Durante, 1557
NAL: MSL/1861/7446

Throwing the pots

The clay used must be as fine and white as possible. Piccolpasso describes how the fluvial clay deposits on the beds of the river Metauro are gathered by the potters of Castel Durante and Urbino. They dig the clay, carried down by the river from the Apennines, mostly during the summer, taking care to keep it free of organic material or stones. They then leave the clay out to dry to purify it. If the clay is dug away from the river beds, it is usually first deposited in dug-out pits to be purified by the repeated action of rain and sun. After the clay has been purified, it is liquefied with water and strained through wide-mesh cloths, large sieves or strainers and stored in biscuit-fired vessels. For common pottery it is not necessary to strain the clay, which is simply beaten and kneaded to make it smooth.

Most plates, bowls, dishes and pots are thrown on the wheel and Piccolpasso describes its construction in some detail. The potters use a so-called kick-wheel with a heavy wooden flywheel about four feet in diameter (pl. 10). Through the middle of this is fitted a shaft made out of wood or iron. The wheel is supported above the floor by a steel peg resting on a flat flint stone or steel plate, so that it can rotate freely. The wheel-head, on which the pots are thrown, is fixed to the top of the shaft. The potter powers the wheel-head by kicking the flywheel, its weight providing momentum ensuring swift and even rotation. The same type of wheel remained in use throughout Europe until well into the twentieth century.

For most shallow hollow shapes, such as plates, dishes and bowls, the potter attaches a convex 'hump mould' to the wheel-head with some clay. This is a turned wood 'negative' mould, which matches the interior shape of the piece to be thrown. The potter places a ball of well-kneaded clay on top of this mould and throws it by pressing and shaping it with his hands. The interior will follow the exact shape of the mould and the exterior will be shaped using a wooden template (pl. 11). The 'chatter-marks' we can see on the back of some maiolica dishes are caused by the template rhythmically bouncing across the surface of the rotating pot (pl. 12). Deeper, open shapes, such as storage jars, jugs and bottles are thrown directly on the wheel-head from a ball of clay. The potter shapes the clay with his hands while turning the wheel. To give the pot its detailed shape he puts his left hand inside the pot while using a wooden template in his right hand, 'with the fingers always opposite to the stick'; he lets it 'be guided as neatly as possible, for in this consists the beauty of the work' (pl. 13).[7]

12 Chatter marks on the reverse of a dish
Deruta, 1530–50
Diam: 40.1 cm
V&A: 646–1884

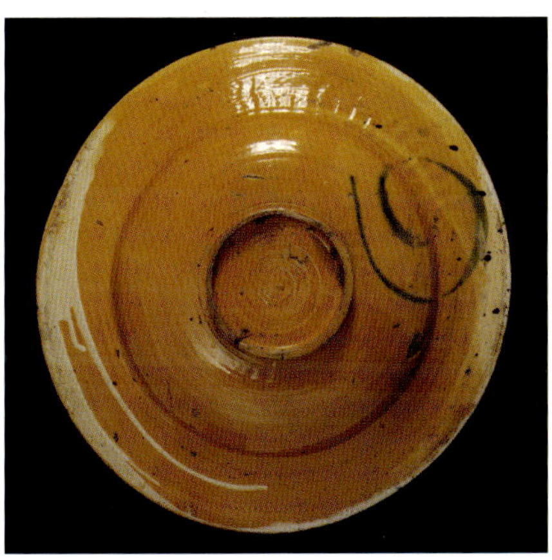

After throwing, all fine wares are also turned. Removed from the wheel-head, they are partially dried and then transferred to a turning block, a negative form of the vessel made in clay. The potter attaches this block to the wheel-head and places the leather-hard vessel on top, upside-down. Pieces of paper, laid in between, prevent it from sticking to the block. By holding special turning irons against the wall of the pot as it is rotated, the potter removes a considerable quantity of clay, until the pot acquires the desired, even thickness. Different irons are used to turn the foot ring (pls 14, 15). This method gives the potter great control over the shape and thickness of the wares. Finally, in this partially dry state, handles or a separately thrown foot can be stuck to the pot with a liquid clay 'slip' mixed with some cloth fluff.

Complex shapes are often press-moulded rather than thrown. The plaster moulds for this are taken from an original model, often made of fresh (still damp) clay. Piccolpasso describes how baskets and ewers and vessels with raised bosses are made in moulds. Depending on the object, the mould can be in one piece, or in several sections. The moulds are concave, shaping the outside of the object to be made (pl. 17). The potter

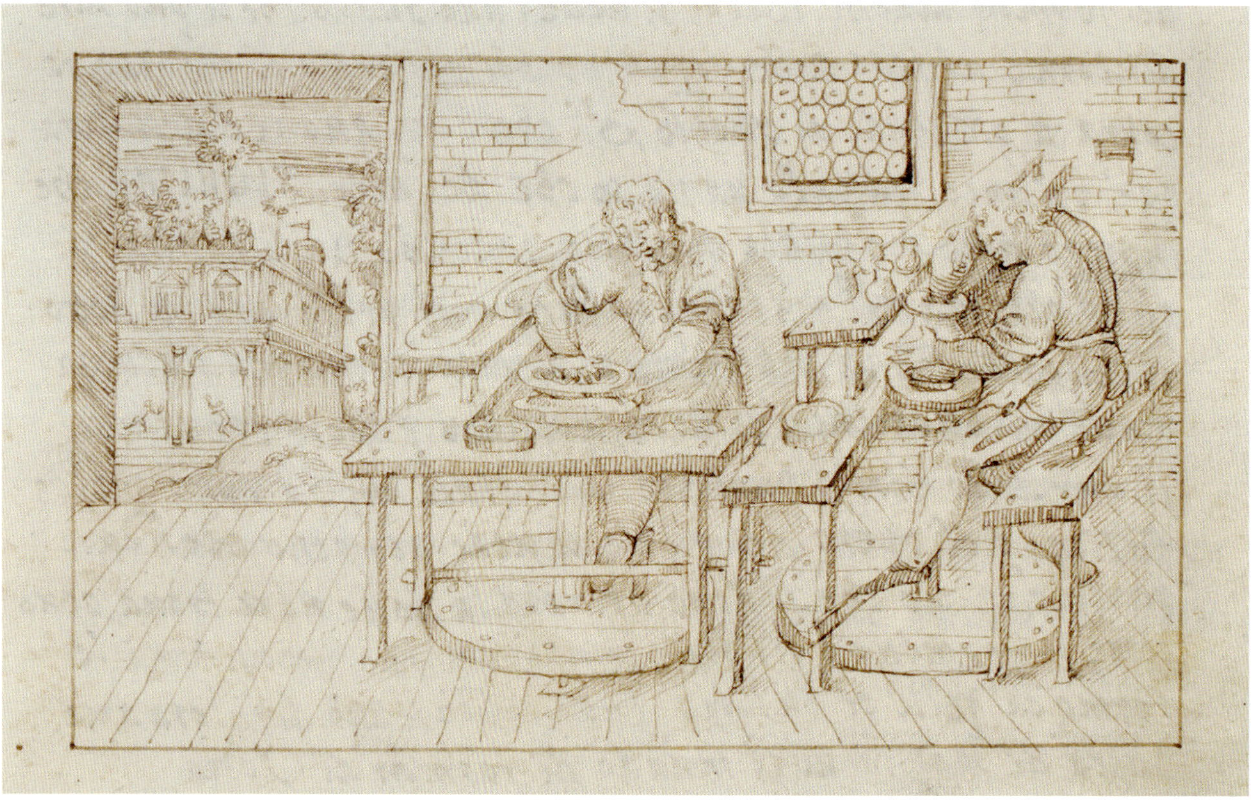

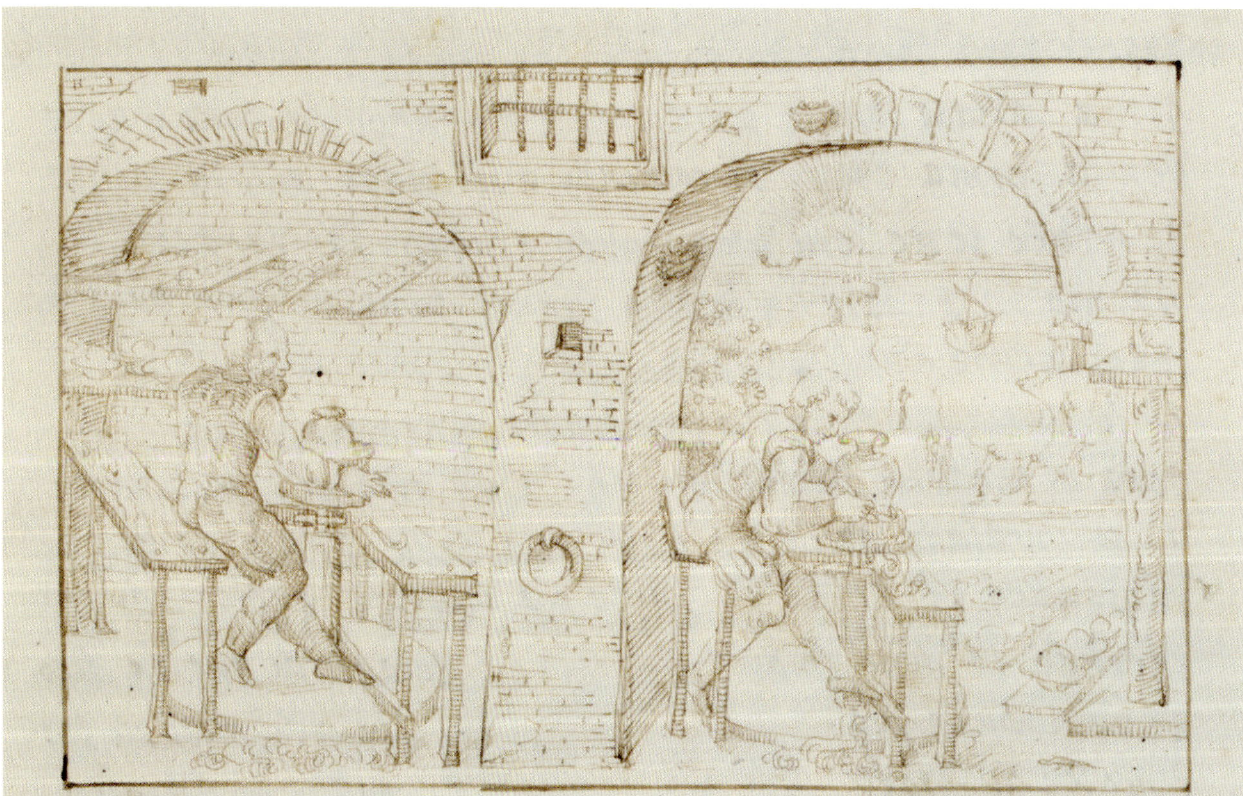

13 Throwing pots
***The Three Books of the Potter's Art*, fol.16r (detail)**
Cipriano Piccolpasso
Pen and ink
Castel Durante, 1557
NAL: MSL/1861/7446

14 Turning pots
***The Three Books of the Potter's Art*, fol.19v (detail)**
Cipriano Piccolpasso
Pen and ink
Castel Durante, 1557
NAL: MSL/1861/7446

15 Turning irons
***The Three Books of the Potter's Art*, fol.14r (detail)**
Cipriano Piccolpasso
Pen and ink
Castel Durante, 1557
NAL: MSL/1861/7446

16 Cutting a slab of clay
***The Three Books of the Potter's Art*, fol.17v (detail)**
Cipriano Piccolpasso
Pen and ink
Castel Durante, 1557
NAL: MSL/1861/7446

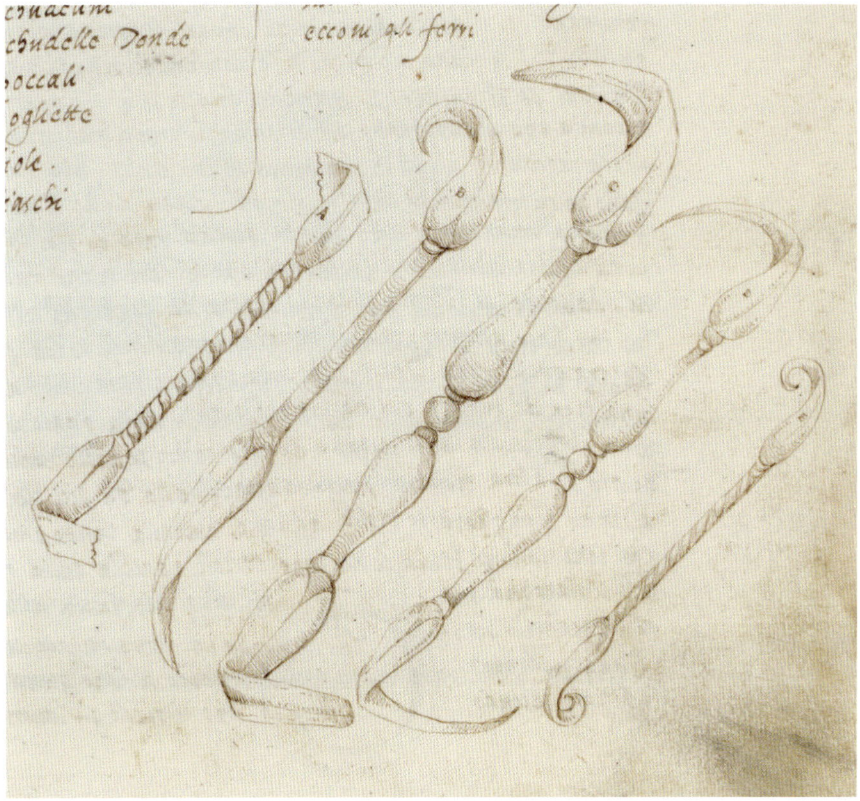

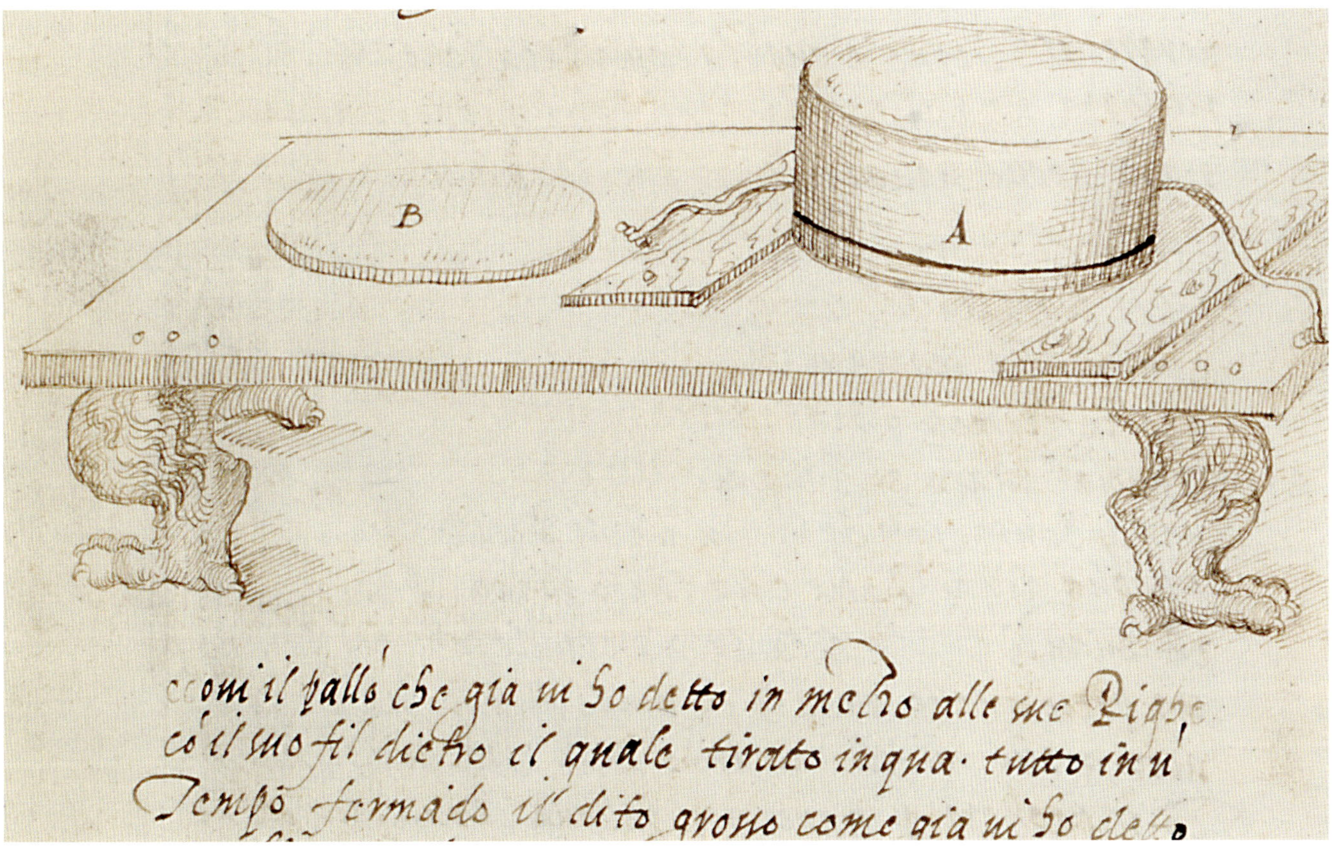

takes a large round 'cake' of well-kneaded clay and cuts off a thick slice with a metal wire (pl. 16). The diameter of this slice corresponds to the size of the mould. This is then pressed down into the mould with the fingers, either in one piece or in sections, so that the outside takes on the shape of the interior of the mould (pl. 19). In the case of multi-part moulds, different parts of an object are moulded separately and joined while still in their separate moulds. The excess clay, sticking out above each mould, is cut away with the string of a bow. The cut edges are then wetted with slip before they are joined. For vessels with a narrow opening, such as ewers, the potter uses a bent and rounded-off stick to smooth the joins together from the inside.

To make an open-work basket, the potter first uses a convex 'hump' mould to make the overall shape of the interior. This is then placed in a convex wooden 'basin' mould, after which sections of the clay wall can be cut out to achieve the open-worked effect (pl. 17). The foot can be turned or moulded separately and joined to the body with slip. Alternatively, the foot can also be attached at a later stage with glaze.

Before the finished clay vessels can be covered with a layer of white tin-glaze they need to be fired: otherwise the glaze would 'crawl', leaving bare patches. We call this first firing the biscuit firing.

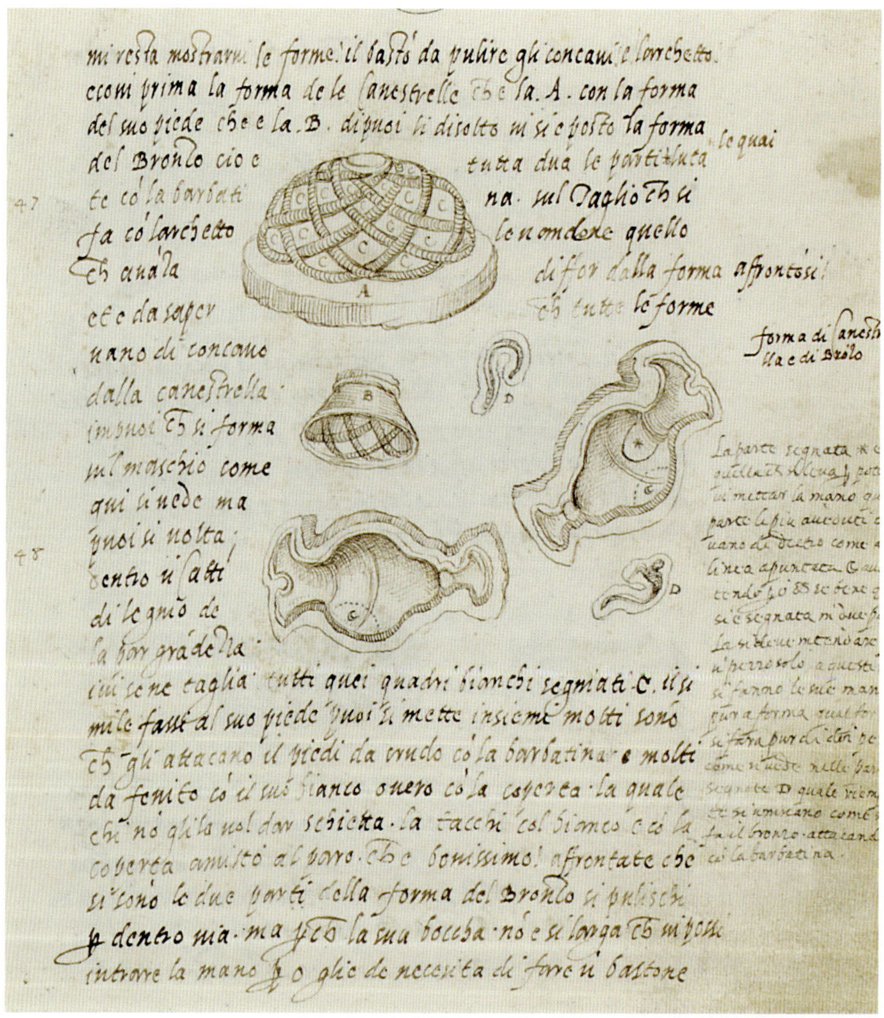

17 Plaster moulds
***The Three Books of the Potter's Art*, fol.18r (detail)**
Cipriano Piccolpasso
Pen and ink
Castel Durante, 1557
NAL: MSL/1861/7446

18 Bowl with the arms of Pope Julius II
Gubbio, before 1513
Salting Bequest V&A: C.2197–1910

19 Evidence of press-moulding on the reverse of pl.18

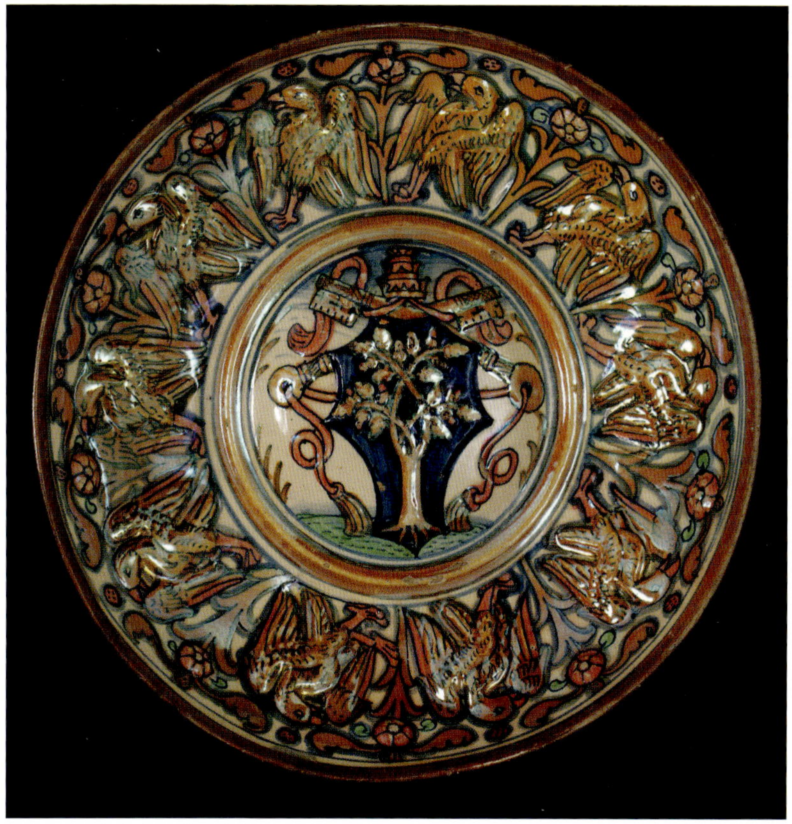

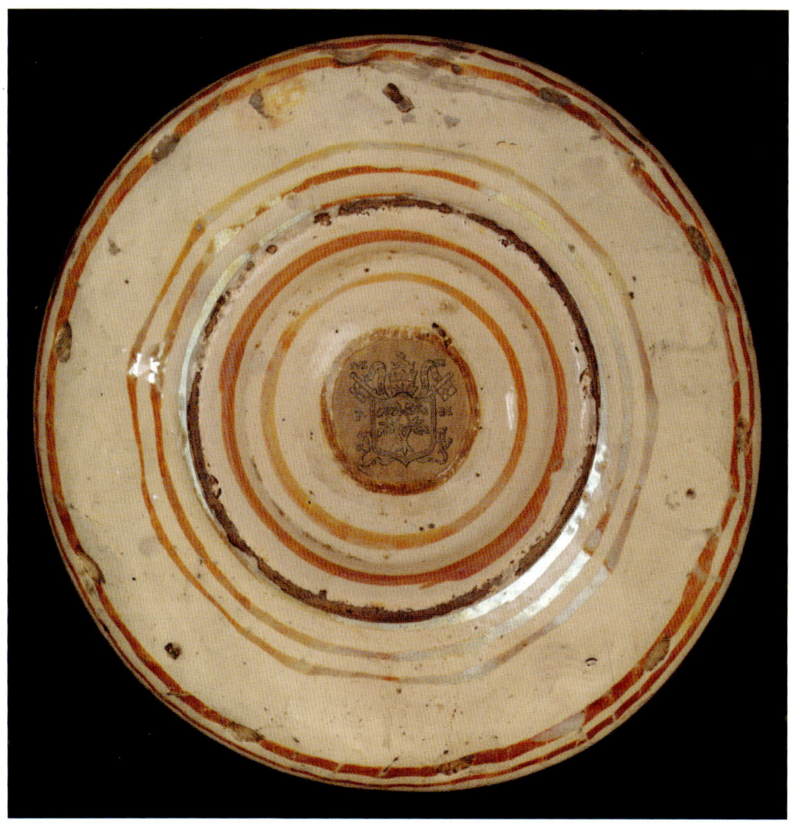

First firing

Piccolpasso describes in detail the kiln type commonly used in Castel Durante, but also mentions seeing a kiln of almost twice this size at the house of a Durantese potter in Venice. The best furnaces are made of unbaked bricks. They consist of two spaces: a lower space, or fire-box, used to burn the fuel, and an upper 'chamber' for firing the pots. The furnace is about five feet wide and six feet long and stands about eight and a half feet high above the ground. The fire-box is four feet high, but continues for another one or one and a half feet underground. At the front there is an opening for stoking the fire. About three arches span the width of the fire-box, supporting the floor of the chamber, which is perforated to let the fire and the hot air rise from below. This type of kiln is known as an up-draught kiln. The chamber has four spy holes along one side, and nine ventilation holes in the vault (pl. 20). A tall, arched opening at the front gives access to the chamber.

For the biscuit firing, the whole kiln is filled with well-dried pots. Firing the kiln is a complex and costly process, requiring huge amounts of fuel, and it makes economic sense to pack the kiln as tightly as possible. When the chamber is full, the entrance is bricked up and small gaps are covered with soft mortar. The spy holes are also covered and small disks or broken roof-tiles are used to cover the vents on top. The fire is lit with straw and built up gradually for four hours with dry wood. It then needs to be kept up for about 12 hours, until the kiln interior appears white through the spy holes, which would be at about 1000°C. At that point stoking is stopped and the fire is left to die out for an hour, when the embers are raked out and made into charcoal by pouring water over them. Piccolpasso mentions that this charcoal is used during winter to heat the workshop of the painters, who have to sit for hours and need to keep their hands steady.

20 Firing the kiln
***The Three Books of the Potter's Art*, fol.35r (detail)**
Cipriano Piccolpasso
Pen and ink
Castel Durante, 1557
NAL: MSL/1861/7446

21 Pounding the frit
***The Three Books of the Potter's Art*, fol.38v (detail)**
Cipriano Piccolpasso
Pen and ink
Castel Durante, 1557
NAL: MSL/1861/7446

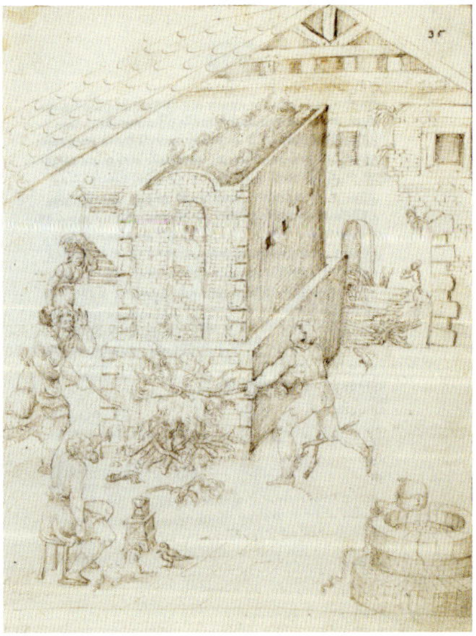

Tin-glazing

The biscuit-fired pots are covered with a layer of white tin-glaze, or 'the white' as Piccolpasso calls it. He lists various recipes for tin-glaze and gives a detailed account of all the processes involved in its preparation. The four main ingredients are sand, potash, tin and lead. The first two are combined to form the alkaline frit, or *marzacotto*, and the last two make the 'tin ash'. The potash for the frit is derived either from tartar, collected from wine-barrels, or from lees, the dregs filtered from wine during November and December. Both lees and tartar are dried and burned before being brought to the pottery.

Sand of high silica content makes the best and purest frit, so potters sought sand that was as white and clear as possible. The sand found in San Giovanni, near to La Terina in Tuscany, reputedly the best in Italy, is 'white, glittering like silver, heavy, clear and clean'. But other sands were used in different regions as well as pulverized quartz pebbles.

Sand and lees are mixed together at a weight ratio of about 30 to 12, making sure that any lumps of lees are pulverized. This mixture is placed in pots of unfired or biscuit-fired clay against the back wall of the fire-box and fired along with the pottery placed in the chamber above. The frit comes out as hard as stone and is released from the pots by smashing them with a hammer. It is then pounded in a hollowed tree trunk or a large stone mortar with an iron-tipped rod or iron mallet, and sieved and pounded again until it is totally pulverized (pl. 21). Finally it is weighed, washed and mixed with the tin ash and this mixture is ground between heavy millstones.

The tin ash itself is a mixture of tin and lead to a weight ratio of about 1 to 6. The best and purest tin, mined in Cornwall in England, was imported into Italy from

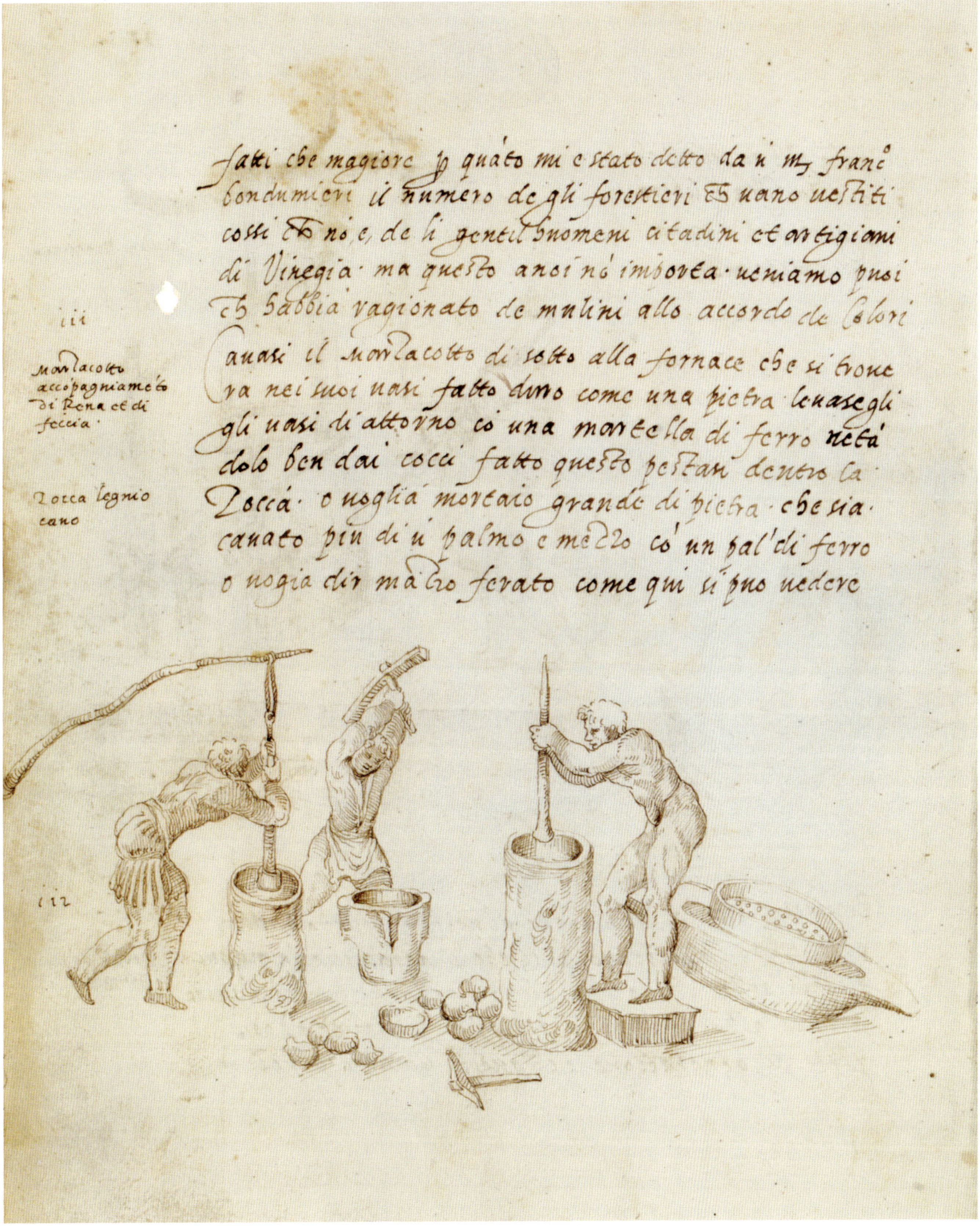
fatti che magiore per quanto mi è stato detto da m. m. Franc.
bonduminieri il numero de gli forestieri che vano vestiti
cossi che no è, de li gentil huomeni citadini et artigiani
di Vinegia. ma questo ancor nò importa. veniamo poi
che habbia ragionato de mulini allo accordo de Colori

iii

Cavasi il marzacotto di sotto alla fornace che si trova
ra nei suoi vasi fatto duro come una pietra levasegli
gli vasi di attorno có una martella di ferro nettan
dolo ben dai cocci fatto questo pestasi dentro la
Rocca o voglia mortaio grande di pietra che sia
cavato piu di u palmo e mezzo có un pal di ferro
o voglia dir maltro ferato come qui si puo vedere

Marzacotto accopagniamento di Rena et di feccia

Rocca legnio cavo

112

Flanders at great expense.[8] Old pewter could be used instead of imported ingots, but more of this was needed as it already contained a percentage of lead. The mixture was turned into tin ash in a special small kiln.

To make normal, 'common' white, the frit and tin ash are mixed at a weight ratio of 30 to 12, but Piccolpasso gives alternative recipes for different types of white. A special 'inside white' for instance contains less tin and an additional percentage of lead. This cheaper, less opaque glaze was ideally suited to making the interior of drug pots and other vessels impermeable to fluids.

The combined frit and tin ash are further ground in a mill with water and repeatedly sieved until they form a milky white liquid without lumps. To glaze the biscuit-fired pots, the finer wares are dipped into a tub full of this glaze, or when only the outside or the front needs a coating the glaze is poured over them using a bowl (pls 22, 23). If the mix is of the correct consistency, this process leaves a layer of tin-glaze on the pot of the 'thickness of the leather used to make gloves'. The pots are then carefully dried prior to painting.

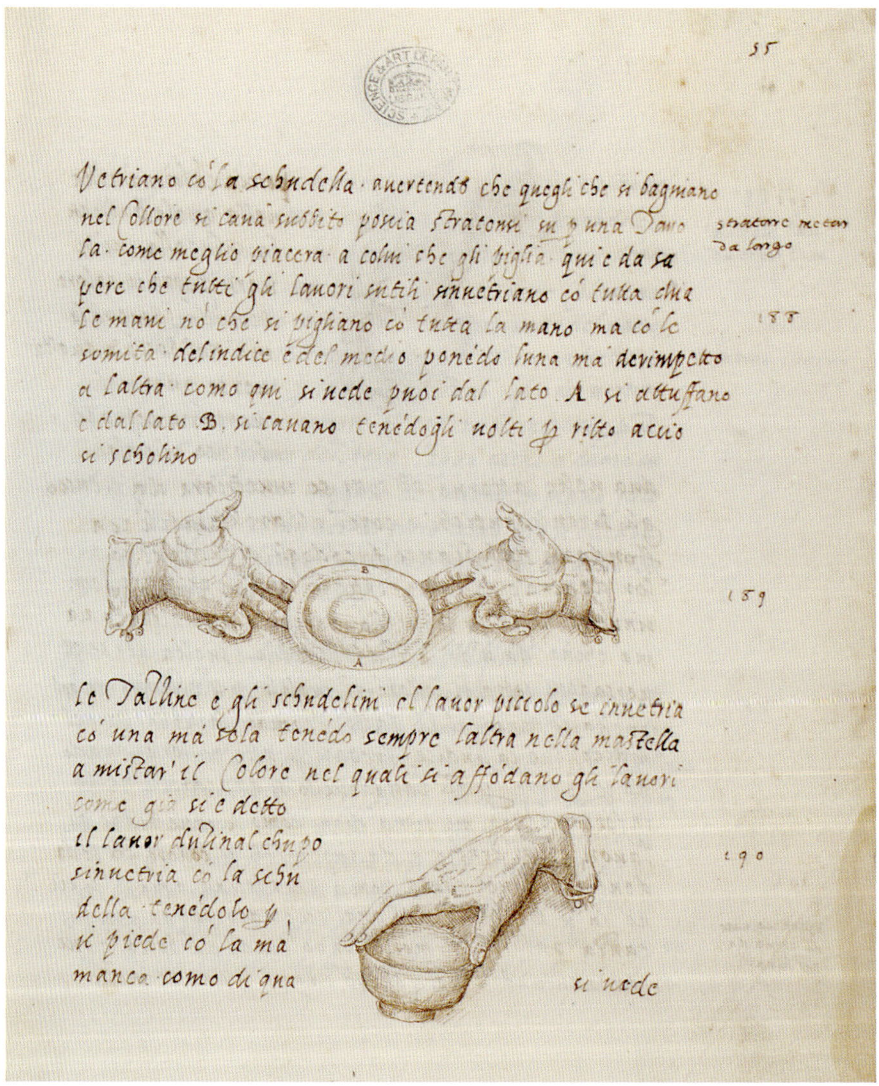

22 Tin-glaze dipping
***The Three Books of the Potter's Art*, fol.55r**
Cipriano Piccolpasso
Pen and ink
Castel Durante, 1557
NAL: MSL/1861/7446

23 Drug jar
Florence, 1420–40
H: 36.3 cm
V&A: 2562–1856

This drug jar was held upside-down, at an angle, and turned repeatedly while the tin-glaze was poured over it from a bowl. This process has left four triangular bare sections at the base of the jar.

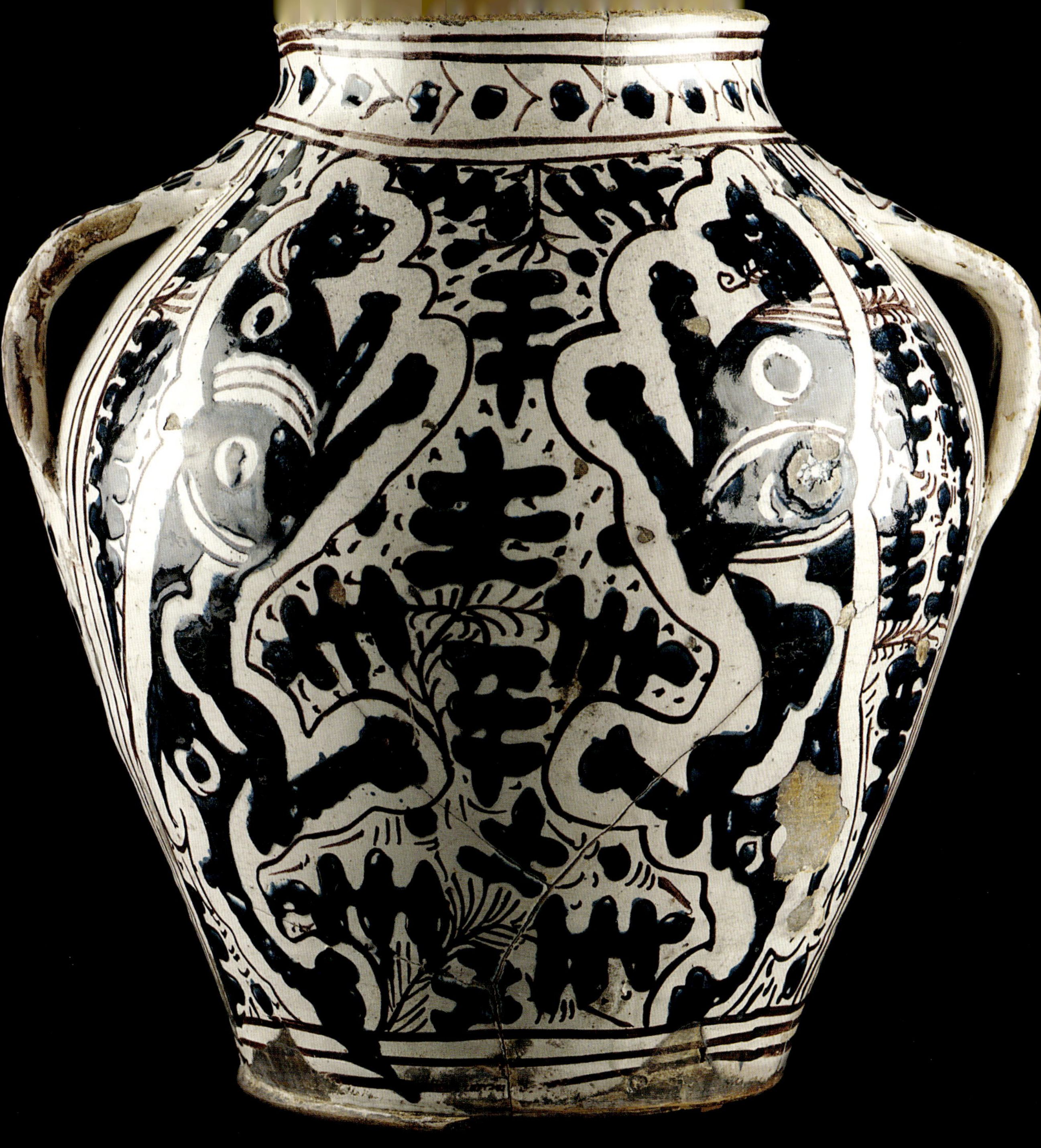

Painting

The 'pigments' used by the potters of Renaissance Italy are blue, purple, brown, green, orange, yellow and white. The first three are made with naturally occurring compounds of cobalt and manganese. The other colours are prepared very much like 'the white' by pounding and burning the ingredients in various ways. All colours contain lead. Green is made with copper and antimony; yellow with iron and antimony; and light yellow with antimony, lead, lees and common salt. Red was very hard to achieve and therefore used by only a few potters and always sparingly. It was made by grinding a dark-brown earthy clay called Armenian bole, which is rich in iron oxide, with red vinegar. This mixture was painted over light yellow, and after firing the resulting dark-brownish red would lie thick and rough on top of the otherwise smooth tin-glaze.

Piccolpasso also describes in detail how the various brushes are made from goats' hair and asses' manes. These are bound onto a pointed stick with waxed yarn and then cut into the required shape (pl. 25). For painting the finest *istoriato* maiolica, covered with elaborate pictorial scenes, some painters mix in whiskers of mice with the hair on their brushes.

A dish made at Cafaggiolo about 1515 is decorated with a wonderful depiction of a maiolica painter at work (pl. 8). The scene may be idealized, showing the painter in elegant attire and watched by his patrons, but it corresponds with Piccolpasso's description of the process. The painter sits on a stool or chair, with the vessel he is painting on his lap. He would hold ordinary plates at the bottom, resting them on his left hand, and hollow wares on his lap with the left hand inside (pl. 26). Fine wares, which are tin-glazed all over, are placed on a wooden pan, slightly larger than the object and held in place with a little tallow. This enables the painter to maintain control of his work, while helping to protect the raw tin-glaze, which can easily be wiped away.

He applies the colours straight onto the absorbent glaze surface, and there is very little room for error. Horizontal lines on pots and concentric circles on plates and dishes are applied with the aid of a turntable or 'banding wheel', an example of which can be seen behind the maiolica painter's chair on the dish described above.[9] (pls 8, 24). By spinning the vessel he can create a perfect circle or band by applying the brush at a fixed point. Faint lines in blue, visible on many pieces of Renaissance maiolica, show how the painter often started by marking out his composition, dividing the area for decoration into equal parts. Piccolpasso does not explain how standard designs could be transferred from a paper drawing to the tin-glazed surface by 'pouncing'. In this method, a tracing of the original design is made on thin paper and the outlines are pricked through with a pin. The tracing is placed on top of the pot and dabbed with a 'pounce', a small cloth pouch filled with fine charcoal dust. The charcoal passes through the pin-holes onto the tin-glaze, creating faint outlines for the painter to follow.

24 Concentric rings on reverse of pl.8

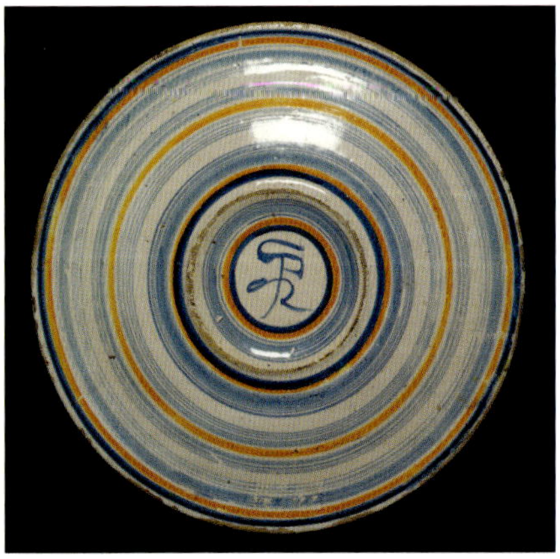

The painter has the different colours diluted in water in small bowls, and uses a separate brush for each colour to avoid contamination (pl. 25). However, on fine wares he mixes the basic pigments in order to achieve the desired tonal effects. Piccolpasso gives some examples, but hastens to add that painters vary the recipes to suit their needs. For drawing the outlines of figures and adding shade, yellow should be mixed with cobalt blue. 'To simulate a dawn, dead flesh, rocks and certain roads that are in bright light' he suggests mixing light yellow and white pigment. It is important to realize that the colours of the unfired pigments are completely different from the fired colours on the finished vessel. The painter's skill and experience in imagining the final result is of crucial importance.

25 A wooden brush handle and two types of brushes
***The Three Books of the Potter's Art*, fol.57r (detail)**
Cipriano Piccolpasso
Pen and ink
Castel Durante, 1557
NAL: MSL/1861/7446

26 Maiolica painter's workshop
***The Three Books of the Potter's Art*, fol.57v (detail)**
Cipriano Piccolpasso
Pen and ink
Castel Durante, 1557
NAL: MSL/1861/7446

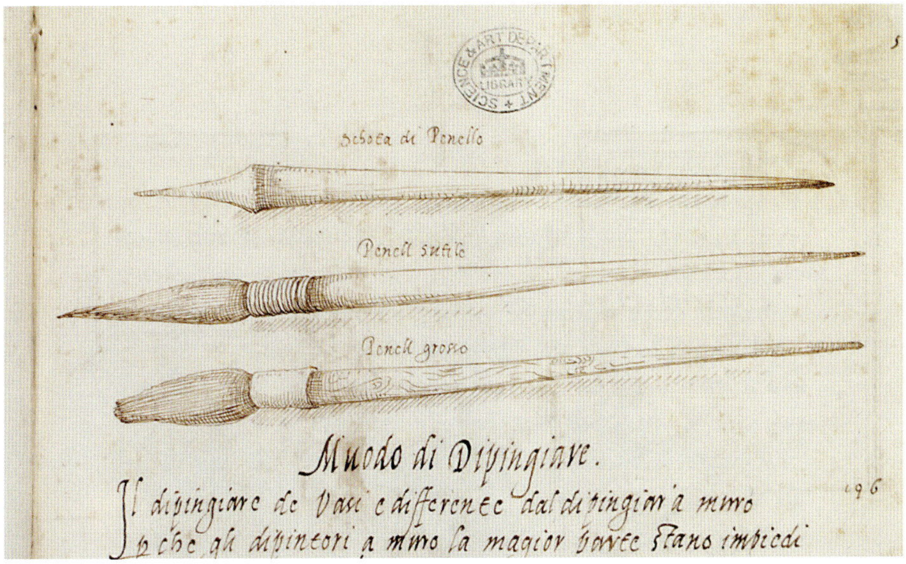

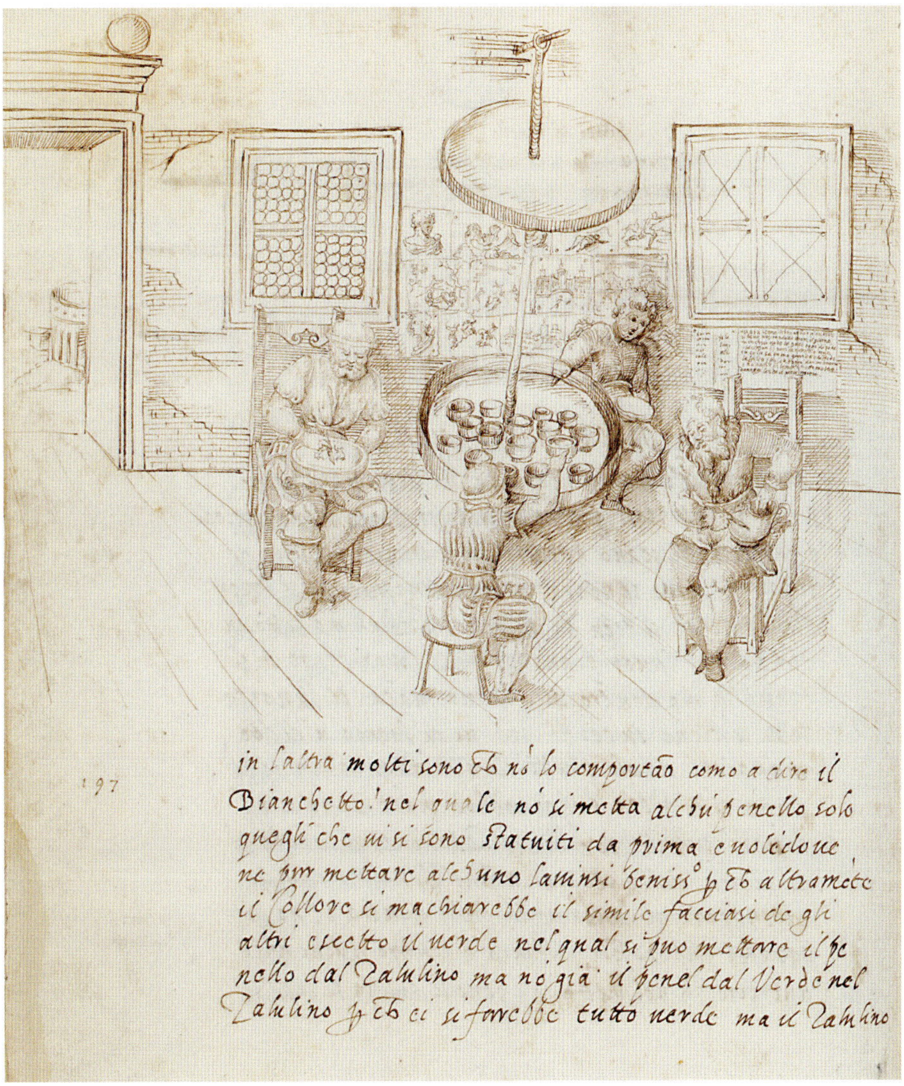

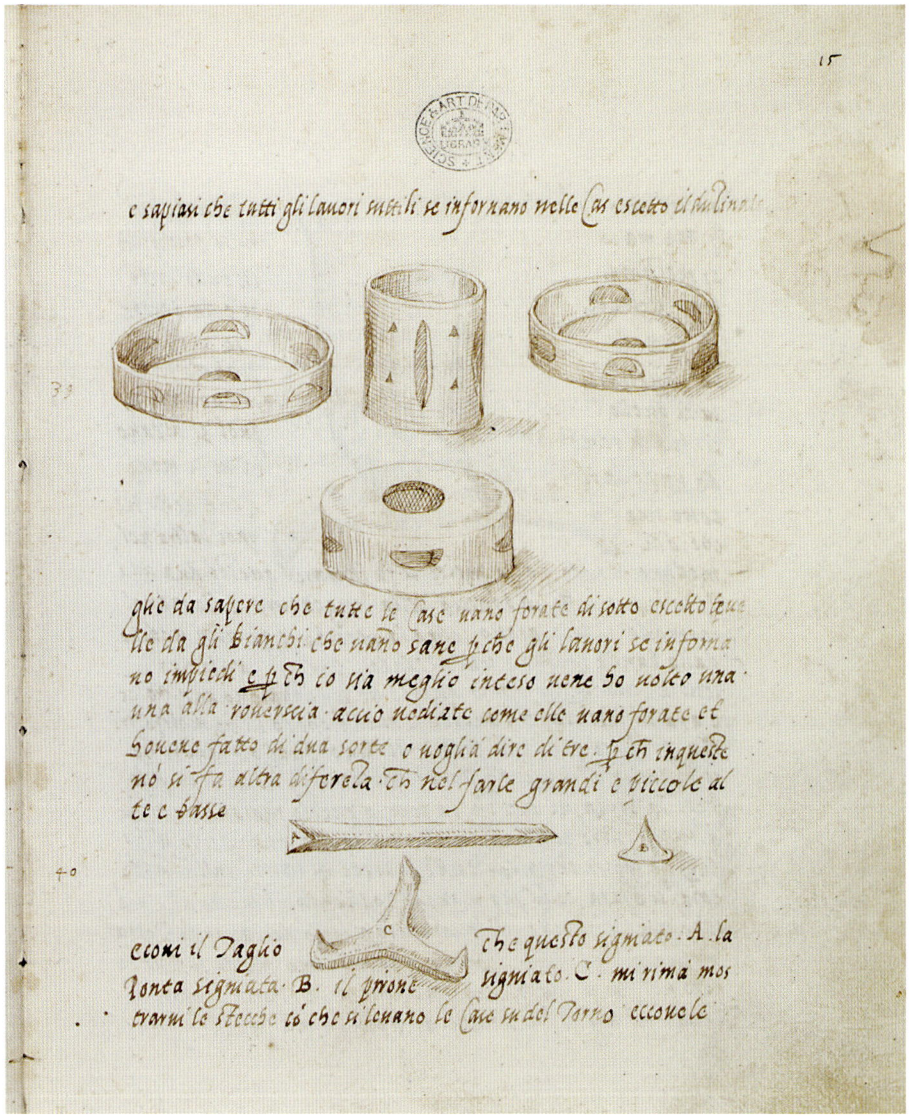

27 A peg (A), a spur (B) and a tripod (C)
***The Three Books of the Potter's Art*, fol.15r (detail)**
Cipriano Piccolpasso
Pen and ink
Castel Durante, 1557
NAL: MSL/1861/7446

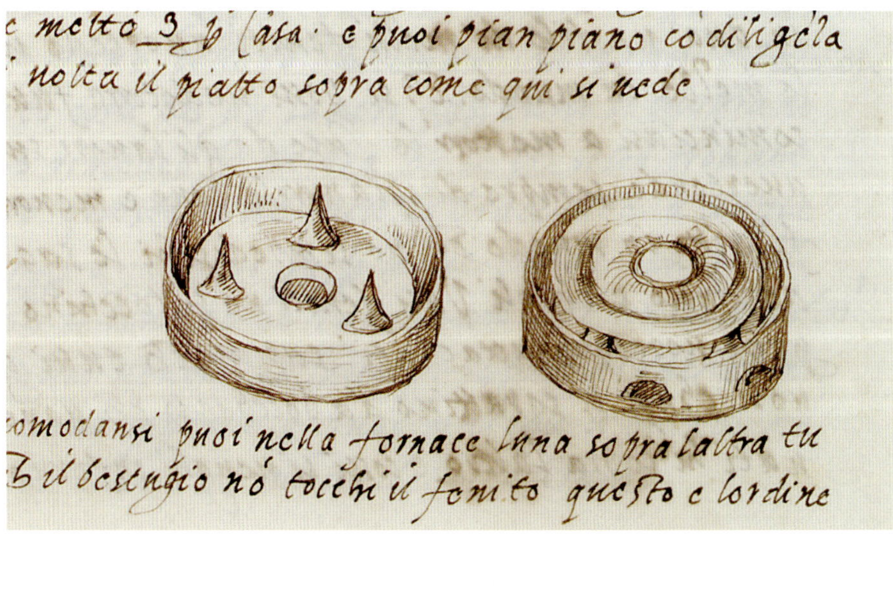

28 A saggar with three spurs (left) and with an upside-down plate placed on the spurs
***The Three Books of the Potter's Art*, fol.62v (detail)**
Cipriano Piccolpasso
Pen and ink
Castel Durante, 1557
NAL: MSL/1861/7446

When the painter is finished, the decorated pots are placed in a clean and dry place. The white can be touched up on the edges, should it have rubbed off. Elaborately painted plates are given a neat light-yellow rim on the banding wheel. If a very smooth shiny glaze is required, painted but unfired wares can be given a cover of clear lead-glaze at this stage. This is applied in liquid form by carefully flicking it on with a brush.[10] The vessels are then thoroughly dried prior to firing.

Firing the finished wares

Stacking the kiln for the glaze firing is one of the most important and precarious of the potter's tasks. The kiln must be stacked as fully as possible and the potter has to take account of many different considerations: the variations of temperature within the kiln; the stability of the stacks of pots; the even passage of the heat from the holes in the chamber floor; and the relative value of the wares. The most elaborate pieces are placed in the safest, most protected, positions, but the potter must still be able to observe them through the spy holes.

To protect them from smoke and kiln debris, all fine wares are fired in 'saggars', which are perforated cylindrical containers made of fire-resistant clay. Shallow dishes or plates are placed face down into the saggar resting on three individual spurs or, for small bowls, on a tripod (pls 27–9). This protects the painted decoration, though the spurs leave three small scars on the front of the dish when they are removed from the saggar. Deeper bowls are placed face down, with their rims resting on three triangular pegs. So-called *bianchi*, or Faenza white wares, are covered with a particularly thick layer of tin-glaze.[11] These must be fired standing on their base, as the thick glaze runs downwards and sticks the pots to their saggars, which leaves unsightly scars when the wares are removed (see pl. 29). Most pieces are placed in their own individual saggars, which are stacked, one on top of the other, reaching up to the vault of the kiln. The stacks are placed in such a way that the fire can play around them, and holes in the bottoms and sides of the saggars ensure that the hot air reaches the ceramics inside. The saggars are used repeatedly until they finally crack and need replacing. In order to reduce the number of different saggars required and to simplify their stacking within the kiln, only a few standard sizes were used. This meant that several types of fine wares made at a single pottery would have the same diameter, so that they could be fired in saggars of a standard size. Piccolpasso gives a diagram to illustrate this way of working, showing that: 'Bowls on foot; salad dishes; dishes for soups derived from silver models; and porringers with a rim of the largest size' were all made to the same diameter of just under 22 cm.

29 Waster with tripod marks
Faenza, 1490–1510
V&A: C.123A-1911

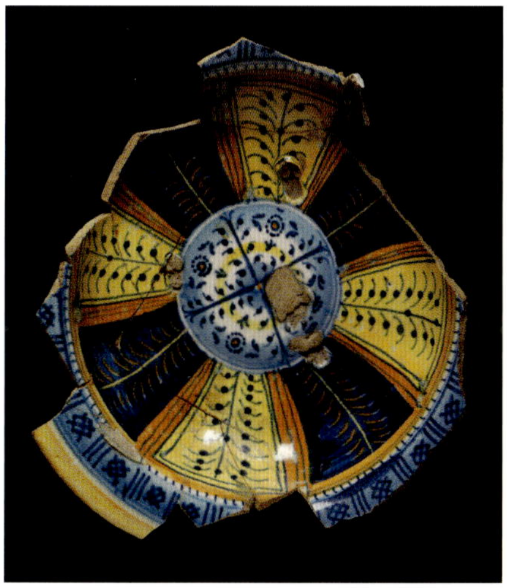

Larger wares such as drug jars and 'ordinary wares', which had less decoration, were stacked face down, one on top of the other. Large dishes were placed on their side in a row, with the first dish facing the side wall of the chamber and the next one leaning against its back. The first and the last row of wares stacked in the kiln were 'raw', unfired pots. When the final row was placed, the kiln opening was bricked up and mortared over.

The actual firing of the finished wares is one of the most important events in the potter's calendar. If something goes wrong during this final stage, the contents of the entire kiln and a whole month's work could be lost. The sixteenth-century potter has no accurate method of controlling the temperature in his kiln, and has to use fine judgment, guided by experience and knowledge handed down from master to master over the decades. Invariably, at the start of each firing, there are prayers to God.

The potter also takes account of the state of the moon and of the weather. In the rainy season especially, a potter would not start his firing when the moon was waning and insufficiently bright. Perhaps there was a belief that this would increase the chance of rain, which could have a negative effect on the firing.

The timber used for fuel must be well weathered and completely dry. Huge quantities of timber are kept at hand, as a single firing can easily need three hundred bundles of wood.[12] Bundles of willow and elm twigs and split lengths of elmwood are the ideal fuel.[13] These allow the potter to build up the fire gradually by continuously adding more wood, while preventing it from burning too fiercely. Firing continued for about 11 hours at which point the kiln would have reached the required temperature of about 960°C. The potter had to judge this by the 'brightness' of the interior of the kiln behind each of the spy holes. In addition he would be guided by other indicators, such as the size of the drips of molten plaster hanging from the vault of the kiln and the ashes appearing on the cracks of the bricked-up kiln mouth. Once convinced the firing is complete, he slackens the fire and rakes out the embers.

Lustreware

For most pots, this would be the end of the making process, and after the furnace had cooled down, they would begin their journey to the customer. The only exception to this was lustreware, as lustre pigments needed an additional firing, at a much lower temperature and under specific oxygen starved kiln conditions. This 'reducing' atmosphere was very hard to control, and the rate of failure was particularly high. Only a handful of specialist workshops, mostly located in Gubbio and Deruta, were able to produce lustreware successfully on a substantial scale. Piccolpasso explains how he could only observe the practice of lustre decoration at the house of Maestro Cencio in Gubbio (this was Vincenzo, the son and successor of the most famous lustre potter of the Renaissance period, Maestro Giorgio Andreoli).

Like other maiolica pigments, lustre works best on a white ground, and if the pot is to be decorated in other colours too, the painter must leave areas in reserve, where the lustre is to be added later. After the tin-glaze and coloured decoration has been fired on, the lustre pigment is applied. Lustre came in three tints at the time: red, gold, and a golden silver. The pigments for these all contain copper and silver as well as red earth (ochre), vinegar and sometimes also Armenian bole or cinnabar. The pigments are painted onto the fired tin-glazed surface and left to dry.

The lustre pigments are fired on in a small specialized kiln, designed to create a good and even draught within the chamber. Fueled by straw and dry willow branches, firing lasts for about three hours, until the interior of the kiln presents 'a certain glow'. This was probably around 600°C, or just around red heat. At this stage, the potter changes the fuel from willow to well dried and seasoned broom or spartium, resinous shrubs that create a lot of smoke during combustion (pl. 30). The smoke starves the kiln of oxygen, causing a reducing atmosphere in which the lustre pigments are transformed into a thin metallic film. This process takes about an hour, during which period the lustre turns from a very pale tone to a fully developed, deep colour. Test pieces are taken from the top of the kiln at regular intervals to ensure that firing can be stopped at exactly the right moment (pl. 31). In order to maximize exposure to the reducing smoke, the objects are placed directly on the kiln floor, not in saggars. First a biscuit-fired bowl is placed upside-down, and a dish is placed onto this, face down and resting on its rim. The next dish rests with its rim on the bottom of the previous dish and so on.

When the ceramics are removed from the kiln, the lustre is covered with a dull layer of ochre which must be washed away and polished to reveal the finished shiny, metallic surface.

Workshop organization

The Piccolpasso manuscript is invaluable for the understanding of Renaissance maiolica techniques, but archival sources give us a greater insight into the organization and size of the ceramics industry. Guild records and protective legislation illustrate how the craft became increasingly organized after 1400.[14] Additional detail on the size and working practice of individual potteries has been gleaned from tax returns, legal documents, inventories and contracts.

Maiolica workshops probably varied in size from a one- or two-man village enterprise to a well-organized manufactory with more than one kiln employing many specialized workers. Workshop inventories list many typical fixtures: a kiln; often also a reverbatory furnace (a special kiln for making tin ash); a well; a mill with several grindstones and a horse in the stable to drive it; usually two mortars; various stools; benches; tubs and sieves; and most commonly two or three potter's wheels and many ware-boards, on which the unfinished pots were placed and carried around.[15] To a large extent, the

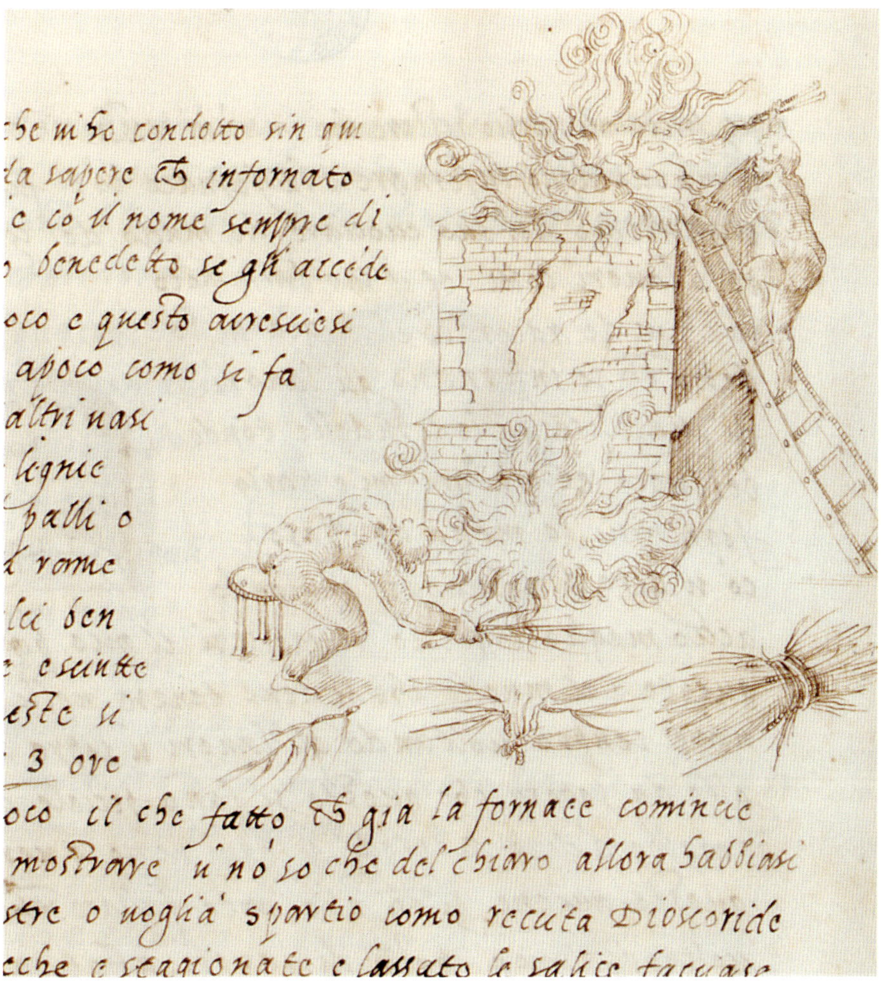

30 Firing the lustre kiln with brushwood. An assistant on a ladder is pulling out a trial piece
***The Three Books of the Potter's Art*, fol.49v (detail)**
Cipriano Piccolpasso
Pen and ink
Castel Durante, 1557
NAL: MSL/1861/7446

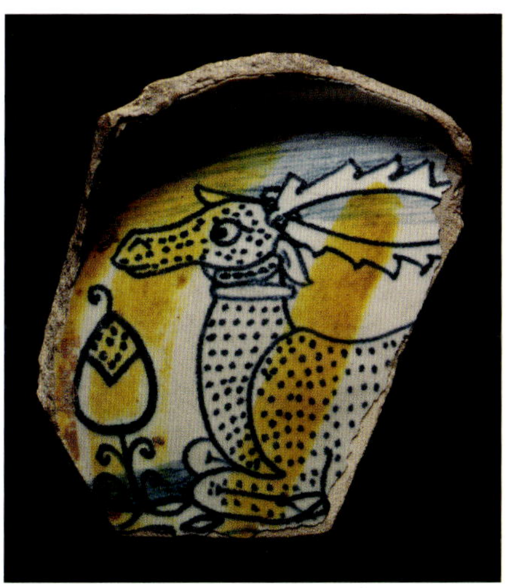

31 Fragment of a dish
Deruta, c.1515
W: 7 cm
V&A: C.632–1917

This was broken in the second firing and subsequently used as a trial piece to see how the lustre developed during reduction-firing.

organization of a workshop was geared to the size of its premises and kiln, which was normally fired only once a month. A well-organized workshop with the size of kiln described by Piccolpasso would probably employ up to nine permanent workers. Apart from the owner/workshop manager, there would have been two throwers, two or more painters and possibly also a kiln-man and one or two general workers. But a large workshop such as that of Maestro Virgiliotto in Faenza, which had two kilns, three horses to drive the mills and six potter's wheels, employed many more.[16]

An experienced potter would have thrown a simple pot or plate in a matter of minutes and two throwers would produce several hundred in a single day. The painters worked at a much slower pace. They would have found it difficult to catch up with the throwers if it wasn't for the fact that most shops produced a mixture of wares, ranging from fine, highly decorated ceramics to pottery for daily use with little or no decoration.[17] Typically, maiolica painters were paid according to the amount of work they produced. Many skilled painters travelled from town to town to find profitable engagement. Giovanni Luca, a painter from Castel Durante, agreed in a legal document of 1525 to lodge with Maestro Giorgio, owner of a large workshop in Gubbio, for one whole year.[18] Other painters worked part-time, sometimes for more than one workshop, perhaps even in two different towns.[19] The Castel Durante painter Giovan Paolo Savini seems to have worked in Rome for a period before he returned to his home town. From a judicial enquiry carried out in Castel Durante in 1606, we learn that he kept a pot with nine paintbrushes in the workshop of Cesare Compagno, where he 'sometimes came to work'.[20] Particularly interesting is a dispute between several workshop owners and a group of skilled workers including painters. The workers made a secret arrangement concerning their pay, and went on strike. They refused to return to work even after the owners offered to increase their salary, and as a result the owners agreed amongst themselves not to employ any of the listed workmen without informing the other master potters.[21]

The Piccolpasso manuscript includes a selection of typical designs, annotated with the payment the painter would receive for executing one hundred pieces. These range from half to two *scudi* for a hundred patterns, depending on their complexity. Two *scudi* represented about three weeks minimum wage at the time.[22] Assuming that a painter would earn the minimum wage during a six-day week, he would need to paint between 5 ½ and 22 plates per day, or 150 to 400 a month. The number would be considerably higher for simple patterns.[23] Needless to say, the most accomplished *istoriato* painters earned more, though their output was necessarily much lower because of the complexity of their work. In 1530, Frederico Gonzaga, the Duke of Mantua, was advised that he could buy almost 100 pieces of Urbino *istoriato* maiolica for 25 *scudi*.[24] His agent explained that the various pieces are 'worth more or less depending on the greater and lesser amount of work'. We do not know what percentage of the price would be paid to the painter, but if we assume it would be half, the painters would have expected the equivalent of over 18 weeks' minimum pay for this job, indicating that they would decorate about three pieces on average each week. The reality was doubtless more complex. It would make sense in the larger workshops for the most skilled painters to paint only the most difficult parts of a design. A plate made at the workshop of Maestro Giorgio Andreoli in Gubbio, has the word *azuro* painted in blue underneath a broad blue area within the design (pl. 32)[25]. This is a clear indication that the principal painter executed the outline and more complex parts of the composition, leaving the colouring-in of background areas to an apprentice painter or a less skilled assistant.

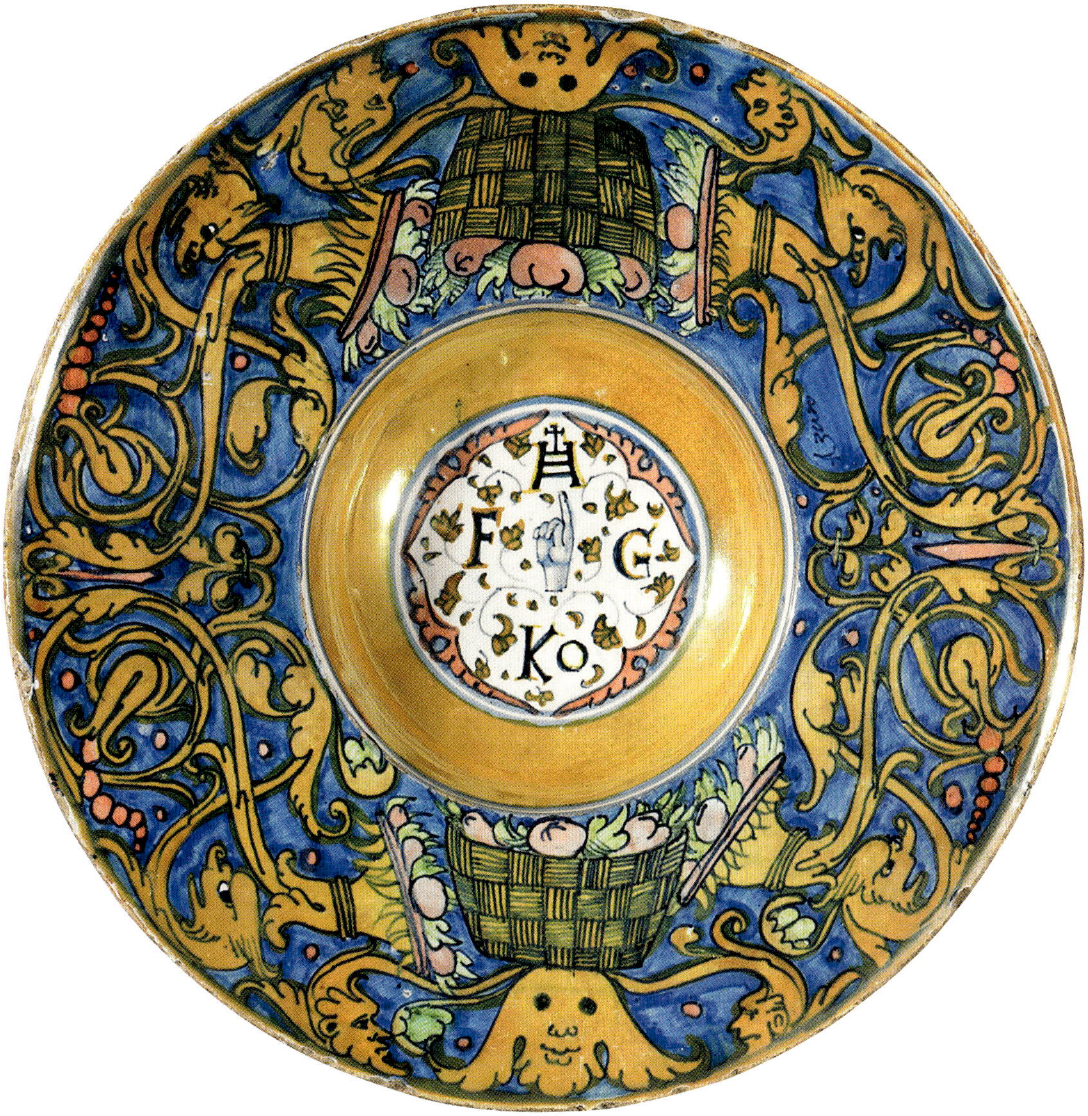

32 Dish with the word 'azuro' [blue] written beneath the blue-hatched background, and detail
Workshop of Maestro Giorgio
Gubbio, 1518
© The Trustees of the British Museum

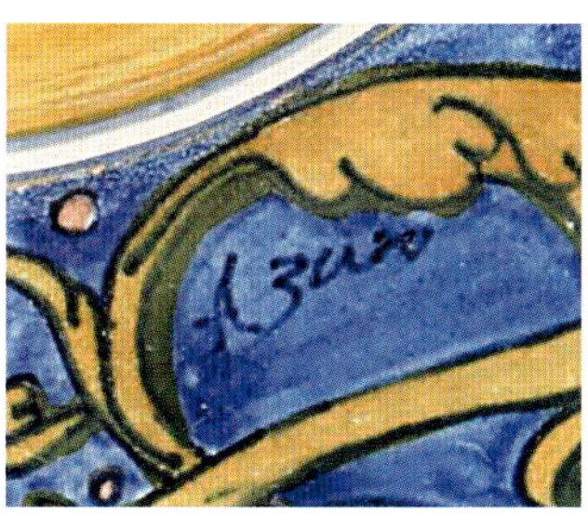

Elaborately decorated pieces were often part of special commissions and sometimes such commissions could be huge. In 1545, Faenza potter Francesco Mezzarisa received an order for 3,500 pieces of maiolica, and in the following year another for 7,025, half of which had to be delivered in 72 days, the rest in a further 61 days. Contemporary evidence shows that large orders could be placed with more than one master, who could work concurrently, and in other instances these must have called for the collaboration of more than one workshop.[26]

By the time that Piccolpasso was compiling his treatise the Italian potters' craft had grown into a large and well-organized industry. Whole towns were dominated by ceramics production, as at Faenza, where one in nine people worked in the potteries during the early sixteenth century.[27] It is striking how many features of pottery production in the sixteenth century – including fixed contracts, price fixing, sub-contracting, industrial disputes and part-time work – sound very familiar to the modern reader.

FOGLIE DA DUZENA

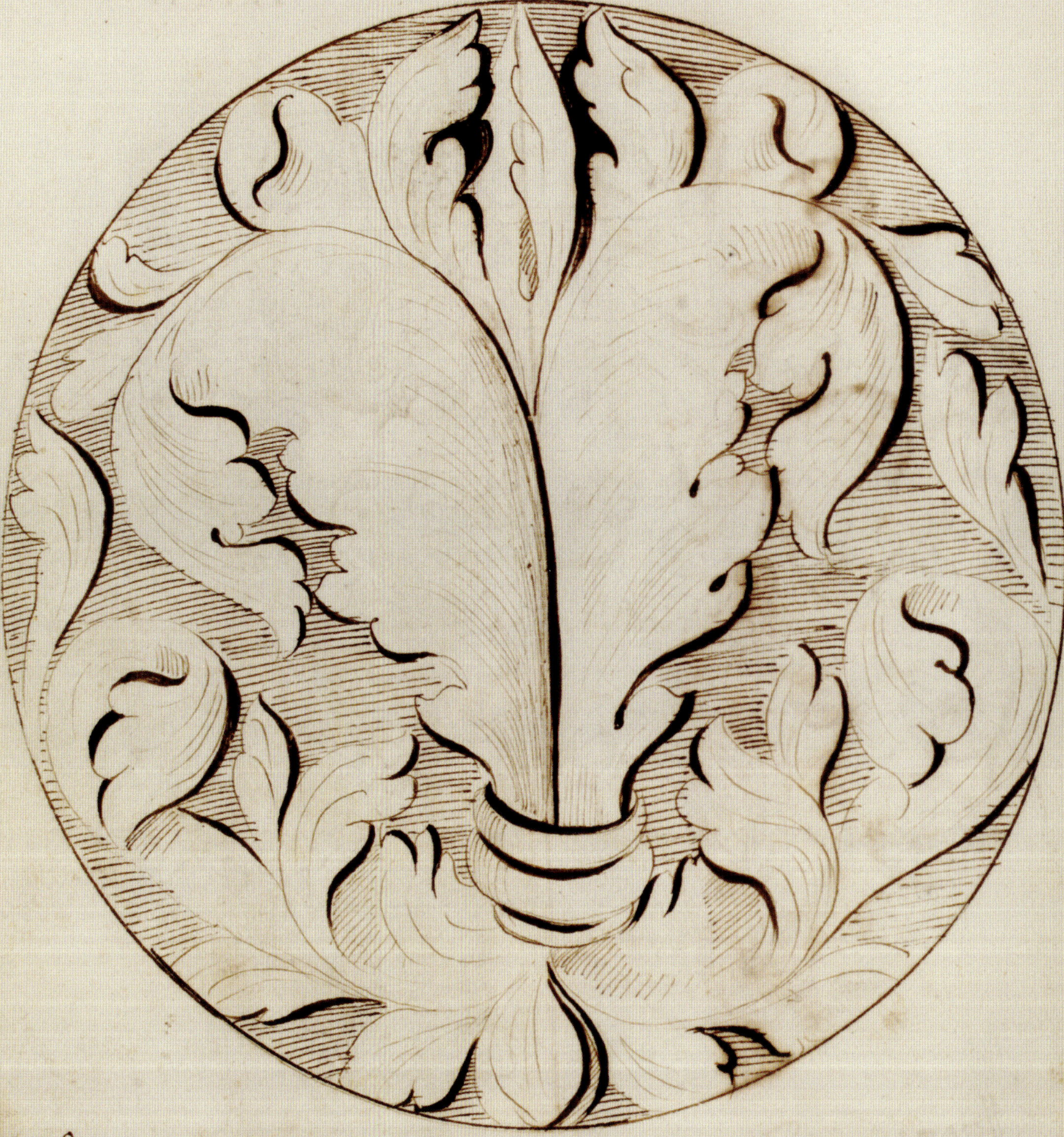

Questa e Pittura chumuna e Pagasi mezo fiorino il cento
in Vinegia 2 lire

2 Stylistic Development

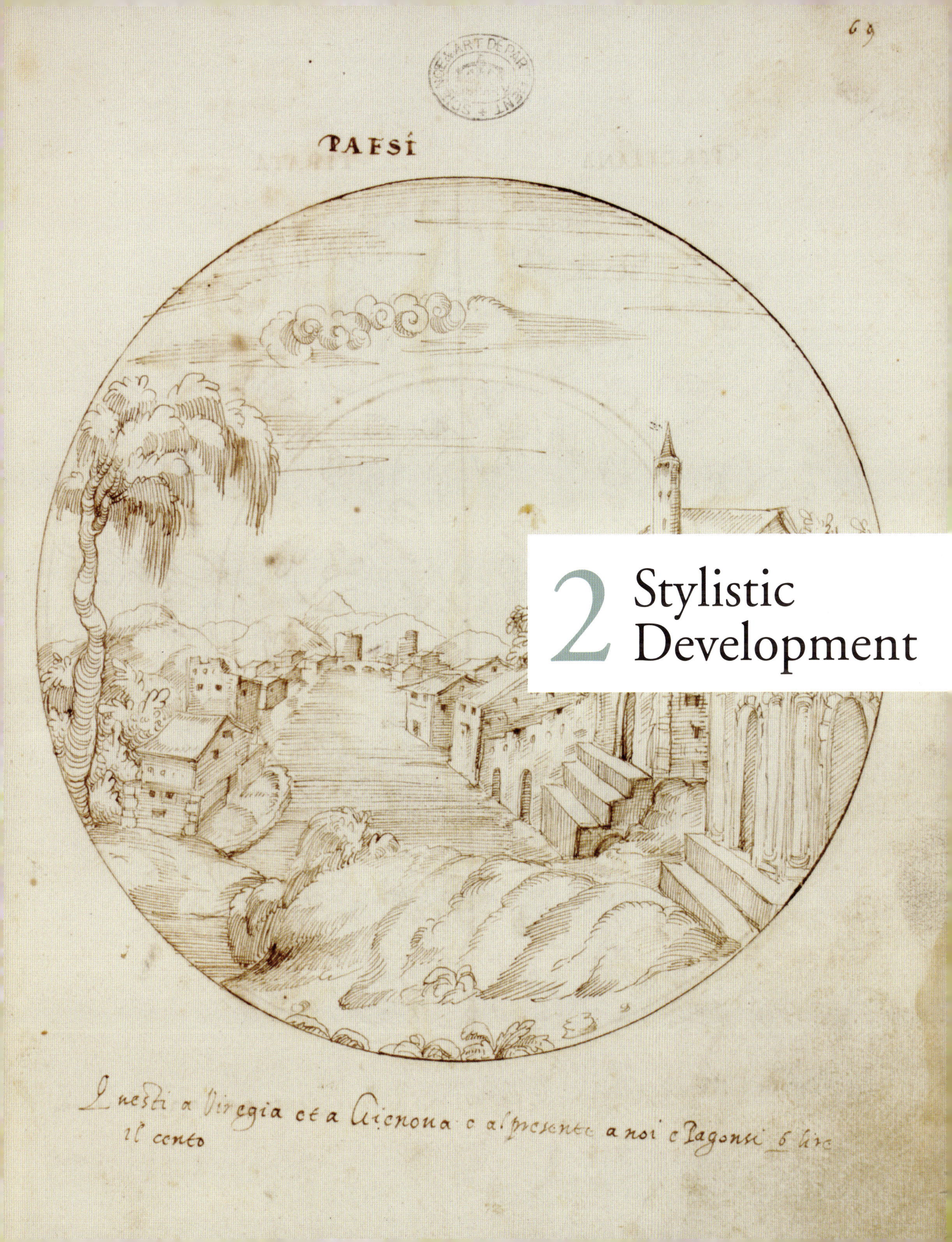

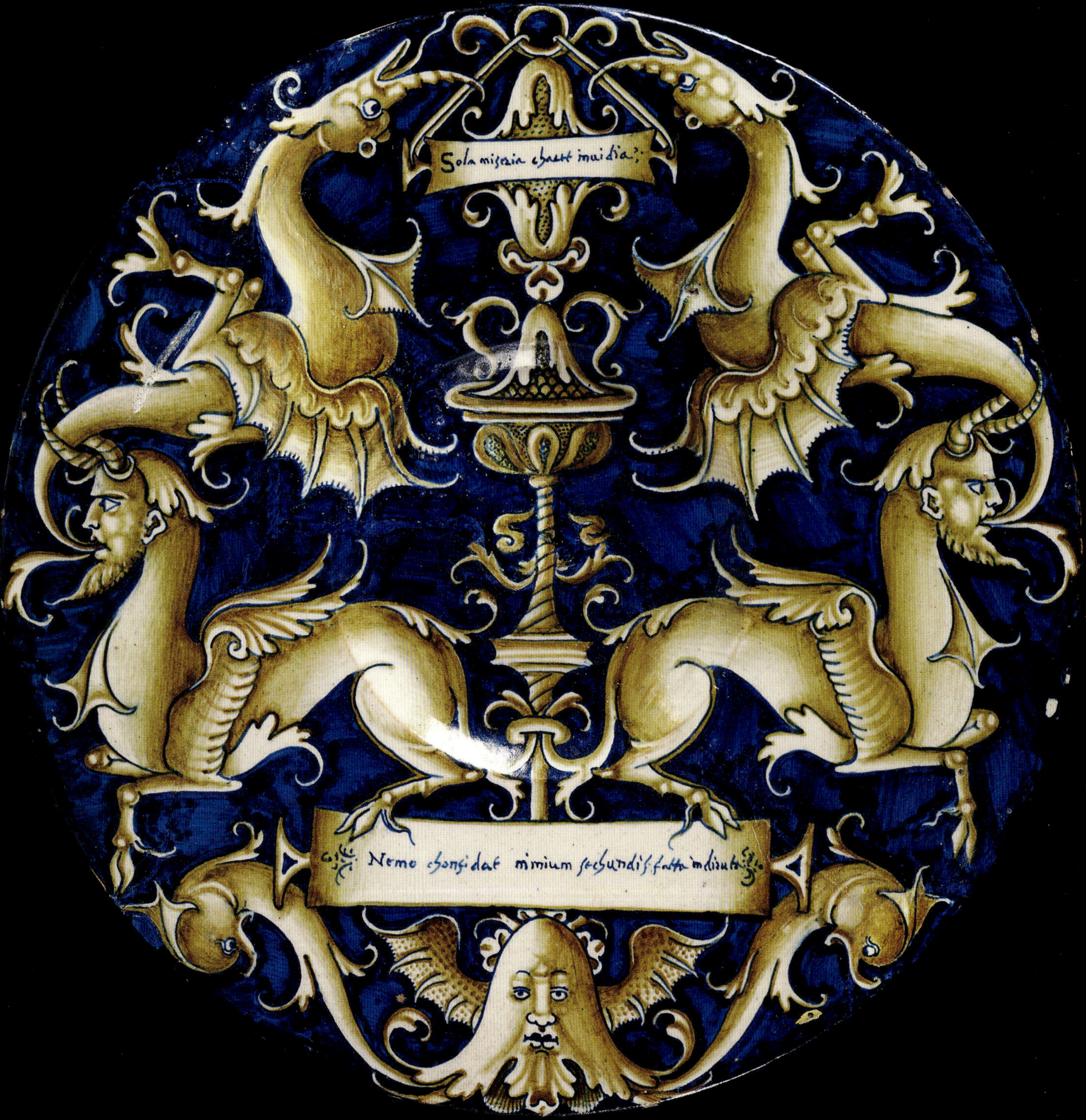
Sola miseria chaett inuidia
Nemo chonfidat nimium sechundis fatta indiruta

Introduction

From the introduction of tin-glaze to Italy around the early thirteenth century, potters explored the possibilities of painting on its white surface. Over time the glaze was developed to give a whiter finish, and more colours became available: gradually, the painted decoration became maiolica's most distinctive feature. The combination of improved technical and artistic expertise, especially from around 1450, resulted in a quintessentially new type of pottery praised for its lightness and vibrancy of colours.

During the fifteenth century, the ceramics industry developed very rapidly in Italy and a number of specialized centres developed. Towns such as Faenza, Deruta and Montelupo became completely dominated by the industry, while places like Urbino, Castel Durante, Pesaro, Gubbio, Castelli, Siena and Naples were also producing significant quantities of pottery.

Each centre developed its own individual style of painting and vocabulary of ornament. In the second edition of his *Lives of the Artists* (1568) Giorgio Vasari paid tribute to the achievement of contemporary potters:

> As far as we can tell, the [ancient] Romans were not aware of this type of painting on pottery. The vessels from those days ... are covered with figures incised and washed in with one colour in any given area, sometimes in black, red, or white, but never with the brilliance of glaze or the charm and variety of painting seen in our day.

Archaeological excavations and archival researches carried out in recent decades have enormously expanded our knowledge of Renaissance maiolica. The increase in production and diversification from the second half of the fifteenth century onwards is reflected in the wealth of examples surviving in collections around the world. Information on where a particular type of decoration was used comes from wares marked with their place of manufacture, potters' marks, signatures and dates. These often show how similar designs were in use in different pottery centres, as artisans moved around taking their repertoire of designs with them.

The development of printmaking in Europe around 1400 and the invention of the printing press in the mid-fifteenth century were crucial factors in the artistic development of maiolica. From the late fifteenth century a wide variety of illustrated books was available in Europe: printed patterns and designs for the decorative arts and even calligraphy manuals offered inspiration to pottery painters.

Motifs used in maiolica designs had a wide range of influences from Chinese, Islamic and Spanish ceramics, to metalwork and textiles.

An invaluable source for the understanding of maiolica patterns is a series of drawings included in the third book of Piccolpasso's pottery manual. For each type of ornament, Piccolpasso, writing in the 1550s, states the price and specifies the location where it was mainly in use at the time.

At the heart of the Italian Renaissance was the revival of Roman antiquity, and from the beginning of the sixteenth century we see potters absorbing its fashionable artistic vocabulary. All these influences resulted in something completely new, a distinctive and artistically accomplished type of pottery different from anything seen before.

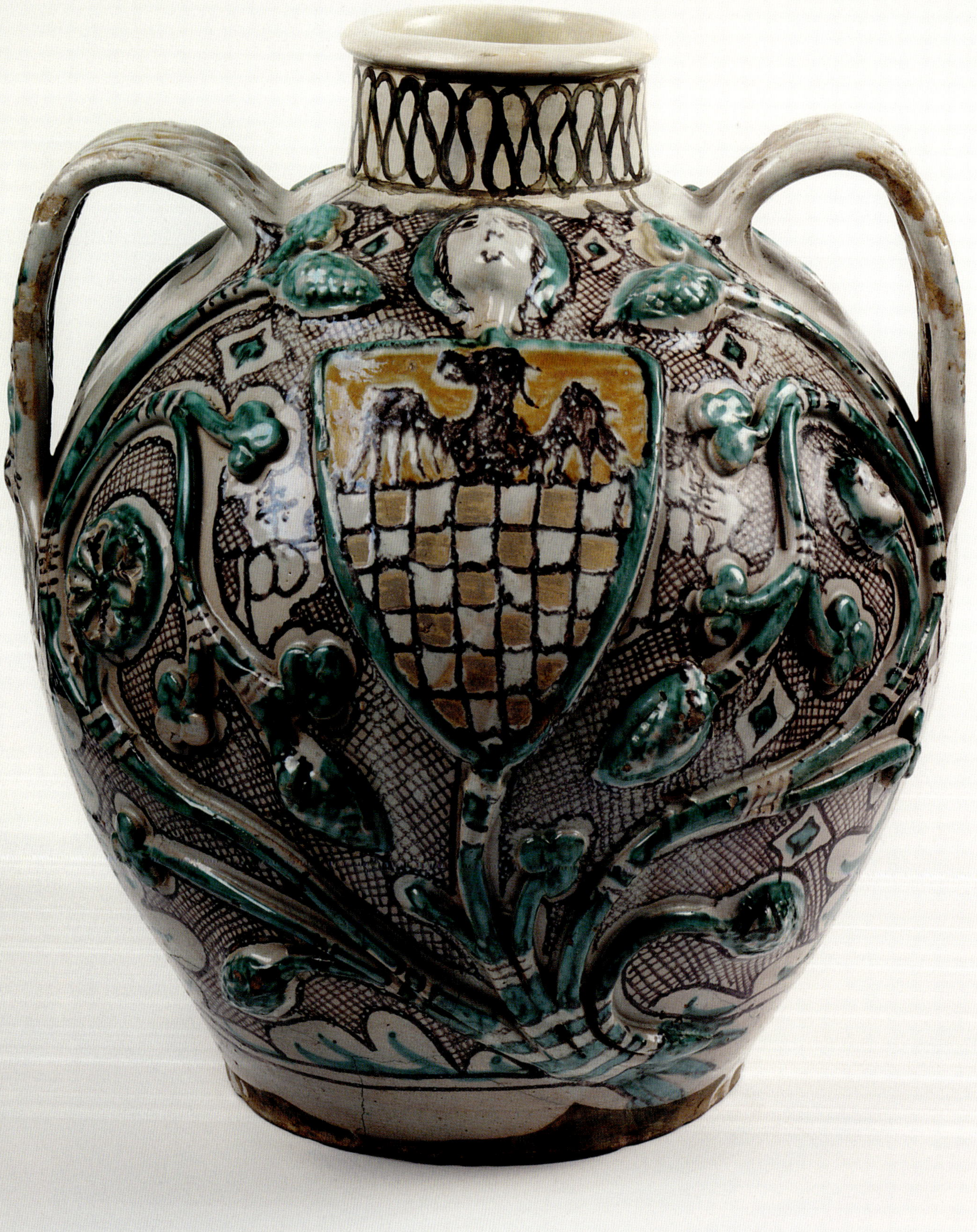

The Ornamental Language of Maiolica

33 (previous spread) 'The Diruta Plate'
Probably Nicola Francioli known as 'Co'
Deruta, c.1525
Diam: 27.5 cm
Salting Bequest V&A: C.2156–1910

34 Two-handled jar with decorations in relief including the coat of arms of Ottoni (?)
Probably Orvieto, 1350–1400, neck modern replacement
H: 35 cm
V&A: 671–1884

Medieval pottery

Early maiolica, dating from the thirteenth to the fourteenth century, is characterized by simple decorations and functional shapes, mostly jugs, dishes and small bowls. The painted decorations are in copper green and manganese brown or manganese purple, which were the first metallic pigments known to potters. The decorations were simple stylized ornaments inspired by nature, leaves or flowers. Simply drawn animals, birds (pl. 37) and heraldic beasts or monsters with human heads are among the first figural elements painted on maiolica, while political and religious symbols, such as the fleur-de-lis or the Agnus Dei, also appear in the fourteenth century.

Geometric motifs, knots and wavy lines cover the background, which is often divided into compartments. A background decoration of heavy cross-hatching in manganese brown is often used on medieval wares from Orvieto and elsewhere. Decorations in relief are visible on the most accomplished pieces, such as the armorial two-handled jar in pl. 34 (1350–1400), one of the most imposing examples of early maiolica production known to us.

A greater diversification in the decoration of maiolica started from around 1400. Cobalt blue, imported from the Middle East, was an expensive addition to the basic palette of brown/purple and green. From the late fourteenth century the use of blue is accompanied by an improved quality of the tin-glaze. One of the first uses of blue involved mixing it with a glassy material to create a relief decoration. This style is known as *zaffera a rilievo* (relief blue).[1] Although relief blue decoration was used in different areas, including Faenza, Viterbo and Orvieto, Tuscany seems to have been the major producer. Some early-fifteenth-century Florentine wares were decorated with a stylized 'oak leaf' relief-blue design outlined in manganese purple. Single figures or animals appeared amid the bold, blue pattern. One of the largest and certainly most ambitious examples is a splendid two-handled drug jar (pl. 35). Its decoration of two rampant beasts in thick blue glaze is reminiscent of contemporary 'Perugia towels', fine cloths decorated with blue thread over white linen (pl. 36).[2]

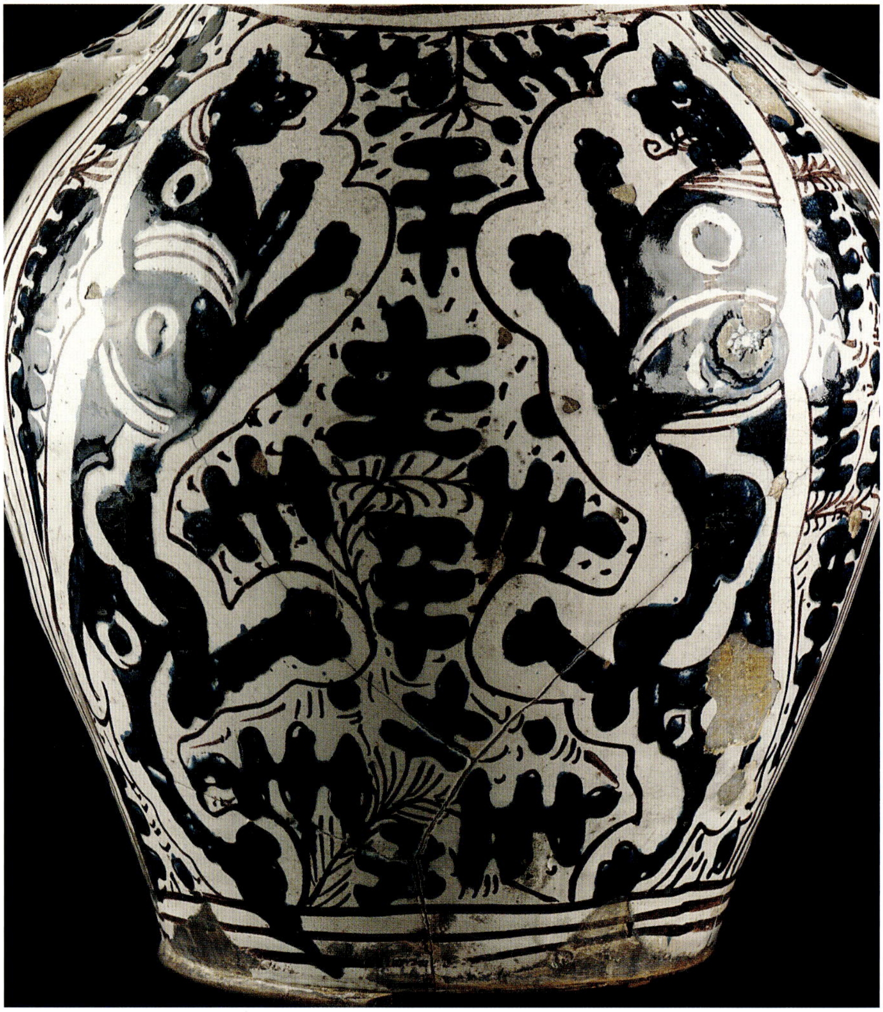

35 Drug jar (detail of pl. 23)
Florence, 1420–40
H: 36.3 cm
V&A: 2562–1836

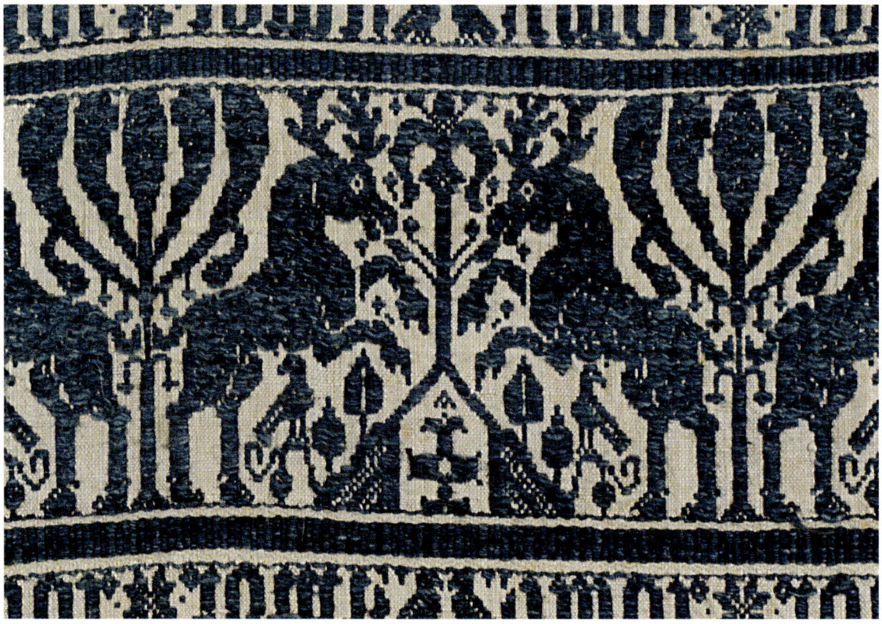

36 'Perugia towel' (detail)
Woven linen
Central Italy (Umbria?),
1400–1500
V&A: 226–1904

37 Dish with bird
Probably Orvieto, c.1350
Diam: 9.5 cm
V&A: C.202–1928

38 Drug jar with vine leaf motif
Florentine area, 1460–75
H: 24.5 cm
V&A: 363–1889

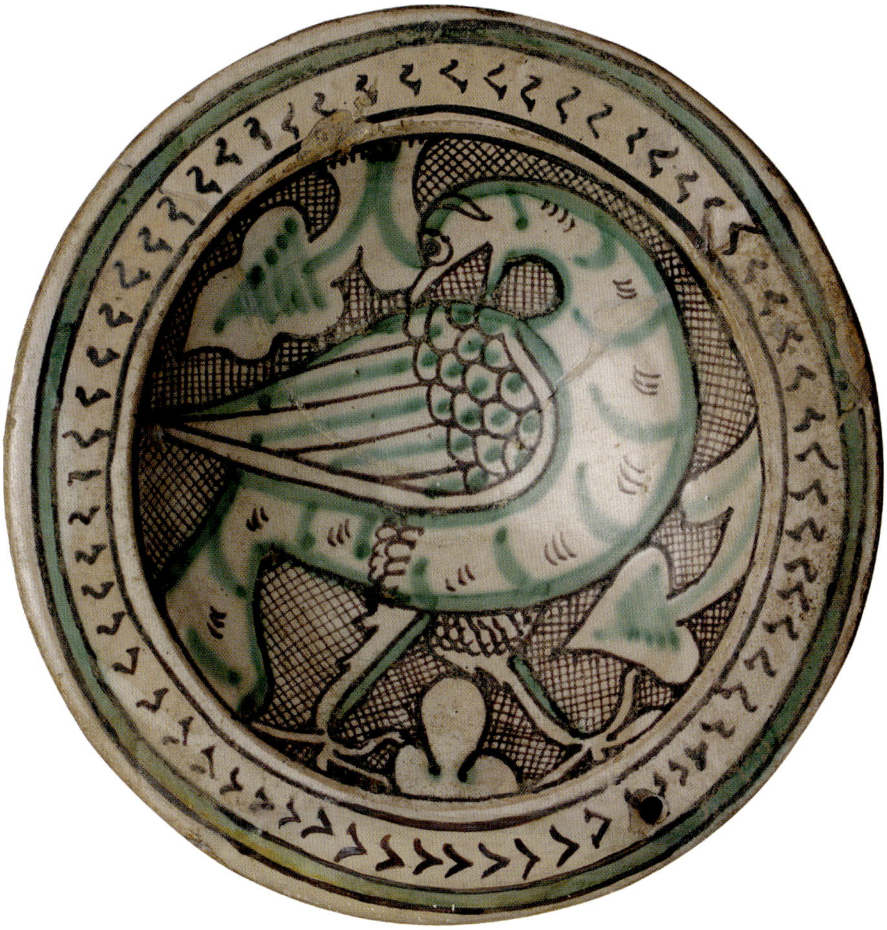

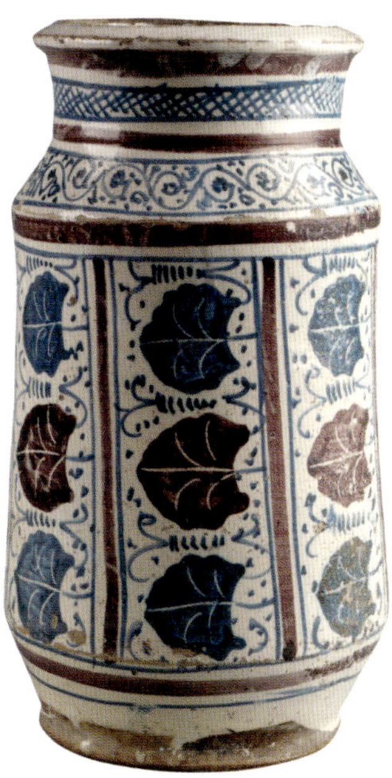

The designs of the early Renaissance

From around 1450 potteries in north-central Italy, including those in Faenza, Deruta, Pesaro, Siena and Montelupo, saw increased production and technological advances. As maiolica became more widespread, designs grew more refined and elaborate. Both the increased demand and the technical and artistic improvements were driven partly by a taste for foreign imports of superior quality. Large quantities of lustred pottery from Valencia in Spain were imported into Italy throughout the fifteenth century. The city of Florence had important commercial interests in Spain and wealthy Florentine families commissioned services of Valencian pottery embellished with their arms.[3]

This prompted imitation from local potters. Unable at first to copy the metallic lustre of the Spanish originals, Tuscan potters produced polychrome imitations. Spanish drug jars decorated with horizontal bands of vine leaves painted in blue and lustre, for instance, were much admired and are often represented in contemporary paintings. Italian potters copied both the shape of the jars and the vine-leaf ornament, substituting brownish purple for the lustre pigments (pl. 38). Another motif derived from Valencian lustred pottery that became particularly popular with Tuscan potters from around the 1460s was a pattern of small stylized leaves; a Pisan inventory of 1480 suggests that Tuscans referred to similar designs as *'fioralixi'* (cornflowers) (pl. 39)[4].

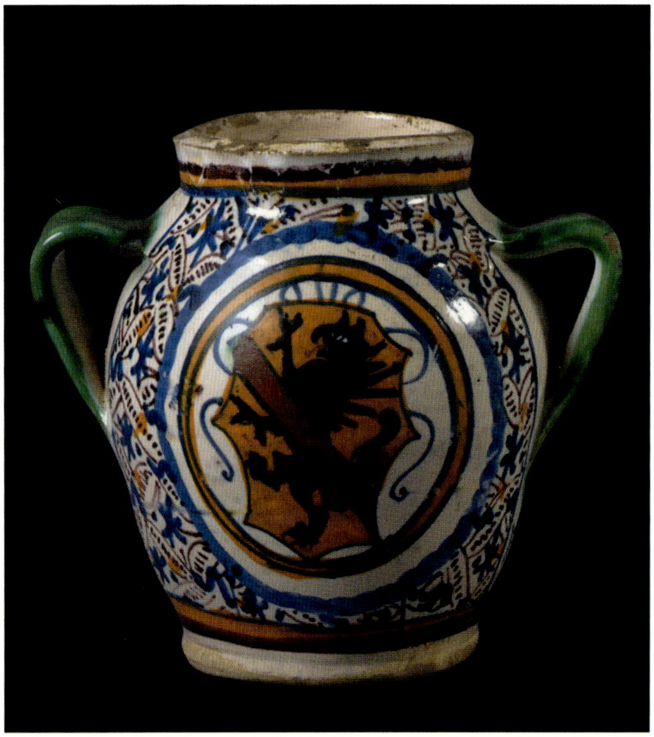

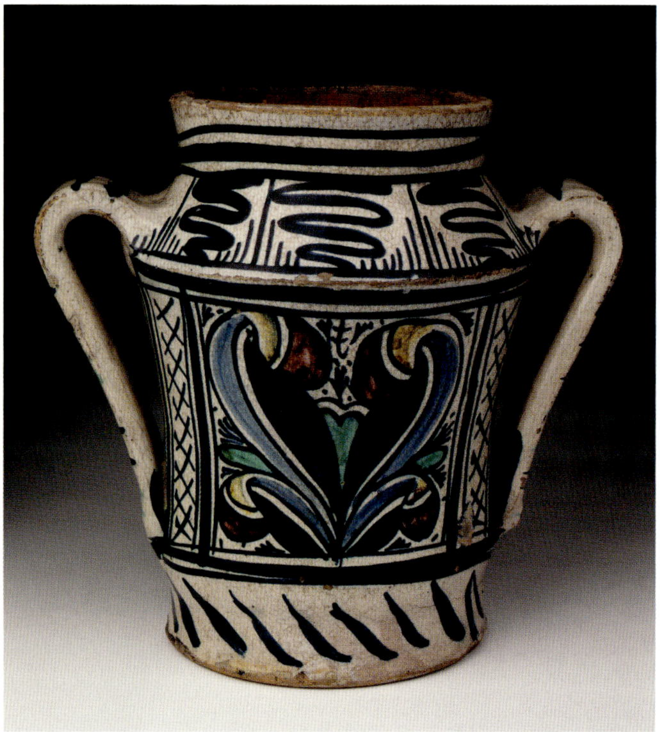

39 Two-handled jar with coat of arms and 'parsley-leaf', *'fioralixi'* decoration
Probably Montelupo, c.1490
H: 13.5 cm
V&A: 433–1906

40 Two-handled *albarello*
Probably Deruta, 1470–90
H: 21 cm
V&A: 834–1903

41 Plate with peacock feather ornament
Perhaps Siena, c.1480
Diam: 20.5 cm
V&A: 2606–1856

These decorations were particularly fashionable amongst the Florentine elite, but similar ornaments were also produced outside Tuscany, for instance in the Urbino region, at Faenza and elsewhere.

During the second half of the fifteenth century the skills of Italian potters continued to improve. They produced vessels of increasingly sophisticated shapes, adorned with boldly painted and highly original ornament. For the first time, we can observe the development of a distinctive Italian style. This emerging style is evident on the tiles made for some of the most prestigious maiolica pavements from the period around 1470–90, such as that of the Vaselli Chapel in San Petronio in Bologna of 1487, probably made by Faenza potters.

One of the most characteristic and widespread designs of the period is the 'Gothic leaf', large curving leaves painted in bold colours on plates as well as vases. Gothic foliage takes a wide variety of shapes and was often combined with coats of arms or figural decorations. A group of late-fifteenth-century two-handled jars, probably made in Deruta but formerly attributed to Faenza and Tuscany, have Gothic leaf as their main ornament on the body (pl. 40). The necks of many of these jars are decorated with another common late-fifteenth-century motif consisting of wavy lines, known as 'San Bernardino rays' because it often appears in a circular arrangement around the sacred trigram IHS which was the device of St Bernardino of Siena.

Other maiolica patterns developed during the second half of the fifteenth century distantly echo oriental motifs. One of the most fascinating of all, the peacock feather, was widely used during the third quarter of the fifteenth century. The lush colours of the feathers are imitated by the pottery painters with a lively palette of orange, green and manganese (pl. 41). This elegant motif is often found on excavated fragments from Faenza and the Marches, especially at Pesaro, but also in Tuscany at Montelupo,

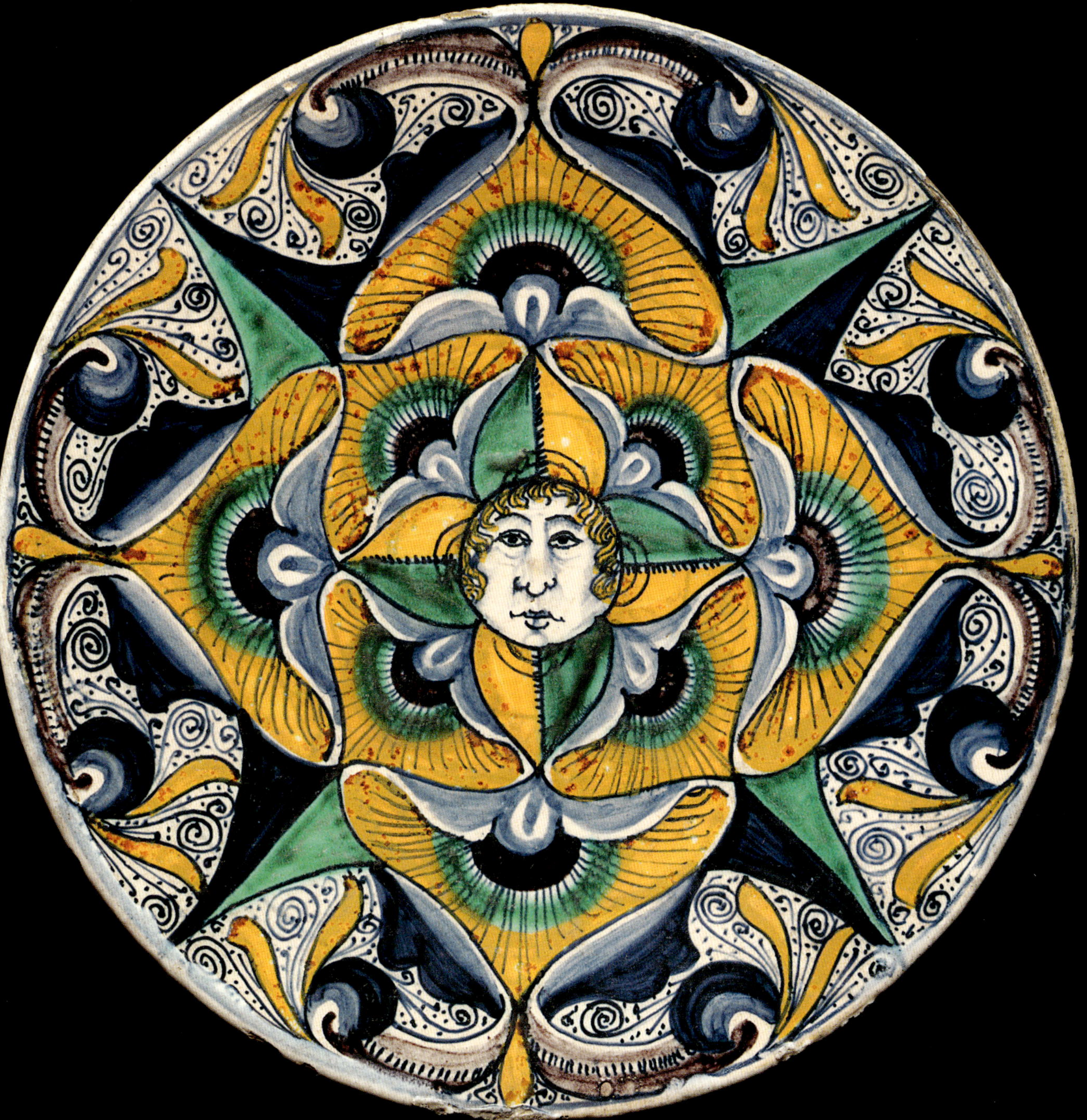

and is also found on maiolica pavements in Siena.[5] At Deruta, the peacock feather was still being used in lustred decorations in the sixteenth century.

Another motif rooted in Islamic art is the *'palmetta persiana'* (Persian palmette) used mainly in the last quarter of the fifteenth century. The motif recalls Egyptian and Iranian ceramics and textiles. It was widely used at Faenza, but also in Tuscany, in various regional adaptations (pl. 42).

Other design elements developed at this time, perhaps also inspired by Islamic decoration, are geometric patterns. In wares produced from the second half of the fifteenth century at Faenza, Montelupo and Deruta, motifs including scale-work, knots, lozenges and zig-zags are often used to frame figural elements or coats of arms (pl. 43).

Potters freely combined motifs from various sources. The superb heraldic jar in pl. 44, dating from the last quarter of the fifteenth century, shows an amalgamation of different designs. The decoration on the neck and shoulder, taken from Valencian lustreware, is combined with peacock feathers and a classically inspired wreath supported by putti. Wreath and putti are enclosed in a cartouche which follows their contour, a common late-fifteenth-century device used to highlight the figural elements of a decoration and separate it from its background.

Armorials and devices

Armorial decorations are a common feature from the fifteenth century, a clear sign of maiolica's increased status. While wares remained primarily functional, the addition of heraldic devices enabled them to convey a political message. The presence of a local court often gave impetus to a town's maiolica production and potters decorated wares with the arms of the dominant family. A relatively high number of jugs with the arms or the initial letter M for the Manfredi, Lords of Faenza from 1313 to 1505, have survived, several having been excavated in the city.[6] An exceptionally beautiful example,

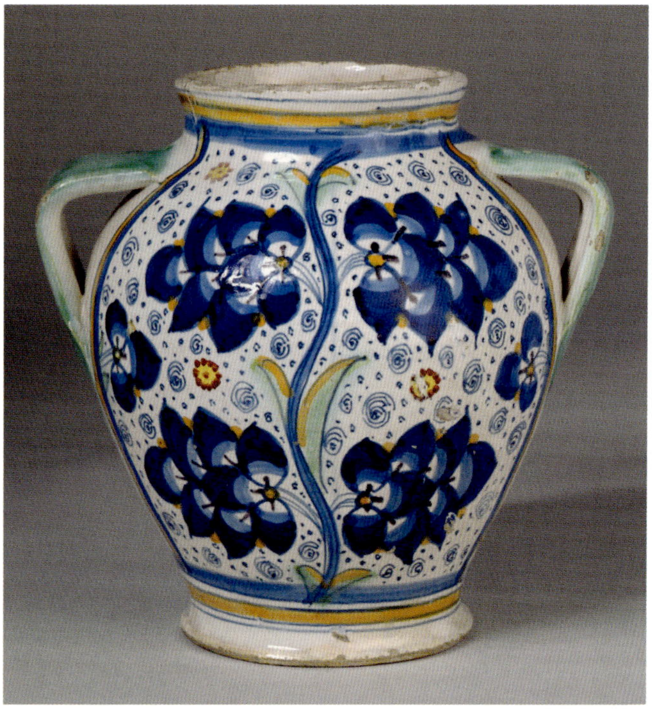

42 Two-handled jar with 'Persian palmette' ornament
Probably Montelupo, c.1490–1510
H: 20 cm
V&A: 375–1889

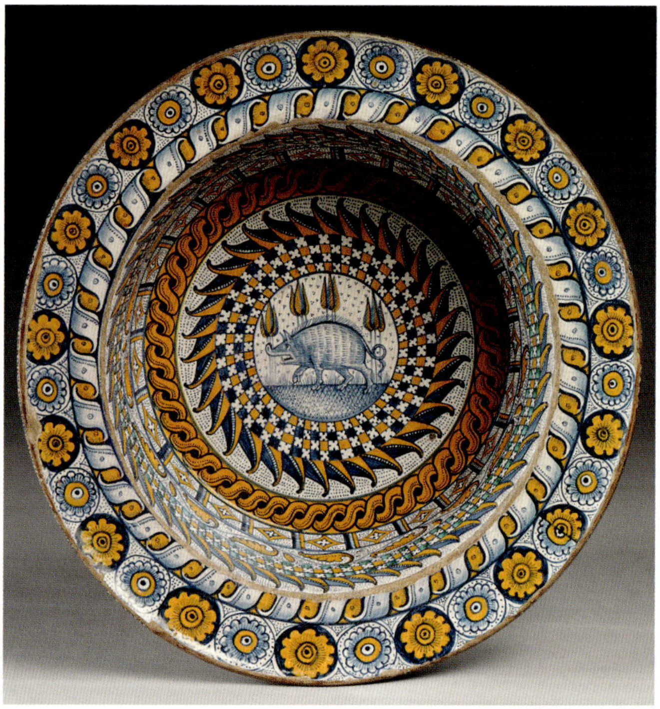

43 Basin with boar and ornamental border
Probably Deruta, c.1480–90
Diam: 47 cm
V&A: 2592–1856

44 Jar with coat of arms
Probably Pesaro, c.1490
H: 37 cm
V&A: 8389–1863

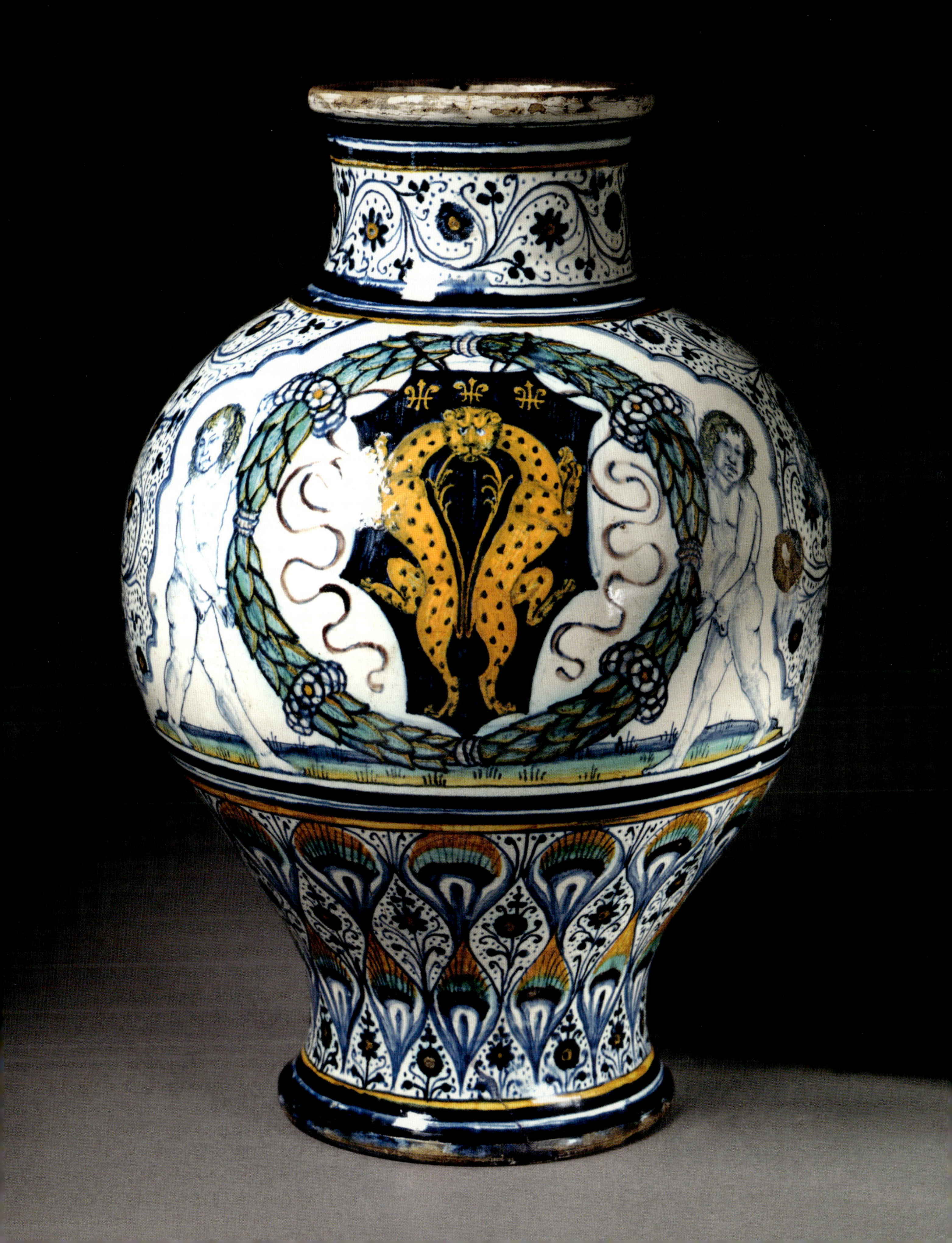

45 Jug with Manfredi arms
Faenza, c.1480
H: 26 cm
V&A: C.5–1922

46 Jug with arms of Pope Leo X and Medici devices
Montelupo, c.1515
H: 45 cm
V&A: 1715–1855

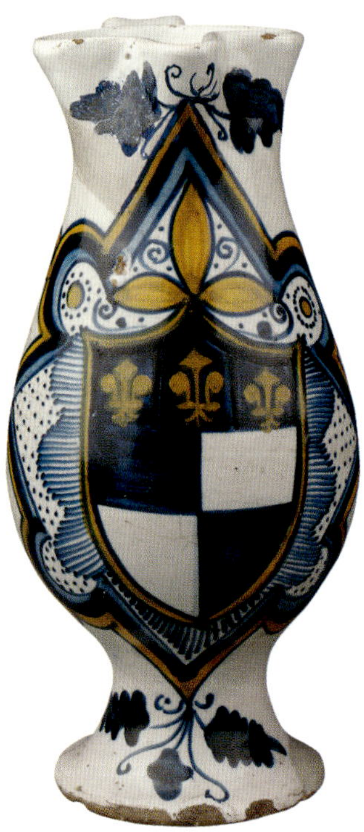

dating from 1480–1500 (pl. 45), represents the highest quality of pottery produced in Faenza at the time, which suggests that it could have been made for an important client, perhaps a member of the Manfredi family itself. The slender jug is of the purest white, made with a high proportion of tin, and features an elaborate Gothic decoration surrounding the arms.

Maiolica indeed became one of the most immediate and ubiquitous media through which to express support for local rulers, and potters were quick to respond to this demand. The arms of the Medici, Lords of Florence, for instance, feature on a large number of surviving ceramics made in Tuscany. A particularly interesting document shows how in 1508, after the fall of the Medici, Piero Soderini, *Gonfaloniere* (ruler) of Florence, ordered the destruction of all vessels for sale bearing the Medici arms, in an unsuccessful attempt to obliterate the visible signs and memory of the deposed rulers.[7] Similarly in 1537 after the fall of the Bentivoglio family, rulers of Bologna, some Faenza potters were caught selling pottery with their arms: the pottery was smashed and the potters maltreated.[8] These contemporary stories clearly illustrate the importance of the propaganda function of maiolica.

Elite Renaissance families sometimes had their personal devices added to maiolica wares. A device (*impresa*) normally comprised a 'motto' paired with a symbol. Learned and cultured courtiers were sometimes involved in this practice, as is documented by a complaint from the famous poet Poliziano, active at the court of Lorenzo de' Medici in Florence. In 1490 he wrote to Gerolamo de Donato complaining about the constant waste of time in having to write for people wanting '*... un motto ... o un verso ... o una impresa... pei cocci di casa*' – a motto, a verse or device for the household crockery.[9]

A monumental jug, probably made in Montelupo (pl. 46), might have been used in connection with the celebration of the election of Pope Leo X (1513–21), the first Medici Pope. The elaborate decoration cleverly incorporates the Medici family devices – the diamond, symbolizing eternity and used by all members of the family; the *broncone* (branch); the yoke, personal emblem of Leo; the motto '*glovis*' (it turns) – as well as emblems of the city of Florence. Armorials continued to be frequent ornaments throughout the sixteenth century.

Classical motifs: 'grotesques'

Classical antiquity had a most powerful and enduring influence on maiolica designs. From around 1500 acanthus leaves, palmettes, laurel wreaths, masks and classical busts started appearing as decorative motifs.

Among the most distinctive ornamental styles to appear was 'grotesque' decoration. The name derives from *grotte* (caves), the term used to describe the Roman palace belonging to the Emperor Nero (subsequently buried by the Baths of Trajan). The so-called *Domus Aurea* (Golden House) had been rediscovered in the 1480s. Artists, especially Pinturicchio, studied its wall decorations intently. Among the names of painters scratched into the walls are also those of a few potters.[10] Important fresco cycles, such as the one in the Piccolomini Library in Siena by Pinturicchio, as well as architectural features incorporating grotesques were produced from the last quarter of the fifteenth century and the style became widely disseminated through engravings in the sixteenth century (pl. 47).

The first phase of grotesque decoration on maiolica features large scale figural elements, mostly winged monsters with human heads, masks and putti. These elements are combined with cornucopia and scrollwork, set against a dark blue

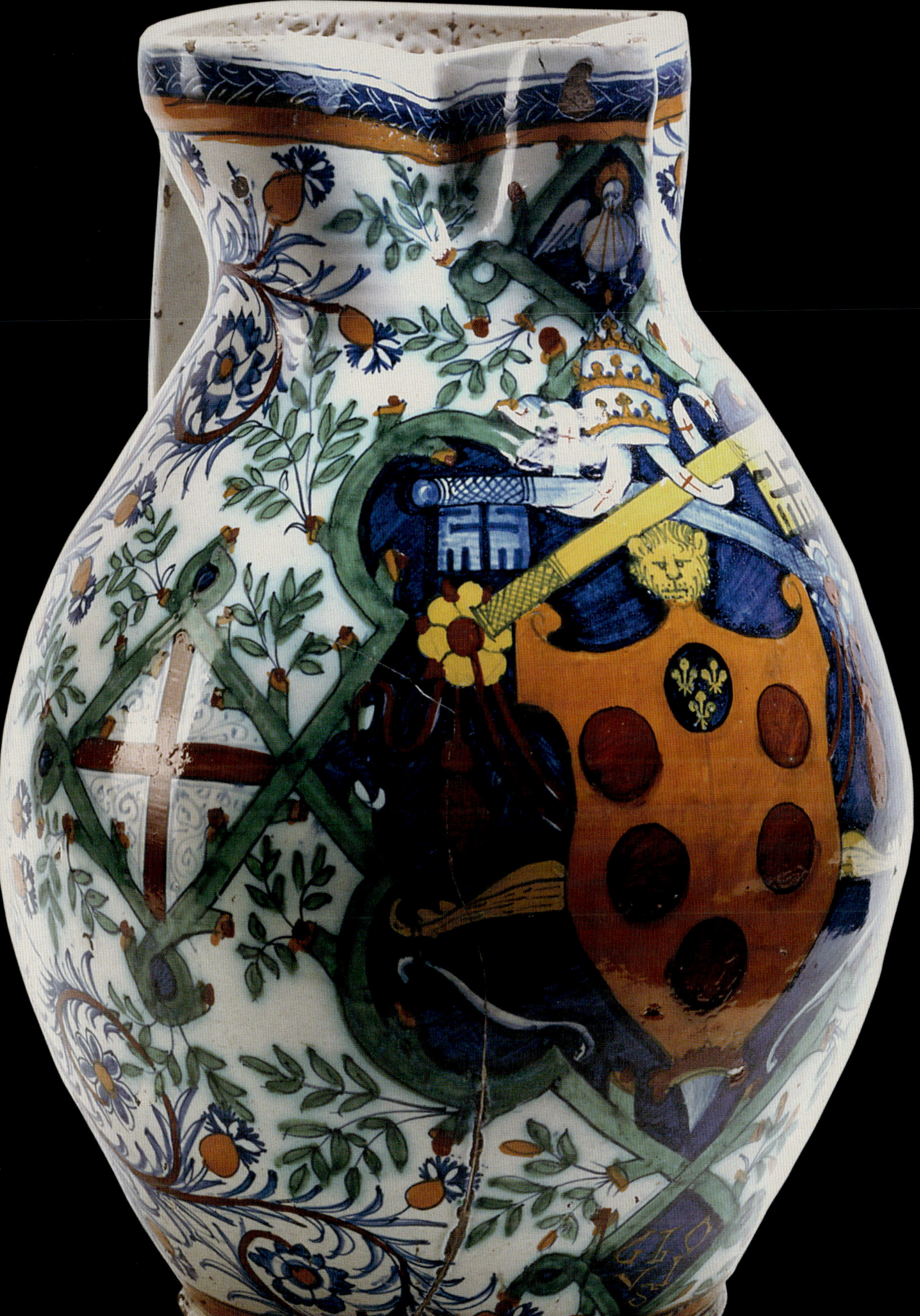

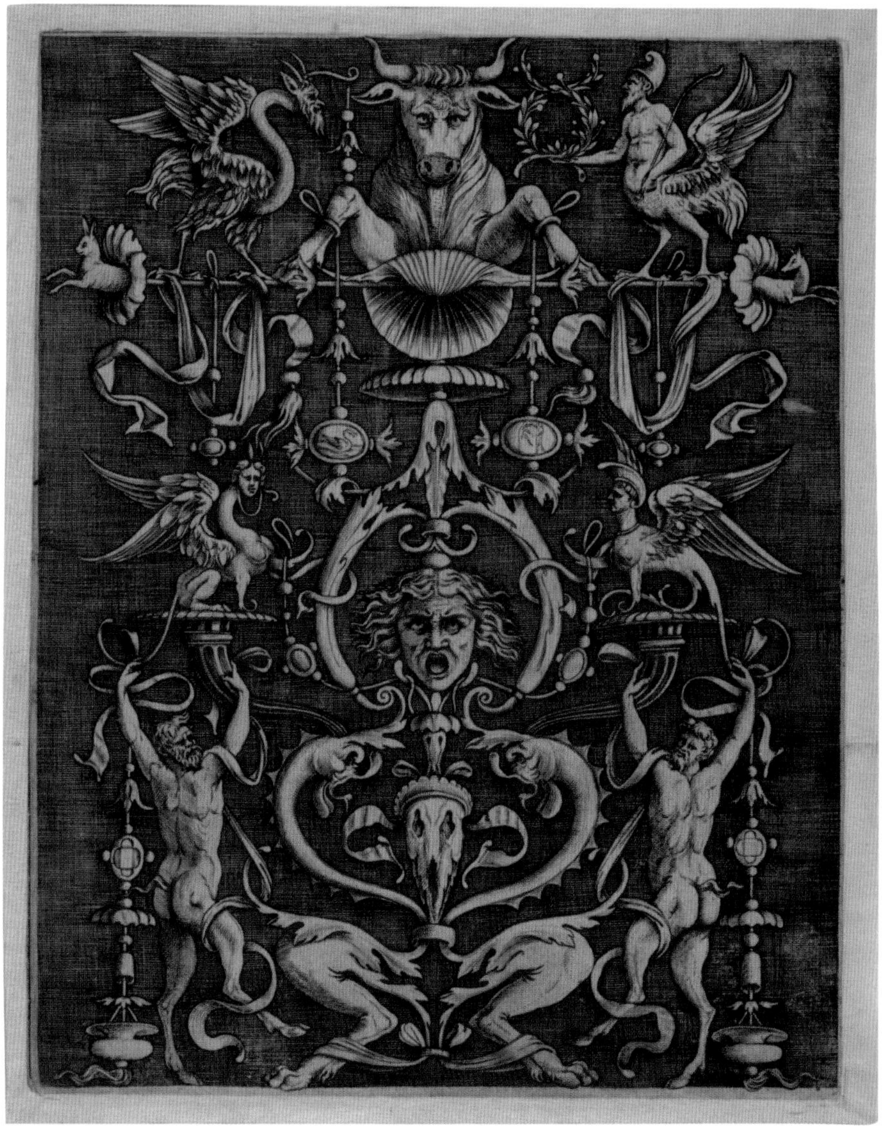

47 Grotesque ornamental panel
Agostino Veneziano
Engraving
Rome, c.1510–20
H: 23.6 cm, W: 18.8 cm
V&A: E.1076–1922

or orange background. Black backgrounds are rare, although they were sometimes used in Siena (pl. 48) where the most important maiolica work featuring grotesque designs, the tiled floor made for the palace of Pandolfo Petrucci, was made in 1509 (see pl. 205). The decoration was widespread on maiolica from the beginning of the sixteenth century but it is often difficult to ascribe a specific type of grotesque to a particular centre due to the rarity of marked pieces. A dish with elaborate grotesques, marked on the front as made in Deruta, has proved that high quality ornamental maiolica was produced in this town (pl. 33).[11]

Faenza was one of the biggest producers of a type of grotesque decoration featuring small and elegant ornamentation. This can be gleaned from a wealth of excavated fragments. A plate from around 1510–15 (pl. 49) shows the apostle St James, surrounded by minute and very finely painted grotesques on an orange ground. Like three other similar plates with saints, it bears the initials 'I.P.' on the reverse (pl. 50), possibly an

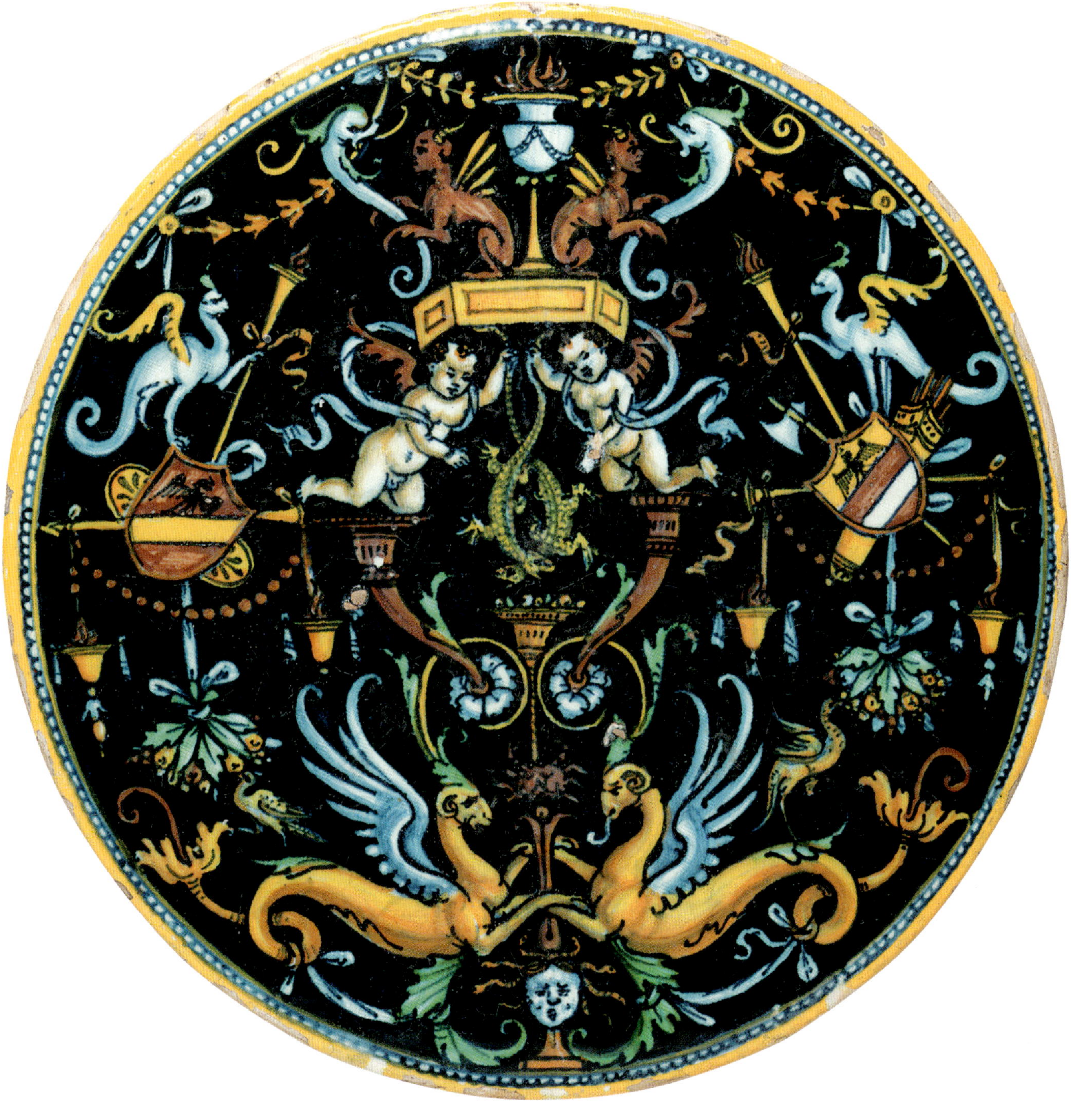

48 Plate with grotesque decoration and shields of arms
Siena, c.1510
Diam: 24.5 cm
V&A: 656–1884

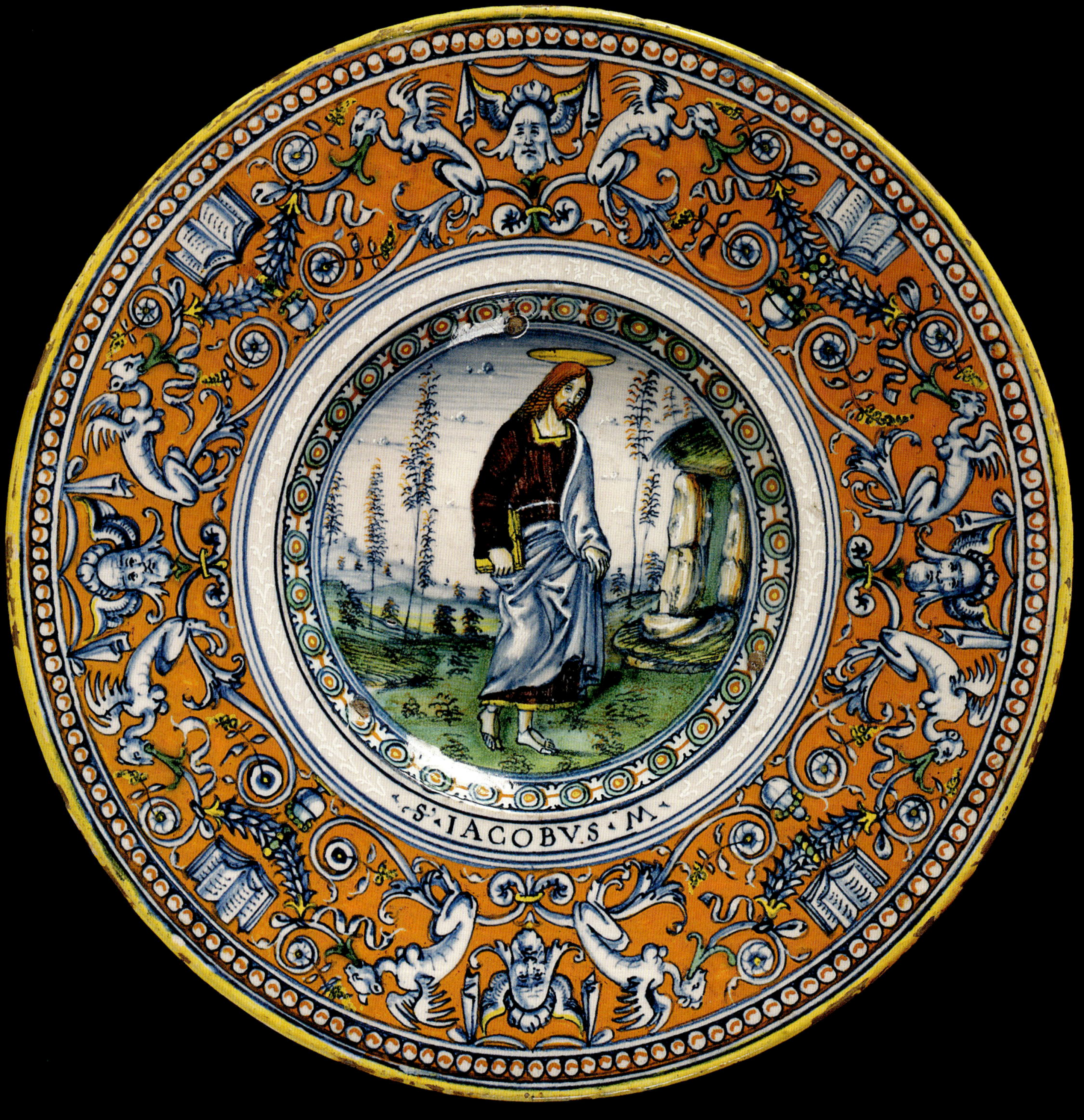
S. IACOBVS M

49 Plate with St James the Greater and grotesques
Faenza or Siena, c.1510–15
Diam: 27 cm
V&A: 11–1867

50 Reverse of pl.49

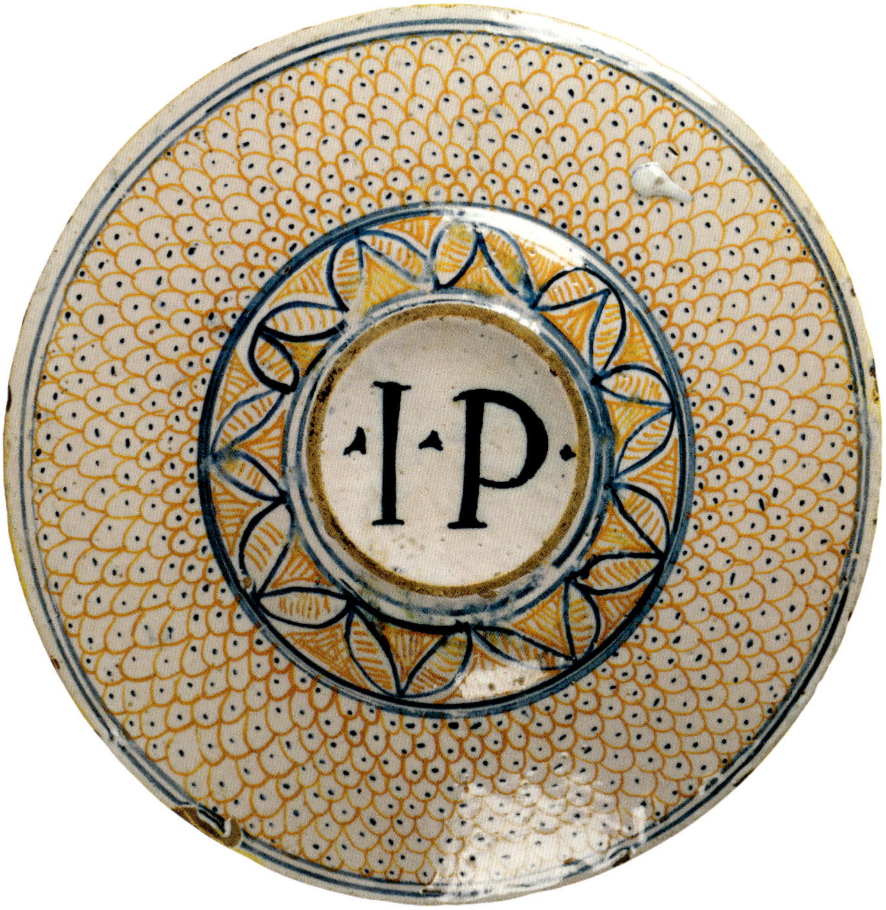

owner's mark. These plates were probably made at Faenza, but both Faenza and Siena produced similar elegant grotesque decoration from the beginning of the sixteenth century and precise attributions are often difficult to make.[12] Grotesque ornaments in blue on a light blue *'berettino'* ground became a particular speciality of Faenza potters between the 1520s and 1540s.

Grotesque decoration on coloured grounds began to fall gradually out of fashion in the 1550s when Piccolpasso commented: 'grotesques have almost fallen out of use, and I do not know why; it is a delicate style of painting'. However in the 1560s it had a new lease of life thanks to potters from Urbino. Their distinct style of elaborate and finely painted grotesques on a stark white ground was highly reminiscent of the decoration designed by Raphael and painted by his pupils in the Vatican Loggias (1519). One of the main workshops in the city, that of the Fontana family, specialized in this type of ornament, which became immensely fashionable. This type of grotesque became the most prestigious form of maiolica decoration for the rest of the sixteenth century. The Patanazzi family, who were related to the Fontana, carried on producing pottery in this style until well into the seventeenth century.

Among the various printed sources inspiring this type of grotesque design on a white ground were *Les Petites Grotesques* by the French architect and designer Jacques Androuet Du Cerceau, published in 1550 and 1562, which synthesized earlier Italian and Flemish examples as well as including original compositions (pl. 51).[13] While some elements are

51 *Les Petites Grotesques*
Jacques Androuet Du Cerceau
Etching
Orlèans, 1550
H: 10.8 cm, W: 7 cm
V&A: 23089:9

52 Vase with snake handles and grotesques (detail)
Fontana workshop
Probably Urbino, c.1560
H: 56.5 cm
V&A: 356–1872

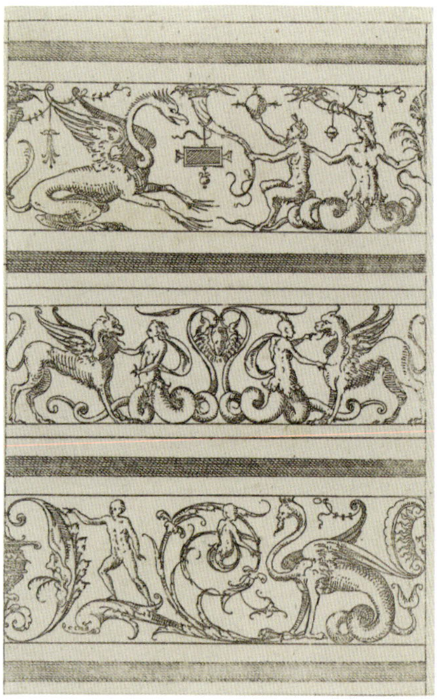

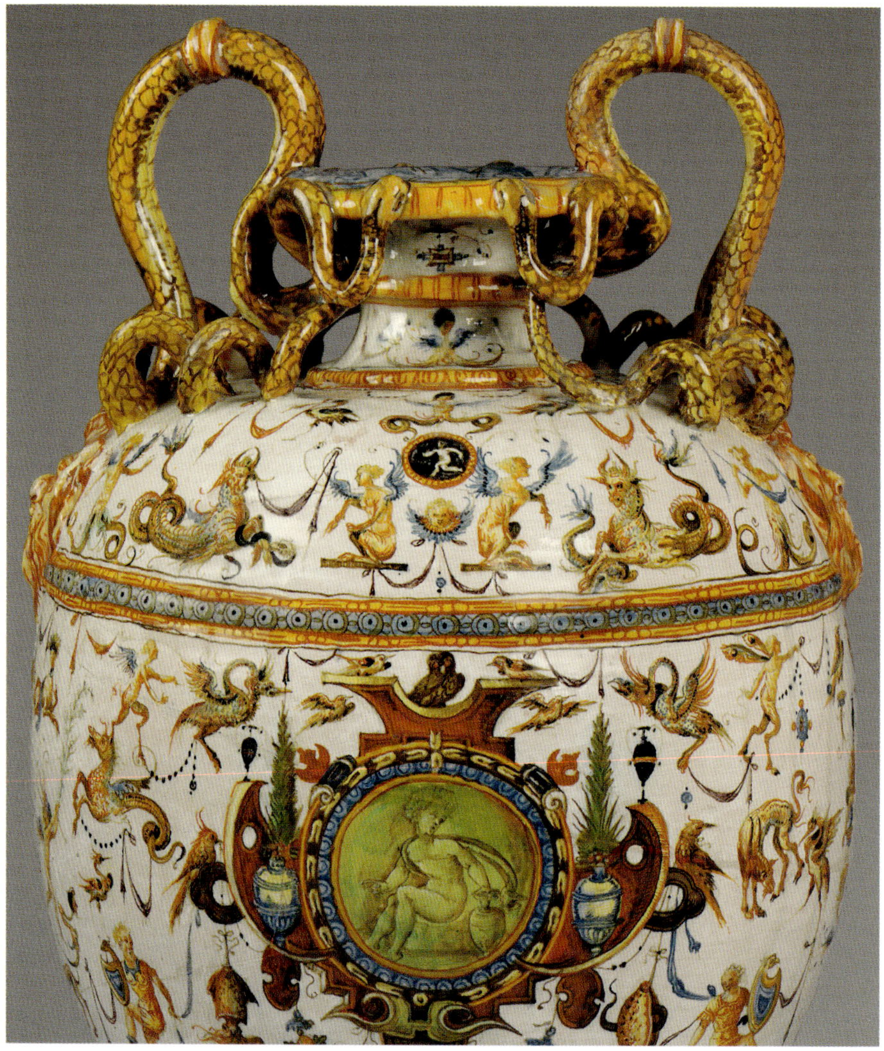

copied from these engravings almost exactly, grotesques on maiolica are generally free interpretations of such designs. Medallions, painted in imitation of Roman gemstones, are sometimes incorporated within these playful and inventive motifs (pl. 52).

Trophies

Military 'trophies', clusters of Roman arms and armour, often accompany grotesque ornament. Maiolica painters from the Marches decorated their wares with such trophies from the beginning of the sixteenth century. A splendid bowl of around 1510 is one of the most accomplished early examples and might have been produced in Castel Durante. It depicts St Jerome, working on his translation of the Bible. The small central image is surrounded by a border of beautifully painted trophies and grotesques on a dark ground (pl. 53).[14]

Around 1515, Maestro Giorgio's workshop at Gubbio started producing wares painted with original motifs of trophies, grotesques and cherubs' heads in ruby red lustre and dark gold lustre on a blue background. The earliest dated work that can be attributed to this highly successful workshop is a dish of 1515 (pls 55, 56). This decorative style,

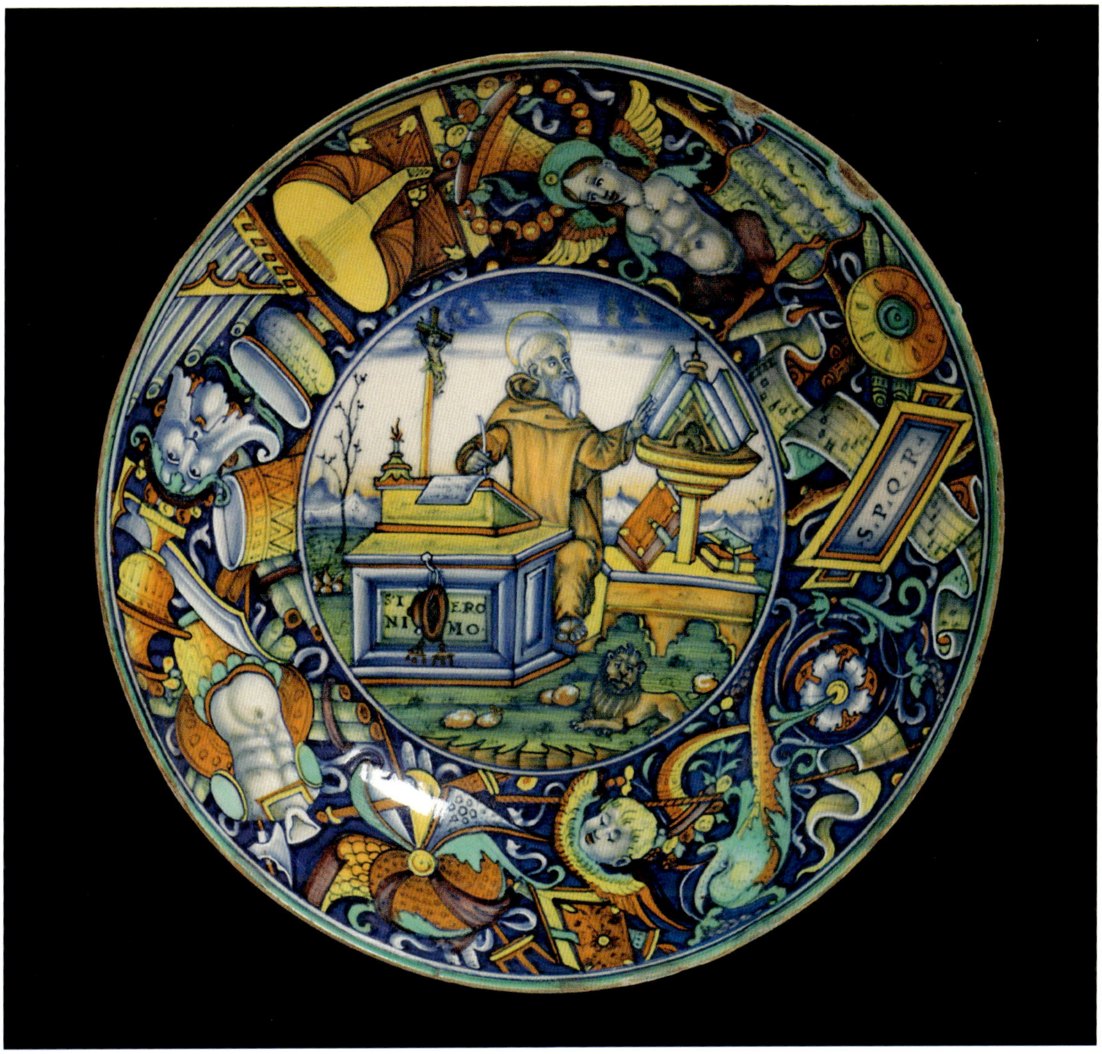

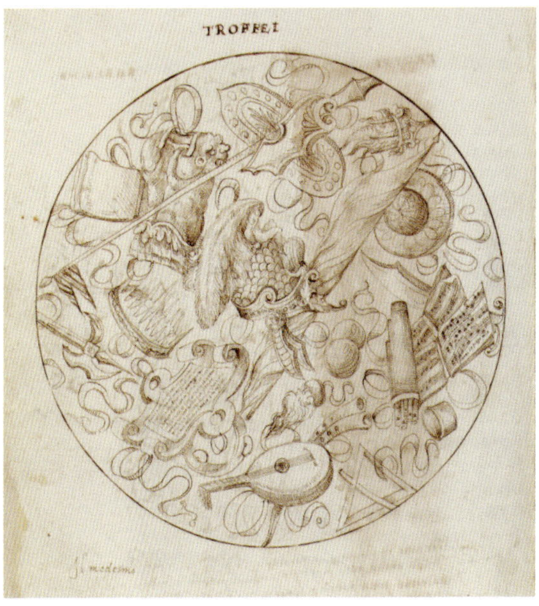

53 Bowl on low foot with St Jerome and a border of trophy decoration
Castel Durante or elsewhere in the Marches, c.1510
Diam: 24.5 cm
V&A: C.2148–1910

54 Drawing of trophies
***The Three Books of the Potter's Art*, fol.67v (detail)**
Cipriano Piccolpasso
Pen and ink
Castel Durante, 1557
NAL: MSL/1861/7446

55 Plate with trophies and cherubs
Probably workshop of Maestro Giorgio
Gubbio, 1515
Diam: 24.5 cm
V&A: C.477–1921

56 Reverse of pl.55

57 Dish with Christ among the Doctors
Workshop of Maestro Ieronimo
Probably Forlì, *c.*1520
Diam: 36 cm
V&A: 4727–1859
The reverse is inscribed: In la botega d mo iero/da forli ('In the workshop of Maestro Ieronimo da Forlì')

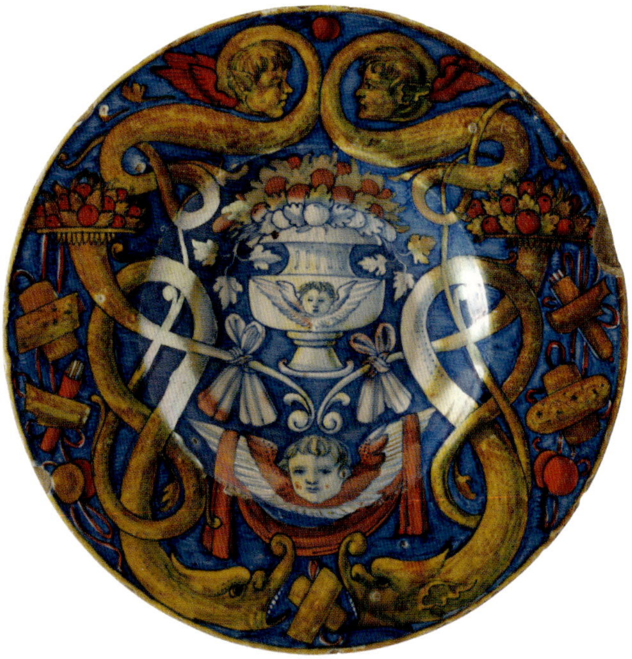

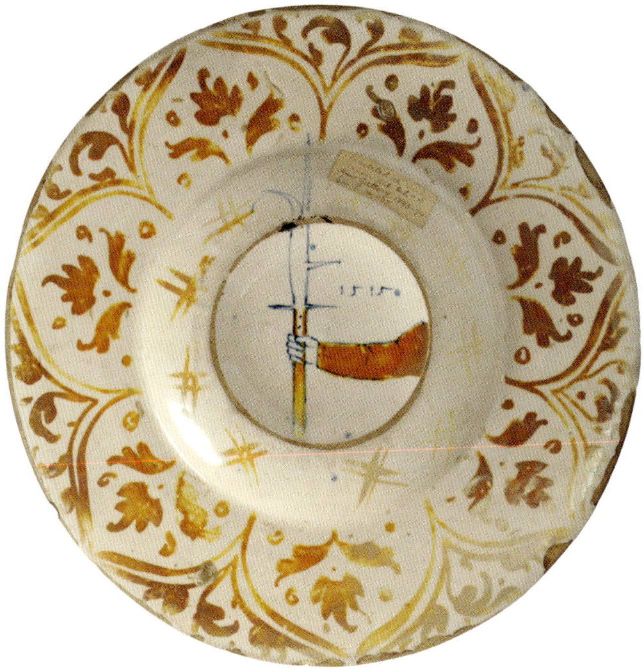

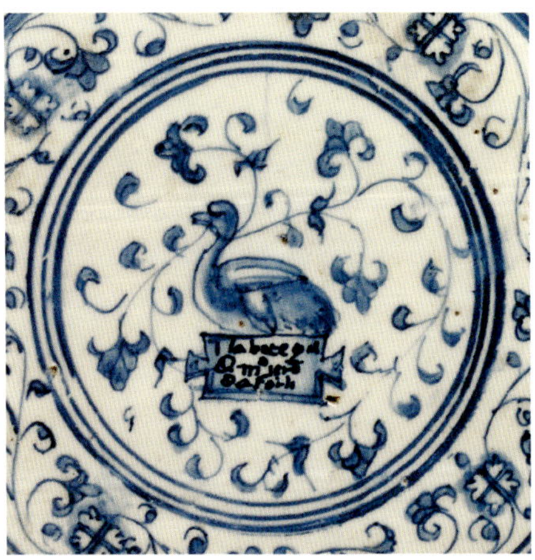

58 Reverse of pl.57 (detail)

perhaps introduced to Gubbio by painters from Castel Durante working in Giorgio's workshop, became dominant up until the early 1520s.

A unique dish, painted in monochrome blue with an elaborate scene showing Christ among the doctors, is marked as made in the workshop of Maestro Ieronimo from Forlì. Its border shows a variety of inventive trophies, including artisans' tools and kitchen implements and even an inkstand.[15] The trophies are on a background with subtle leaf scrolls in imitation of decorations found on Chinese wares, which also cover the reverse of the dish (pls 57, 58).

'Classical' trophies painted on maiolica also often incorporate Renaissance musical instruments, musical scores and books. Music was highly valued in the Renaissance and written compositions were printed for the first time. On an extraordinary bowl featuring the arms of the Gonzaga, dukes of Mantua, a musical score is the main decorative feature (pl. 59). The score is for a *frottola*, an instrumental piece popular in North Italian courts from the end of the fifteenth century.[16]

The continued appeal of painted trophies is illustrated by Piccolpasso's inclusion of this type of ornament in his manual, stating that 'trofei' are in general use, in particular in the Duchy of Urbino (pl. 54).

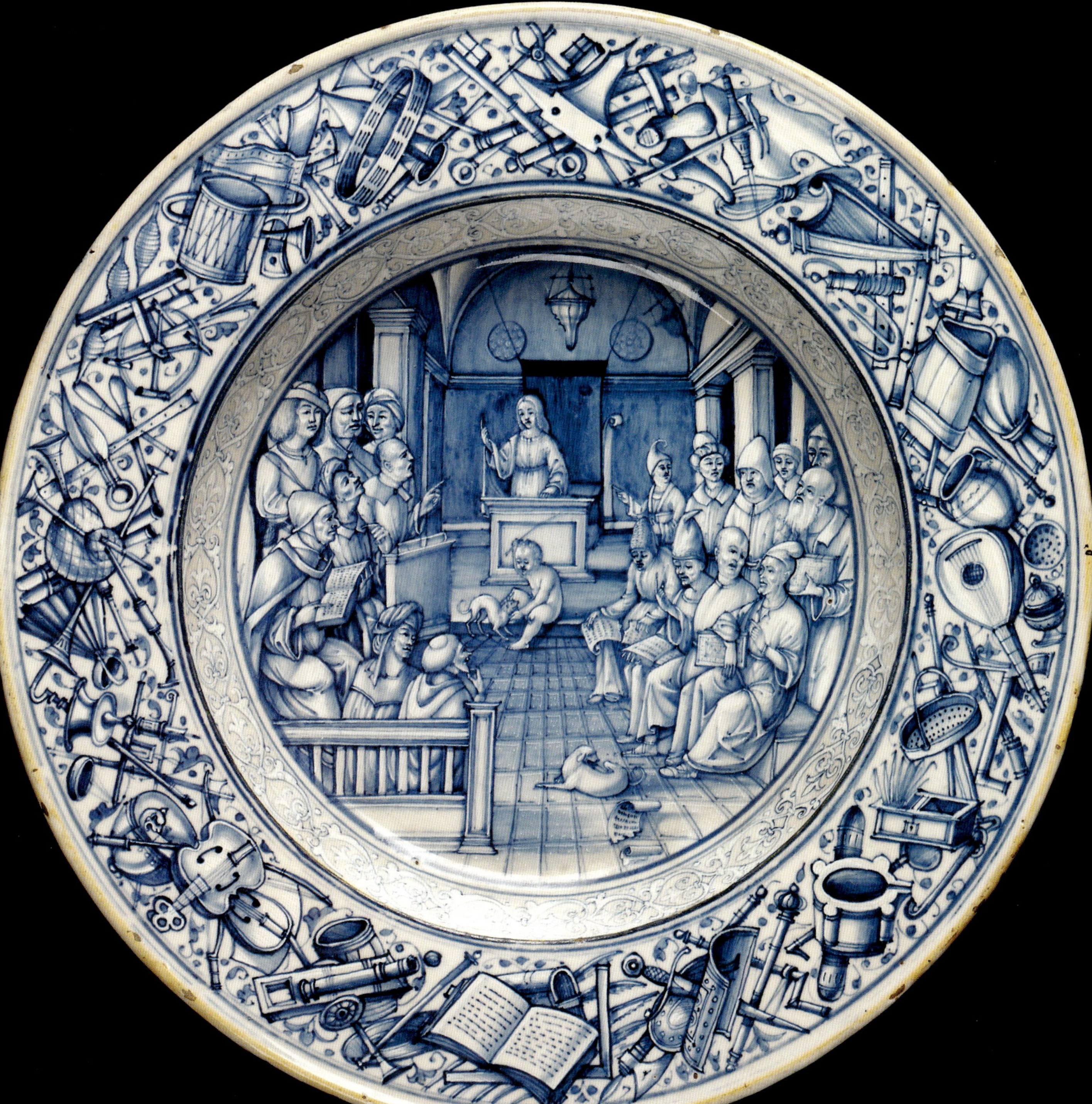

59 Bowl on low foot with the arms of Gonzaga Duke of Mantua
Urbino district, c.1525
Diam: 24.5 cm
Salting Bequest V&A: C.2224–1910

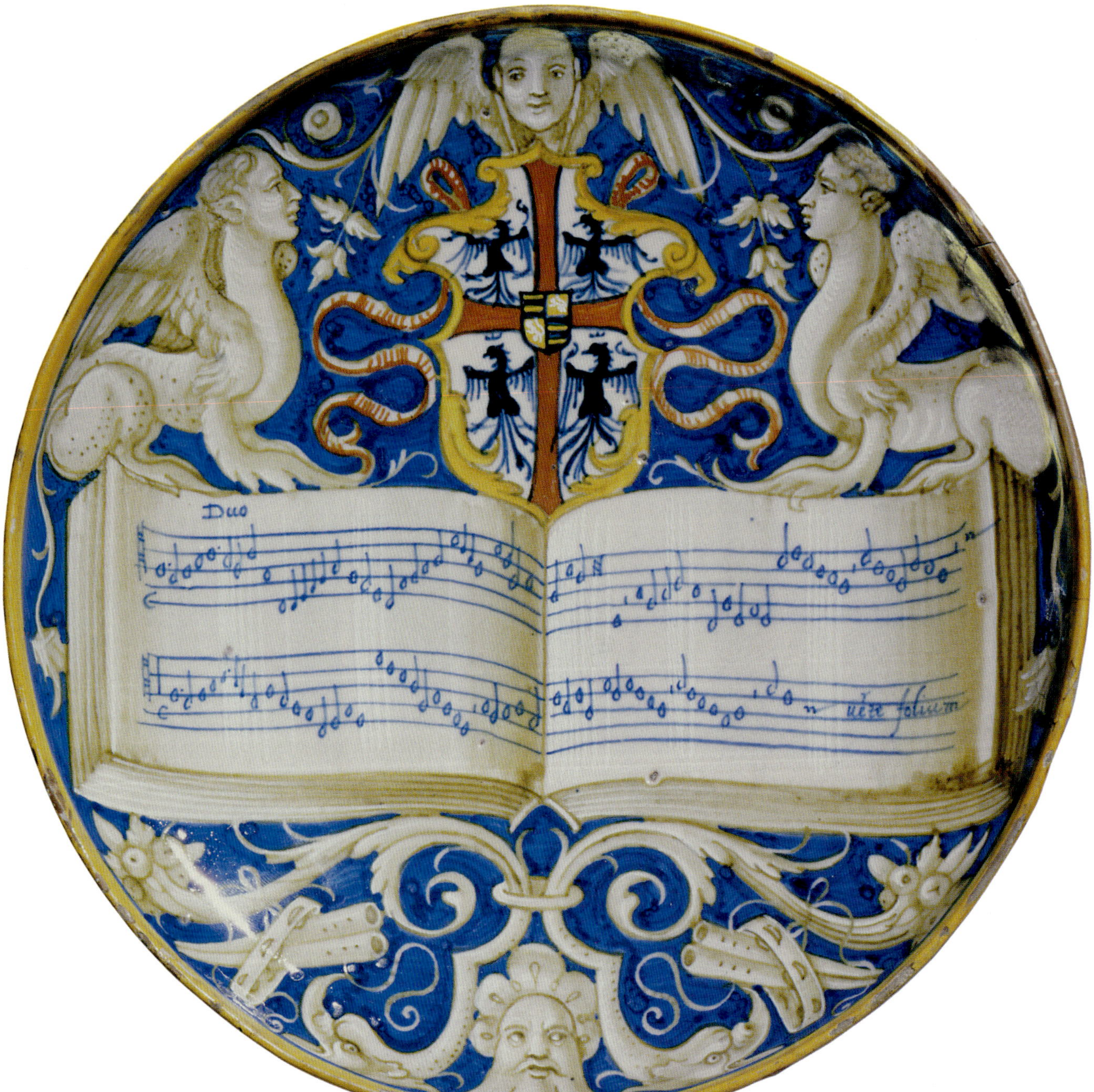

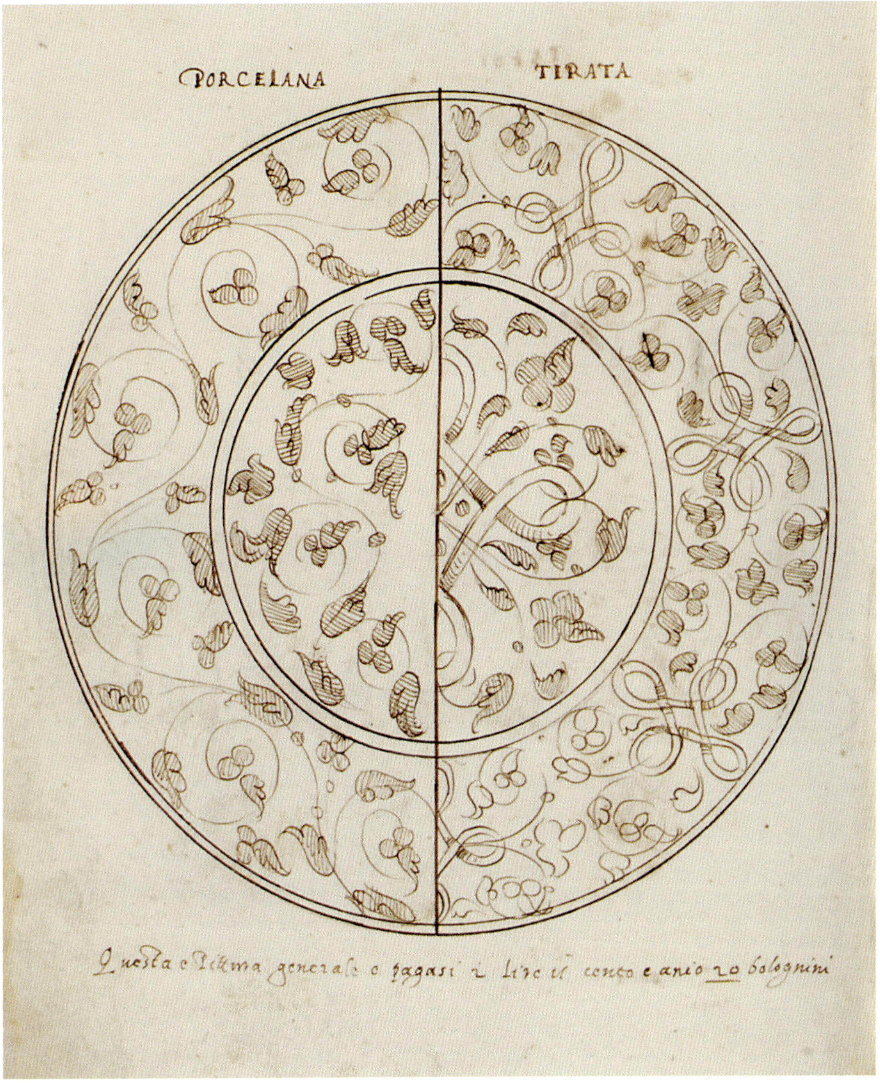

60 Drawing of porcelain motif (*'porcellana'*)
***The Three Books of the Potter's Art*, fol.70v (detail)**
Cipriano Piccolpasso
Pen and ink
Castel Durante, 1557
NAL: MSL/1861/7446

Imitating porcelain

Chinese porcelain of the Ming Dynasty (1368–1644) arrived in Italy in the fifteenth century through trade with the Middle East and was highly prized. Among the first passionate collectors in Europe were Piero de' Medici and his son Lorenzo.[17] Its popularity prompted many different imitations of Chinese originals (*'alla porcellana'*) in maiolica, all painted with subtle foliate scrolls in monochrome blue on a bright white background. Many such wares, produced in Italy from the beginning of the sixteenth century onwards, were of the highest quality and painted by well-known potters, including Maestro Benedetto, who lived in Siena from at least 1503 until his death in 1522.[18] His only known signed work is one of the finest examples of painting on Italian maiolica in existence (pls 61, 62). Painting only in blue, using the occasional highlight in white, the painter has achieved an amazing subtlety of tone. The border shows an elaborate porcelain pattern as well as an Islamic-inspired knot decoration. The finely potted shape and refined white glaze of the plate are closely akin to porcelain.

61 (overleaf) Dish with St Jerome (?)and porcelain decoration
Maestro Benedetto
Siena, c.1510–15
Diam: 24.4 cm
V&A: 4487–1858

62 Reverse of pl.61
Inscribed: fa[t]to i[n] siena da mo[maestro] benedetto

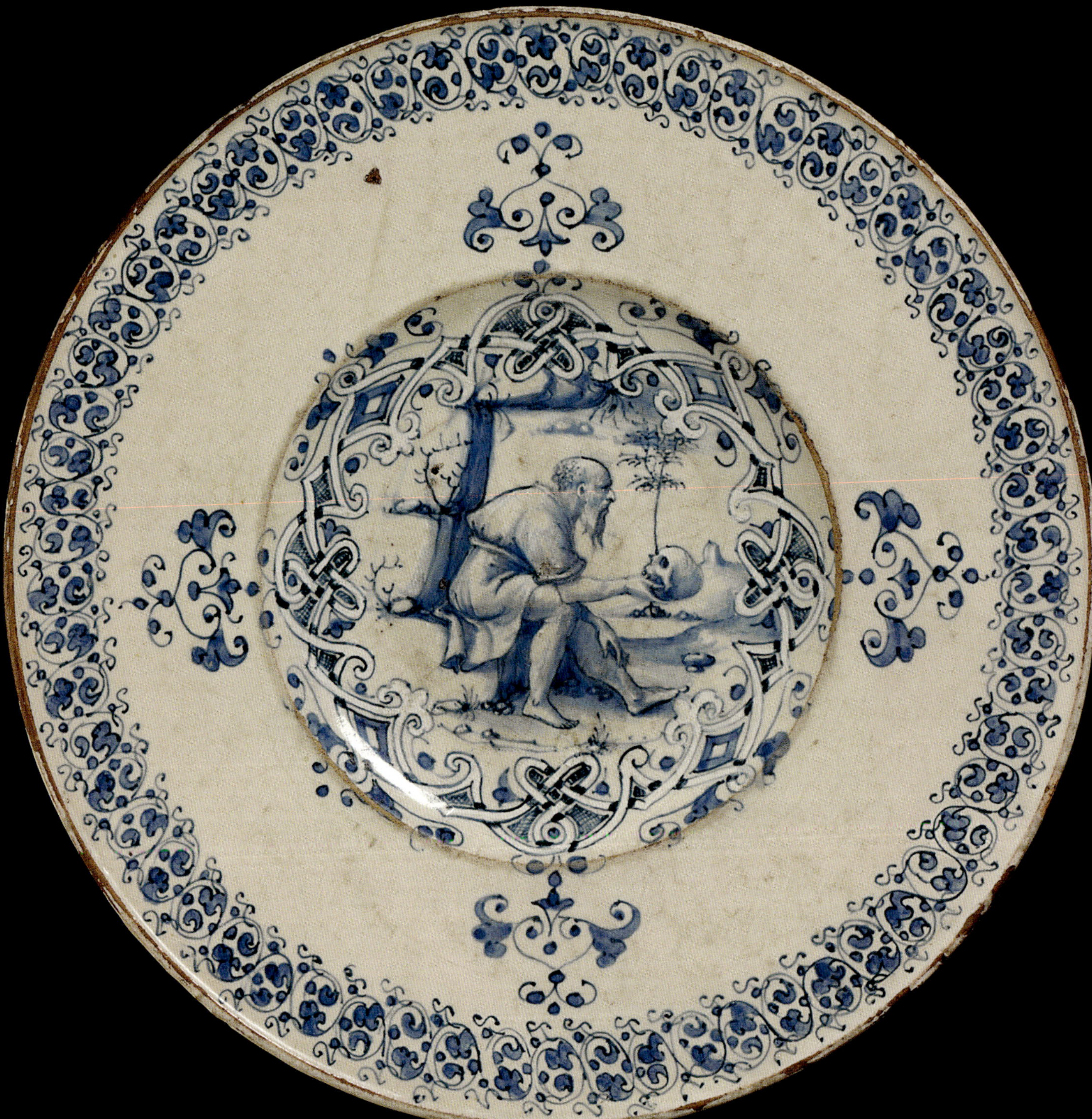

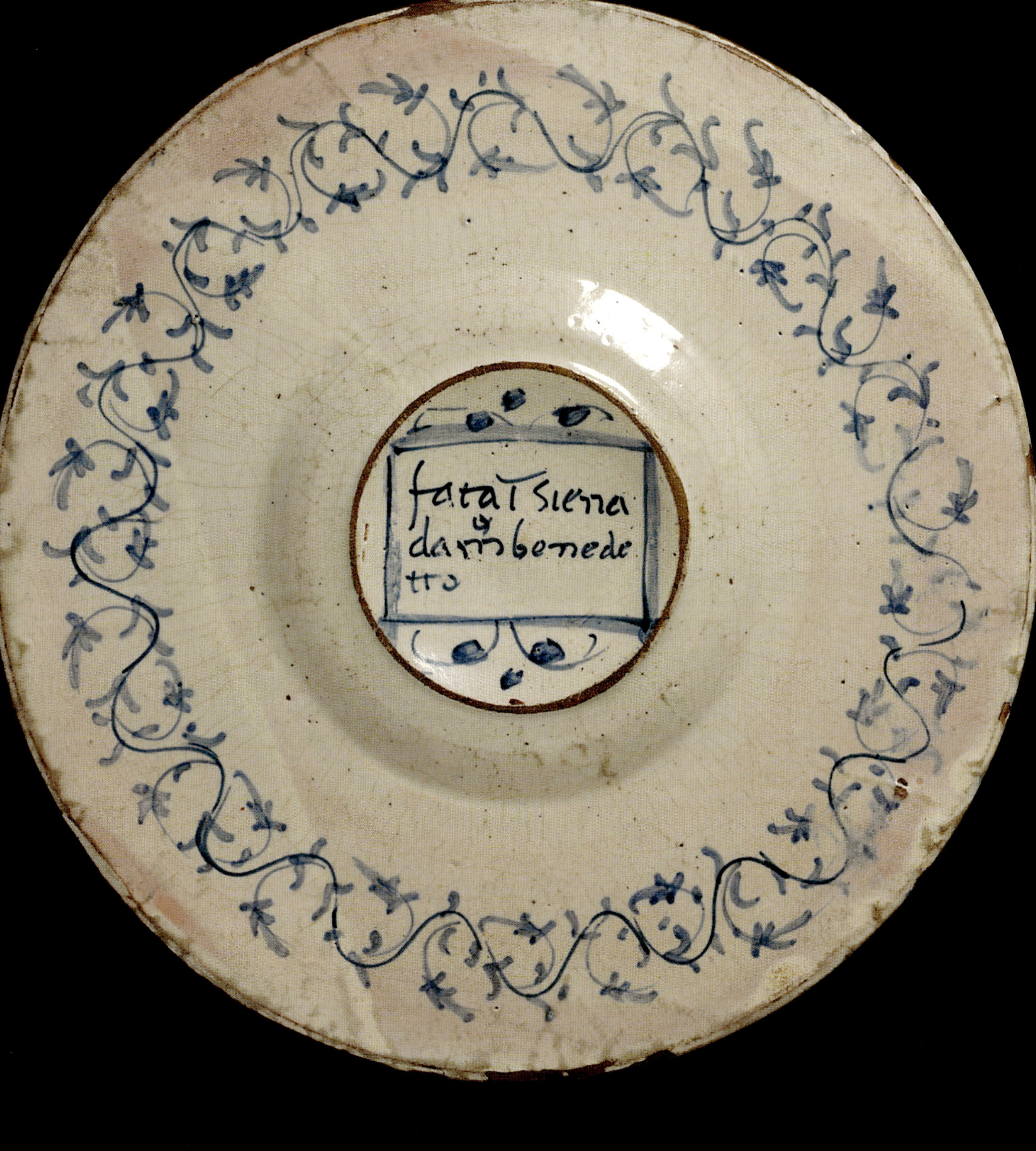
fatai siena
da m° benede
tto

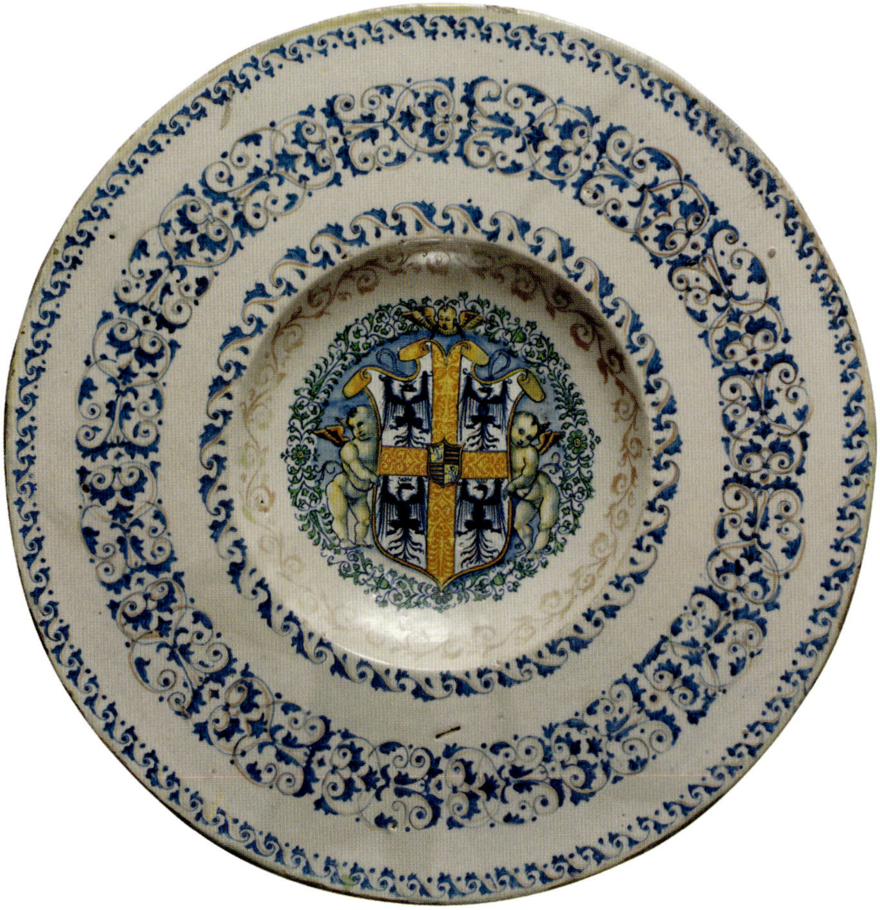

63 Dish with the arms of the Gonzaga dukes of Mantua and porcelain-style decoration
Urbino district, c.1520–25
Diam: 34.5 cm
Salting Bequest V&A: C.2144–1910

In the early sixteenth century maiolica in the porcelain style was fashionable in many parts of Italy, including Forlì where it can be found on the maiolica floor of the Lombardini chapel of 1513–24 (see pls 203, 204). It was in particular demand amongst the nobility. Numerous fragments have been excavated at the Ducal Palace in Urbino. Fine examples of this style, featuring the arms of the Gonzaga, dukes of Mantua, made both at Cafaggiolo and in the Marches, are in the V&A's collection (pl. 63).[19] Potters in Venice, a port with extensive trade links with the East, received commissions from German and Italian nobility, including the Medici Grand Duke Cosimo I and his wife Eleonora of Toledo.[20]

Piccolpasso illustrates this type of ornament, stating that it was in 'general use' (pl. 60). Further evidence of its continued popularity comes from the 1556 inventory of the Virgiliotto Calamelli workshop in Faenza, which lists a large number of wares decorated *'à[lla] porcellana'*. The monochrome blue decoration was particularly suitable for the pure white glaze for which Faenza became famous.[21]

Appreciation of Chinese blue and white porcelain in Italy also led to experiments with the material itself, resulting in the production in the Grand Ducal workshops in Florence of a soft-paste porcelain known as 'Medici Porcelain'. Made only from about 1575 until 1587, surviving examples are now exceptionally rare.[22]

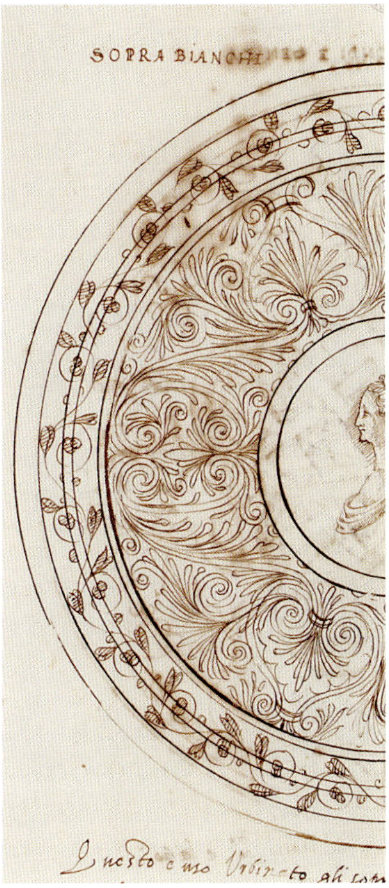

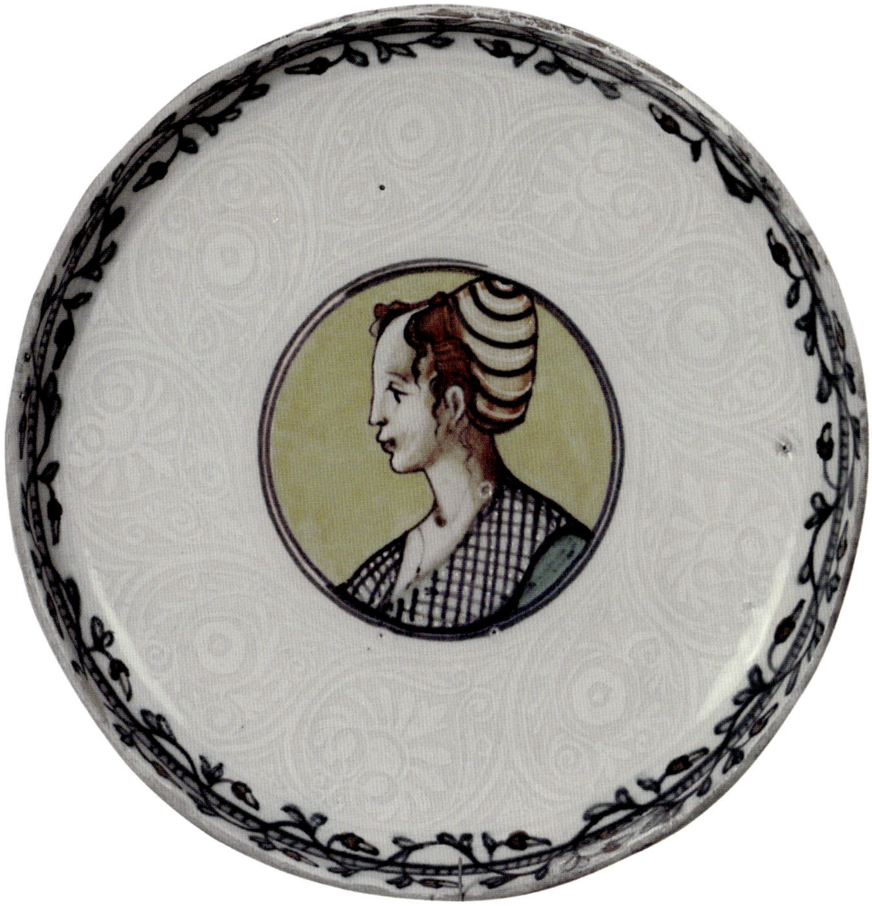

64 Drawing of white on white motif (*'soprabianchi'*) *The Three Books of the Potter's Art*, fol.70r (detail)
Cipriano Piccolpasso
Pen and ink
Castel Durante, 1557
NAL: MSL/1861/7446

65 Bowl on low foot with white on white decoration
Possibly Urbino, c.1545
Diam: 21 cm
Salting Bequest V&A: C.2260–1910

White on white and oak-leaf decoration

One of the more delicate types of maiolica decoration consists of subtle arabesques and foliate scrolls, painted in white on a greyish, off-white ground. This highly refined decoration, recalling intricate patterns in lace, is known as '*bianco sopra bianco*' (white on white). It was often used on decorative borders, separating more ornate and colourfully decorated areas. It first appears before 1490, on the service made for Matthias Corvinus, King of Hungary, and his wife (pl. 145). It seems to have been particularly popular with elites: tablewares decorated in white on white were the first choice of Pope Clement VII (1523–34) when dining informally (see p. 125). A delicate white on white border is used by Nicola da Urbino in combination with elaborate figurative scenes on plates and dishes belonging to the set made for Isabella d'Este in 1524.

White on white decorations were produced in many different centres including Siena, the Marches and Cafaggiolo, and examples dating from the beginning of the sixteenth century have been excavated at Faenza. Piccolpasso calls this type of decoration '*soprabianchi*' and to produce it he recommends using the best quality white, created with high quantities of tin 'from Flanders' (probably Cornish tin imported via Flanders, see p.26) Beneath his illustration of the pattern he states that it was used at Urbino (pls 64, 65).

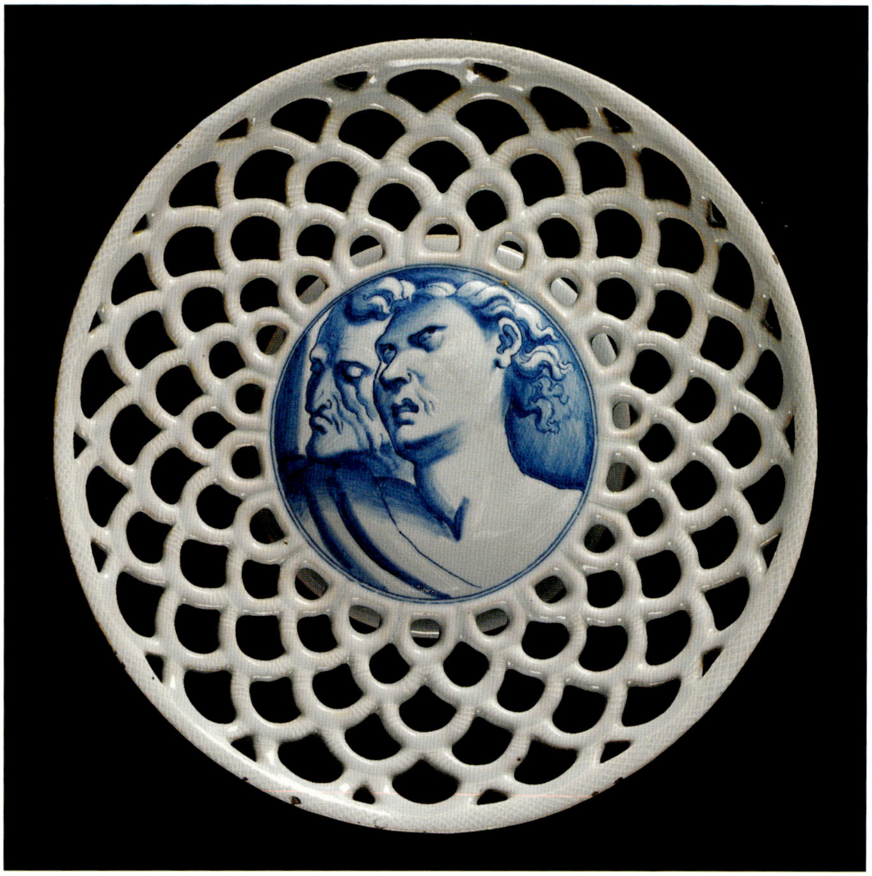

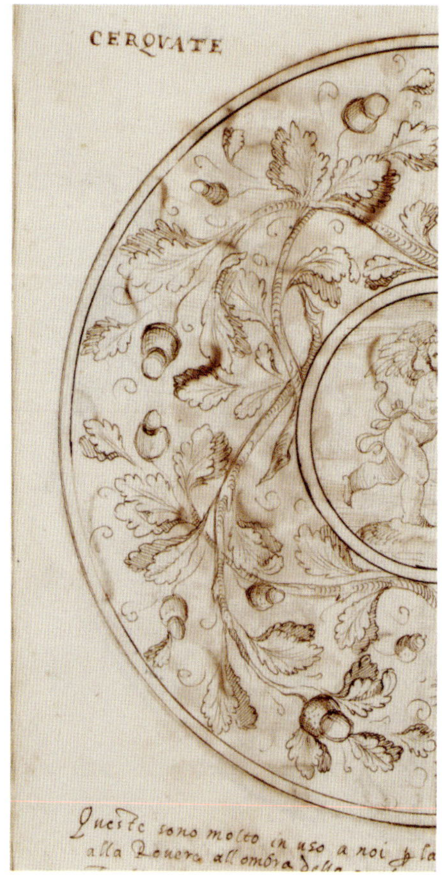

66 Open-work dish with bust of young man and old man and white on white decoration
Maestro Jacomo of Pesaro
Venice, 1543
Diam: 23.5 cm
V&A: C.713–1936

67 Reverse of pl.67
Inscribed: 1543 i[n] Venetia a San Barnaba Mo Jacomo

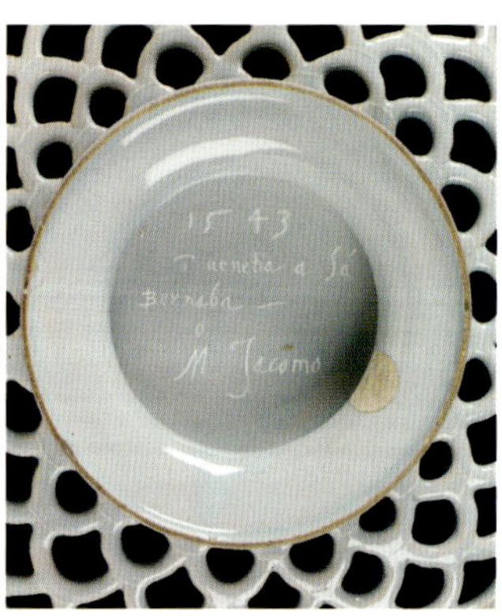

Some of the most delicate white on white decorations, applied on a pale blue-grey ground, were produced in the Venetian workshop of Maestro Jacomo of Pesaro. A bowl on a low foot, with open-work scale pattern, recalling the mould-blown pattern on Venetian glass dishes of the period, is one of only two surviving marked works by Jacomo (pl. 66). It is inscribed on the reverse in white: *1543 i[n] Venetia a San Barnaba / Mo Jacomo*. It is known that Jacomo established a workshop in the St Barnaba district of Venice as early as 1507, but his known signed works belong to the 1540s.[23]

Among the ornaments fashionable from the mid-1520s and sometimes used in combination with white on white decoration is a motif featuring oak-leaf branches with acorns which Piccolpasso calls *'cerquate'* (from *'cerqua'* meaning *'quercia'*, oak tree):

> These are much in use with us [in the Duchy of Urbino] from the veneration and duty we owe to the oak tree [*'rovere'* the family name of the Della Rovere dukes of Urbino, means 'oak tree'], in the shade of which we live happily, so that it can be called the Urbino style of painting.

Used as a tribute to the Dukes of Urbino, this design seems indeed to have been mainly used in the Urbino area. It usually covers the entire surface of dishes, leaving only space for a small central roundel (pls 68, 69). The motif is common on plates but also features on different types of vessels such as pilgrim flasks or three-lobed dishes, sometimes in combination with scenes with figures.

68 Drawing of oak-leaf decoration (*'cerquate'*) *The Three Books of the Potter's Art*, fol.67r (detail)
Cipriano Piccolpasso
Pen and ink
Castel Durante, 1557
NAL: MSL/1861/7446

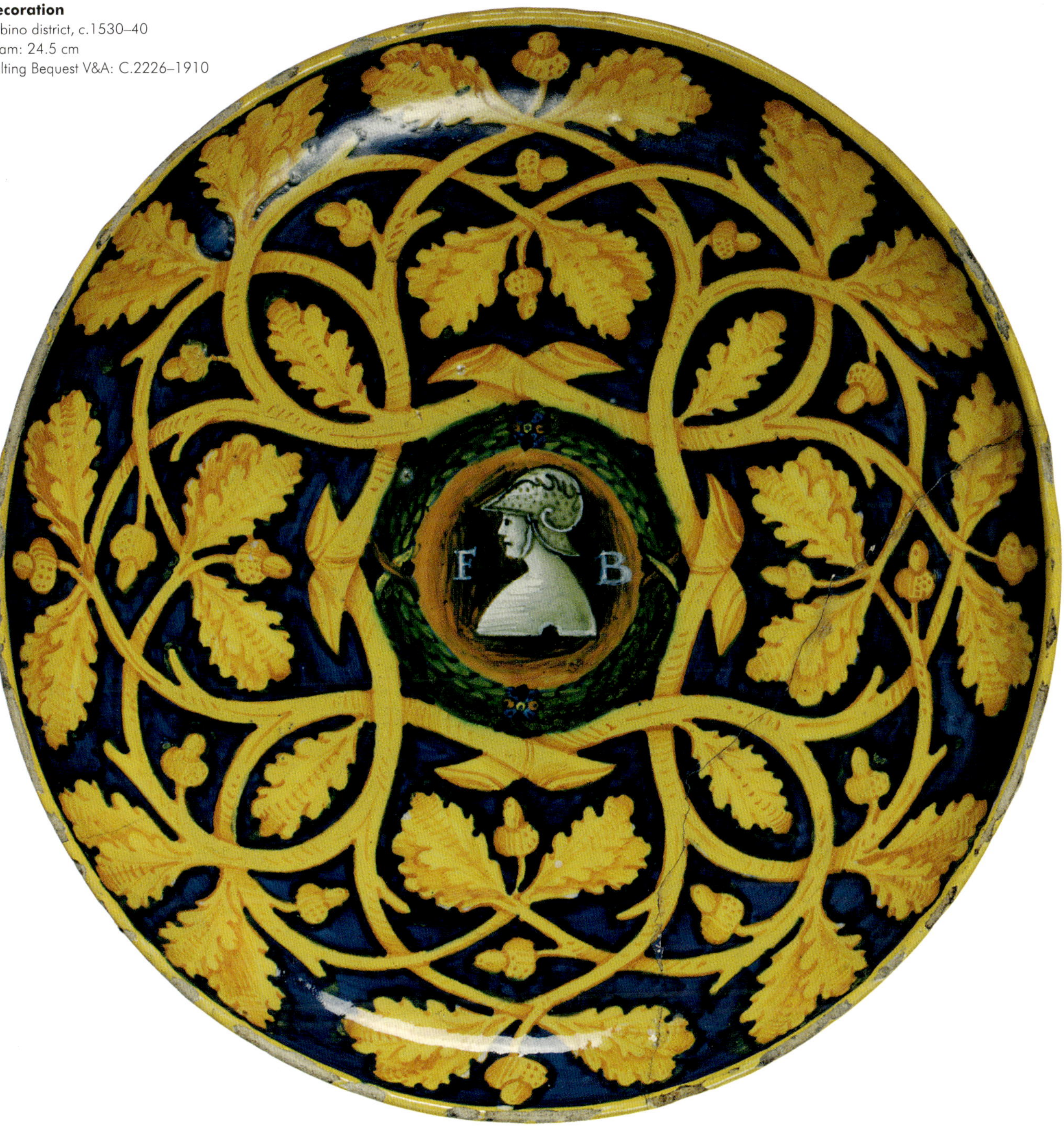

69 Bowl on low foot with bust of a man within oak-leaf decoration
Urbino district, c.1530–40
Diam: 24.5 cm
Salting Bequest V&A: C.2226–1910

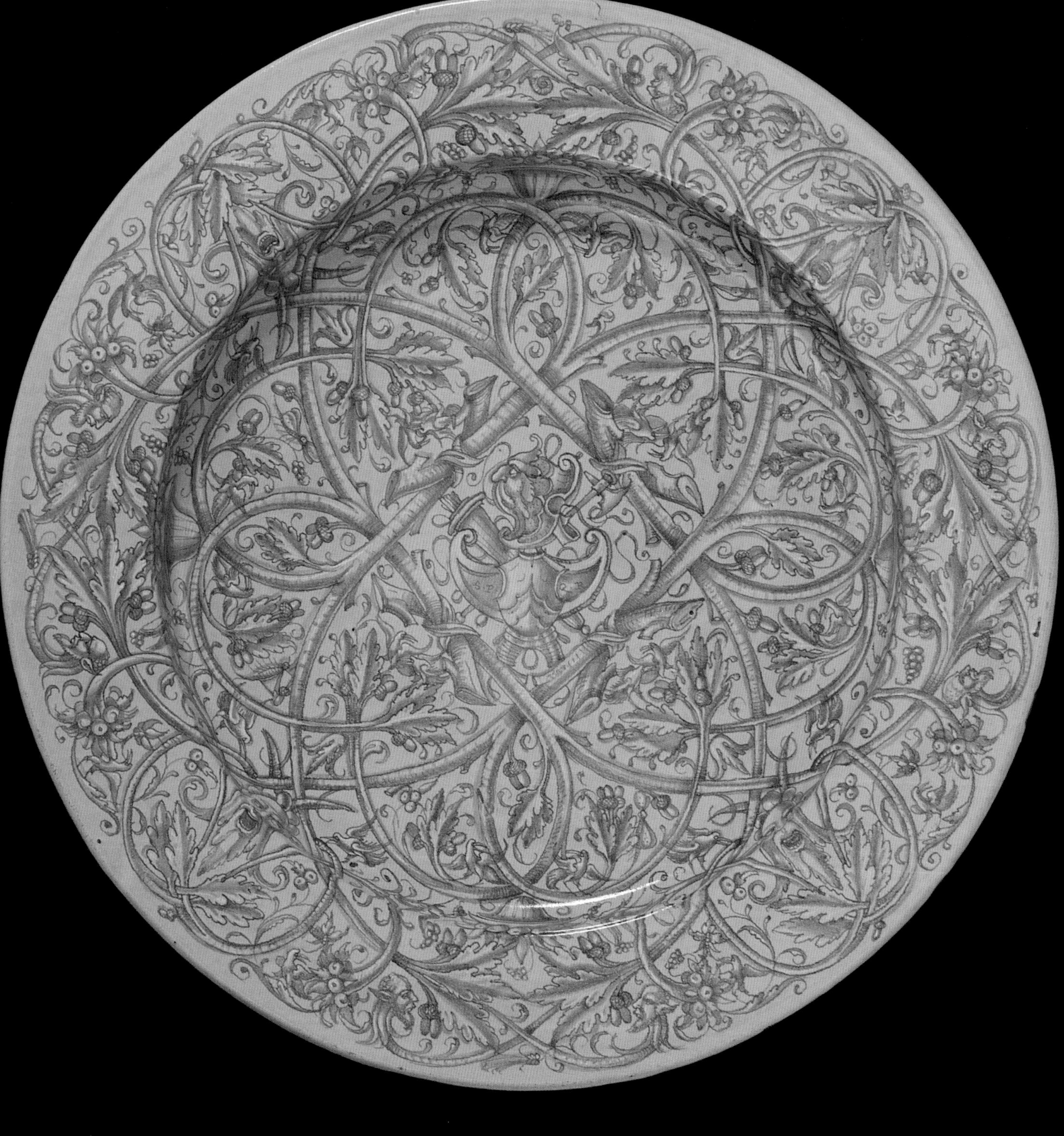

70 Dish with oak-leaf decoration and trophies
Meastro Ludovico
Venice, c.1540
Diam: 51 cm
V&A: 4438–1858

71 Reverse of pl.70
Inscribed: in Venetia. in Co[n]trada dj S. to Polo, in botega dj Mo Ludovico ('In Venice in the San Polo district, Maestro Ludovico')

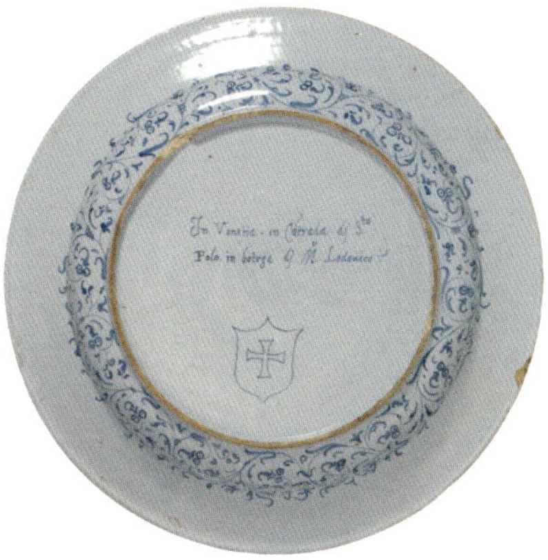

Sometimes the oak-leaf pattern is moulded in relief, especially on lustre-decorated bowls and dishes. Similar decorations with oak branches can also be found on contemporary embroidery.[24] A large dish made in the Venetian workshop of Maestro Ludovico is decorated with a particularly elaborate pattern of interlaced oak branches in blue on a pale blue ground (pls 70, 71). The inscription on its reverse provides the only surviving evidence of the activity of this workshop: *in Venetia. in Co[n]trada dj S. to Polo, in botega dj Mo Ludovico* ('in Venice in the district of St Polo, in the workshop of Master Ludovico').

Faenza potters created a compartmentalized design of scrolling oak foliage, without acorns, divided into sections with alternating coloured backgrounds. They used it from the 1540s to decorate drug jars and moulded dishes, which were produced in large quantities (pl. 72). Wares decorated with the same ornament were exported to Sicily and imitated there, and also in other centres, during the late sixteenth and seventeenth century. Piccolpasso mentions that *'quartieri'* (pl. 73) or 'quartered designs' were used in Urbino, but evidence from surviving pieces is scarce. In Deruta, a different type of quartered decoration was used on the borders of large dishes intended for display.

Sixteenth-century Islamic influences: arabesques and interlaced knot patterns

Middle-eastern ceramics arrived in Italian ports during the Renaissance, alongside other luxury goods such as metalwork, ivories and textiles. In his manuscript Piccolpasso illustrates a pattern he calls *'rabesche'* (arabesques), which is clearly inspired by Islamic ornament (pl. 74). He states that the motif was in use everywhere but that

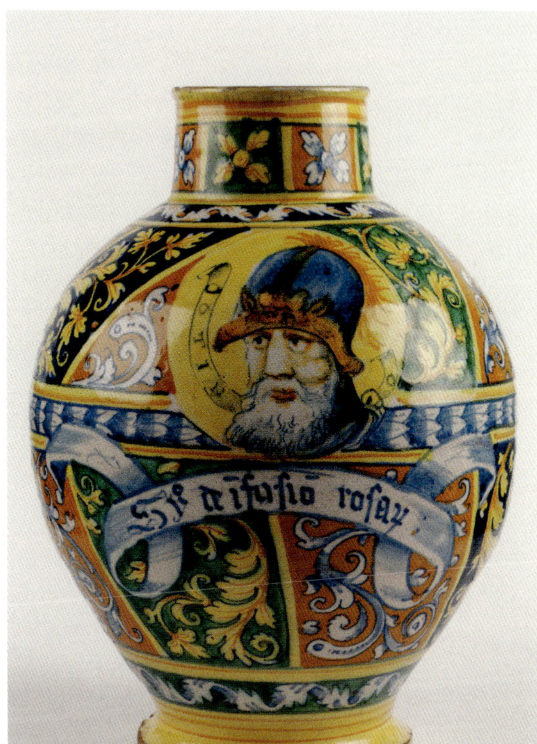

72 Drug jar for syrup of roses with quartered design and bust of helmeted man
Faenza, c.1550
H: 33 cm
V&A: Circ.482–1924

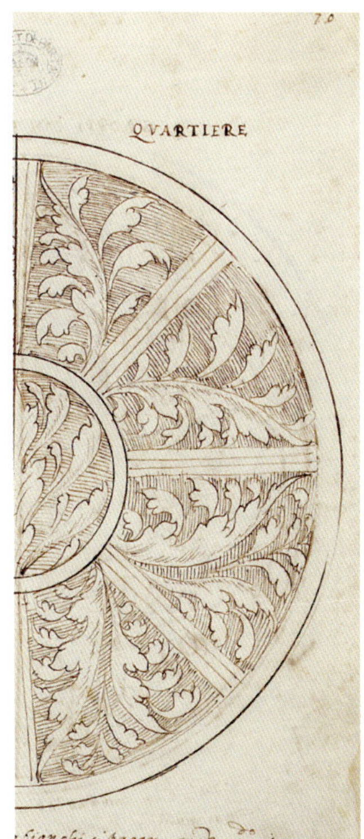

73 Drawing of quartered design (*'quartierie'*) *The Three Books of the Potter's Art*, fol.70r (detail)
Cipriano Piccolpasso
Pen and ink
Castel Durante, 1557
NAL: MSL/1861/7446

74 Drawing of arabesques (*'rabesche'*)
***The Three Books of the Potter's Art*, fol.66r (detail)**
Cipriano Piccolpasso
Pen and ink
Castel Durante, 1557
NAL: MSL/1861/7446

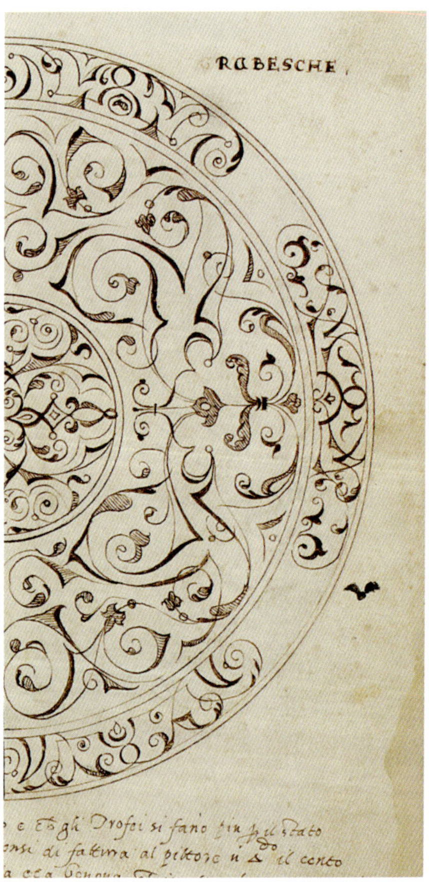

it was most commonly made in Genoa and Venice, the two major ports of the time. The decoration indeed seems to have been a speciality of various maiolica workshops in Venice, a city with particularly strong trading links with the Islamic world. These arabesque patterns closely resemble the engraved and inlaid decoration found on imported metalwork which was highly valued in Italy at the time. Similar motifs decorated book-bindings of the period. Highly decorative arabesque patterns often occupy the background of figurative scenes on Venetian maiolica dishes made in the 1540s (pl. 75).

Lustred versions of arabesques imitated the gold colour of the metalwork originals. Sets decorated with delicate lustred arabesque patterns on a dark blue background and with a coat of arms in the centre were made in Gubbio during the 1520s and 1530s. One such set was made in 1527 for a wedded couple from the ruling family of Città di Castello (pl. 76).

A popular sixteenth-century Deruta lustreware ornament is formed by arabesques on a white ground with small blue flowers, probably inspired by similar ornaments appearing on Valencian lustreware and Islamic metalwork. This motif used on its own can be seen on many vases and large display plates of the period. More rarely it was used as a border for coats of arms or figures. The central figure of an elegant, oriental man in Turkish costume, on a bowl in the V&A collection, is in perfect harmony with the Islamic-inspired decoration on its border (pl. 77).

Interlacing knot patterns, which were popular during the Renaissance period, were also derived from middle-eastern ornament. Leonardo da Vinci's workshop produced an engraved set of such patterns from his drawings around 1498–1500. Inspired by this series, Dürer also made prints with interlaced motifs. Similar motifs can be found on embroidery of the time, and all of these might have contributed to the use and popularity of this type of maiolica decoration.

Piccolpasso illustrates two types of knotted decoration, named *'groppi'* (literally 'knots'), stating that they are 'of general use'. Knotted patterns are indeed widely found. Faentine potters used knots and arabesques combined with leaves, scrolls and wreaths. A dish with the arms of the Medici impaling Strozzi shows that the pattern was deemed suitable for association with two of the most important Florentine families (pl. 78). Montelupo potters also had this pattern in their decorative repertoire. Knotted patterns are often painted on a light blue-grey *'berettino'* ground, which was achieved by mixing a small amount of cobalt blue with the white tin-glaze. These were produced in considerable quantities by potters at Faenza from the 1520s onwards, but also in Venice and elsewhere in the Veneto, in the Marches and in Rome.[25]

Flowers and fruits from Venice

Around the middle of the sixteenth century maiolica with typically Venetian ornaments was in high demand. One of the most popular patterns consisted of *'fiori e frutti'* – brightly coloured fruits or flowers, often yellow lemons and other fruits, leaves and vegetables, painted on a white ground. Piccolpasso associates the patterns with Venice, calling them 'very pretty things'. The motif appears chiefly on wares of typical Venetian shape, such as globular vases and jars for *mostarda,* a fruit pickle which was a Venetian speciality. A spectacular Venetian dish shows a satyr's face appearing among dense foliage and an assemblage of different fruits (pls 79, 80). Similar satyr faces incorporated in rich vegetable borders also appear on tapestries of the period. The reverse of this dish reveals a rarity: the maiolica painter has made an elaborate

75 Dish with arabesques and busts of famous women from antiquity
Marked 'Adi 13 Aprille 1543 AOLASDINR'
Venice, 1543
Diam: 47.5 cm
V&A: 8512–1863

76 Plate with arms of Niccolò Gentilini impaling those of his wife Gentilina Della Staffa
Workshop of Maestro Giorgio
Gubbio, 1527
Diam: 27.5 cm
Salting Bequest V&A: C.2192–1910

77 Lustred dish on low foot with figure in Turkish costume
Nicola Francioli known as 'Co'
Deruta, c.1525
Diam: 25 cm
Salting Bequest V&A: C.2185–1910

78 Dish with arms of Medici impaling Strozzi
Faenza or Montelupo, 1530–45
Diam: 39.5 cm
V&A: 1723–1855

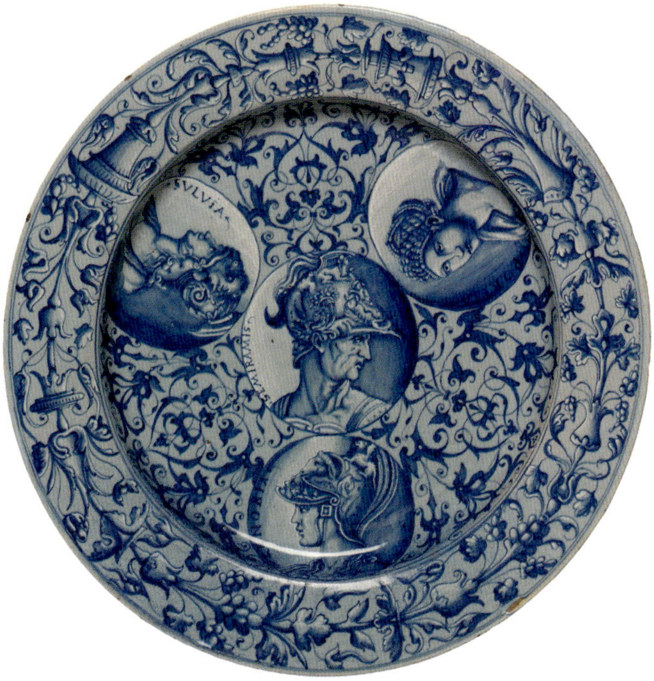

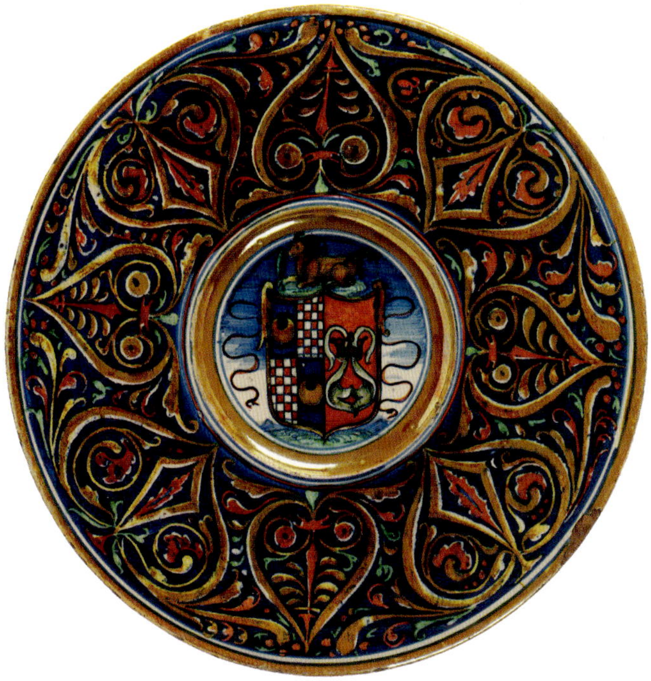

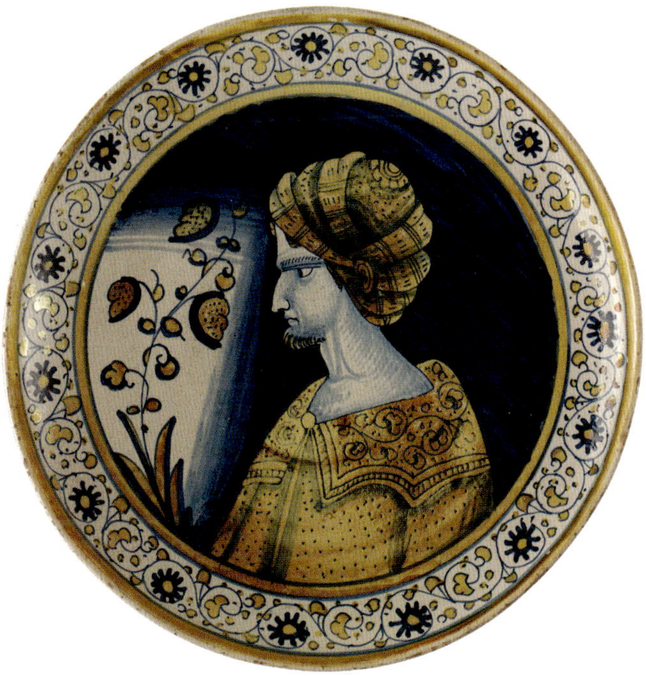

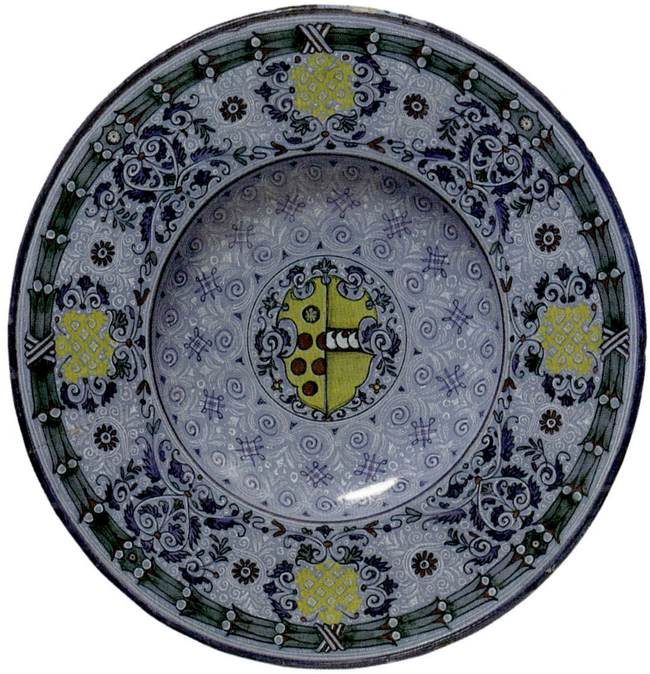

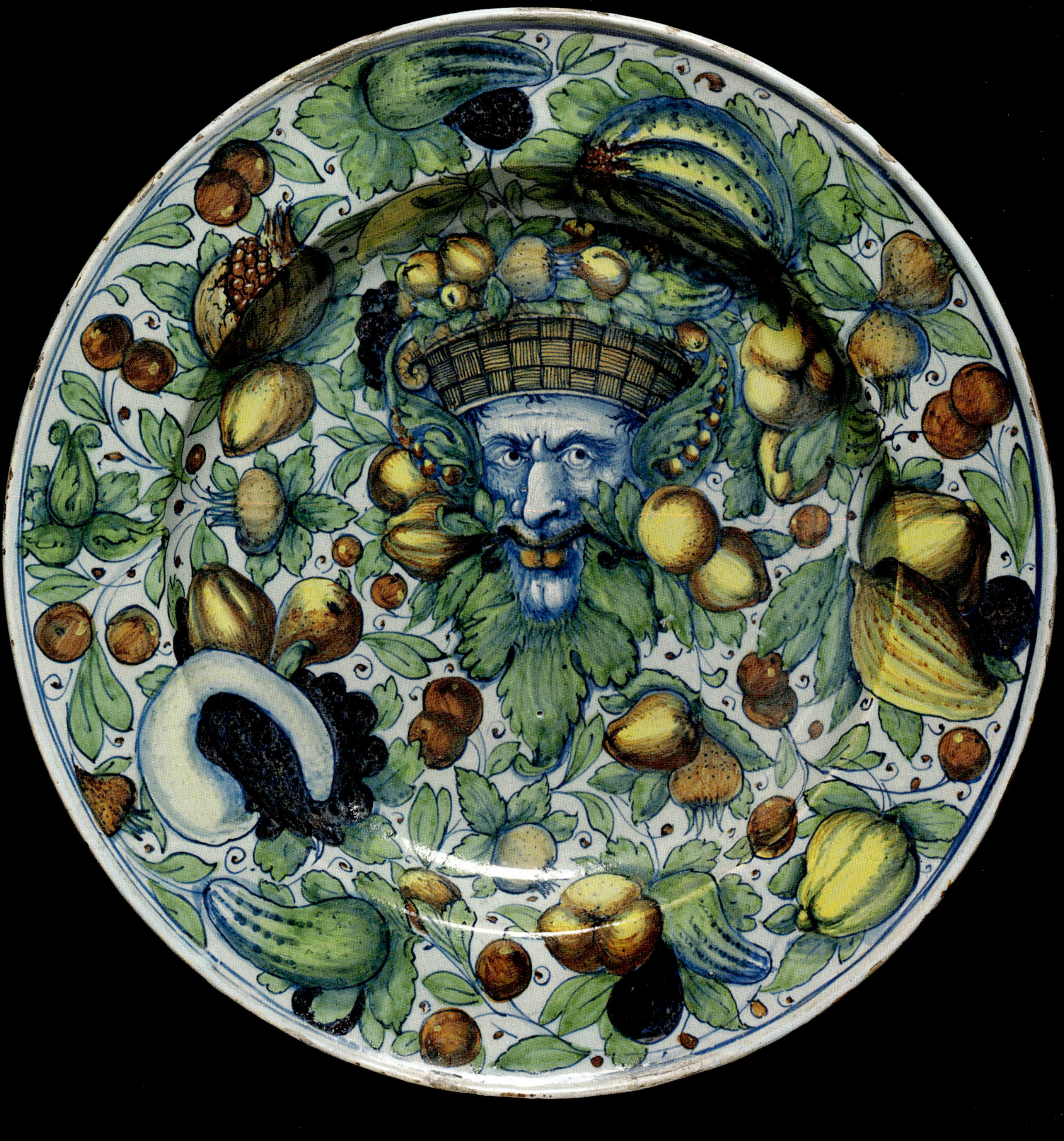

79 Dish with satyr head
Venice, c.1550–60
Diam: 45.5 cm
V&A: 1768–1855

80 Reverse of pl.79

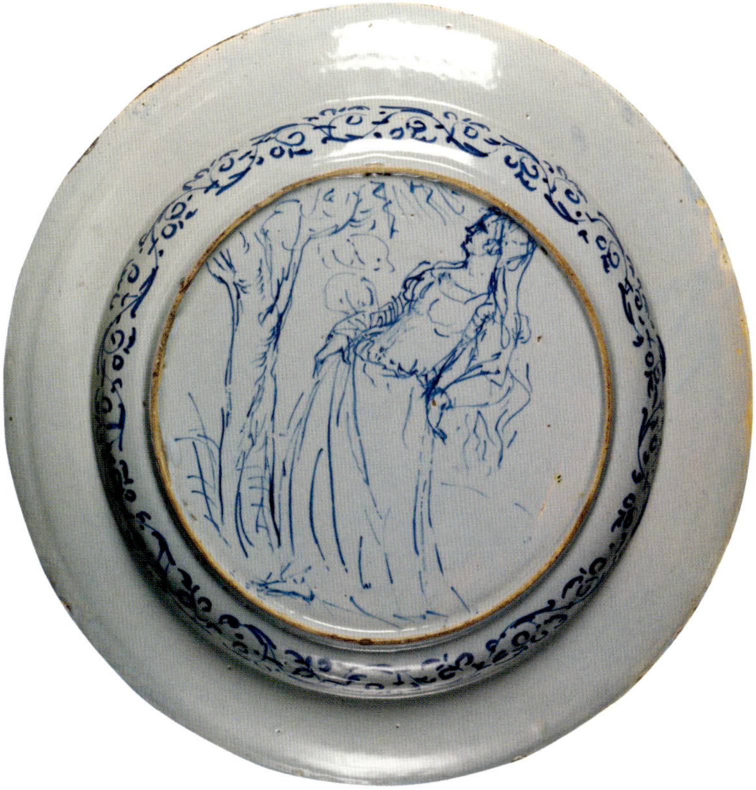

sketch of a woman standing next to a tree. The painting on the dish is closely stylistically related to equally spectacular large storage jars decorated with animals including an elephant, a stag and parrots appearing amongst leafy scrolls, which are attributed to the Venetian workshop of Maestro Domenego.[26]

Faenza white and late sixteenth-century ornament

Towards the middle of the sixteenth century, potters in Faenza took the lead in developing a revolutionary type of maiolica, covered with a thick layer of pure white tin-glaze. Piccolpasso states that 'the milky white today wrongly called Faenza white' was actually invented by Alfonso I Duke of Ferrara. Whether or not this is true, it is clear that a small number of potters from Faenza played leading roles in developing the glaze, including Francesco Mezzarisa, who in 1540 engaged a glaze specialist on an exclusive contract for five years, specifically to mix the white glaze for the workshop. Virgiliotto Calamelli was another of the main producers: the inventory of his workshop taken in 1556 included over a thousand pieces of white wares.[27] The thick white glaze was sometimes left completely undecorated, but this type of plain pottery is almost exclusively known from excavated examples. Often the brilliant white surface was decorated in a rapid, sketchy ('*compendiario*') manner of painting in a limited range of colours, enabling fine tablewares to be produced on a large scale relatively quickly and therefore more cheaply (see pls 135, 159, pp.132–4).

This style became very successful and soon afterwards spread to other Italian regions, throughout Europe and even to South America.[28] '*Compendiario*' painting became the dominant style of the second part of the sixteenth century and services decorated this way were made for foreign nobility such as Duke Albrecht V of Bavaria.

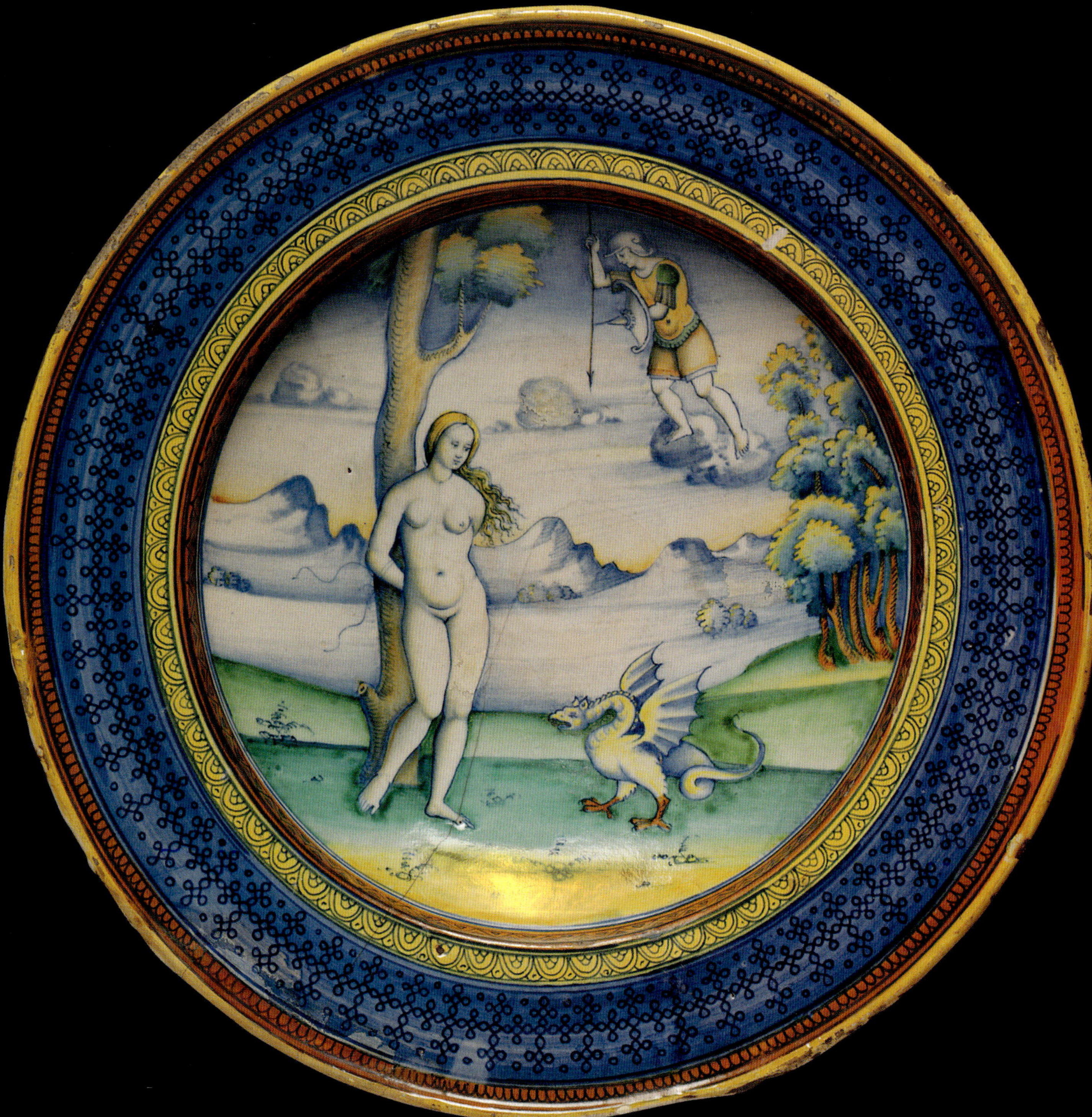

Narrative Painting (*Istoriato*)

81 Dish with Perseus and Andromeda
Faenza, 1510–20
Diam: 37.7 cm
Salting Bequest V&A: C.2118–1910

Around 1500 maiolica painters began to explore the possibilities of painting narrative subjects. Influenced by engravings and book illustrations, which were increasingly available, they developed an extraordinary new style, *istoriato* or *figurato* (story or figure painting), treating plates, jugs and other wares as a 'canvas' for illusionistic narrative painting. The subject-matter was varied and reflected the interests of Renaissance society. Images were taken primarily from recently rediscovered classical literary works or from the Bible, with contemporary events only rarely represented. The best *istoriato* maiolica deserves a place among the finest pictorial art of the Renaissance period. Furthermore, unlike oil, fresco or tempera, its colours remain as fresh as when they were first painted and they can be enjoyed today exactly as 500 years ago.

Subject-matter

The most popular single literary source for *istoriato* maiolica was Ovid's *Metamorphoses* (8 AD), which appeared in several illustrated editions during the late fifteenth and the sixteenth centuries. Eye-catching stories from the ancient poem – such as Diana transforming Actaeon into a stag, or Daphne being changed into a tree to escape the amorous attentions of Apollo – made excellent source material. A beautiful dish probably painted in Faenza around 1510–20 shows the very popular tale of Perseus rescuing Andromeda from a sea-monster (pl. 81). The precisely outlined figures on this dish are probably taken from an early woodcut illustration. Ovidian subjects remained common on maiolica until the end of the sixteenth century.

Religious subjects were popular on maiolica, but were always less common than mythological ones. The scenes chosen were normally seminal stories from the Bible, such as the life of Christ, the Saints or Moses, while episodes of religious devotion are less common. A delightful example is a bowl showing a lively scene with Franciscan friars playing at the organ and singing (pl. 82). A sheet of music shows the title of the piece they are playing: 'Hear, O Heaven, my lament', a *'frottola'* by Bartolomeo Tromboncino. A dog accompanies the singers, while a man on the right operates the organ's bellows. Biblical themes became especially common in the second half

82 Lustred bowl on low foot with Franciscan monks playing an organ
Deruta, 1520–35
Diam: 27 cm
Salting Bequest V&A: C.2183–1910

83 Dish with Pope Leo X in procession
Montelupo, c.1515
Diam: 49 cm
V&A: 8928–1863

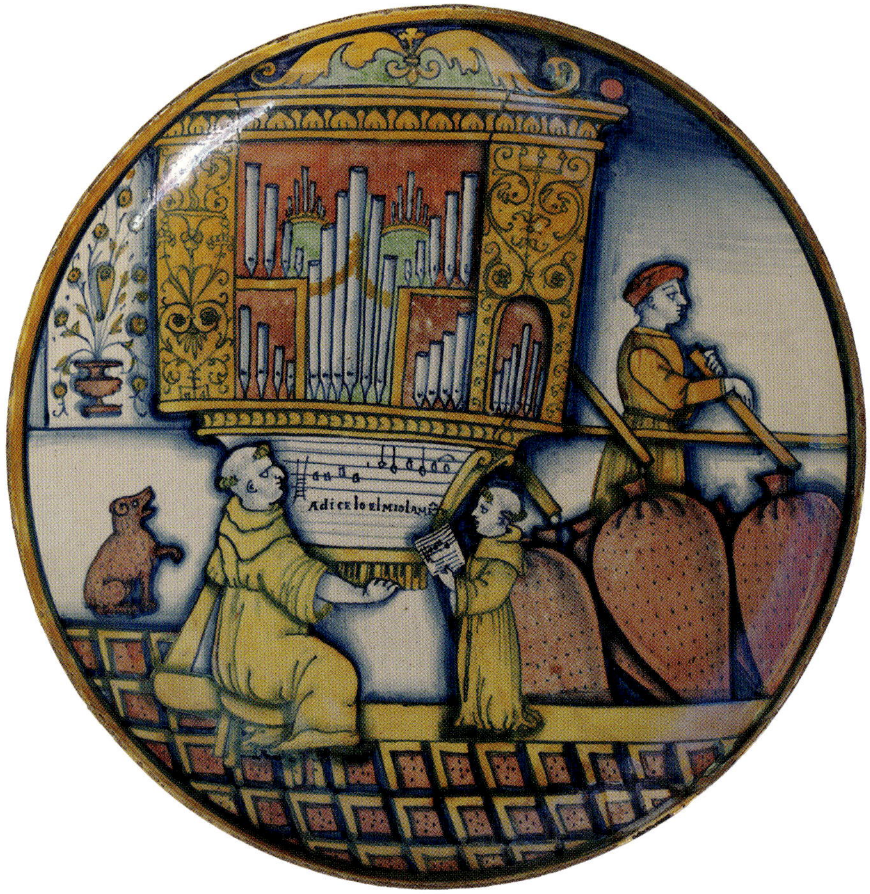

of the century, perhaps under the influence of the Council of Trent (1545–63), which sought to refocus the Catholic church in response to the Reformation. Several Bible picture books were published in Lyons from the 1550s and their illustrations were widely used by maiolica painters.

Contemporary events appear only occasionally on Renaissance maiolica. One of the most extraordinary surviving examples is an unusually large dish showing Pope Leo X (1513–21) in procession (pl. 83). It was probably made in Montelupo, and is thought to represent the triumphal entry of Leo X, the first Pope from the Medici family, into the city of Florence in 1515. This event, of crucial political significance as a celebration of the restoration of Medici rule in Tuscany, was the subject of numerous depictions in different media. However, the scene on the plate seems to be partially imaginary: the presence of Hanno, the Pope's pet elephant, given to him by the King of Portugal in 1514, has not been recorded elsewhere.[29]

Graphic sources

One of the crucial factors in the diffusion of narrative subjects on maiolica was the invention of the printing press. The dissemination of printed images from the second half of the fifteenth century onwards meant that potters could easily turn to these graphic sources for guidance or inspiration. A drawing in Piccolpasso's manuscript treatise on the potter's art shows pottery painters working from prints or drawings pinned to the wall (pl. 26). The painters used images in different ways, probably

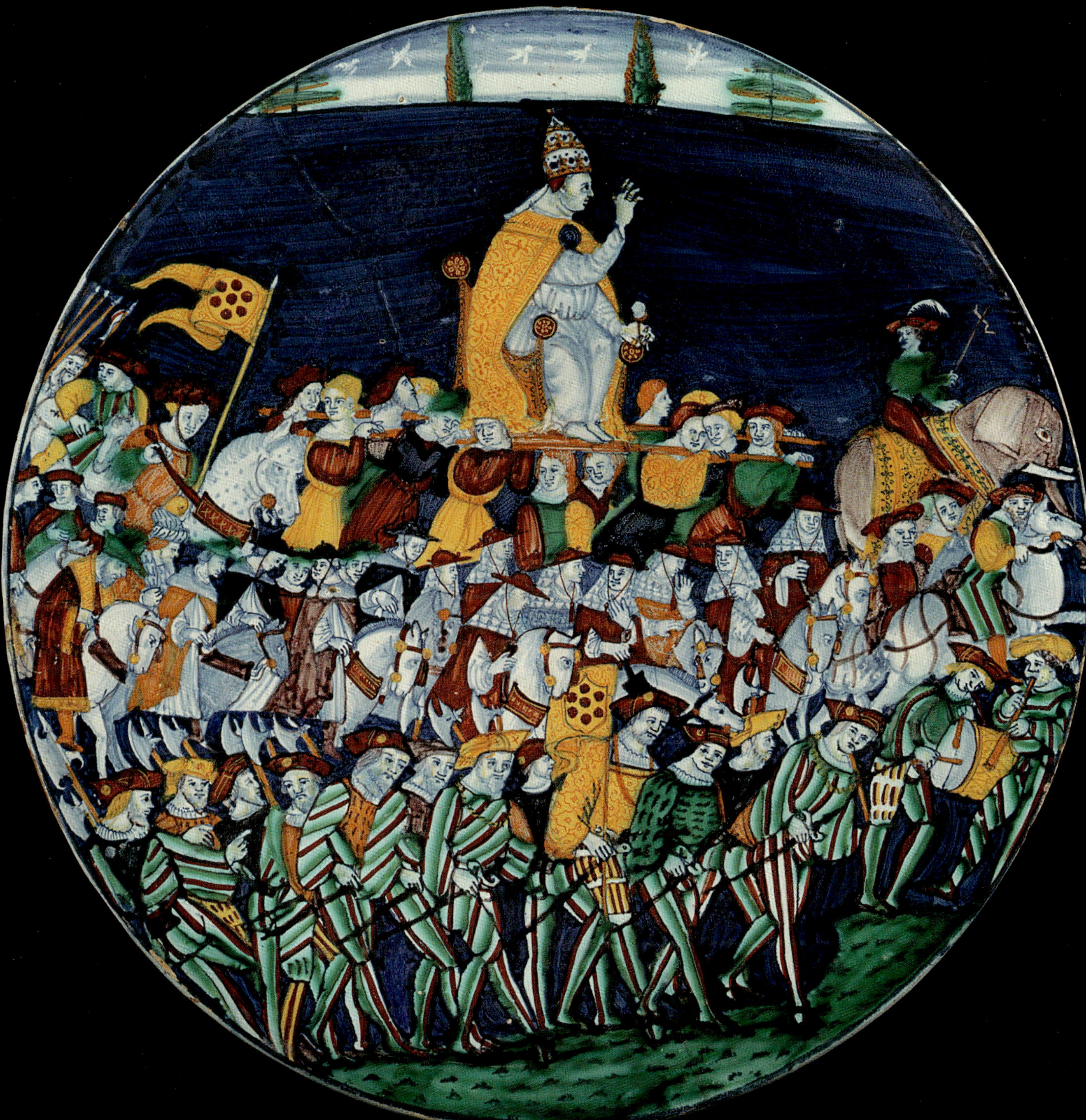

starting by making a working copy of the design. A rectangular or square composition would have to be adapted to the round shape of a vessel, and a scene would often be reduced in the process. Every workshop must have kept a stock of working drawings, but virtually none of these have survived.

The images copied by potters reflect technical innovations in the print-making industry. Wood-blocks were the earliest means of printing images on paper. The process involves making a drawing on a smoothed block of wood. The lines of the design are left standing in relief on the block while the wood on either side of them is cut away with a knife. An impression is then taken by laying a sheet of paper over the inked block. Woodcut illustrations were used increasingly from the 1490s to illustrate printed books since the wood-block and raised type could be printed simultaneously. When maiolica painters turned to this important graphic source their bright colours gave new life to the mostly black and white world of prints.

Early narrative scenes on maiolica often follow their woodcut sources very closely. A dish of 1514 shows part of a Roman triumphal procession (pl. 84). The scene is interrupted rather abruptly at the plate edges, cutting the figures at both sides in half. The image duly derives from one of a set of 12 woodcuts forming *The Triumph of Caesar*, published in Venice in 1504.[30] The dish shows two horses drawing Caesar's chariot, surrounded by incense-bearers, musicians and a jester. It is marked with a capital 'I' on the front. The existence of a dish showing another part of the scene

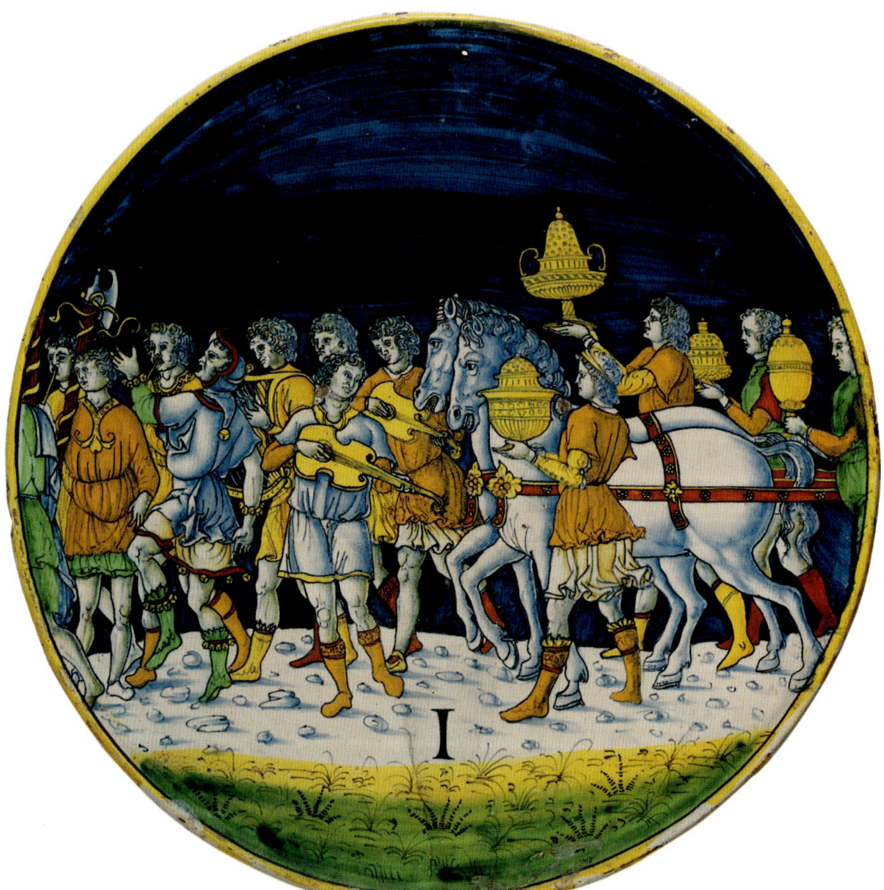

84 Dish with a sequence from the Triumph of Caesar
Close to Jacopo's style
Perhaps Montelupo, 1514
Diam: 41.5 cm
V&A: 6664–1860

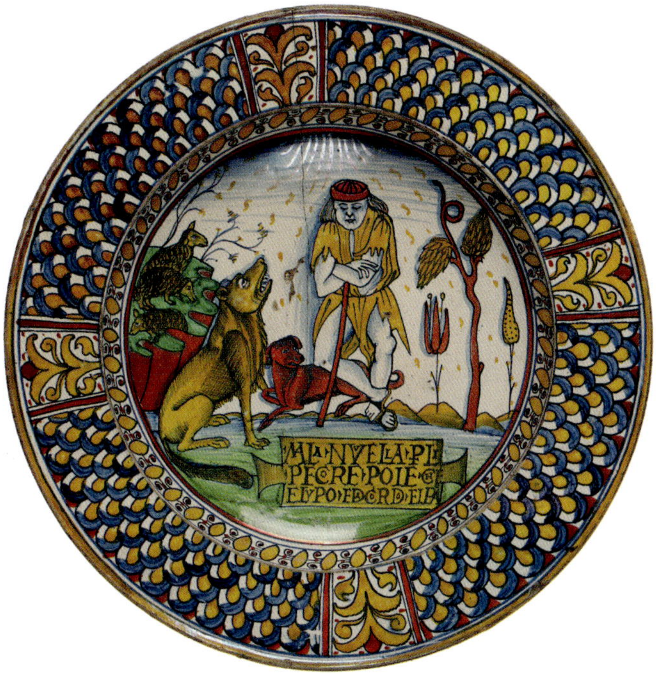

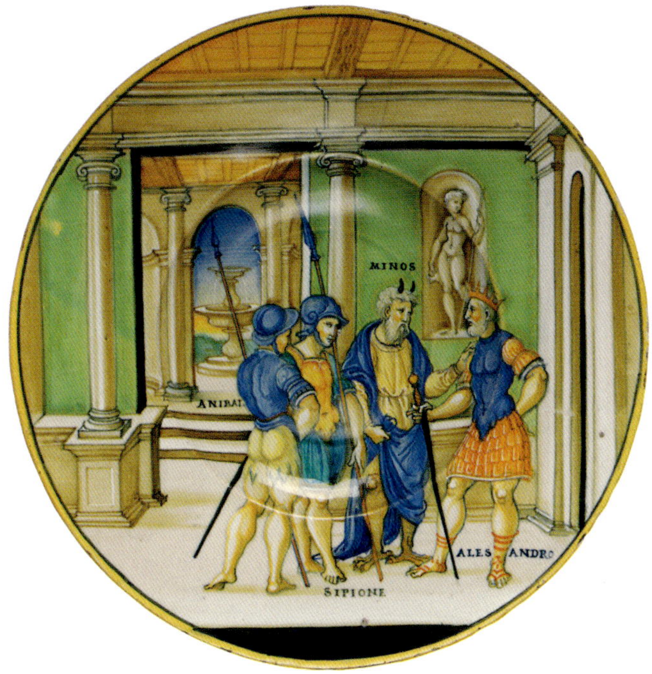

85 Lustred dish with Aesop's fable of the Shepherd and the Wolf
Probably Gubbio, c.1510
Diam: 39 cm
Salting Bequest V&A: C.2171–1910

86 Dish with the dialogue between Minos, Alexander, Scipio and Hannibal
Nicola da Urbino
Urbino, c.1530–35
Diam: 26 cm
Salting Bequest V&A: C.2225–1910

marked with 'H', at the Fitzwilliam Museum in Cambridge, suggests that the two dishes might have been part of a series of 12, one for each of the woodcuts.[31]

Aesop's *Fables* was a popular choice for moral education and often featured in medieval and Renaissance art and architecture. A woodcut illustration in one of the first complete Italian translations of the fables, published in Naples in 1485, made an exemplar for the decoration of a lustred maiolica dish from around 1510, probably one of the earliest attempts at narrative painting made in Gubbio (pl. 85). It shows the fable of the Shepherd and the Wolf, the inscription on the front of the dish explaining the visual message: 'bad news for the sheep as the shepherd is in league with the wolf'.

Woodcut illustrations used by pottery painters as source material were often quite bold and the best maiolica painters learned how to work around this. A dish by Nicola da Urbino (see page 100) probably executed in the early 1530s (pl. 86) draws on another classical work, a woodcut in the Italian translation of Lucian's *Dialogues of the Dead*, published in Venice in 1525. The skill of the painter is shown in the adaptation of his source. Nicola has moved the scene from a bare exterior to a lavish classical interior, although the influence of the woodcut can be seen in details such as the presence of names of the characters in capital letters.[32]

Illustrations from contemporary literary works such as Ariosto's extremely popular poem *Orlando Furioso* were sometimes reproduced on maiolica, for example by Xanto in the 1530s (see pl. 121). Giacomo Mancini (also known as El Frate), the most important *istoriato* painter in Deruta, illustrated many scenes derived from the woodcut illustrations of the Venetian edition of this poem, only three years after its publication in 1542. These works are often signed, and six of them are dated 1545.[33] The dish shown in pl. 87 shows an episode from the fourth canto of the poem, the heroine Bradamante about to fight and defeat the magician Atlante. Text from the poem is written on the reverse of the dish (pl. 88).

For the German painter and printmaker Albrecht Dürer (1471–1528) the production of engravings and woodcuts was a major source of income. His woodcuts were copied by Italian engravers, notably Marcantonio Raimondi, and these in turn became a source for maiolica painters. An example of this practice is a beautiful bowl made in Faenza showing the Presentation in the Temple (pl. 90). The scene derives from Marcantonio's engraving after Dürer's woodcut of about 1504, part of a series illustrating *The Life of the Virgin.* To fit the round shape of the bowl a figure of a man with a tall hat derived from an entirely different woodcut by Dürer (*The Betrothal of the Virgin*) has been introduced at the far left of the bowl.

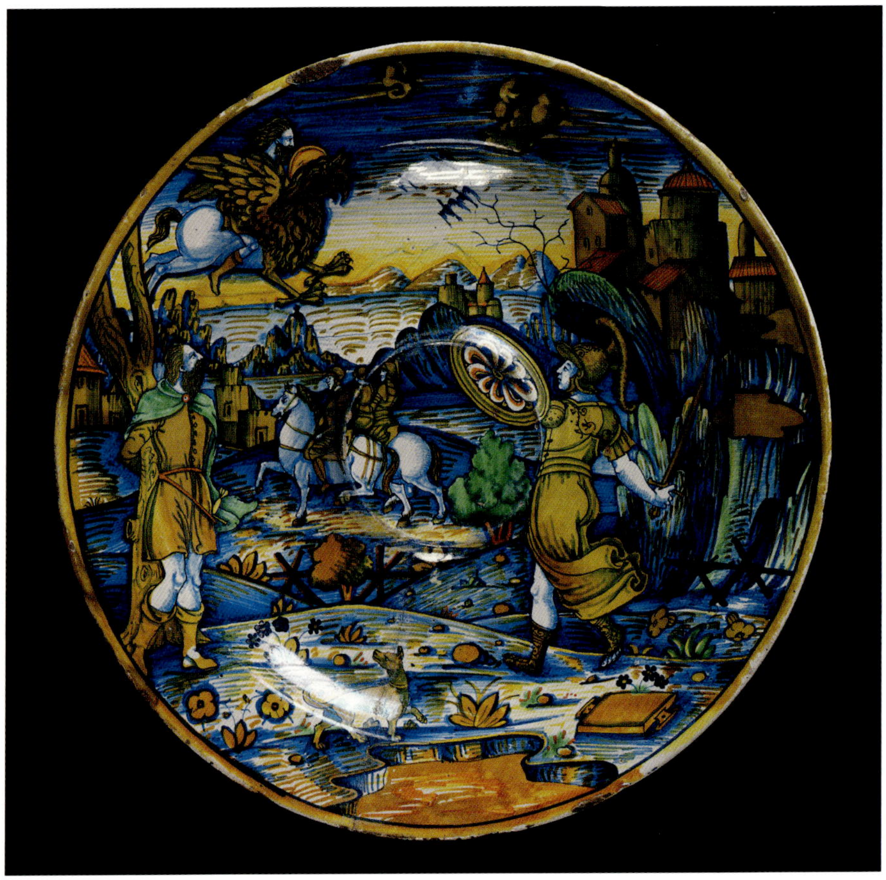

87 Lustred basin for a ewer depicting Bradamante and Atlante from the fourth canto of Ariosto's poem *Orlando Furioso*
Giacomo Mancini known as El Frate
Deruta, 1545
Diam: 37 cm
Salting Bequest V&A: C.2198–1910

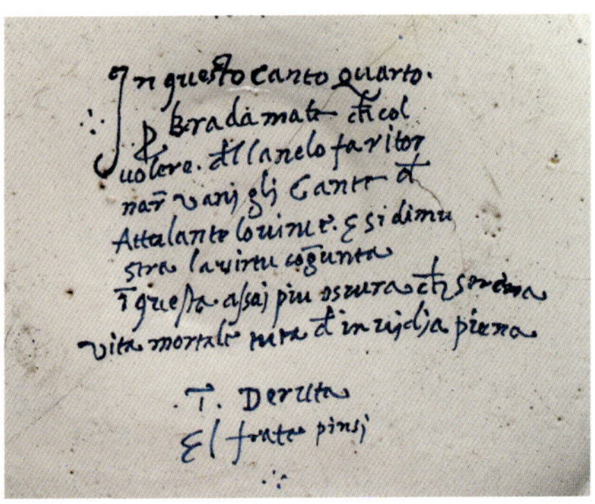

88 Reverse of pl.87
Inscribed with description of episode and signature: 'In Deruta painted by El Frate'

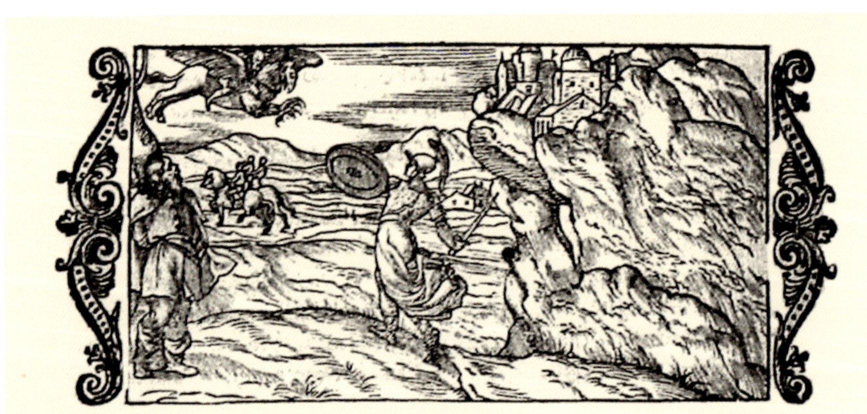

89 Woodcut illustrating Ariosto's poem *Orlando Furioso*
Gabriele Giolito de' Ferrari
Venice, 1550
NAL: A.L.648-1885, drawer 51

90 Bowl on low foot with the Presentation in the Temple
Faenza, c.1520–30
Diam: 25.5 cm
V&A: C.159–1937

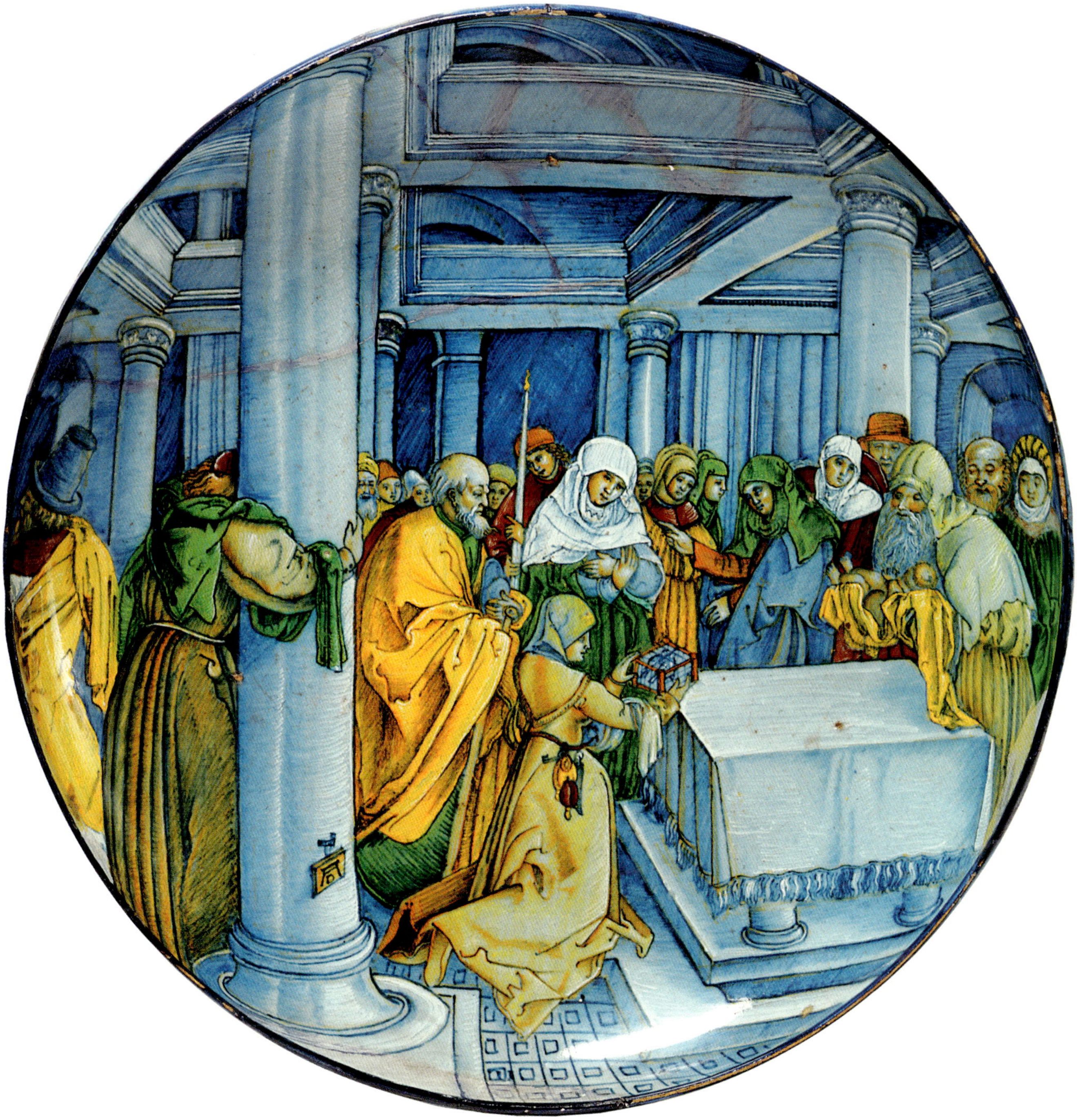

91 Plaque with the Entombment
Probably Urbino, 1523
H: 31 cm, W: 29.5 cm
Salting Bequest V&A: C.2119–1910

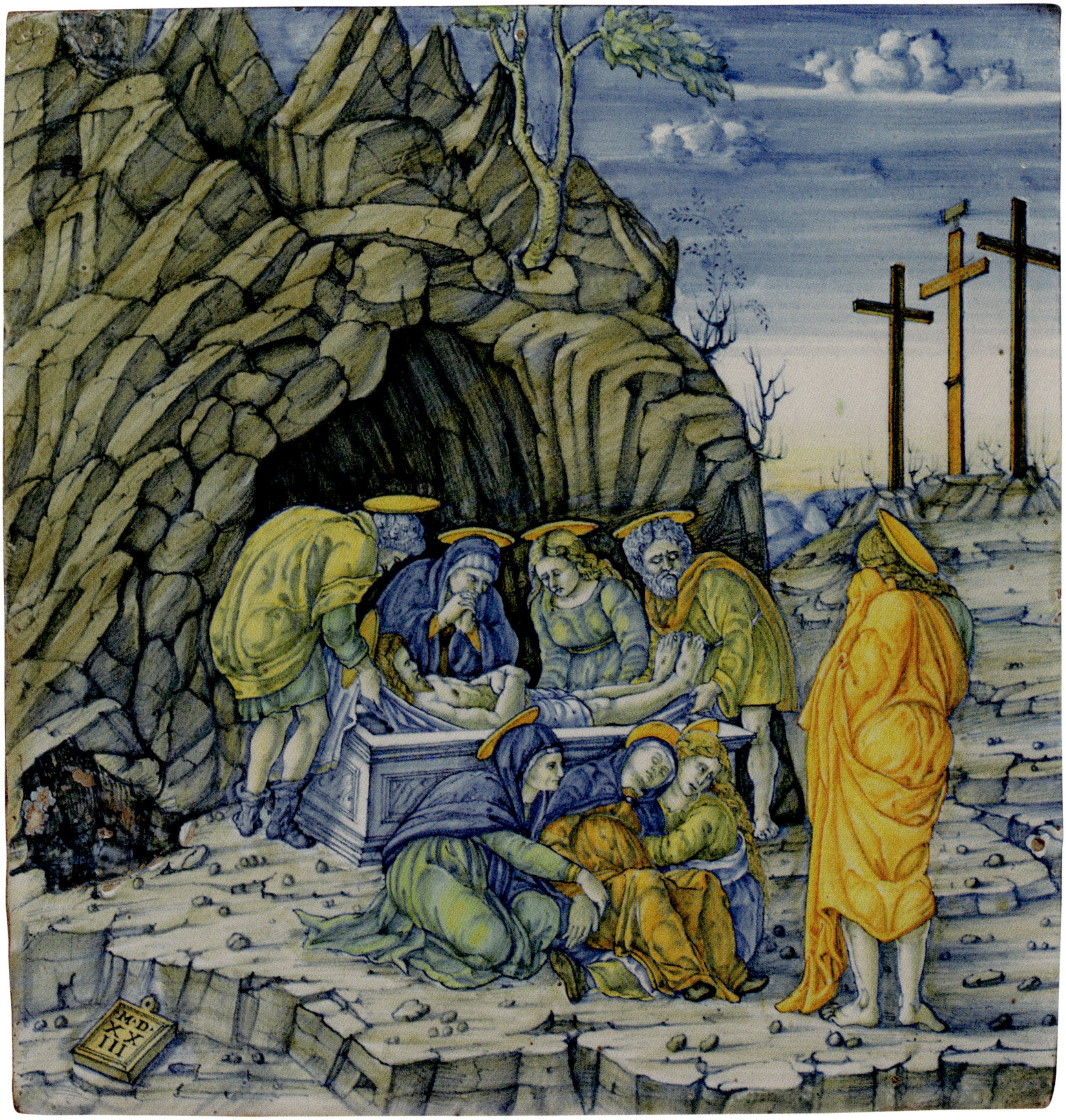

92 The Entombment
Andrea Mantegna
Engraving
Italy, 1475–1500
V&A: Dyce.989

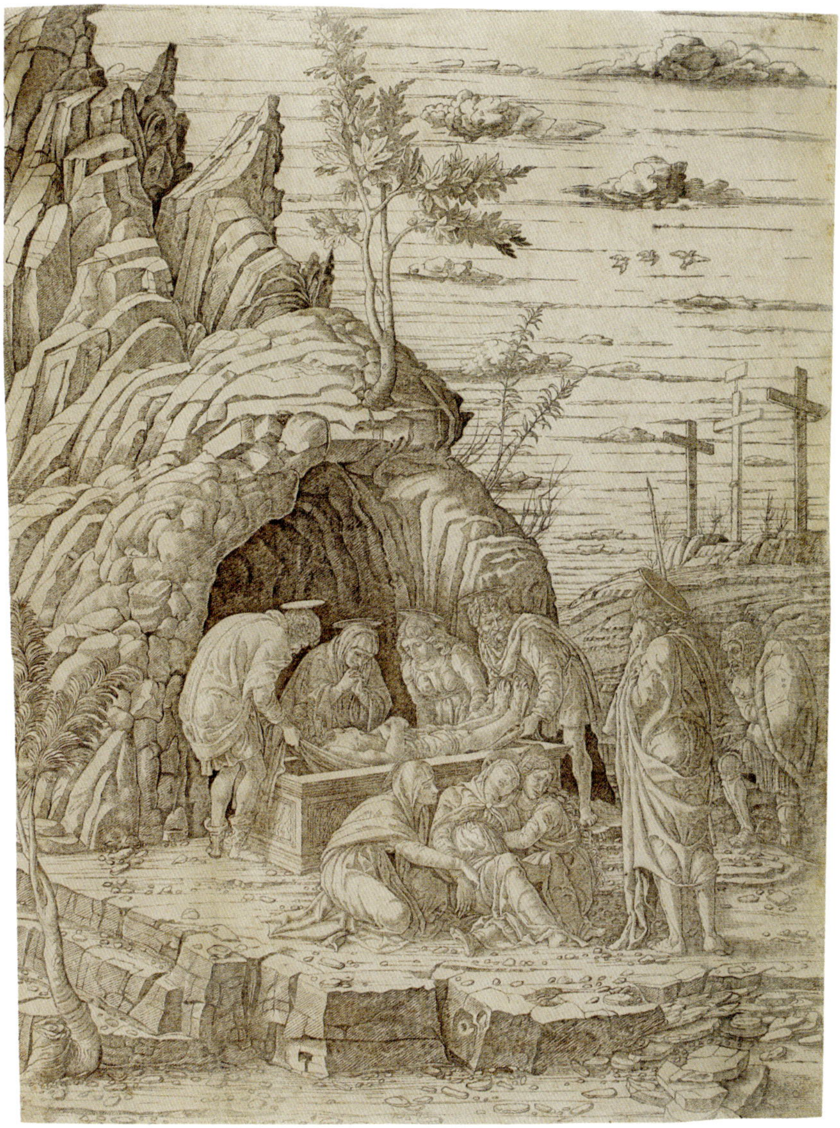

Engravings printed from copper plates, which were more detailed and enjoyed higher status than woodcuts, soon became the most important graphic source for maiolica painters. The northern Italian painter Andrea Mantegna (1431–1506) was responsible for a number of highly influential prints. An important example of *istoriato* painting deriving from one of his compositions is an extraordinary panel dated 1523 representing the Entombment (pls 91, 92). The unknown painter has succeeded masterfully in following closely the detailing of the rectangular print while adapting it to the square shape of the panel.

The taste for northern prints dominates the first phase of *istoriato* painting, especially in Faenza. From the 1520s however Italian prints became the most widely used as models. Of these the most influential were prints after compositions by Raphael (1483–1520) and his school. Raphael did not make prints himself but understood their commercial potential. He started collaborating with Marcantonio Raimondi around 1510, supplying him with drawings and in all likelihood supervising the production

93 Dish with the Marriage of Ninus and Semiramis
Francesco Xanto Avelli
Urbino, 1533
Diam: 46.5 cm
V&A: 1748–1855

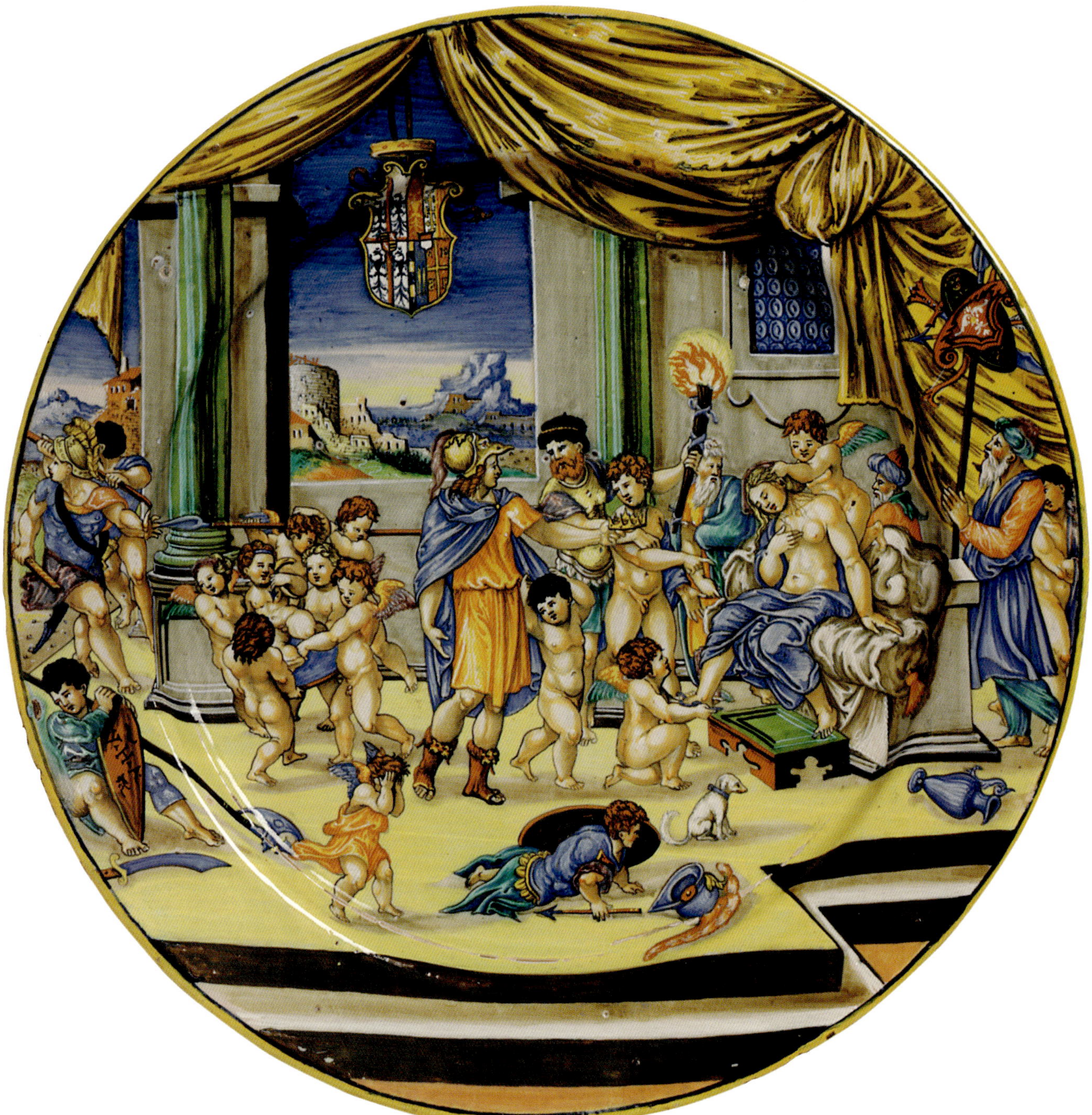

94 Reverse of pl.93

95 Broad-rimmed dish with the Death of Leucothoe
Francesco Xanto Avelli
Urbino, 1540
Diam: 27.5 cm
V&A: 1695–1855

96 Illustration of sonnet nine of Pietro Aretino *I Modi*
Marcantonio Raimondi after
Giulio Romano
Engraving
Italy, c.1524
Reproduced in *Sonetti sopra i 'XVI modi'*, edited by Giovanni Aquilecchia
Rome 1996

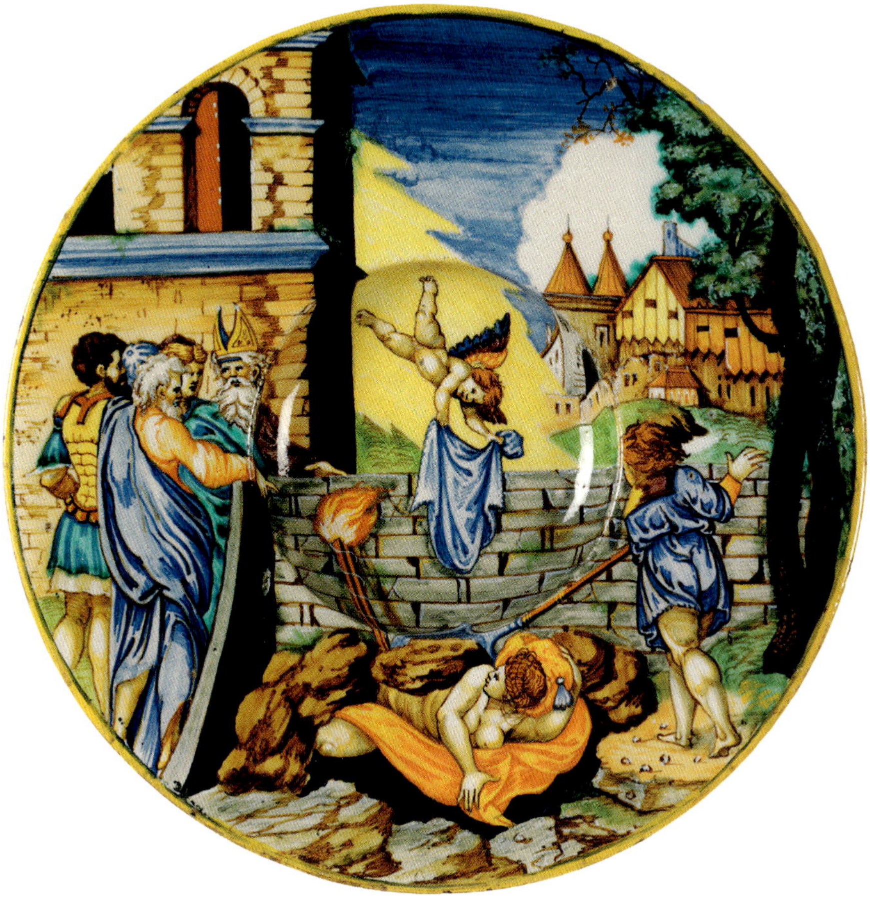

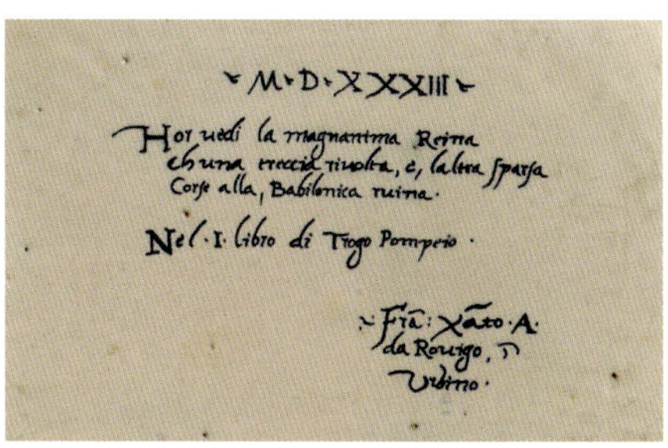

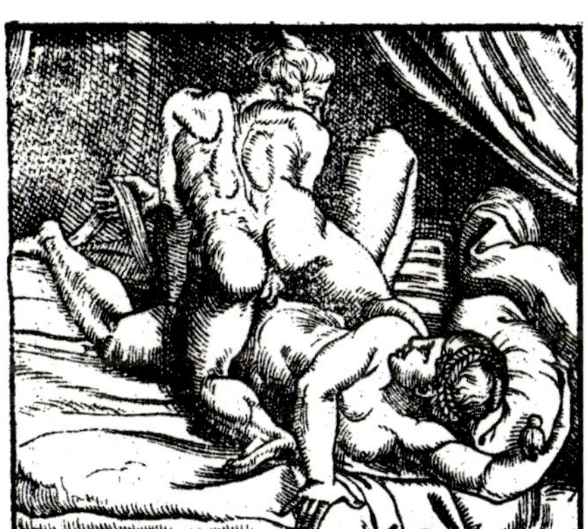

of prints.[34] Pottery painters began to transpose such prints onto maiolica from the 1520s, abandoning fifteenth-century sources for the pictorial language of the High Renaissance.[35]

The pottery painter Francesco Xanto Avelli, active in Urbino from the late 1520s up to his death in 1542, made extensive use of engravings, especially those after Raphael. The central group on a large dish probably representing the marriage of Ninus and Semiramis, dated 1533, derives from an engraving by Gian Giacomo Caraglio after Raphael, while figures from other prints are used to extend the composition (pl. 93). Xanto would effectively 'cut and paste' figures from numerous engravings to create new compositions. He added inscriptions on the reverse of wares, sometimes taken from literary sources (pl. 94), including, in one instance, his own poetry.

Conventional printed sources were not the only images used by this resourceful painter. On a dish representing the tragic death of Leucothoe, buried alive (pl. 95) a subject from Ovid's *Metamorphoses*, Xanto incorporates various figures from compositions by Raphael, while the figure of the victim is taken from a notorious set of Renaissance erotic prints, *I Modi* (*The Positions*), made by Marcantonio from a set of now-lost drawings by Giulio Romano dating from 1524, illustrating sonnets by Pietro Aretino. The drawings were first banned and then destroyed, but a few fragments of the prints made after them survive. On the dish the dying Leucothoe even has under her head the bed cushion that features in the print (pl. 96).

A pottery-painter might use the same print in different ways. *The Allegory of Envy* by Cristofano Robetta is copied in its entirety on a large dish dated 1525, while only three of the figures (the young couple with a baby) appear on a smaller dish produced in the same year and in the same workshop, that of Maestro Giorgio in Gubbio (pl. 97).

Besides prints, drawings and sketches relating to paintings were also used by potters. The subject of a delicately painted plaque (pl. 98), was unclear until its source was identified in a fresco which formerly decorated the walls of the Camera Bella of the Sienese palace of Pandolfo Petrucci. The fresco, depicting Coriolanus persuaded by his family to spare Rome, was made about 1509 and is attributed to Luca Signorelli (pl. 99).[36] The maiolica panel, one of the highest achievements of early narrative painting from Faenza, probably derives from a lost drawing of the fresco, as some details of the background differ from the original.

One of Raphael's most influential projects was his full-scale designs for tapestries for the Sistine Chapel, commissioned from him by Pope Leo X in 1515. These cartoons are now in the Royal Collection and have been on loan to the V&A since 1865. The dish shown in pl. 100 represents the subject of one of these cartoons: *The Healing of the Lame Man* (pl. 101). The scene was not engraved during the sixteenth century so the pottery painter must have known the composition through another source.

The influence of Florentine art on the talented pottery painter Jacopo (active briefly at Cafaggiolo around 1510–15) is illustrated by an extraordinary dish (pl. 103). In this rare case, the central figure is closely based on a public sculpture: the *Saint George* by Donatello on the facade of Orsanmichele in Florence (pl. 102). The plate shows the saint holding in his right hand a thrusting dagger, which is now missing from the original sculpture. Jacopo, a skilled artist, might have sketched the sculpture himself in order to use it on one of his plates.

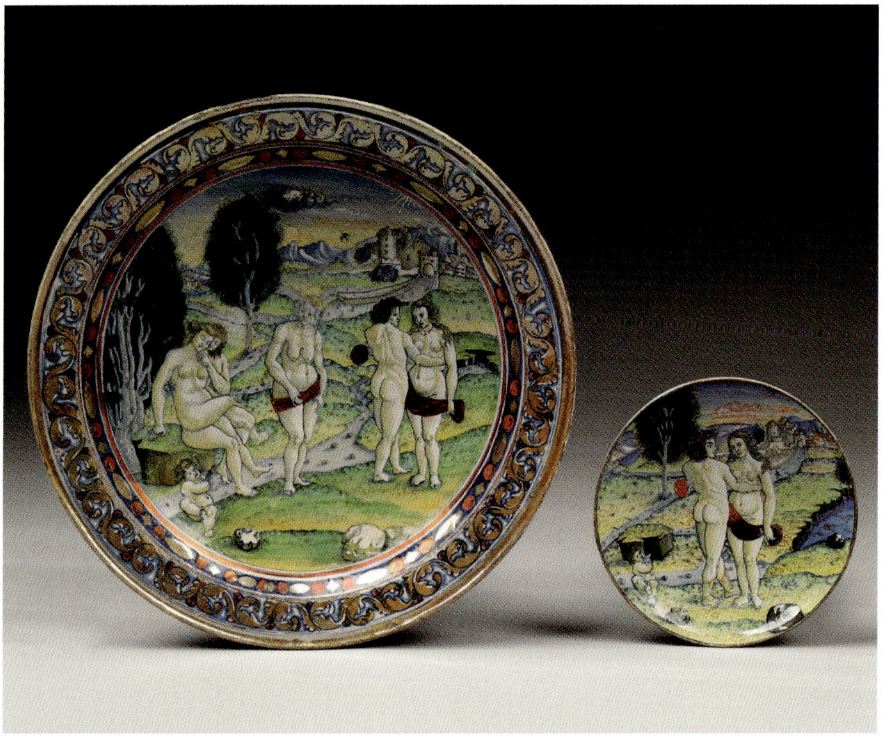

97 Lustred dishes with the Allegory of Envy
Workshop of Maestro Giorgio
Gubbio, 1525
Diam: 40.5 cm and 20 cm
Salting Bequest V&A: C.2200–1910 and 8939–1863

98 Panel with Coriolanus persuaded by his family to spare Rome
Faenza, c.1510–20
H: 38.5 cm, W: 38.5 cm
V&A: 4277–1857

99 Coriolanus persuaded by his family to spare Rome
Luca Signorelli
Fresco transferred onto canvas
From the Petrucci Palace, Siena, c.1509

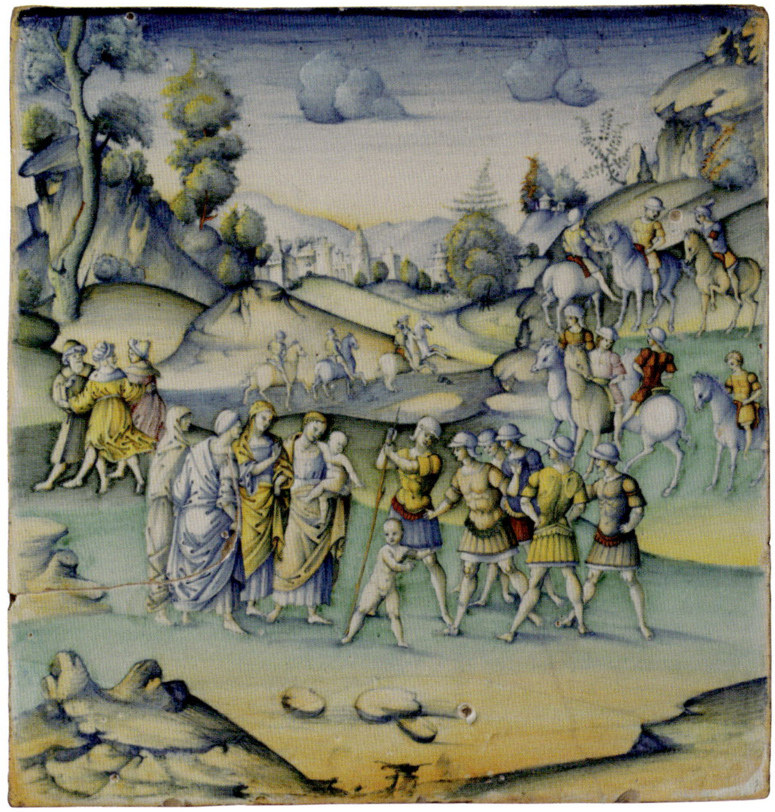

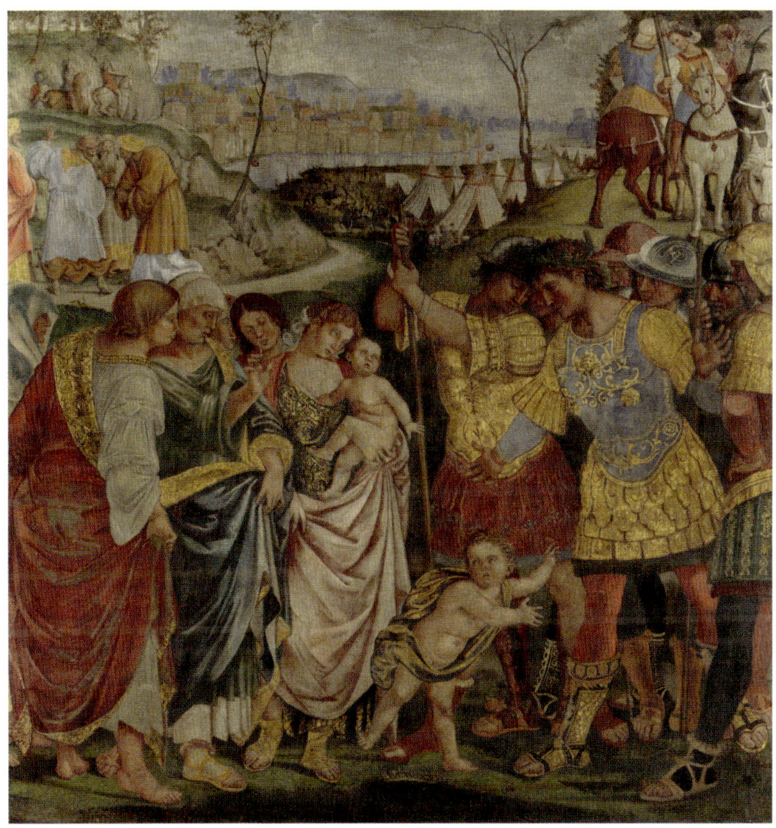

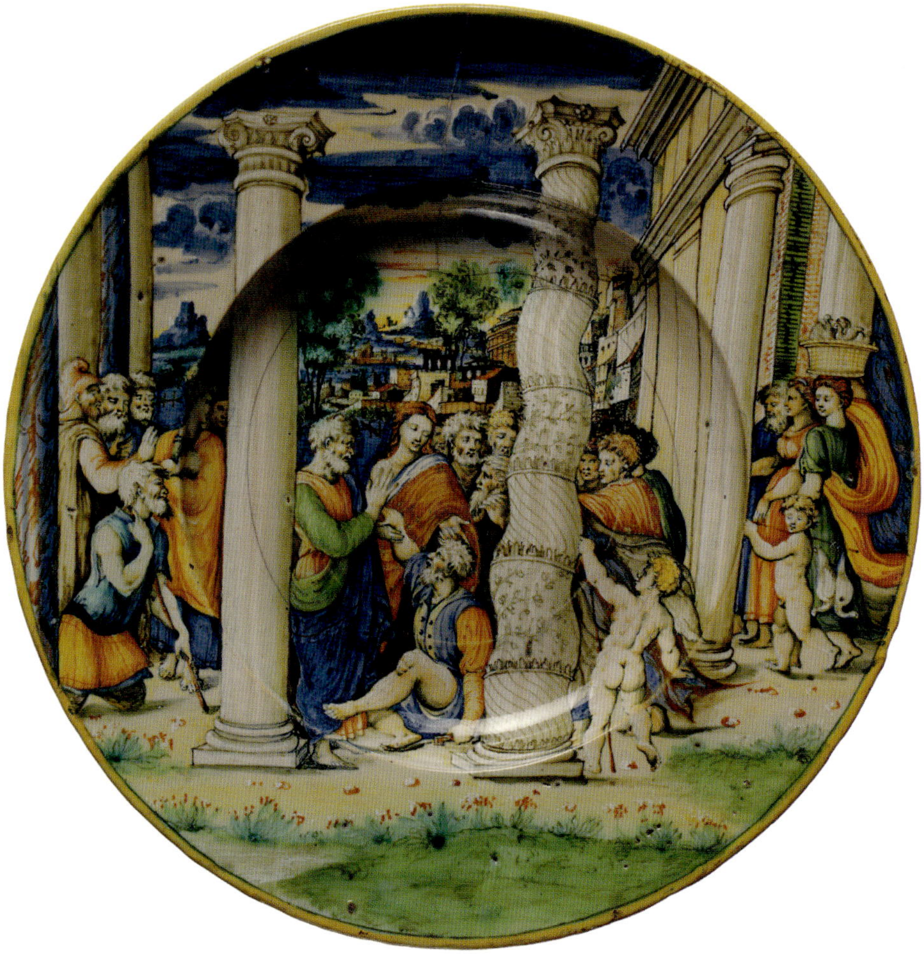

100 Dish with the Healing of the Lame Man
Urbino, 1540–50
Diam: 38 cm
Salting Bequest V&A: C.2251–1910

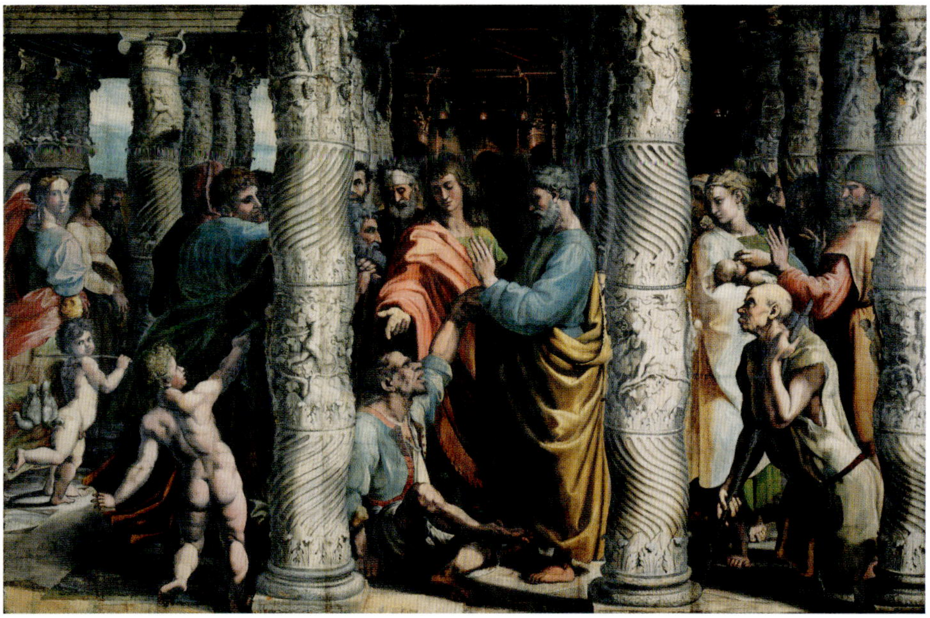

101 Cartoon for tapestry
The Healing of the Lame Man
Raphael
Rome, 1515–16
On loan to the V&A from the collection of Her Majesty the Queen
V&A: RoyalLoans.4

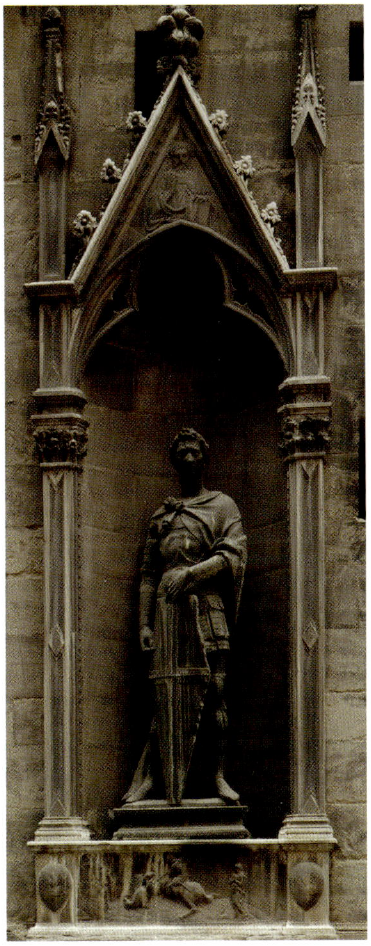

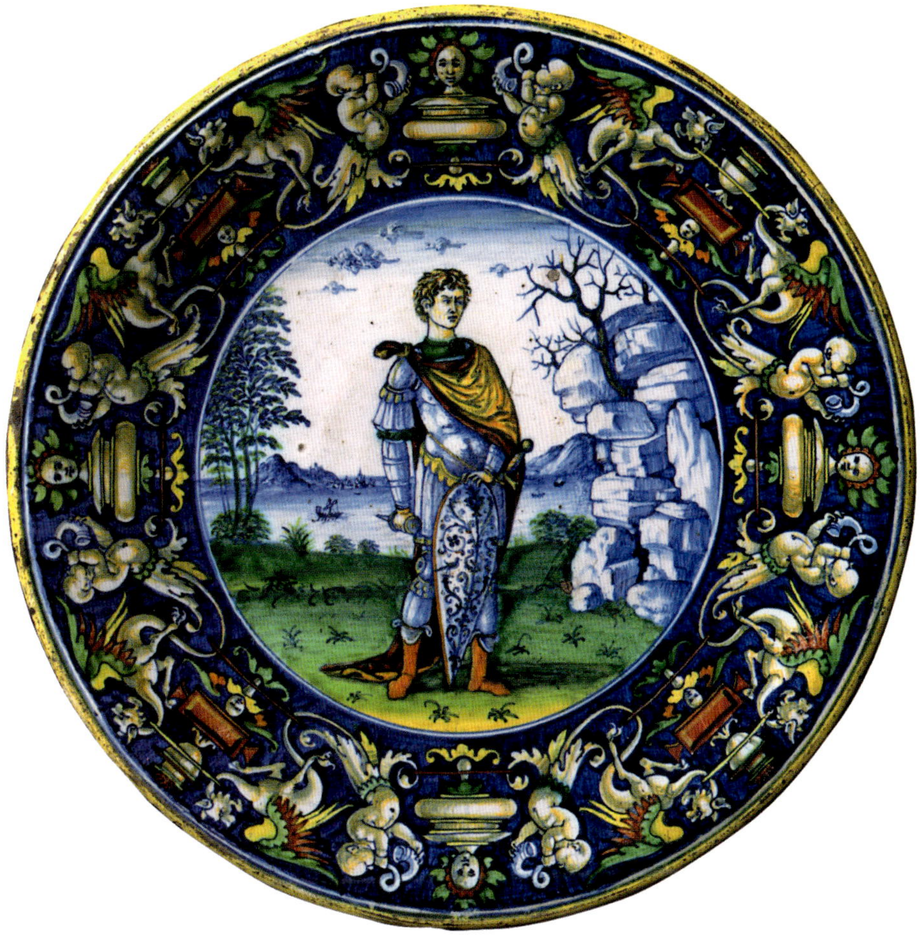

102 Marble Sculpture of St George
Donatello
Orsanmichele, c.1415
Bargello Museum, Florence

103 Plate with St George after Donatello
Maestro Jacopo
Cafaggiolo, 1510–15
Diam: 32 cm
V&A: 1726–1855

Special orders

On rare occasions leading painters were asked to create designs especially for maiolica decoration. This practice is described by the painter-biographer Giorgio Vasari in the second edition of *Lives of the Artists* (1568), in his account of the painter Battista Franco:

> The Duke [Guidobaldo of Urbino] ... thinking that his designs would be very successful if put into effect by those who made excellent pottery vessels at Castel Durante, and who had made much use of engravings of Raphael of Urbino and of other men of talent, had Battista make a very large number of drawings which, adopted for that most elegant of all Italian wares, emerged as something exceptional. From them were made many and various sorts of pottery, enough to make and do honour to a royal service ... Duke Guidobaldo sent a credenza of this pottery to the Emperor Charles V and one to Cardinal Farnese, brother of his wife Vittoria.[37]

A surviving drawing for a maiolica dish by Battista Franco, probably made for one of these sets, shows a scene from the Trojan war, with King Priam receiving a warrior (pl. 104). The border decoration with putti appears on only one side of the drawing,

104 Drawing with the reception of a warrior by King Priam
Battista Franco
Urbino, 1530s–40s
V&A: 2404

105 Dish with King Priam welcoming Helen back to Troy
Urbino or Castel Durante, 1540–50
Diam: 41 cm
V&A: C.31–1973

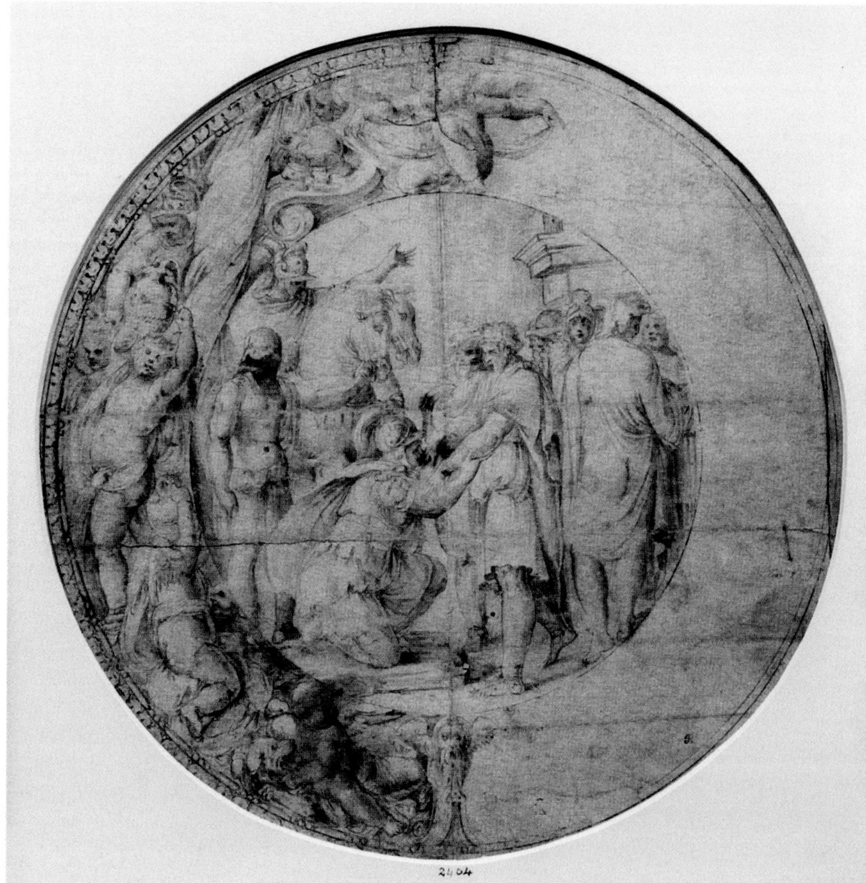

as is common in maiolica designs: the border on the other side of the dish was created as a mirror image by reversing the design through the use of an outline transferred to the pot by 'pouncing' (see p. 30). A dish depicting King Priam welcoming Helen back to Troy derives from one of Franco's designs and is likely to have been part of one of the sets made for the duke (pl. 105).[38]

Other well-known painters provided designs for prestigious maiolica commissions. Vasari also records that around 1560 the artist Taddeo Zuccaro produced drawings for a service that the Duke Guidobaldo sent to King Philip II of Spain. This is likely to be the service described by Paolo Mario in a letter of 1562:

> I have found that more care has been taken over the making of that earthenware service than if it had been made of precious stones. The drawings were brought here from Rome, drawing by drawing, by the hand of the celebrated painter … and in the end it was all complete and so perfect that you can learn from it the arts of sculpture, painting and miniatures, and the history of Caesar, for which Muzio of Constantinople, secretary of his Excellency, a learned and excellent man, dictated the verses or quotations on the back of all the pieces. His Excellency had sent them with an experienced master who has packed them in ten crates and he will be as careful as possible to transport them unbroken and intact (God grant that he may) and to free them from the hands of the Aragonese custom's men.[39]

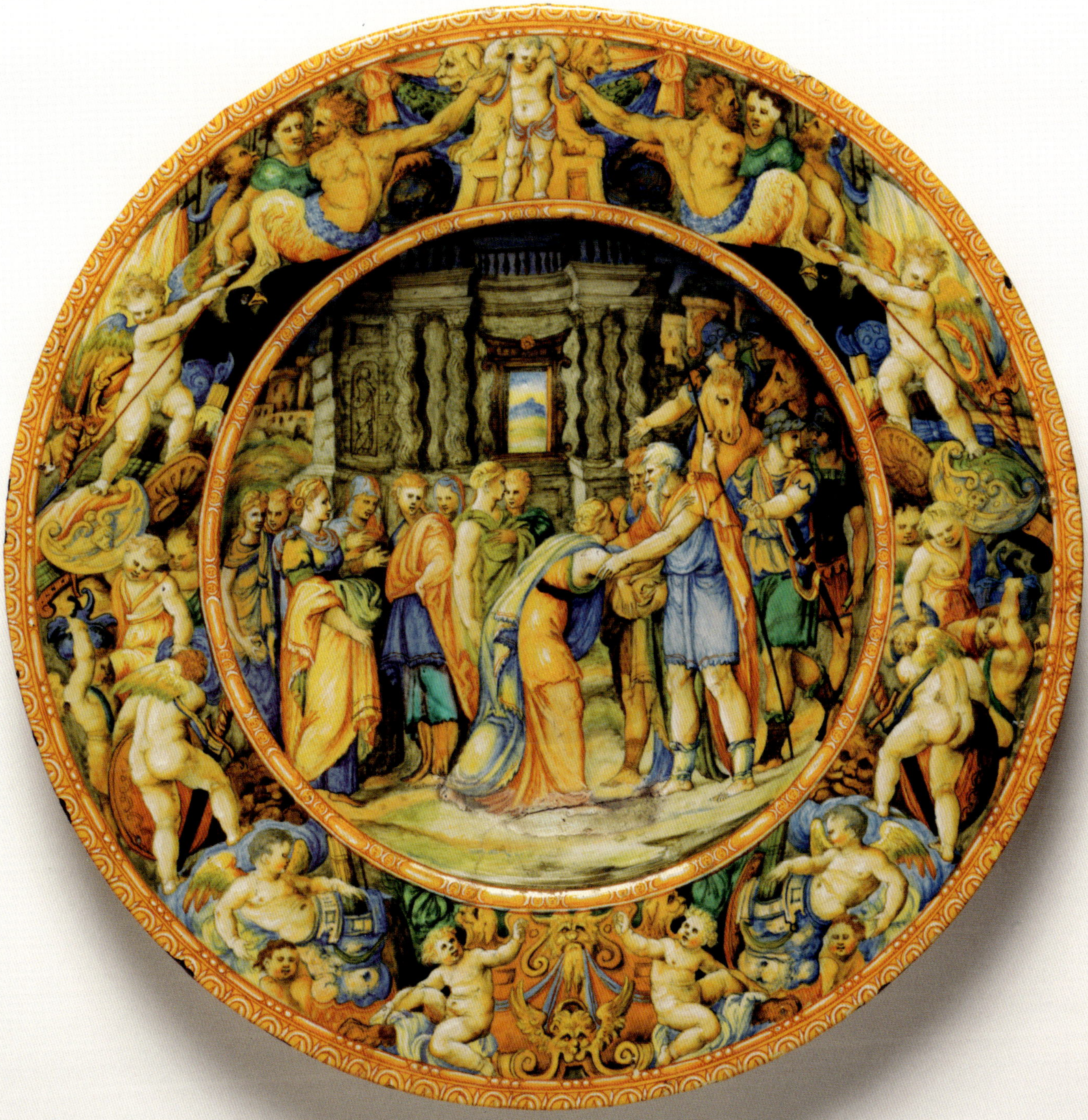

106 Dish with Caesar destroying the bridge at Geneva
Fontana workshop, c.1560
Diam: 44 cm
V&A: 7159–1880

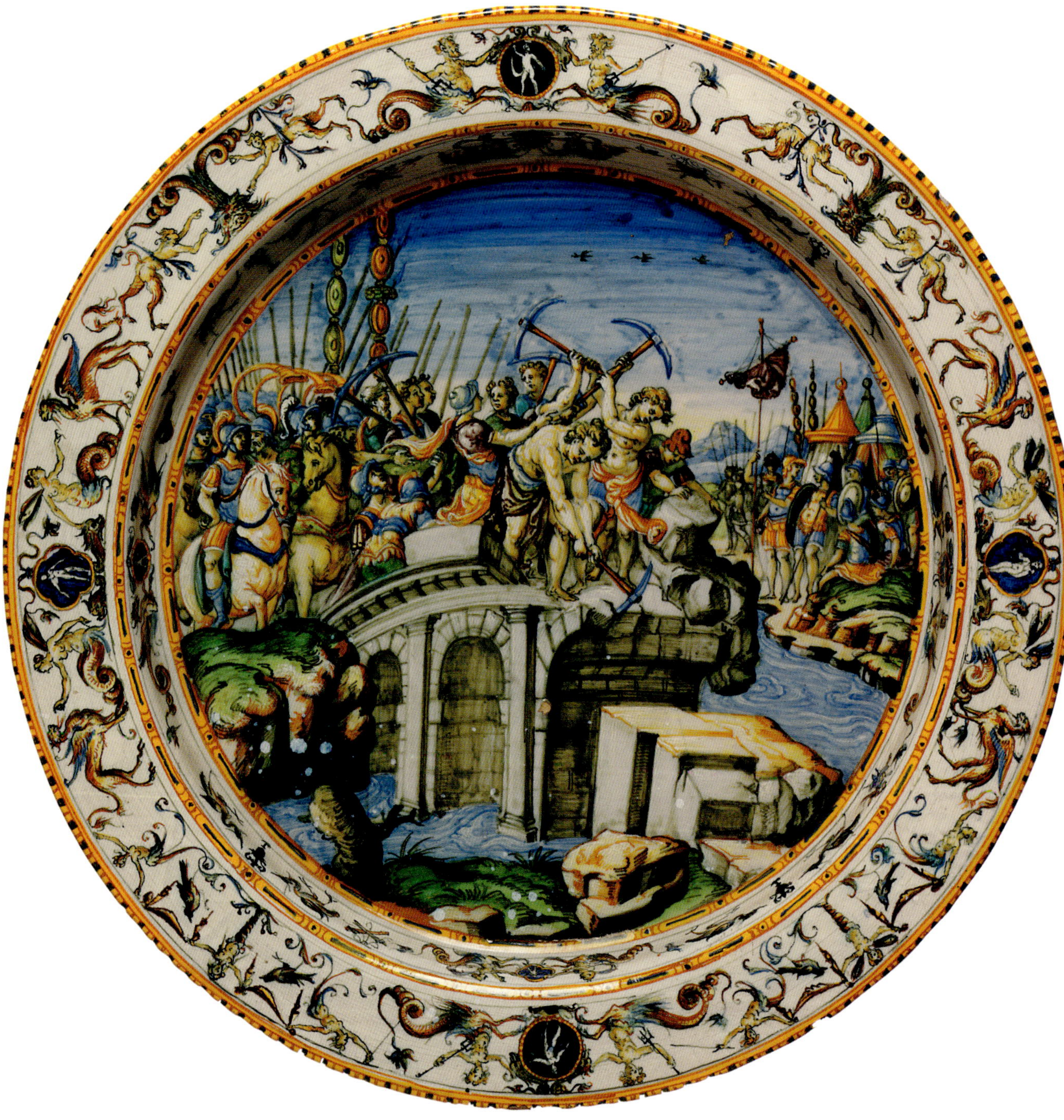

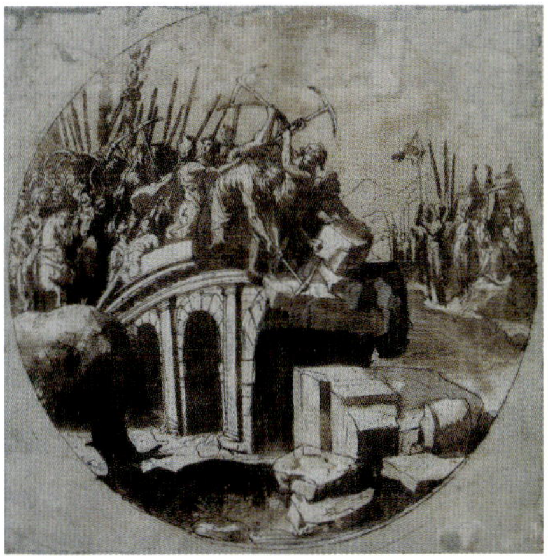

107 Drawing of Caesar destroying the bridge at Geneva
Taddeo Zuccaro
Rome, 1550s
By kind permission of Viscount Coke and the Trustees of the Holkham estate

108 Bowl with satyr looking at nymphs bathing
The Marches, dated 17 November 1503
Diam: 28.8 cm
V&A: 36–1989

109 Reverse of pl.108

From Mario's letter we can appreciate the care put into the design, production and transportation of an exceptional maiolica service. A large dish showing Caesar destroying the bridge at Geneva, might have been part of the service for the king of Spain, known as the Spanish Service (pl. 106).[40] The design by Zuccaro for this dish survives at Holkham Hall in Norfolk (pl. 107) and nearly 50 other known drawings relate to this service, one of the most ambitious of all sixteenth-century maiolica commissions. The dish bears an inscription recalling that on the drawing, 'Caesar breaks down the bridge near Geneva', which might have been one of those provided by the duke's secretary, as mentioned in the letter above. Zuccaro's drawings were copied and continued to be used by maiolica painters for some decades, as many versions can be found on surviving ceramics.

The development of narrative painting

The earliest examples of narrative or *istoriato* painting on maiolica from the years around 1500 are invariably anonymous. A few rare dated works help us to chart the chronological development of the style.

The earliest intact dated example of narrative decoration can be found on a superb bowl dated 1503 (pls 108, 109). Its central image of a satyr observing two nymphs bathing is charged with subtle eroticism. Mythological themes in pleasant outdoor settings are very frequent on narrative maiolica. The bowl might have been made in Castel Durante or Pesaro, both in the Marches. It was once supposed that potters in Faenza took the lead in developing *istoriato* decoration, but recent scholarship has left the question more open: it is likely that the style emerged in all the major pottery centres in northern-central Italy at the same time.[41]

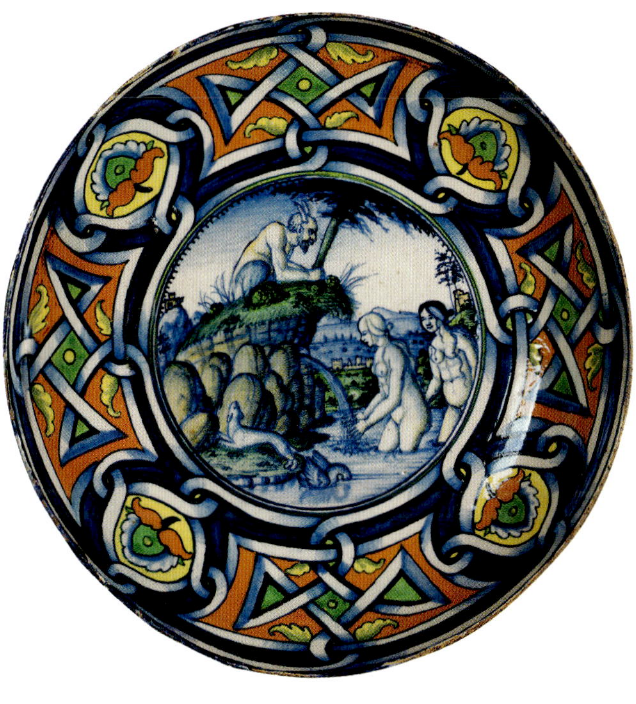

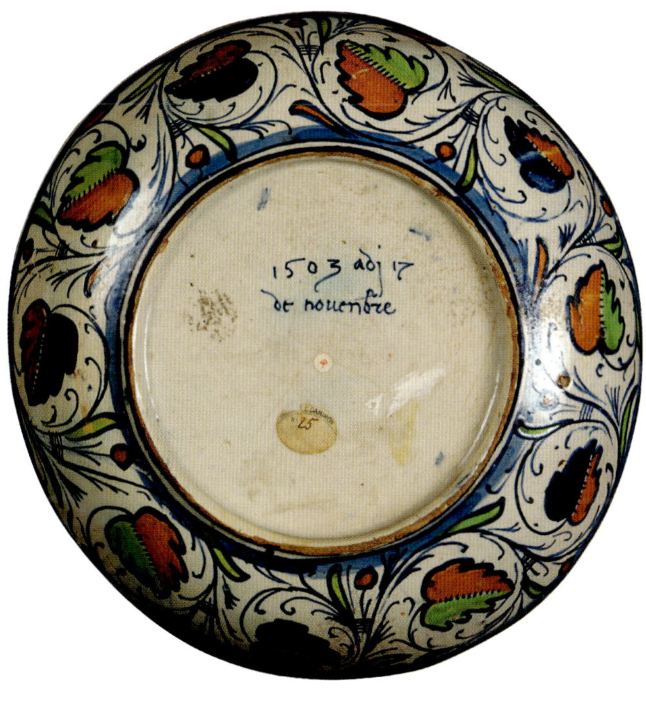

110 Dish with Vulcan at the forge
Probably Jacopo
Cafaggiolo or elsewhere in Tuscany, 1510–15
Diam: 39.4 cm
V&A: 2990–1853

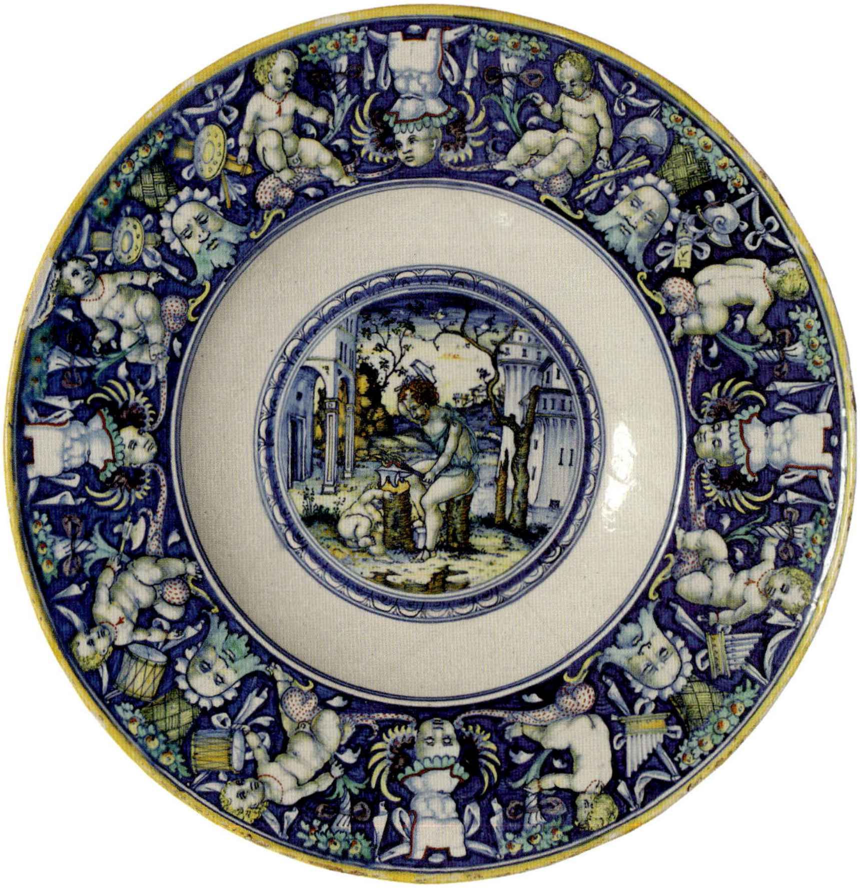

111 Dish with Judith with the head of Holofernes
Jacopo
Cafaggiolo, c.1510–15
Diam: 32.5 cm
Salting Bequest V&A: C.2151–1910

112 Reverse of pl.111
with Jacopo's signature: 'ja[co]po in cafagguolo'

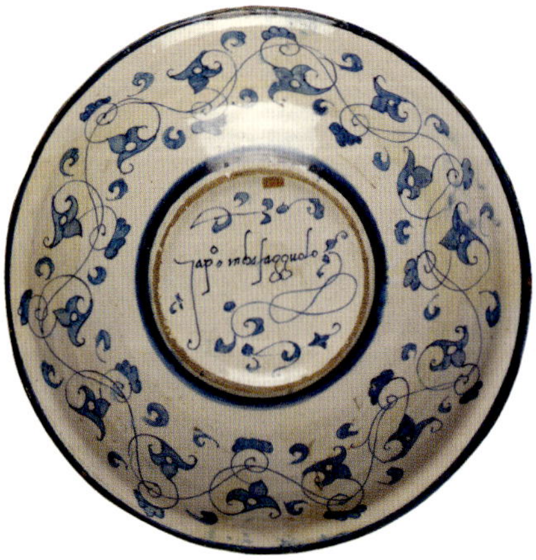

Initially narrative decorations were confined to the central part of dishes or the front part of the body of jugs and jars and framed by ornamental devices such as cartouches, wreath or grotesque borders (pl. 110).

A painter named Jacopo working around 1510 at Cafaggiolo, a maiolica workshop based in the outbuildings of a villa just outside Florence owned by Lorenzo di Pierfrancesco de' Medici, was one of the first to paint the entire front of his dishes with 'narrative' scenes. Jacopo's name is known to us from a single signed plate, depicting the Biblical Jewish heroine Judith and her servant riding home with the head of the Assyrian general Holofernes. It is marked on the reverse: 'japo'(short for Jacopo) 'in cafagg[i]uolo' (pl. 111, 112). Stylistic particularities of the painting on this dish, such as the rendering of the landscape, help to attribute other works made at Cafaggiolo to the same master. Jacopo is a very competent painter, executing the figures on the Judith plate with a masterly hand, showing the influence of major Florentine painters including Ghirlandaio and Botticelli. As so few works by his hand have survived in maiolica, it is conceivable that Jacopo might have worked as an easel- or fresco-painter as well. He certainly had an elevated view of himself. An iconic plate, marked 'SP' for the Cafaggiolo workshop, can be attributed to him on stylistic grounds (pls 8, 24). It shows a maiolica painter (Jacopo himself?) at work, fashionably dressed, watched by two wealthy patrons.

With increased confidence in their status, some pottery painters started signing their narrative wares. We know a single dish signed by Jacopo, but soon a few painters in the Duchy of Urbino in the 1520s, in particular Francesco Xanto Avelli, started to inscribe

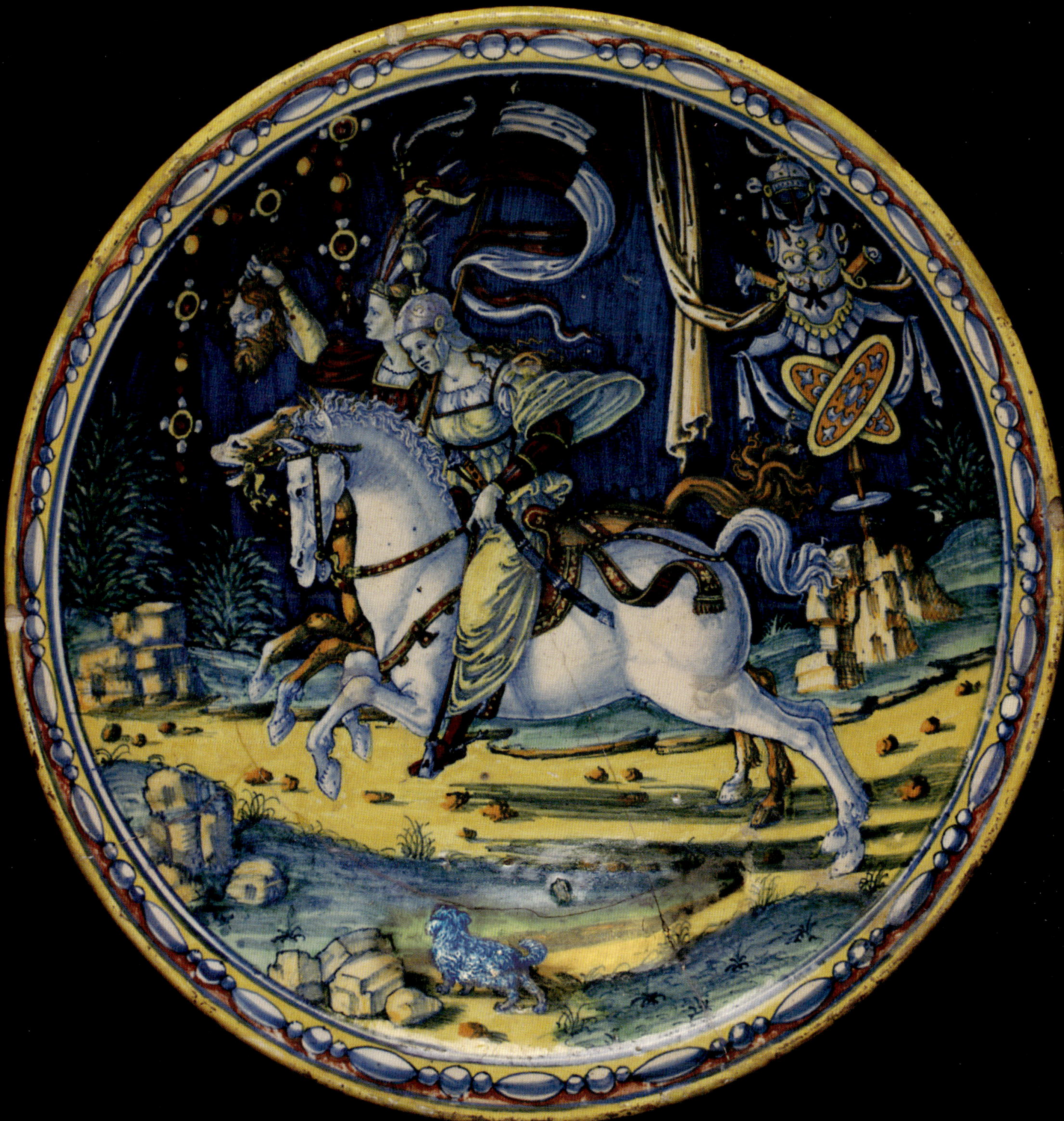

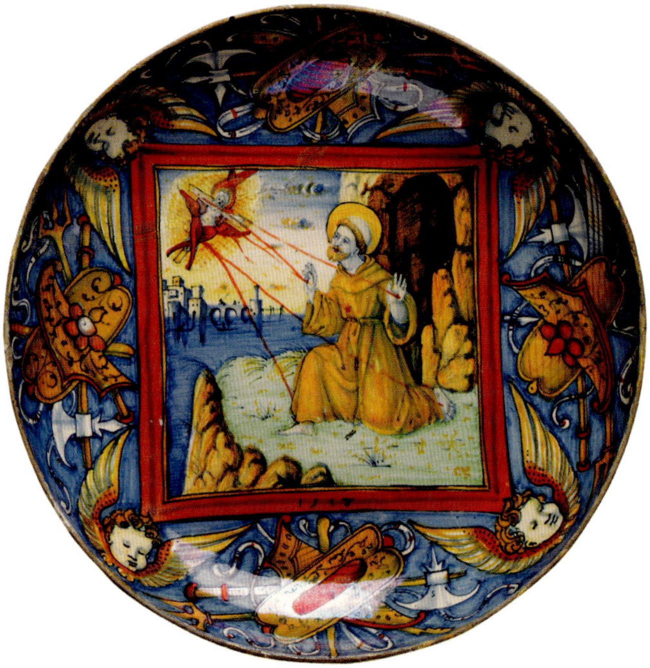

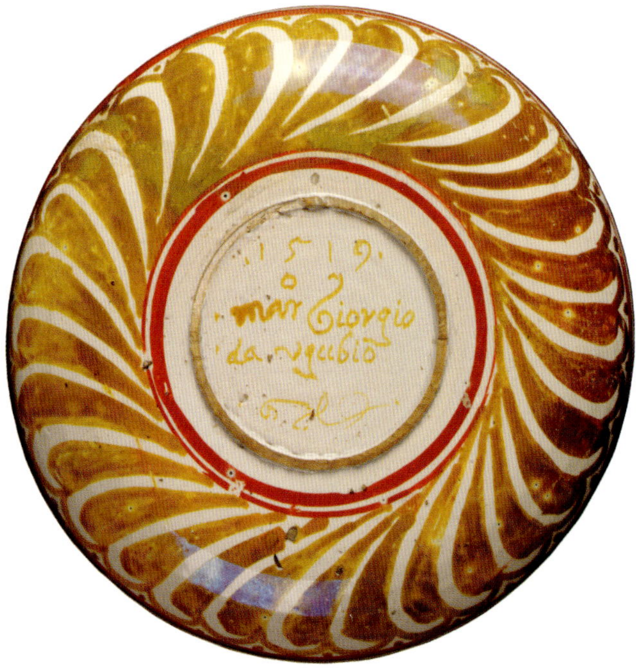

113 Bowl on low foot with St Francis receiving the stigmata
Workshop of Maestro Giorgio Andreoli
Gubbio, 1518–19
Diam: 23.5 cm
V&A: 401–1854

114 Reverse of pl.113

115 Bowl on low foot with figures in front of the tomb of St Ubaldo
Gubbio, 1521–22
Diam: 25.5 cm
V&A: C.476–1921

the underside of their work with the subject depicted, sometimes adding their initials, or their name.

Maestro Giorgio of Gubbio, a shrewd man of business, arranged that from 1518 onwards his name alone should be used as a brand-name for wares of the family workshop, regardless of who had painted or lustred them. We can assume that Giorgio was an expert in the making of lustre, but there is no evidence as to whether he was himself a painter. Pieces bearing his mark show a wide variety of hands, as painters from other centres were attracted by the success of the workshop. We have archival evidence that Maestro Giorgio hired painters on short contracts: a document of 1525 for example shows that Giovanni Luca from Castel Durante agreed to paint pottery for him for one year.[42]

Maestro Giorgio's workshop was responsible for the earliest dated *istoriato* works marked with their place of manufacture. One of the first examples is a bowl depicting St Francis receiving the stigmata in a frame surrounded by cherubs and trophies (pls 113, 114). It is dated 1518 in blue on the front, and 1519 in lustre on the reverse, along with the signature of Maestro Giorgio, showing that there was a period of time between the execution of the painting and the application of lustre.

One of the earliest dated and marked examples of overall narrative decoration represents a scene at the tomb of Gubbio's patron saint St Ubaldo, a place of local veneration (pl. 115). St Ubaldo was thought to have worked many miracles and among the people gathered around his tomb are a crippled man and a woman with a small devil, painted in black, escaping from her mouth. This work also bears two dates: 1521 in blue on the front and 1522 on the back, in lustre.

The earliest examples of *istoriato* produced in Maestro Giorgio's workshop, from around 1520–5, seem to have been deliberately designed for lustred decoration. These early pieces show a trademark dark red lustre used in conjunction with a very dark golden lustre. The relatively large areas of lustre on these early works are an integral

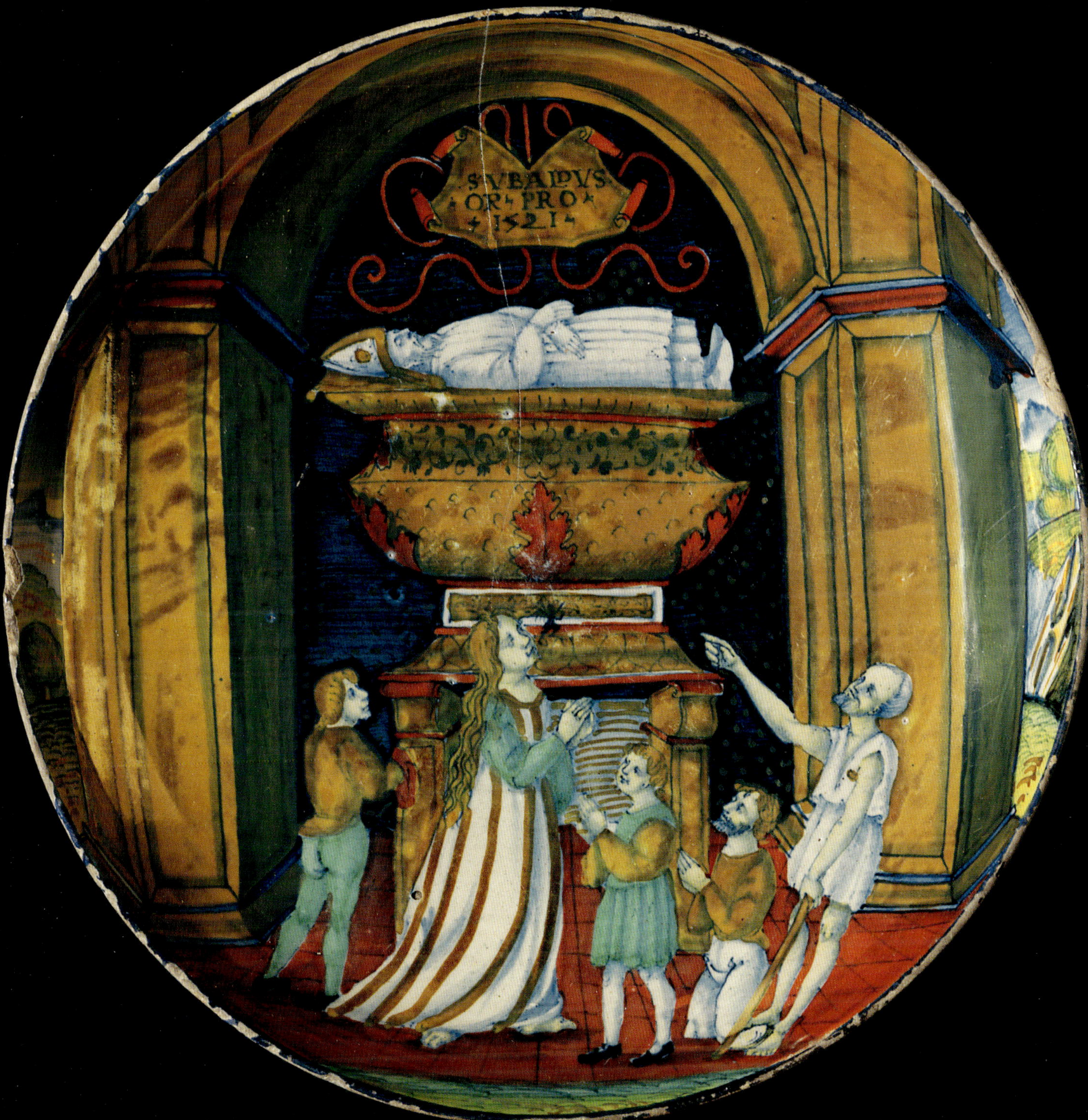
S·VBALDVS
OR· PRO·
1521

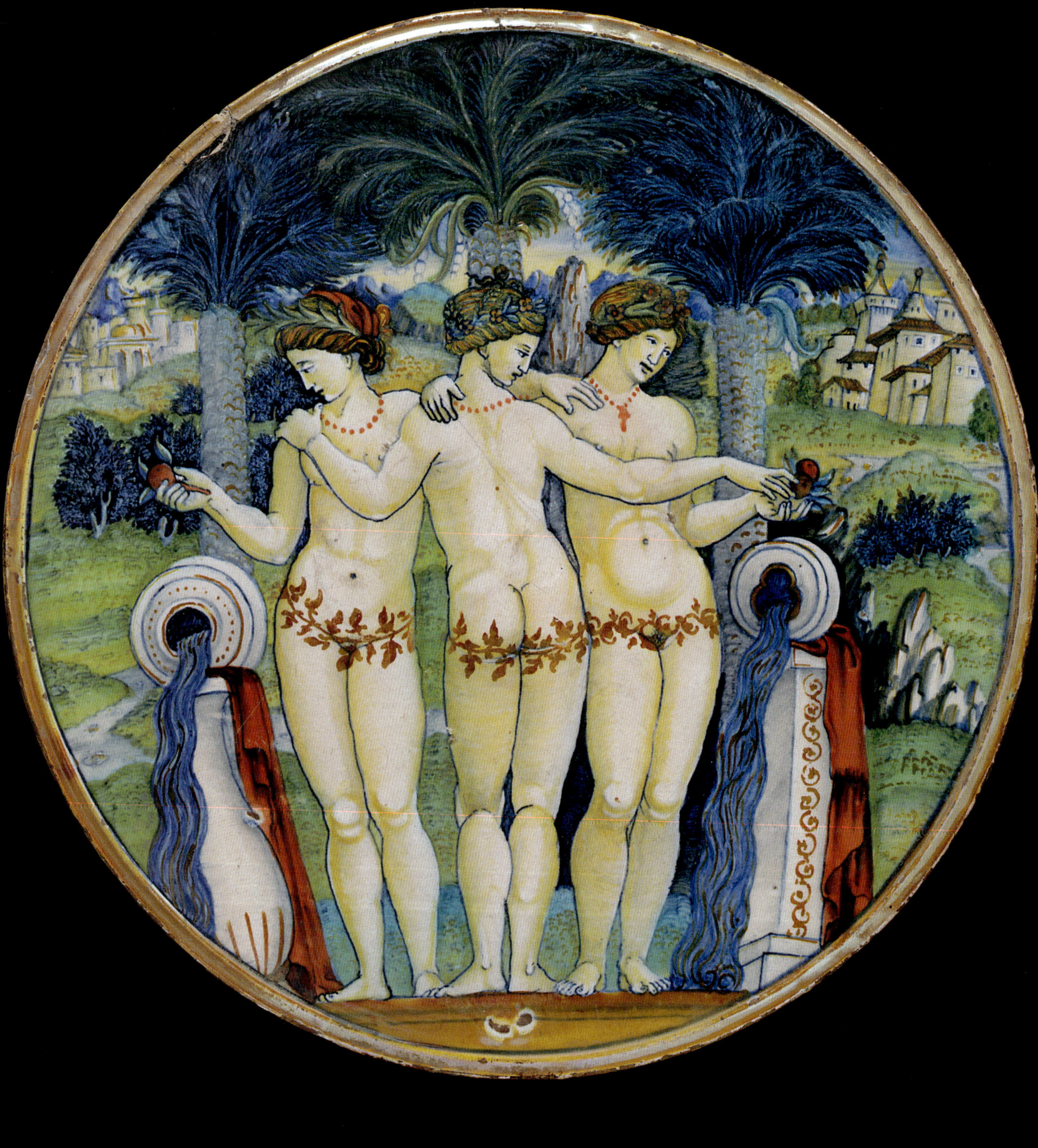

116 Roundel with the Three Graces
Workshop of Maestro Giorgio
Gubbio, 1525
Diam: 30.5 cm
V&A: 175–1885

117 Dish on low foot with the Death of Tarpeia
The 'In Castel Durante' Painter
Castel Durante, c.1525
Diam: 26.5 cm
Salting Bequest V&A: C.2263–1910

part of the painted decoration. Later on, lustre was often used only in small quantities, added as highlights to an otherwise already completed painted decoration.

Some of the best works produced in the Gubbio workshop are from the year 1525. One of the most famous pieces of *istoriato* maiolica ever made, the extraordinary roundel with the Three Graces, was painted in that year (pl. 116). The composition of the Graces, personifying grace, beauty and beneficence, is based on an engraving by Marcantonio Raimondi after an ancient relief.

Istoriato took deepest root in the Urbino district, which included many important pottery centres, such as Urbino, Castel Durante, Pesaro and Gubbio. Its development can be traced in the region from the early 1520s.

Among the first generation of *istoriato* painters there is only one that we can link with the small centre of Castel Durante (later renamed Urbania by Pope Urbano VIII). From the phrase this painter used to mark his pieces he has been named the 'In Castel Durante Painter'.[43] All we know of him are his works – plates, and especially bowls on a low foot, dated between 1524 and 1526. He belongs to the first generation of *istoriato* painters from the Marches, whose style no longer includes ornamental borders, but solely narrative scenes. A dish on a low foot with a Roman scene shows the vestal virgin Tarpeia crushed to death by the shields of Sabine soldiers (pl. 117). The works of the 'In Castel Durante Painter', with their imperfect perspective, pale colouring and lack of surface shine, have an unearthly, primitive beauty close to certain fresco decorations.

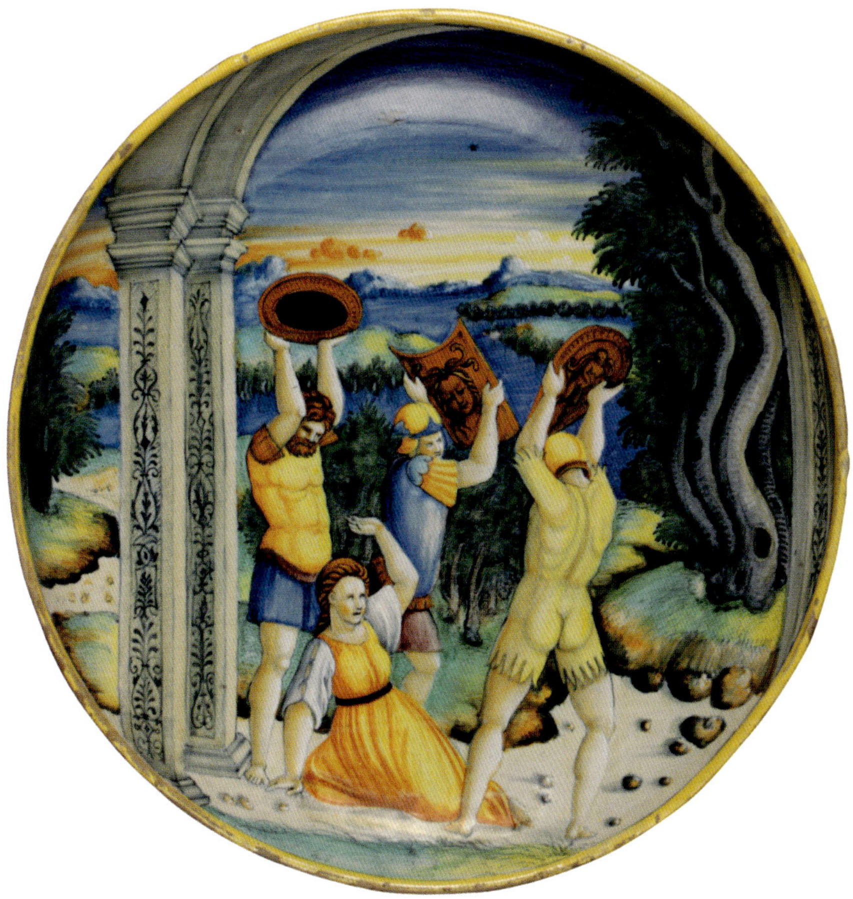

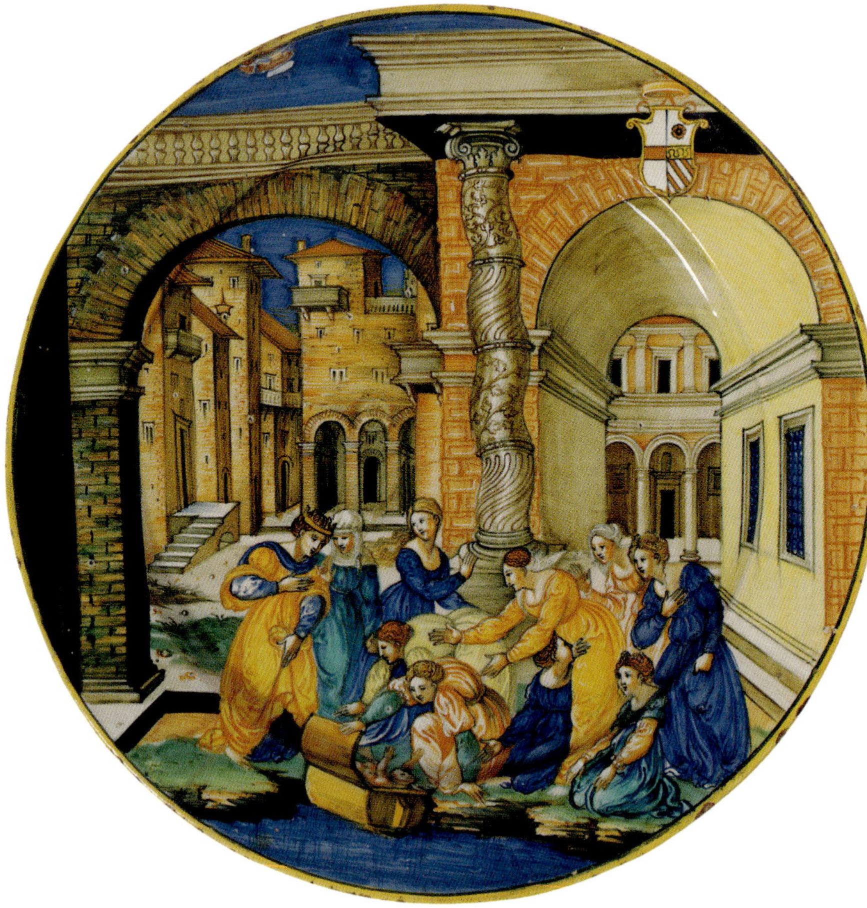

118 Large plate with the Finding of Moses with arms of Sanseverino impaling Orsini
Nicola da Urbino
Urbino, c.1530–35
Diam: 45.5 cm
V&A: 2825–1856

From about the 1520s a pottery painter in the city of Urbino led an extraordinary phase of *istoriato* painting, setting the standard for the next generation. He is known from a few pieces marked with different versions of his name, 'Nicola', in one instance followed by 'da U.', presumably 'from Urbino'. His earliest known piece is dated 1521, and there is documentary evidence that he was a master potter in the city from 1520. Some of the most beautiful maiolica services ever made can be attributed to Nicola (see pl. 148), who must have worked at the high end of the industry for his entire career, mostly on commissions for important families.

Nicola deployed a variety of graphic sources and showed a full understanding of the style of Raphael. A plate depicting the Finding of Moses by the Pharaoh's daughter shows a gathering of excited women around the newly-found baby boy (pl. 118). The fluidity of painting and the graceful mannerism of the figures are typical of Nicola, as is the elaborate architectural setting. Nicola's workshop must have been one of the busiest in Urbino until his death in 1537/8.[44]

An enigmatic, anonymous painter who must have worked in Urbino around 1522–5 included his painted initials 'F.R.' on the front of a handful of dishes (pl. 120).[45] 'F.R.' created exceptional compositions, skilfully adapted to the round shape of the wares he was decorating. A dish on a low foot, illustrating the Biblical scene of the Israelites gathering the manna, is painted with wonderful detail showing 'F.R.'s' great painterly skills (pl. 119). Even when he copies his images quite closely from prints after Raphael

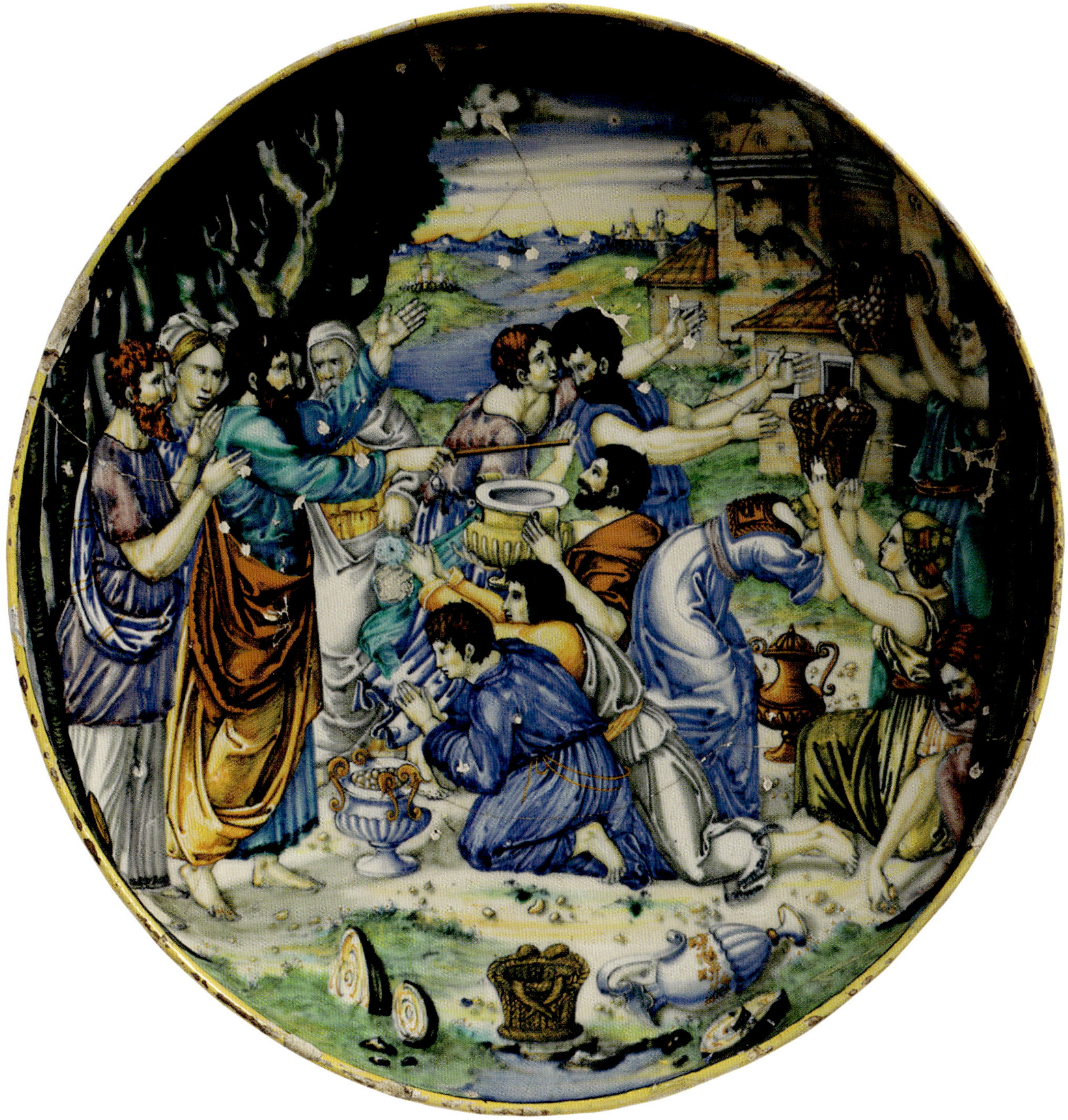

119 Dish with the gathering of the manna
'F.R.'
Urbino, c.1520–25
Diam: 41 cm
V&A: 7680–1861

for instance, 'F.R.' manages to give his paintings a highly original character. The figures, often clad in heavy drapery and with elaborate hairstyles, have a classical allure and distinctive facial features (pl. 120).

'F.R.'s work has influenced the next generation of pottery painters in Urbino. It has close similarities to that of one of the most prolific *istoriato* painters, Xanto Avelli, and 'F.R.' might have been a mark used by this painter in his early career.[46] Other examples are known of artists using two different names or monograms during the Renaissance period.

Francesco Xanto Avelli was originally from Rovigo, but from documents and from his signed pieces it is known that he worked in Urbino from 1530, although he was probably active in the area a few years earlier.[47] There are dishes dated 1528–9 that are clearly by him, unsigned but often distinguishable by a flourish or punctuation mark resembling a 'y' or the Greek letter 'phi' at the end of the inscription. From 1530 until 1542 (the last date that appears on his works) Xanto signs his work constantly, using different versions of his name, adding inscriptions that explain or comment on the subject represented (see pl. 94). Unlike Nicola (with whom he collaborated) Xanto was never a workshop owner and seems to have worked for others, earning his wages solely through his skill with the brush. As a result, he is one of the most prolific painters of *istoriato* maiolica. Over 400 pieces, most of them signed and dated, survive today, including at least 14 dining sets for important families (pl. 93).[48]

120 Plate with Dido entertaining Aeneas
'F.R.'
Urbino, c.1520–25
Diam: 25.5 cm
Salting Bequest V&A: C.2117–1910

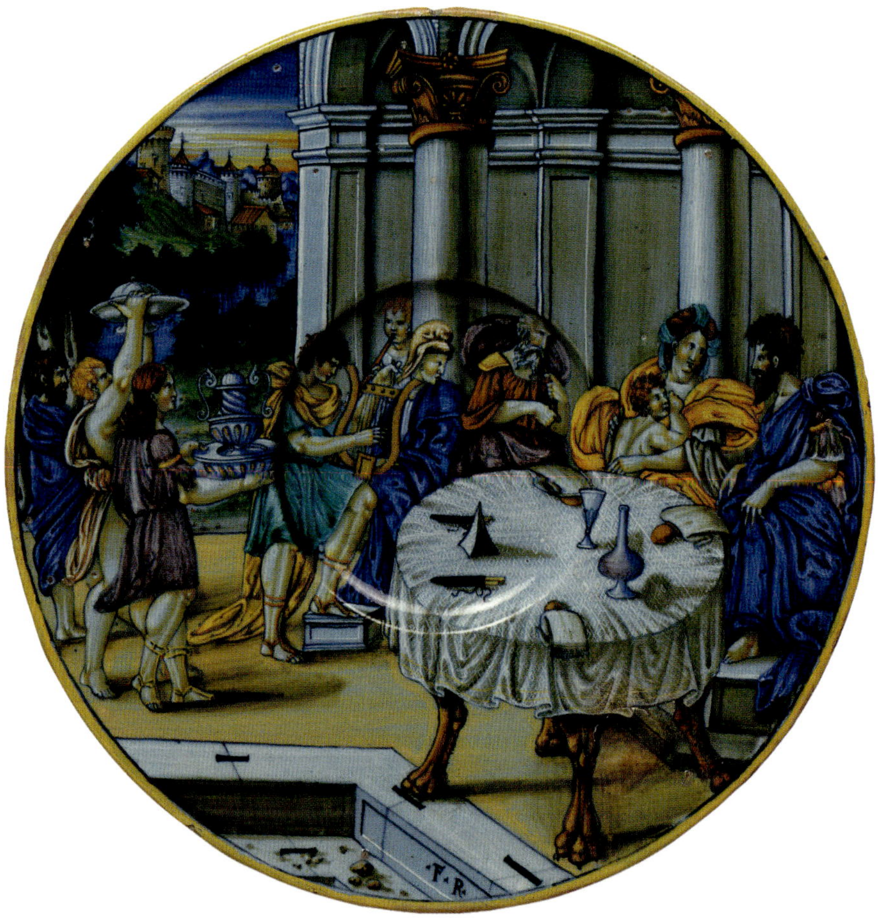

121 Lustred dish with Astolpho chasing the Harpies
Xanto, lustred in the workshop of Maestro Giorgio Andreoli
Gubbio or Urbino, 1532
Diam: 26 cm
Salting Bequest V&A: C.2201–1910

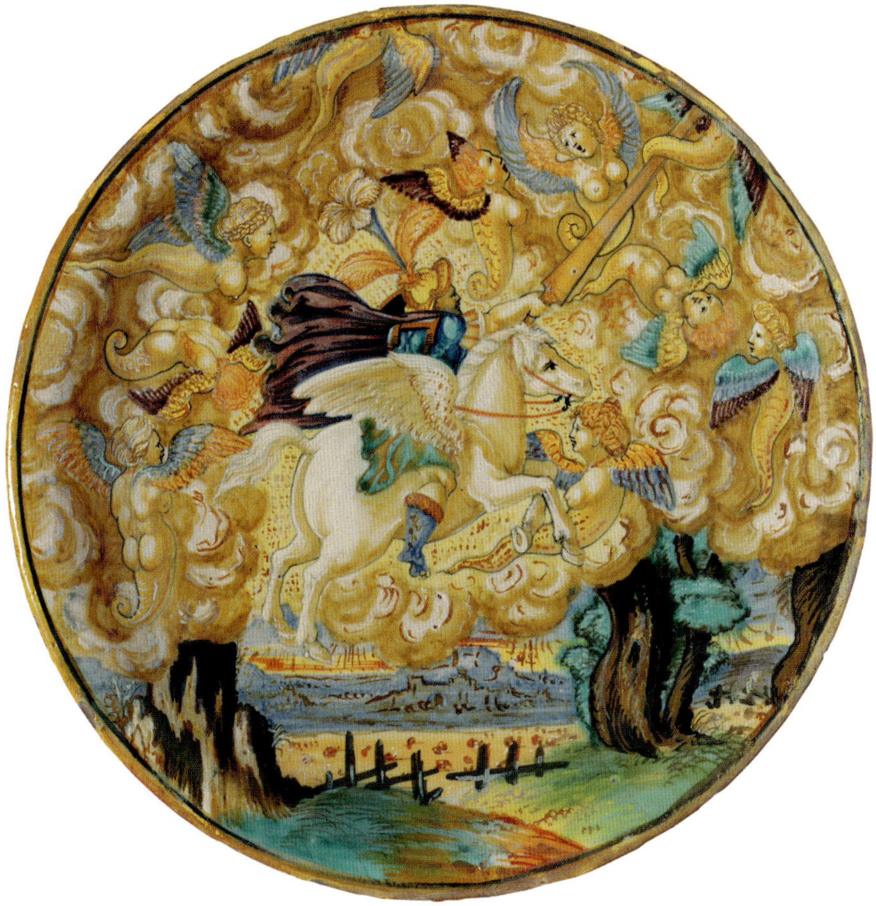

During the late 1520s through to the 1540s Maestro Giorgio's workshop often added highlights in lustre, sometimes poorly integrated with the design, to otherwise finished wares painted by Urbino-trained potters. It is not always clear if these finished wares were also made in Gubbio or made in Urbino and brought to Gubbio to be finished in lustre.[49]

122 Reverse of pl.121

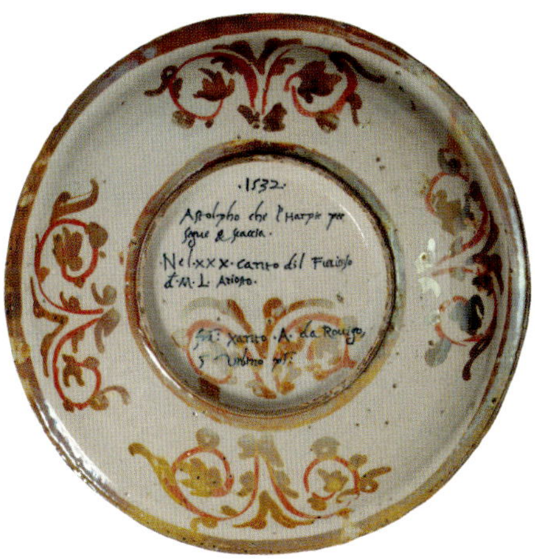

Many *istoriato* dishes painted by Xanto in Urbino were lustred, especially those made between 1532 and 1535. One example showing a somewhat confused scene from Ariosto's *Orlando Furioso*, with Astolpho chasing the Harpies, is dated 1532 (pls 121, 122). Xanto's signature and the place of manufacture, Urbino, have been partially obscured by one of Maestro Giorgio's painters with a lustre scroll, perhaps to avoid custom duties.[50]

Only a few works painted by Nicola da Urbino are lustred. A dish showing the Roman hero Camillus and the Gauls has only a few touches of added lustre and it is not known if this was done under Nicola's control (pl. 123). It is likely that some *istoriati* were lustred in Urbino itself. After Nicola's death in 1538, his widow leased his workshop for three years to Maestro Giorgio's son Vincenzo, who set up a lustre kiln there.[51] The presence of Vincenzo at Urbino is evidence of the close artistic and commercial links between the Gubbio workshop and Urbino.

A second wave of *istoriato* maiolica painters in Urbino is represented by the Durantino family, who by 1541 had taken the surname Fontana. Their workshop

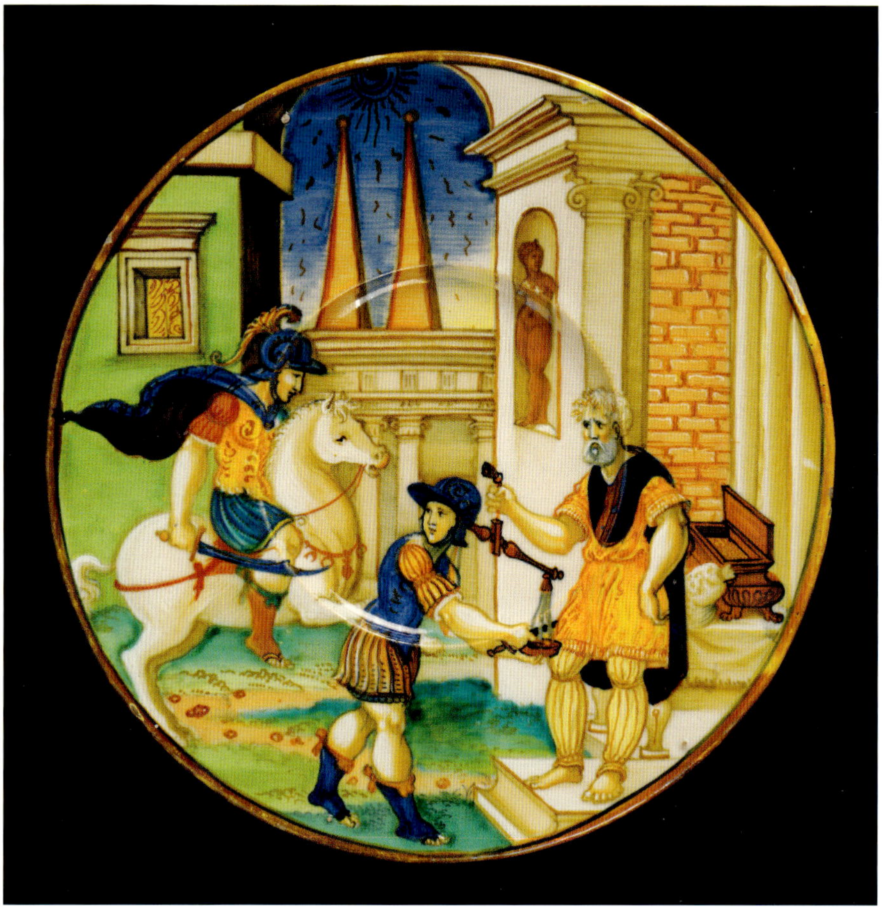

123 Plate with Camillus
Nicola da Urbino, lustred in the workshop of Maestro Giorgio
Gubbio or Urbino, c.1535
Diam: 26 cm
Salting Bequest V&A: C.2203–1910

appears to be the most successful and prolific centre of *istoriato* production in Urbino from the 1530s to the 1560s (see pp.129–30). The workshop's founder Guido Durantino (Guido from Castel Durante) employed several of the best painters of the time and it is often hard to attribute works to individual painters within the workshop.

Potters from the Urbino district in due course took the *istoriato* style to other regions. An interesting example is Francesco Urbini (Francesco from Urbino), who went to work in Gubbio for Maestro Giorgio between 1531 and 1536. A crucial piece of evidence for his later career, a basin for a ewer with scenes from the story of Apollo signed 'Francesco Urbini in Deruta 1537', shows that he subsequently moved to Deruta, introducing *istoriato* in the Urbino style to that town (pls 124, 125).[52]

Another painter known as Francesco Durantino provides one of the best illustrations of the mobility of *istoriato* painters from the Urbino district. Having previously worked in some of the most important *istoriato* producers' workshops in Urbino, notably that of Guido di Merlino, Francesco Durantino moved to the outskirts of Perugia, at Monte Bagnolo, where he worked from 1547 to 1556. His works from Monte Bagnolo include some original oval-shaped wine coolers of different sizes, some signed and marked. One features six different scenes from the story of Moses, including the crossing of the Red Sea, a subject particularly suitable for a vessel that was to be filled with water (pl. 126). After his period in Monte Bagnolo Francesco moved on to work in Turin and Rome.[53]

124 Basin for a ewer with the Story of Apollo
Francesco Urbini
Deruta, 1537
Diam: 34 cm
Salting Bequest V&A: C.2157–1910

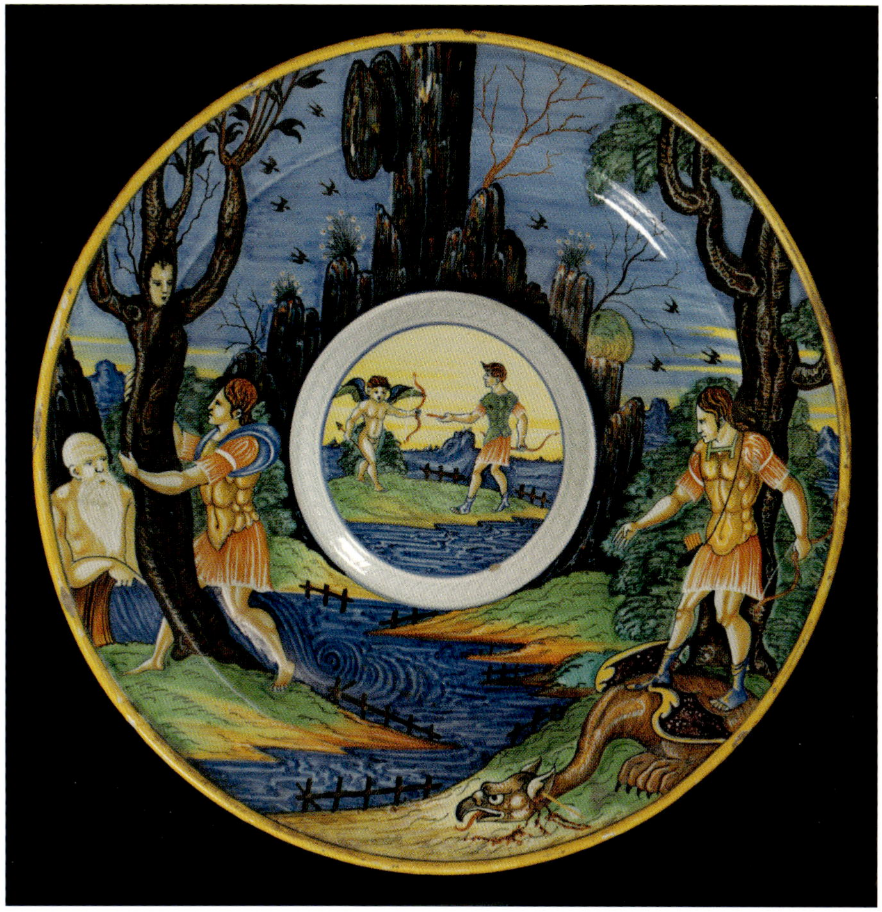

125 Reverse of pl.124
Inscribed: 'This is she who with her golden hair once fired with love the sun [Apollo] whom the world beholds and through him still bears heavy burdens. Francesco of Urbino, at Deruta.'

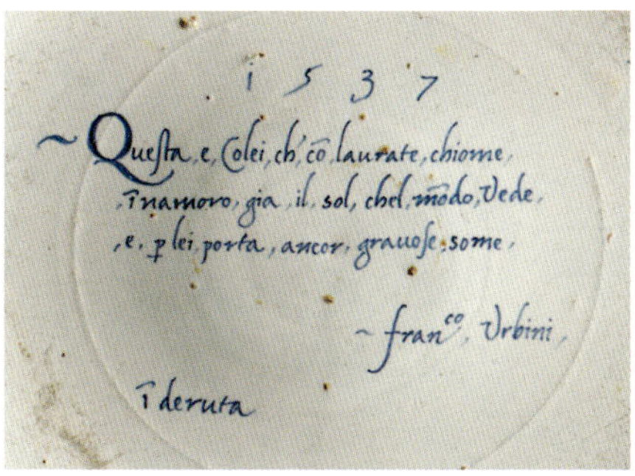

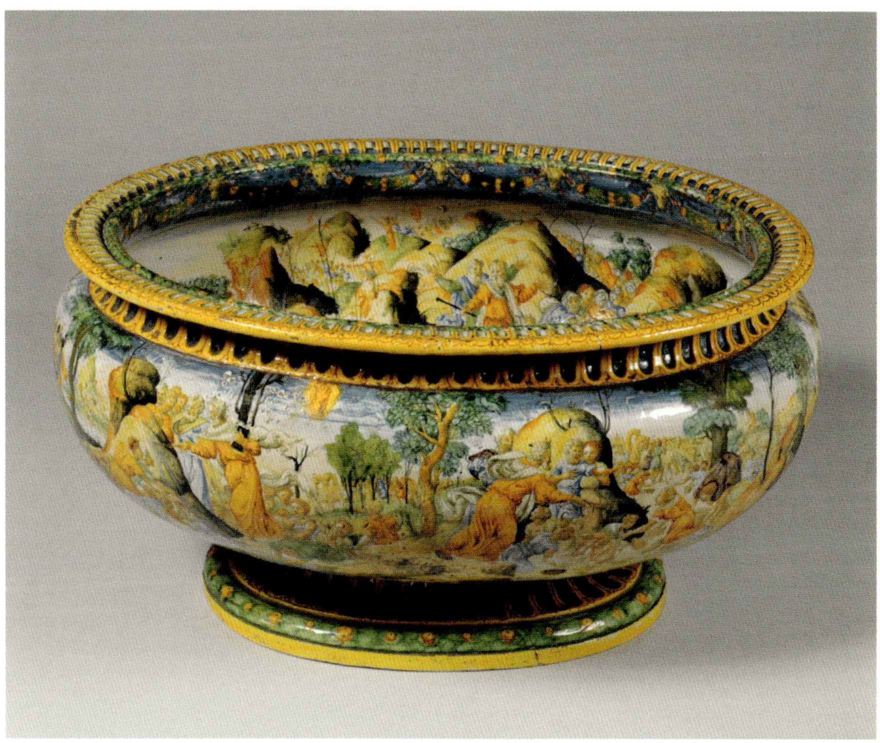

126 Wine cooler with the History of Moses
Francesco Durantino
Montebagnolo (Perugia), c.1550–55
L: 54.5 cm
Salting Bequest V&A: C.2294–1910

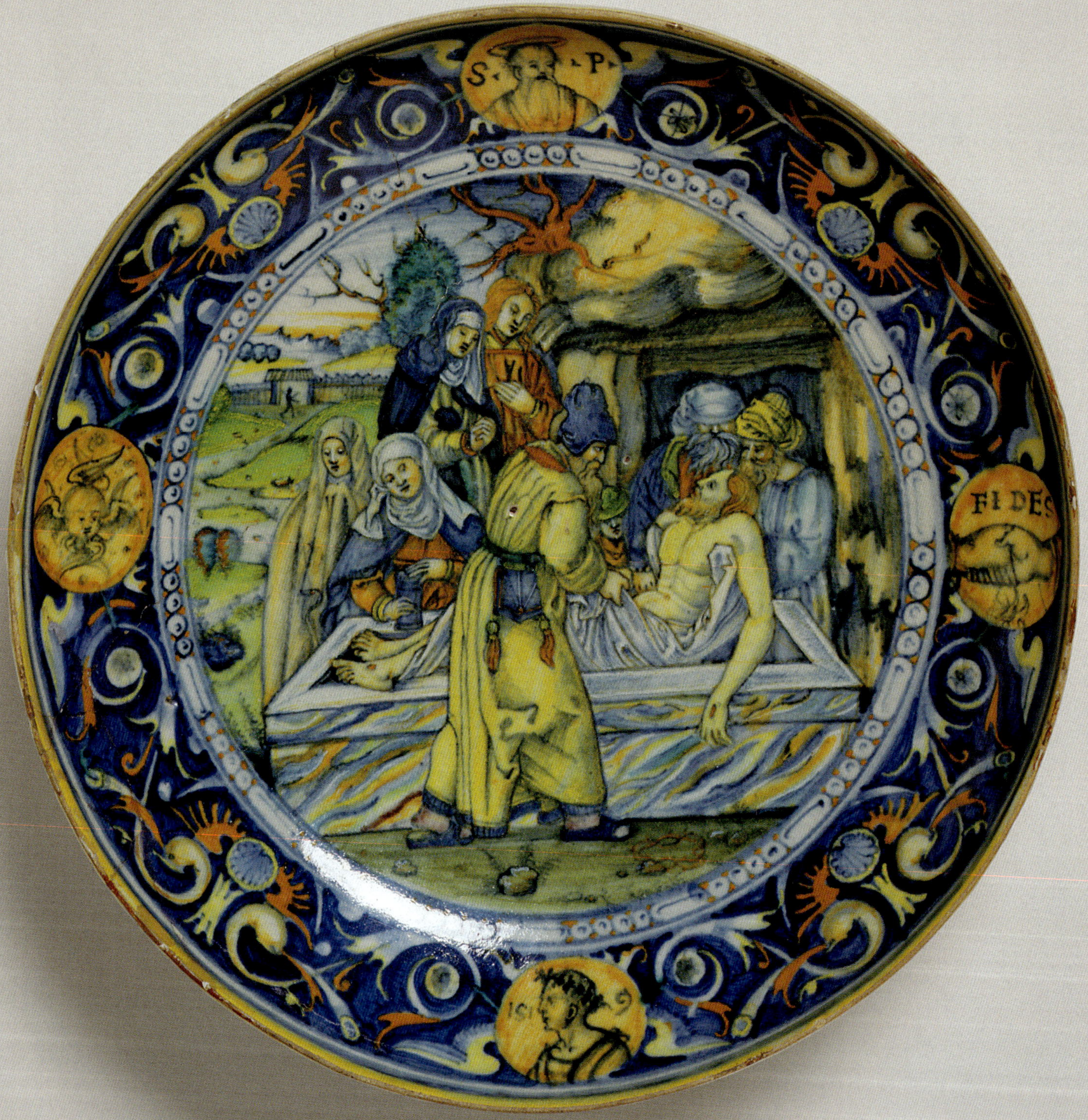
S · P
FI DES

127 Dish with the Entombment
Faenza, 1519
Diam: 21 cm
V&A: 75–1885

128 Dish on low foot with the Devotion of Marcus Curtius
Faenza, c.1525
Diam: 25 cm
V&A: 354–1872

129 Reverse of pl.128

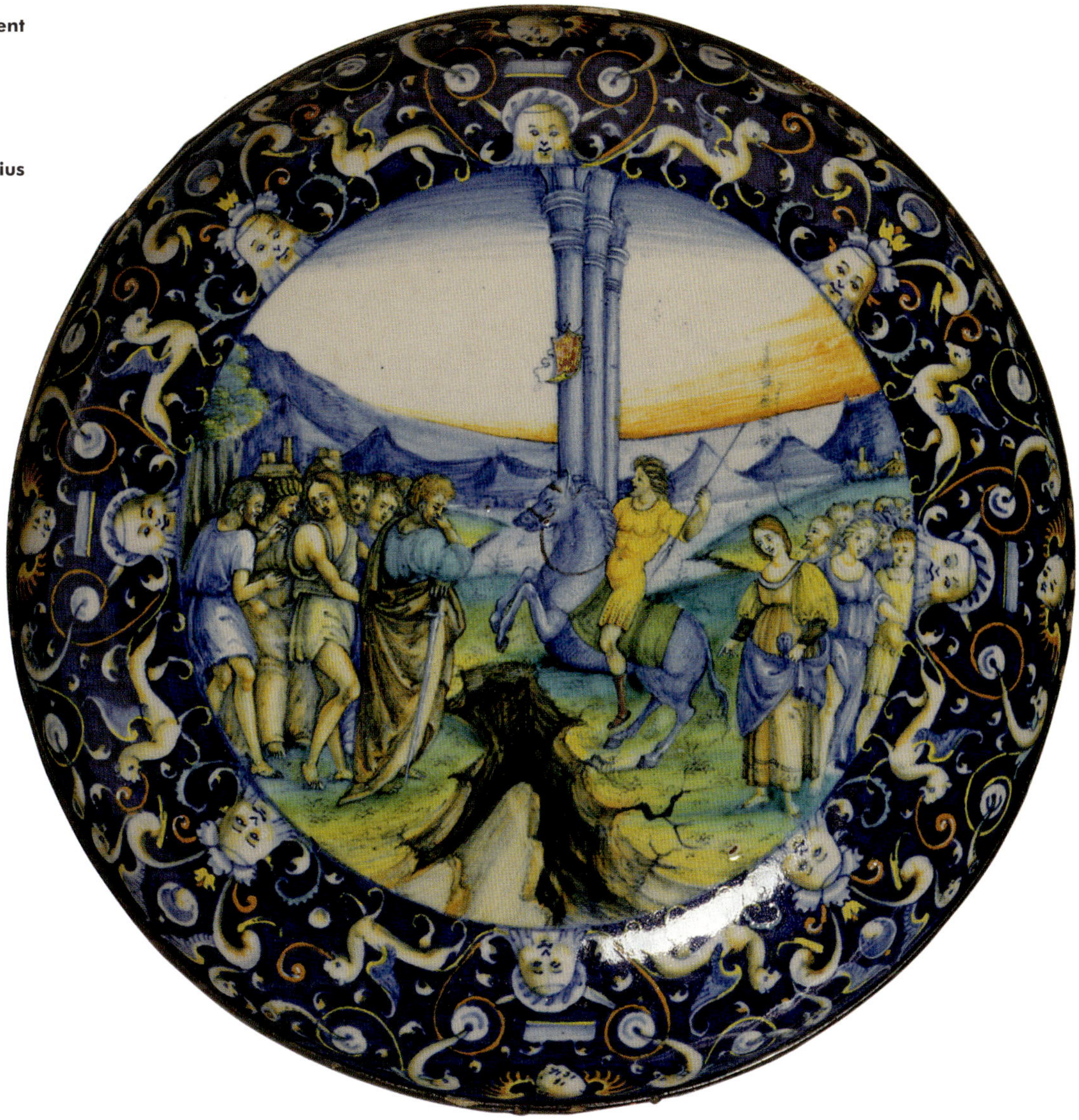

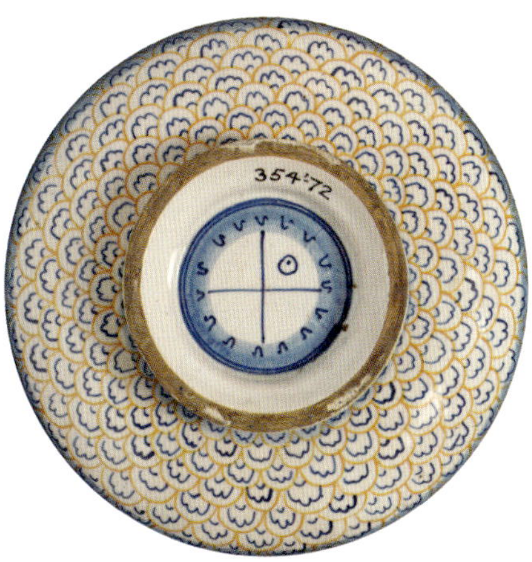

Potters from the leading centre of Faenza produced wares of outstanding quality over a long period of time, including extraordinary examples of narrative painting. Pottery painters from Faenza very rarely add their names or date their works. A rare dated example is a bowl of 1519 decorated with the Entombment after a composition by Albrecht Dürer (pl. 127). Faenza *istoriato* painters often preferred Biblical subjects from engravings by northern artists. The delicate scene is framed by grotesques on a blue ground, and this combination became extremely popular in Faenza maiolica. Scenes are also often painted on a light-blue ground-glaze (see pl. 147).

The names of many workshops at Faenza can be gleaned from archival sources. The workshop of Pietro and Paolo Bergantini, documented from 1503 to 1558, is thought to have been one of the major producers of *istoriato* maiolica. The dish shown in pls 128 and 129 illustrates a popular example of Roman virtue, the Devotion of Marcus Curtius, the young soldier who sacrificed himself to close a chasm in the

130 Bowl on low foot with the Resurrection
Baldassarre Manara
Faenza, 1535
Diam: 23.5 cm
V&A: 62–1876

131 Reverse of pl.130

132 Dish with Venus removing a thorn from her foot
Venice, c.1540
Diam: 26.8 cm
Given by Mrs A. Lane in memory of Arthur Lane V&A: C.62–1963

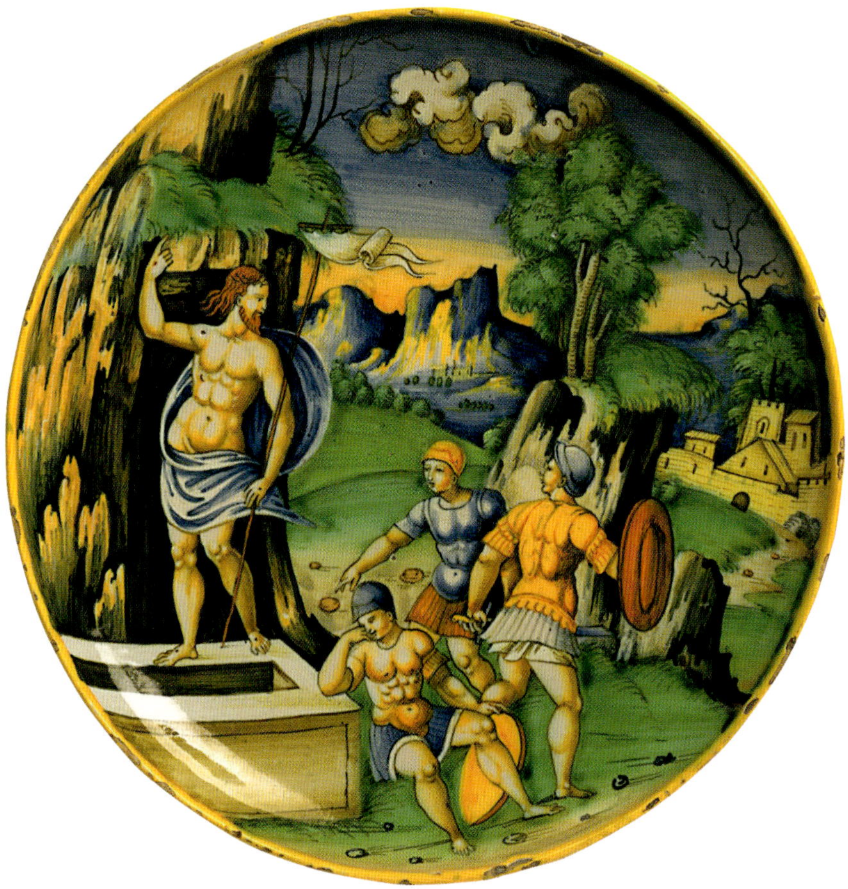

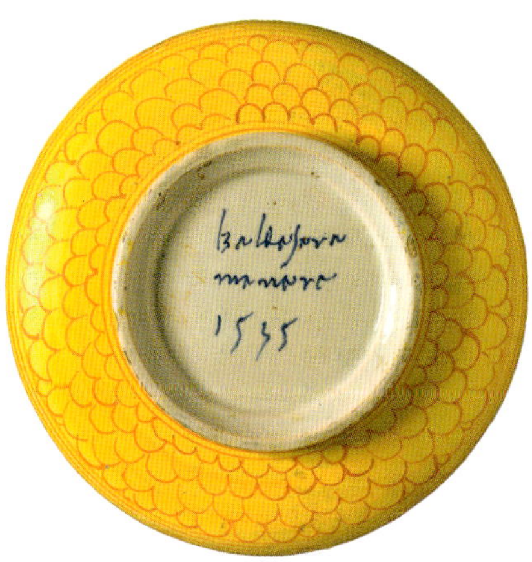

middle of the Roman Forum. On the reverse is a mark resembling an inflatable ball which is frequent on Faenza maiolica. The mark was thought to be connected with the workshop known as 'Ca Pirota'; however the bowl was more likely produced in the Bergantini workshop.

Baldassarre Manara is one of the few *istoriato* painters from Faenza whose name is known, because he took up the Urbino custom of fully signing his work (pls 130, 131). He is documented from 1526 until his death in 1546–7.[54]

In Venice the trend for narrative compositions was probably imported by masters from other regions, such as Faenza (which was for a brief period under Venetian rule) and particularly the Urbino district. A distinctive Venetian style developed during the 1540s. Characteristic figures are set in a marine landscape, sometimes painted in monochrome blue on a light grey-blue *berettino* ground. A typical dish shows Venus removing a thorn from her foot, framed by a delicate ornamental border (pl. 132).

A fully polychrome *istoriato* style appears on Venetian works from around the middle of the sixteenth century, which often have a maritime theme. The dish shown in pl. 133 features Theseus and his companions feasting with the river god Achelous, as a long inscription on the back explains, in a scene taken from Ovid's *Metamorphoses*. With its warm and fluid colours, the decoration is stylistically close to works attributed to Maestro Domenego, who operated one of the leading workshops in the city until

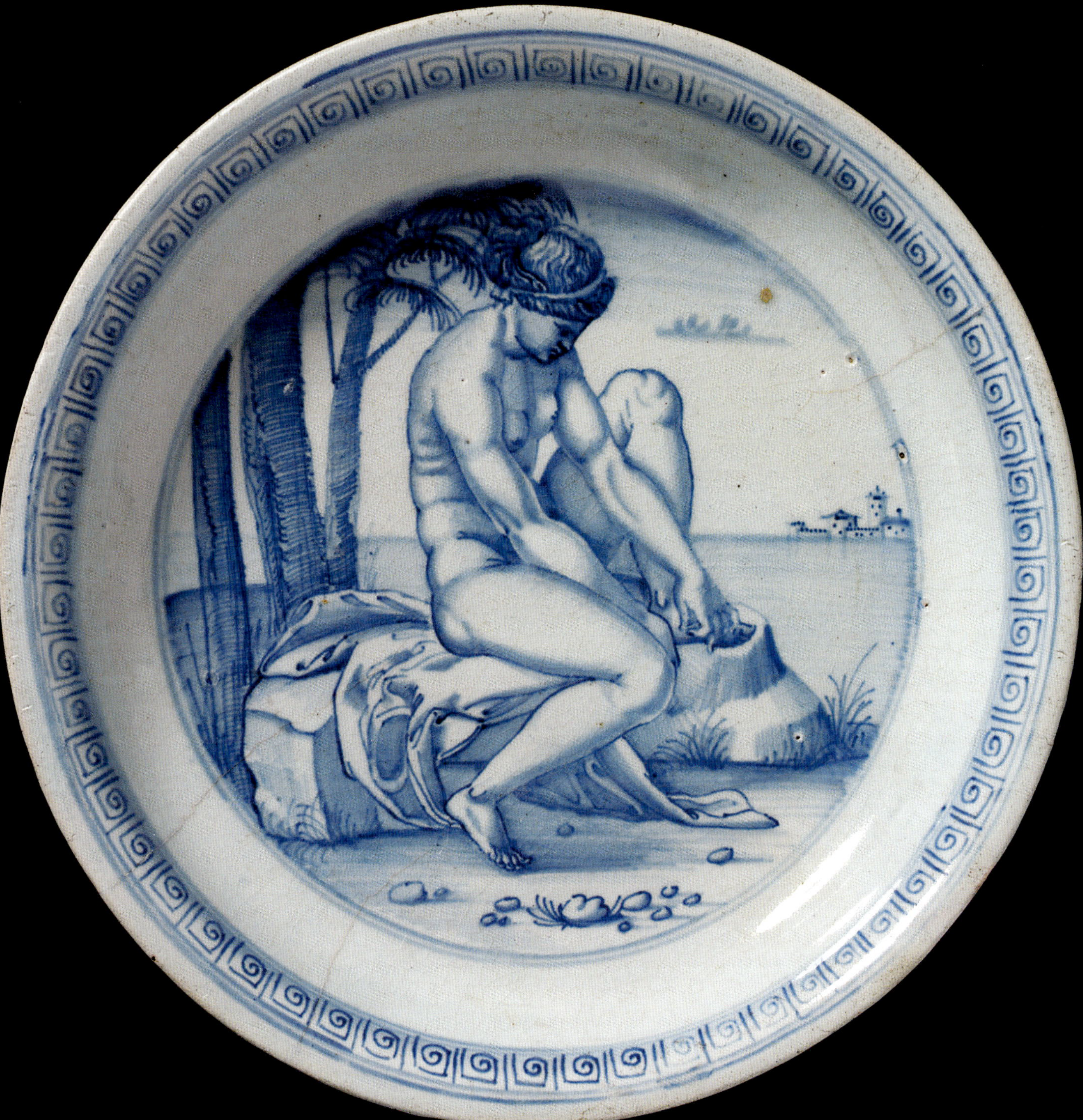

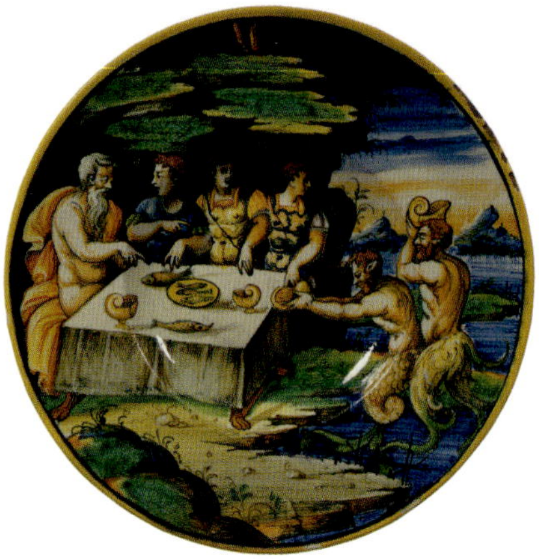

his death in 1574. Only a handful of his signed works are known, dating from 1562 to 1568/9, but his distinctive style, influenced by Venetian painting, can be seen on a large number of wares. A dish probably made in Domenego's workshop after 1560 shows two magistrates of Venice, the figures derived from a Venetian print by Matteo Pagani of 1550 (pl. 134).[55] The painter has transposed the figures into a characteristic coastal landscape.[56]

The increasing demand for wares covered solely with pure white tin-glaze which had been developed in Faenza around 1540 but soon spread to other centres, began to impact on narrative painting in the second half of the sixteenth century. Dense, overall *istoriato* painting was gradually replaced with a much lighter, sketchy style. Typical is a dish depicting Moses striking water from a rock, a scene from the Old Testament, which is lightly painted in blue, yellow and orange, revealing much of its brilliant white surface (pl.135).

During the second half of the sixteenth century, *istoriato* painting began to decline in quality and quantity. Elaborately painted narrative scenes were unsuitable for large scale production and the style gradually lost its status as a novelty and fell out of fashion. However, its influence continued to be felt in Europe and narrative painting in the style of the Italian Renaissance was produced abroad, especially in France.

133 Dish with Theseus and his companions feasting with the river god Achelous
Perhaps workshop of Maestro Domenego
Venice, c.1560–70
Diam: 30 cm
V&A: 1722–1855

134 Dish with two Venetian magistrates
Perhaps workshop of Maestro Domenego
Venice, 1560–70
Diam: 24.5 cm
Salting Bequest V&A: C.2252–1910

135 Plate with Moses striking the rock
Perhaps Virgiliotto Calamelli
Faenza, 1550–70
Diam: 45.5 cm
V&A: C.293–1938

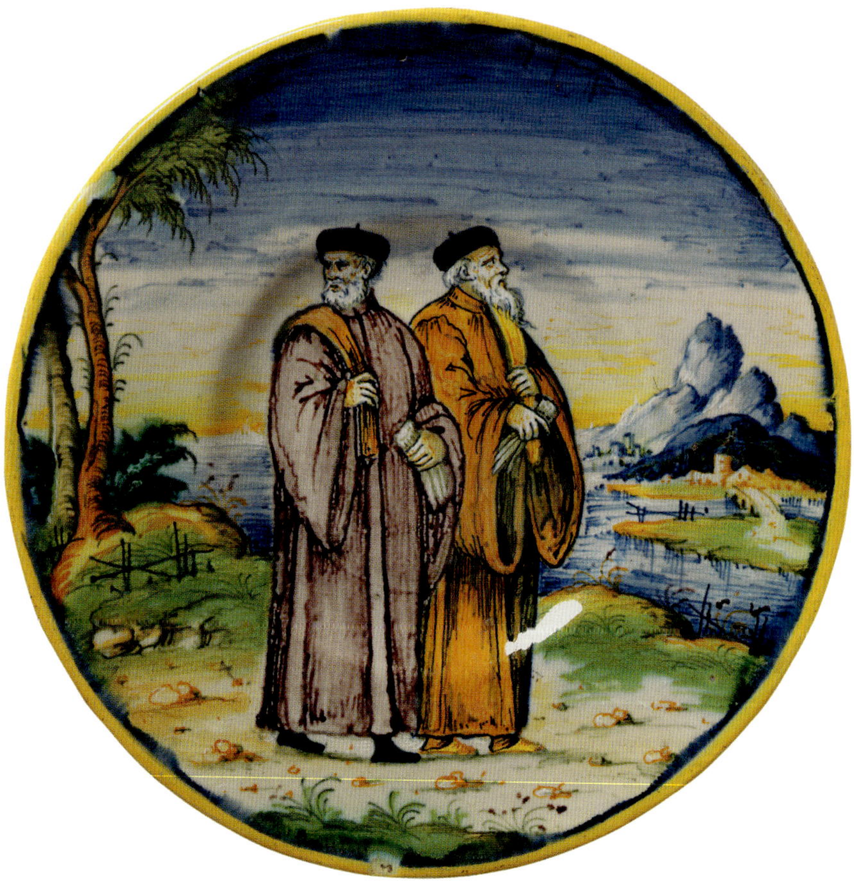

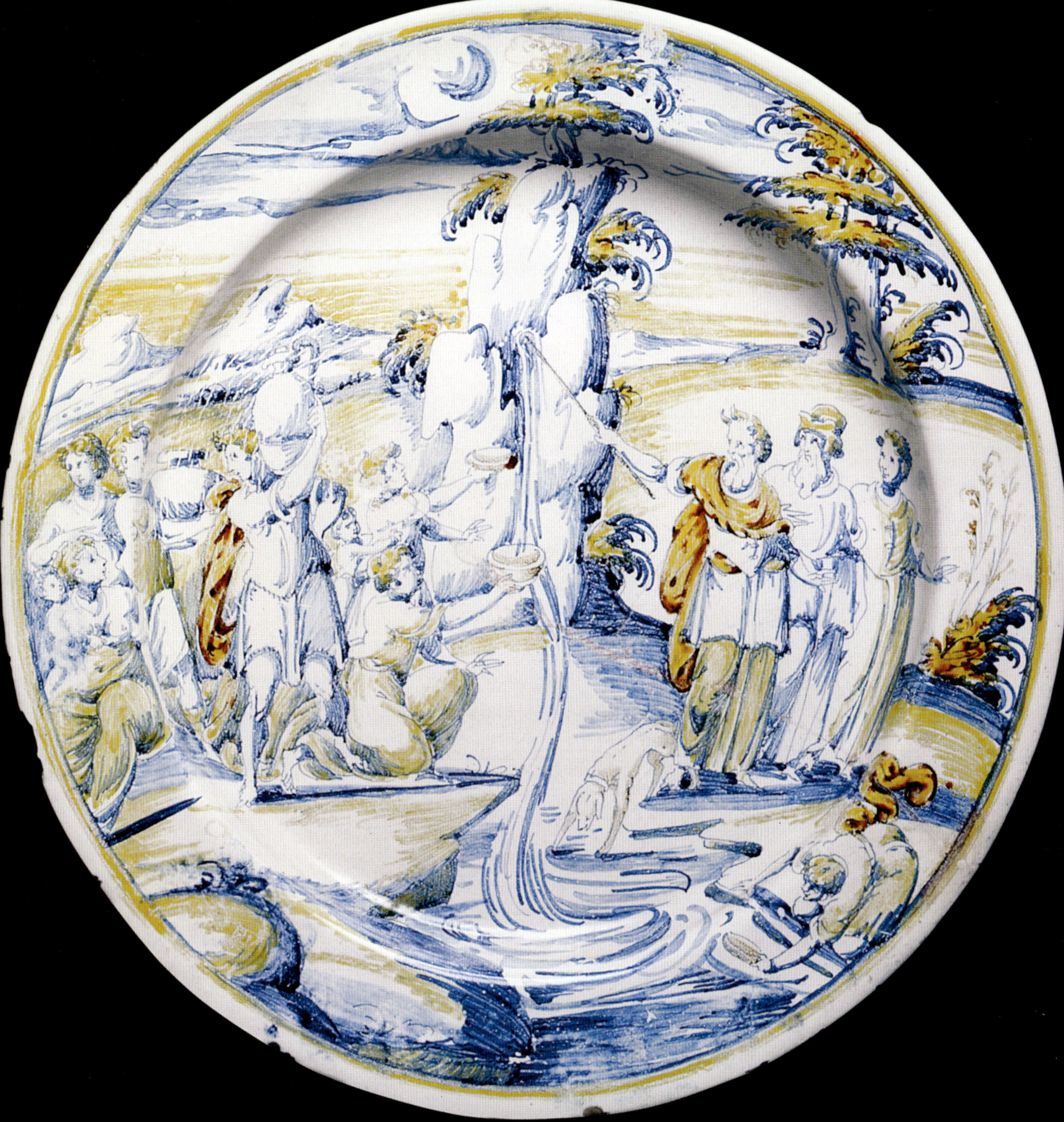

Tornai propriamẽte quegli ch lauora di legnio al torno

Tornai. alquanto incauate dalla banda di sotto come si uede
a quella. lo oue termina la linia. C. ora questa e la differē
za che e tra la scudella e il muginolo. e mi puoi ei mugio
lo piano ch e quello del qual si e ragionato ch ua nel
ferro. questo nō si caua mai ora diremo degli lauo
ri ch si fanō su la scudella. quegli che si fano sul
muginolo e sul muginol piano

27 Talloni o uoglia dir Confetiere
Coppette
Ongaresche o uoglia Piadene
Piatti strati cō il fondo e senza.
Tondi
scudelle
scudelini } sutili
scudelle
Taze } da limpagliata.
Talline o uoglia Ciotolette

Tutti questi lauori si fano su la scudella cō la Palla della quale si ragionera piu oltre ma prima intendo dire de tutti gli altri lauori asegniādo le sue misure come si uedra tra questi ue ne e di dua sorte ch si fano di dua pezi come le scudelle dal impagliata alle quai ua il suo coperchio e parimēte alle Taline che ui ua la manica. molti sono che uene fano dua. ma ame nō piace.

28 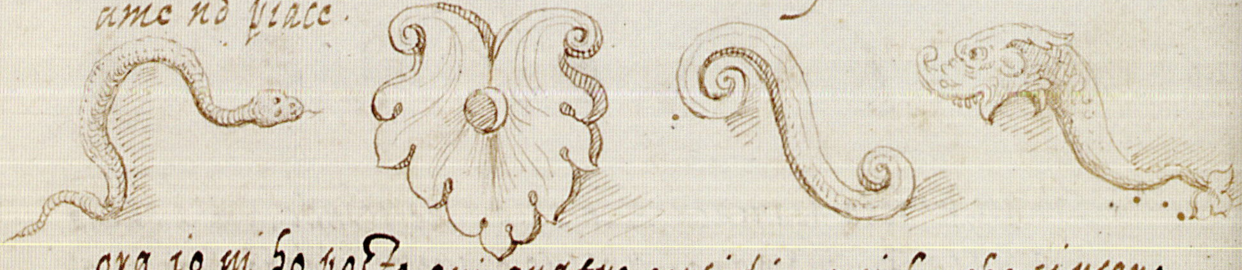

ora io mi ho posto qui quatro sorti di maniche che si usano

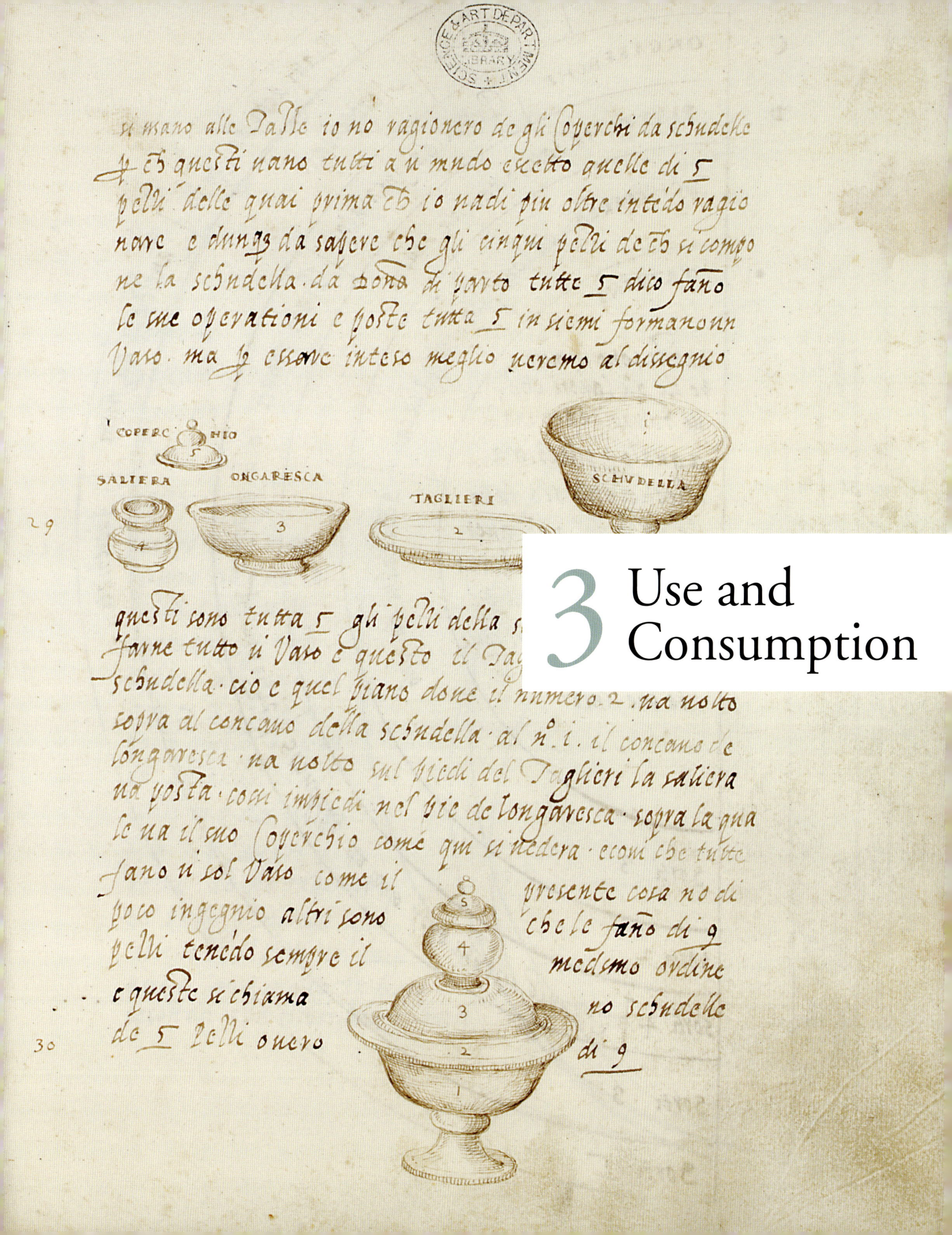

3 Use and Consumption

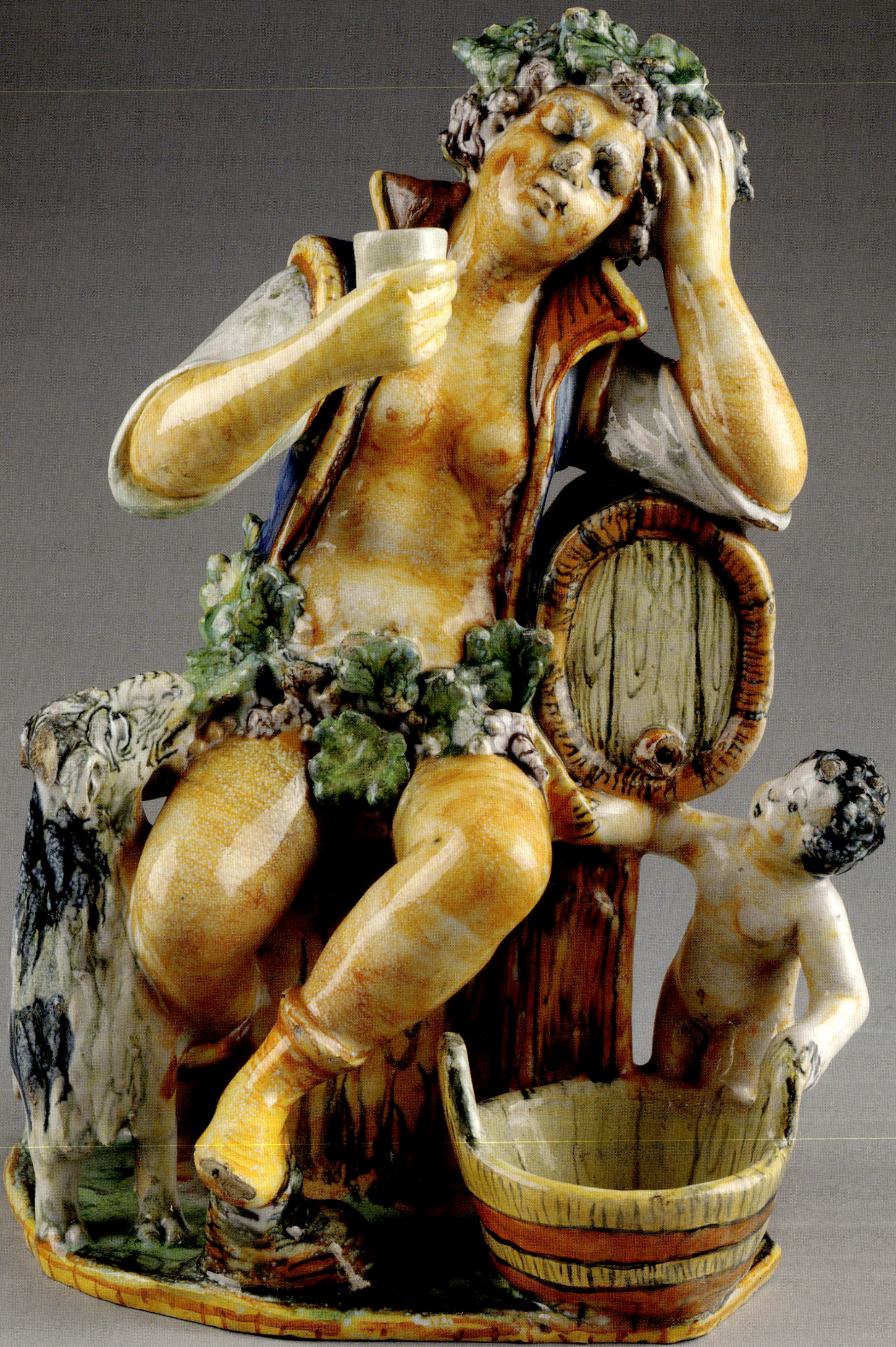

Introduction

It is important to remember that the fine Renaissance maiolica we find in museum collections today is not representative of what was commonly made and used at the time. Elaborately decorated examples were used infrequently, treasured by their successive owners, and from the eighteenth century onwards collected by individuals and museums, which is why they survive today in relatively high numbers. The more ordinary and relatively sparsely decorated vessels were generally used until they were broken and are now known mainly through archaeological finds.

During the Renaissance an enormous increase in maiolica production ran alongside major improvements in techniques of manufacture. Ceramics were an ideal medium for creating new and inventive shapes, satisfying the demand for a greater variety of household goods. Specialized pottery workshops met this demand by producing maiolica that was beautiful as well as useful – not just for eating and drinking but for all aspects of life. Inventories of potters, such as that of Virgiliotto Calamelli of Faenza made in 1556, list tablewares of all sorts as well as inkstands, shaving bowls, so-called puzzle cups, torches, candlesticks, basins, ewers and flower vases.[1]

Contemporary inventories of noble households show the presence of maiolica objects in every room of the elite Renaissance house, from the dining room and the kitchen, to the bedroom (where tableware was sometimes stored) and the study. These included devotional plaques, statuettes and other decorative objects. Pharmacies, often run by religious orders, required large numbers of containers for drugs and spices. Finally floor tiles were commissioned for churches and palaces.

In the past it has been assumed that Renaissance maiolica showed too few signs of wear to have been used for eating. However, cutlery was used relatively sparingly in the Renaissance: eating with one's hands was quite customary. Even the most beautifully decorated maiolica tableware, perhaps infrequently used, had a functional purpose.

The 1596 inventory of the Ducal Palace in Urbino lists maiolica wares according to their function: 'broth bowls', 'eggcups and salts', 'basins for washing hands', 'fruit bowls', 'wine flasks', 'flasks for oil and vinegar', as well as plates for salads or 'Indian chickens', dishes for sweetmeats and many others. These were all wares of the best quality, painted with narrative scenes or grotesques.[2]

Renaissance elites surrounded themselves with highly decorated objects. In 1490, Lorenzo de' Medici received a gift of maiolica from Galeotto Malatesta (Lord of Rimini from 1467 to 1492). In sending thanks Lorenzo stated that he valued the ceramics: '… more than if they were of silver, being excellent and rare … and a novelty to us here. I assure you it was not necessary to put your coat of arms on these vases to make my remembrance and recollection of your lordship more lasting.'[3]

Lorenzo had a long-standing interest in ceramics.[4] A fragment of a small dish bearing Galeotto's arms flanked by his initials was perhaps part of that precious consignment from Pesaro (pl. 138). The fragment shows the refined wares produced in the Marches at the time. Beautifully painted maiolica was esteemed among the cultured elites for its excellence in craftsmanship and design, even if its value never equalled that of silver or Chinese porcelain.

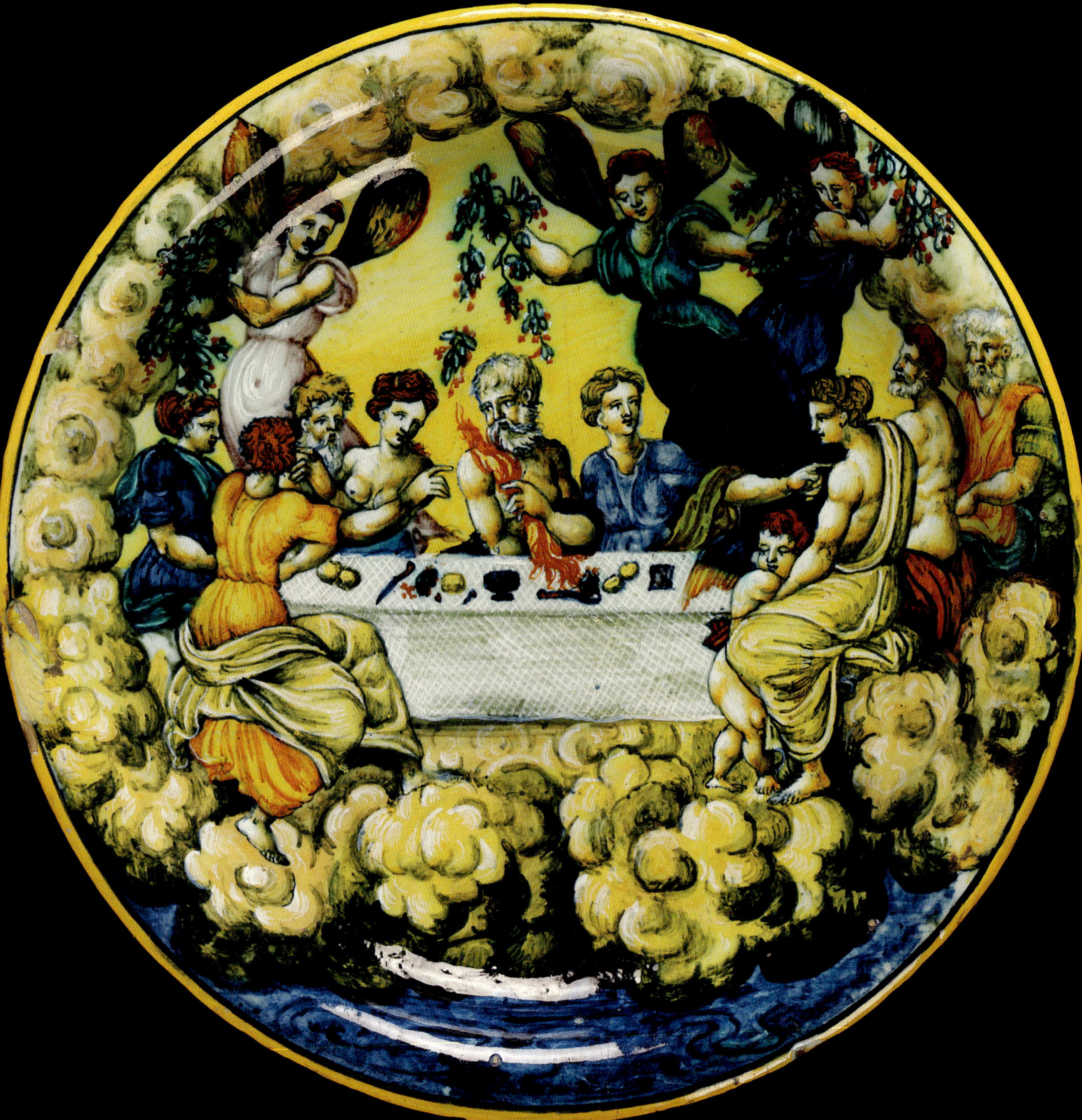

Tableware

136 (previous spread) Fountain in the form of Bacchus
Patanazzi family workshop
Urbino, c.1580–90
H: 29.5 cm
Gift of Lieutenant-Colonel Kenneth Dingwall through The Art Fund V&A: C.665–1920

137 Bowl with the Marriage Feast of Cupid and Psyche
Urbino, 1541
Diam: 28 cm
Salting Bequest V&A: C.2237–1910

Tin-glazed pottery is ideally suited to use on the table: it is impermeable, adaptable to various shapes, and capable of bearing detailed decoration. From its introduction to Italy in the twelfth to thirteenth centuries it found a place on the table together with objects made of wood, metal and glass. Medieval paintings featuring table settings, generally in depictions of the Last Supper or the Marriage at Cana, help us to understand the range of maiolica vessels used for dining (pl. 139). The medieval table was sparsely laid, mainly with jugs and cups of different sizes, while large wooden platters usually holding meat also appear in the middle of the table. Individual plates do not appear until the fifteenth century, and cutlery was restricted to a few knives.

The first maiolica tablewares were very limited in range. Small bowls, of roughly the size of a palm, are common survivals from the thirteenth to fifteenth centuries (pl. 140). They would probably have been used for soups and for dipping bread, and their shape was simple and utilitarian. Maiolica jugs, made in different sizes and shapes of body, handle and spout, became ubiquitous for the measuring, transporting and serving of liquids. Several could be used at table during a banquet for both water and wine (pl. 141).

From around 1450 a greater diversification of forms is visible. A primitive and strongly functional appearance gave way to more refined shapes and decorations. Dates never appear on pottery of this period but the presence of armorials can sometimes help with dating. The whitish bowl shown in pl. 142 is the earliest known maiolica decorated with papal arms, in this case those of Calixtus III, who was Pope for only three years, between 1455 and 1458. The simple shape of the bowl, which probably corresponds to what appears in fifteenth-century inventories as a *'scodella'*, is a rare example bearing arms of a type that was probably produced in large numbers. The bowl is said to have been found in the river Tiber in Rome, and was probably made locally. It is unlikely that it was made for the use of the Pope himself, and his arms could have been added simply as a sign of loyalty.

With growing prosperity and larger quantities and greater variety of foods available, dining rituals became more complex during the fifteenth century, requiring

138 Fragment of a dish with arms of Galeotto Malatesta
Probably Pesaro, c.1490
H: 7 cm; W: 9.5 cm
V&A: 6981–1860

139 Panel from an altarpiece with the Marriage Feast at Cana
Duccio di Buoninsegna
Siena, 1308
Museo dell'Opera Metropolitana, Siena

140 Bowl with bird
Perhaps Orvieto, late 14th or early 15th century
Diam: 12.5 cm
V&A: C.175–1912

141 Jug
Latium or Umbria, late 14th or early 15th century
H: 19.5 cm
V&A: 391–1889

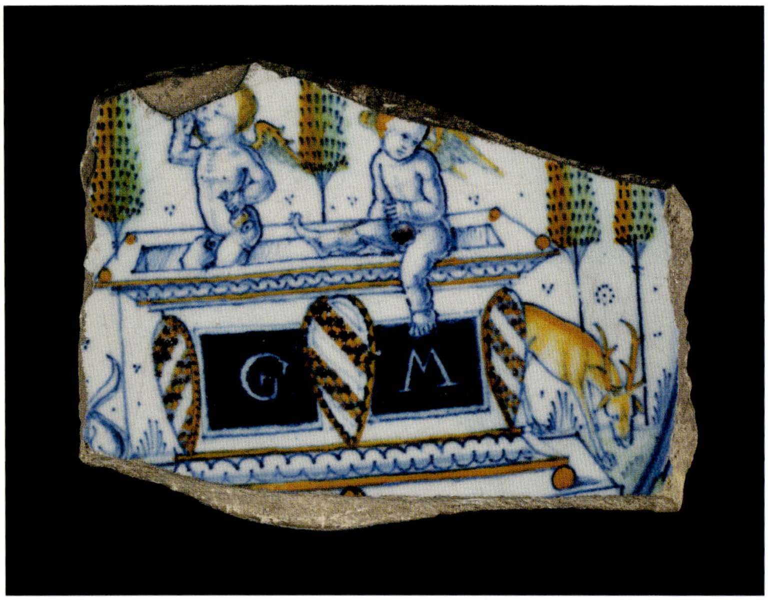

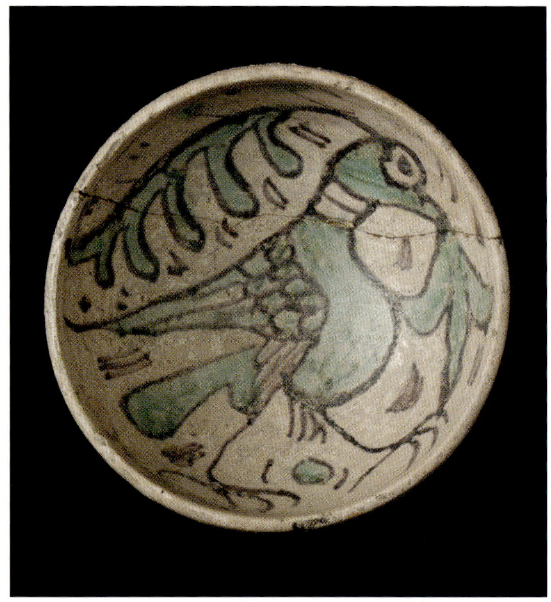

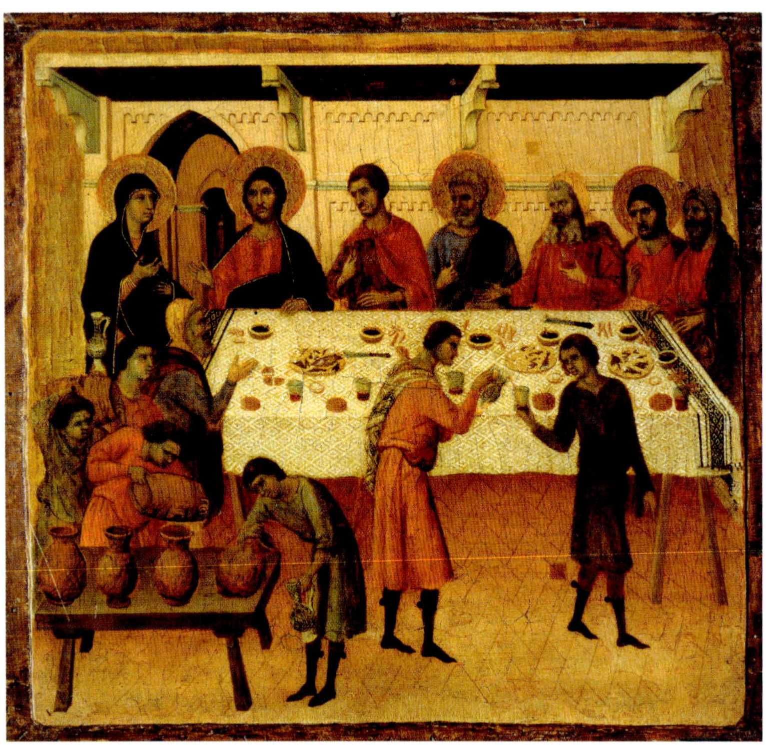

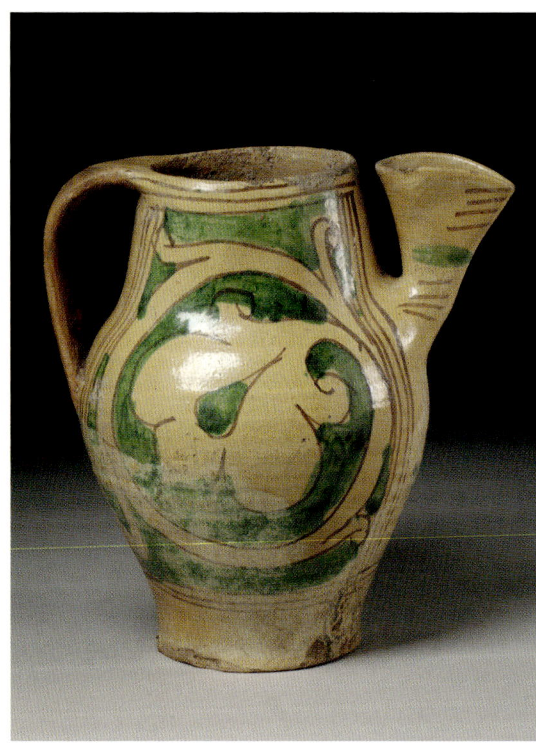

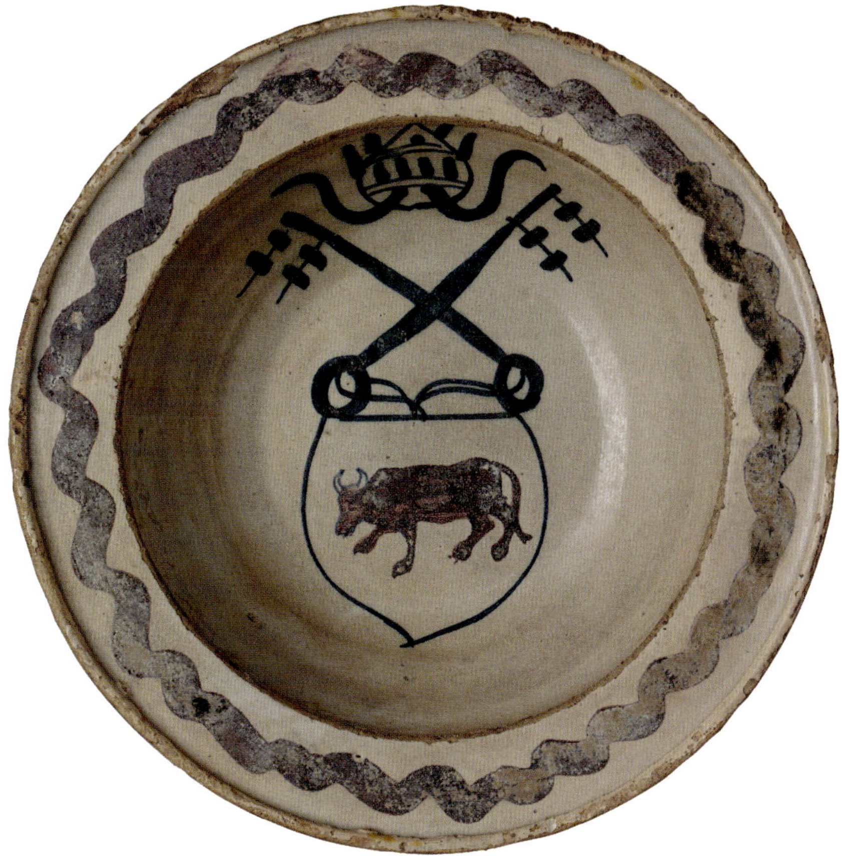

142 Bowl with arms of Pope Calixtus III
Perhaps Rome, 1455–58
Diam: 21 cm
V&A: C.7–1922

a proliferation of forms used for different types of food and particular activities, from plates and bowls in various sizes to large cooling vessels, flasks, ewers, salts and candlesticks. The shapes of these new types of ceramic tablewares were often copied from contemporary gold and silver wares.

Among the new types of wares probably introduced during the fifteenth century were elegant maiolica ewers and basins, referred to in contemporary inventories as *'bacini con mesciroba'*. They were used in the ceremonial rinsing of hands before and between courses at banquets. As most people ate with their fingers, rather than with cutlery, hands were washed frequently, often using water scented with rose petals, rosemary or camomile. One of the earliest survivals is a beautifully decorated basin bearing the arms of Giovanni Della Rovere, Duke of Sora and Arce and Lord of Senigallia, and his wife Giovanna da Montefeltro, daughter of Federigo Duke of Urbino and his wife Battista Sforza (pl. 143). The coat of arms on the basin which is missing its matching ewer, is surrounded by a diamond ring and dragon wings, both devices of the Sforza, rulers of Pesaro.

A complex array of serving dishes is reflected in Renaissance cookbooks, such as the monumental treatise on gastronomy by Bartolomeo Scappi, chef of Pope Pius V, where a wide range of terms describe the vessels each recipe required. By the early sixteenth century the number of courses had increased dramatically. Cristoforo Messisbugo, the *scalco* (carver) at the Ferrara court, in his manual on banquets of 1549 describing the special occasions of the Este court, mentions from seven to nine dishes for each of the many courses of a banquet (pl. 144).[5]

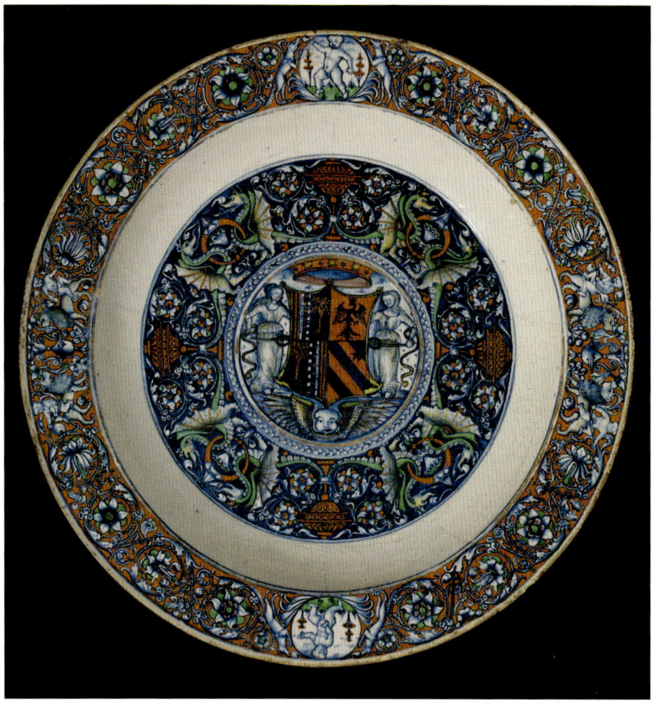

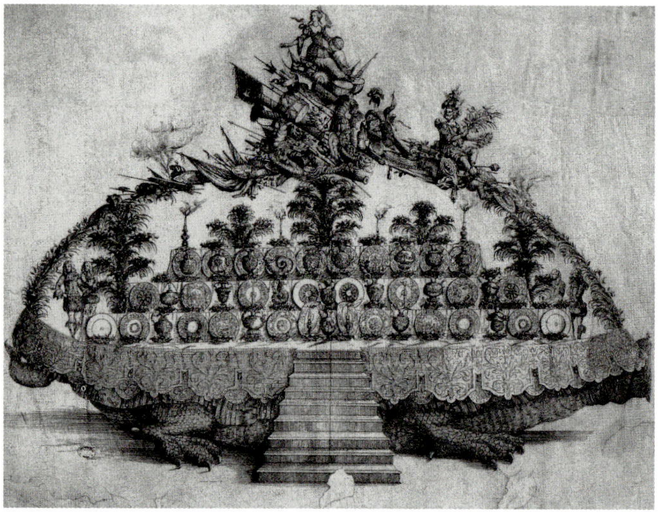

143 Basin with arms of Giovanni Della and his wife Giovanna da Montefeltro
Probably Pesaro, c.1500
Diam: 44 cm
V&A: 5475–1859

144 Banquet
Banchetti, Composizioni di vivande ...,
Christoforo Messisbugo
Engraving
Ferrara, 1549
Modena University Library

Maiolica services

The changing habits and etiquette of dining led to a growing range of tableware with specific functions. The ceramic dinner plate for individual use was introduced, as well as whole sets of tableware with matching decoration.[6] Ordered by elite families, initially from potters in Spain but soon also from local maiolica potters, such sets represented the height of fashion. Their lavish decoration often incorporated the arms of their owners. These sets were intended to be used at banquets, where they would be put on the table or perhaps displayed on a tiered sideboard known as a *credenza*, as was customary for silver. We know from contemporary inventories and account books that the word *credenza* soon came to refer to the sets of tableware that the sideboards were designed to display.

Very few pieces from fifteenth-century Italian dining sets have survived. From a documentary source we know that in 1478 Lorenzo de' Medici received a small maiolica set sent from Pesaro by Costanzo Sforza. This *'tavoletta'* (small set) was intended to be used in the summer at Lorenzo's villa at Careggi. At court, etiquette would probably dictate the use of gold and silver; however, at this time eating off these novelty maiolica wares was a sign of the owner's sophisticated taste and civility, even if their value was far less than that of silver.[7]

From the description of Lorenzo's set we can gain an idea of the component parts of a late fifteenth-century service:

> *6 scodelle* [bowls], *6 scodellini* [small bowls]... *2 piattelli grandi* [large plates] *e 2 piattelli mezzani* [medium size plates], *4 piattelletti da posare* [small trenchers], *6 tazze* [cups], *1 baccino colla miscrirobba* [basin and ewer], *2 coppe da frutti* [fruit bowls], *2 confettiere col coperchio* [sweetmeat dishes with covers], *2 candellieri* [candlesticks], *1 rinfrescatoio* [cooling vessel], *2 saliere* [salts][8]

The service made for the King of Hungary Matthias Corvinus and his second wife Beatrice of Aragon, daughter of the King of Naples, whom he married in 1476, is the earliest datable Italian maiolica service known to us. Only four pieces remain from what must have been one of the most prestigious maiolica commissions ever made: three large, deep basins, presumably serving dishes, and one small broad-rimmed bowl, probably for individual use. Both shapes are represented in the V&A collection (pl. 145). All four pieces show the arms of husband and wife, joined together by a knot under a crown.

Maiolica services made for couples (with the impaled arms of husband and wife) are relatively common; however, it is extremely difficult to find firm evidence of a set made specifically for a wedding. The Corvinus set bears allegorical images strongly linked with love and marriage: the basin shown below features boys picking fruit, symbolic of abundance and fertility; another shows a girl combing the mane of a unicorn, an image associated with feminine chastity, with a couple of stags in the background, symbols of fertility and love. Stylistically the set is unlikely to be as early as the date of their wedding in 1476, but certainly the set was made before Matthias's death in 1490, the year in which Beatrice remarried.

While Matthias was a great patron of the arts, it is known that Beatrice had a particular appreciation of maiolica: the Ferrarese ambassador in Hungary wrote to Beatrice's sister Eleonora, Duchess of Ferrara in 1486, to say that 'earthenwares from Faenza' would be a welcome gift and that 'Beatrice will be more delighted than if they were of silver'.[9]

A document relating to the commission in 1501 of a maiolica service for a cardinal gives insight into the attention given to such prestigious work. The Urbino potter Francesco Garducci was contracted to make 91 pieces: 'Beautiful and well painted and of good colours with the arms of the said cardinal and other paintings to gain praise

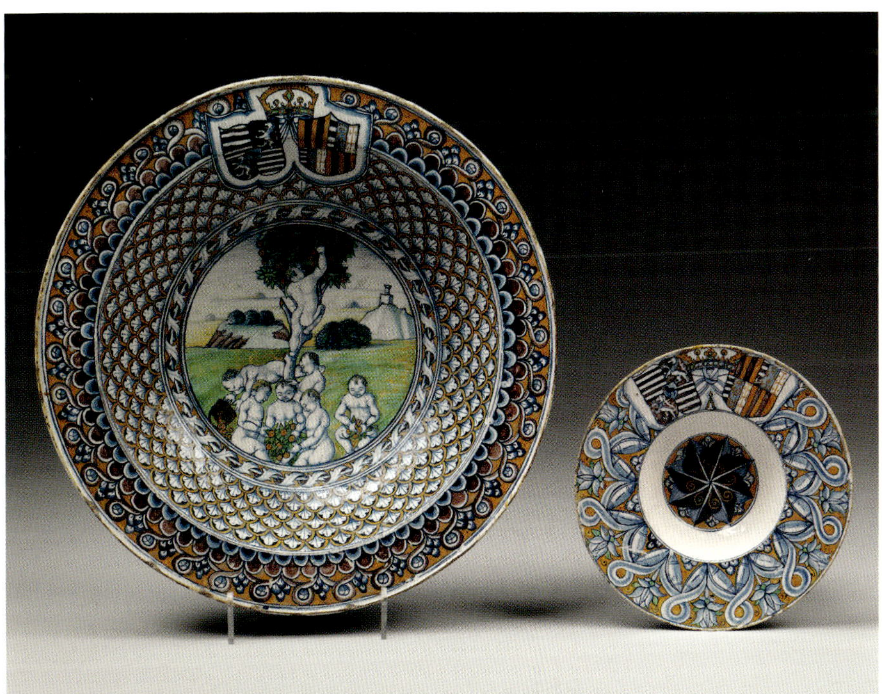

145 Basin and broad-rimmed bowl with arms of Matthias Corvinus, King of Hungary and his wife
Probably Pesaro, before 1490
Diam: 47.5 cm; 25 cm
V&A: 7410–1860; 1738–1855

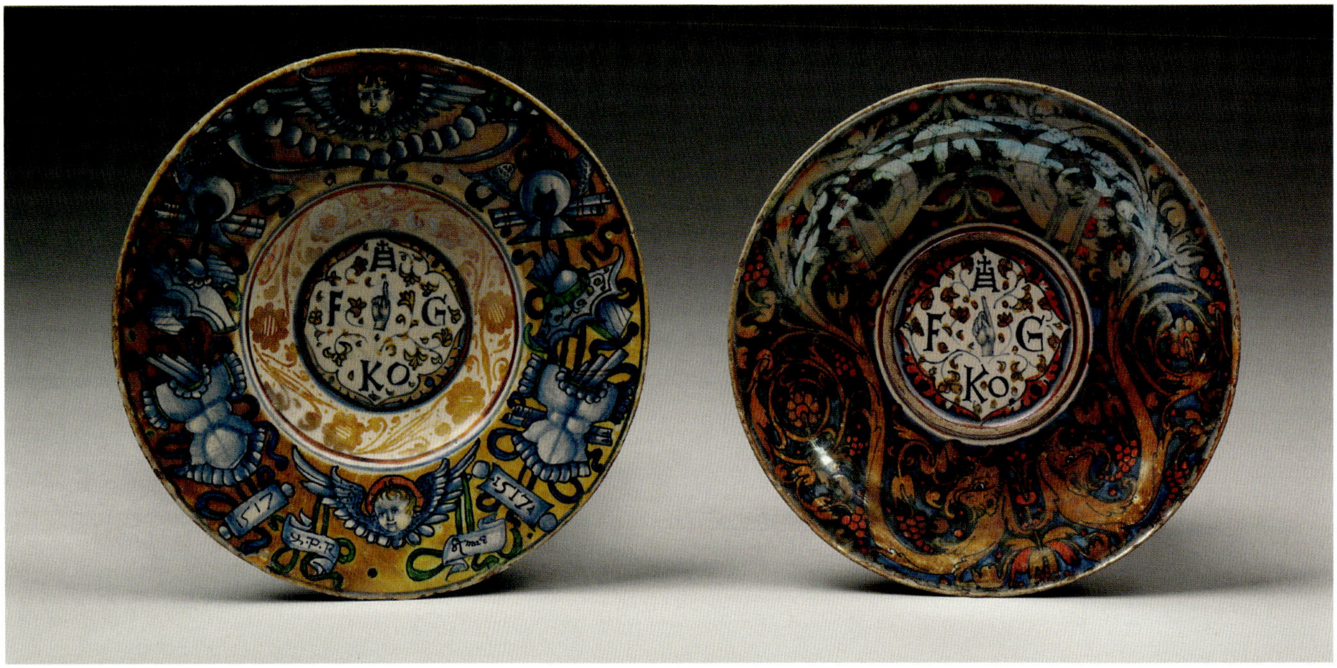

146 Plates with trophies, grotesques and badge
Workshop of Maestro Giorgio
Gubbio, 1517–18
Diam: 24.5 cm; 23 cm
Salting Bequest V&A: 800–1877; 2199–1910

and approval of one knowledgeable about art.' The service had to include several 'well painted' vessels including wine coolers, fruit dishes and basins painted differently from each other. The level of detail in the requirements is noteworthy.[10]

By the first quarter of the sixteenth century, all major pottery centres were involved in the production of armorial services, both for local and foreign consumption. Such sets were commissioned by or for distinguished patrons and were often intended as gifts.

The earliest dated 'armorial' set known was produced by the highly successful workshop of Maestro Giorgio of Gubbio. The surviving pieces are all decorated with lustre and dated '1518' in lustre on the back. One of the two plates in the V&A collection also has the year '1517' painted on the front (pl. 146). Each plate of this set has a central badge of a hand pointing upwards accompanied by the letters 'FG KO' and an emblem of a ladder surmounted by a cross. The badge is surrounded by a border of trophies and grotesque ornament which is different on each of the surviving pieces. The emblem of the ladder and cross belonged to the hospital of Santa Maria della Scala, in either Florence or Siena, and the badge with initials might be that of a chamberlain of the hospital.[11]

Maiolica services with coats of arms on a blue ground were also produced at Faenza from the early 1520s. One of the most popular Faentine patterns, small blue grotesques on a light blue ground called *berettino*, features in many armorial sets. This type of decoration seems to have been particularly popular with powerful Florentine families in the 1520s and 30s.[12] Among the surviving examples of this style of armorial service are tablewares with the impaled arms of various married couples, including Roberto Strozzi and Maria Ridolfi (*c.*1524–30),[13] Bindo Altoviti and Fiammetta Soderini (1524), and Francesco Guicciardini and his wife Maria Salviati (1525).

These fashionable Faentine blue services included many elegant yet functional vessels. A jug from a set made for the Florentine Salviati family has a cartouche just above the arms with the inscription *'ollio'* (oil) specifying its use as a cruet (pl. 147).

The cruet is dated 1531, as are various other pieces from this set. The Salviati were an important family who are known to have ordered several maiolica dinner services.[14]

Pl. 147 shows the range of wares which might have been included in such Faenza sets. Maiolica candlesticks, their shape derived from bronze prototypes, were also part of table services. Indeed maiolica tablewares often took their shapes from metalwork models. A highly original bowl on high foot, decorated in high relief with a diamond pattern, recalls a type of footed bowl illustrated by Piccolpasso. He calls them *'confettiere abborchiate'* (embossed sweetmeat bowls) and mentions that they were moulded in imitation of gold and silver vessels. The moulded diamond motif of the bowl, which probably had a matching lid, also recalls glass vessels.[15] Some of these armorial sets made in Faenza, decorated with blue-ground grotesque borders, include a few pieces painted with narrative scenes.

Istoriato maiolica services

The Renaissance courtier, diplomat and author Baldassare Castiglione (1478–1529) wrote about the importance of the art of conversation in his famous *The Book of the Courtier* (1528). Like the paintings and tapestries that covered walls during the Renaissance, maiolica services could carry a decoration reflecting the owner's erudition, social standing and, occasionally, wit. The scenes depicted on maiolica plates, often explained in an inscription on the back, could be used to stimulate erudite conversation at banquets.

Isabella d'Este (1474–1539), Marchioness of Mantua and one of the most distinguished art patrons of the Renaissance, was a widow when her daughter,

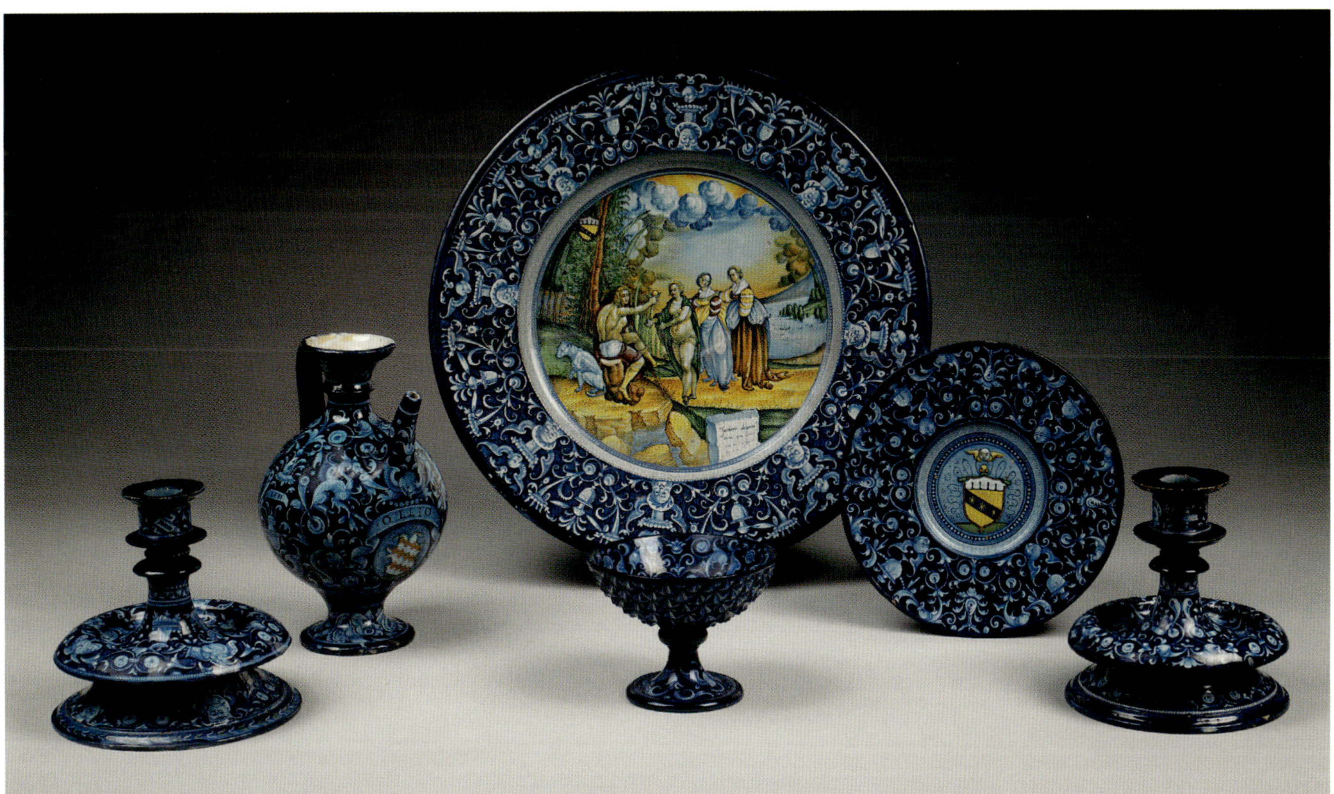

147 Cruet for oil with Salviati arms, candlesticks with grotesques, high-footed bowl, plate with Judgement of Paris and Zannoni arms, and dish with grotesques and Zannoni arms
Faenza, 1531; c.1520–30; c.1520–30; 1527; probably 1527
H: 25 cm; 17.5 cm; 11 cm; Diam: 45.5 cm; Diam: 24.1 cm
Salting Bequest V&A: C.2123–1910; C.2103–1910, 2104–1910; C.2100–1910, C.2110–1910; 1732–1855

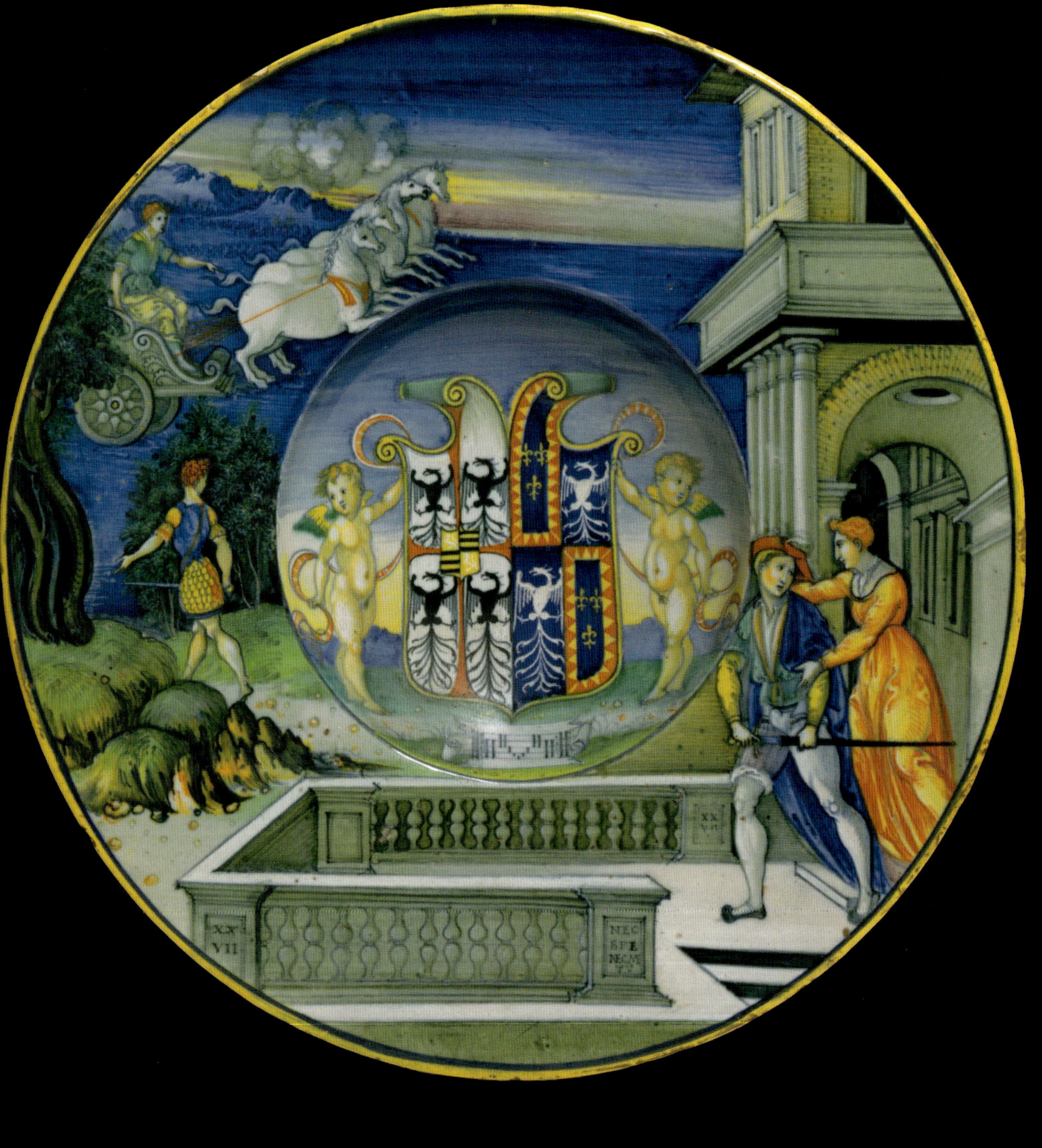
XX VII

148 Broad-rimmed bowl with Hippolytus and Phaedra and arms and devices of Isabella d'Este
Nicola da Urbino
Urbino, c.1524
Diam: 27.2 cm
Salting Bequest, V&A: C.2229–1910

Eleonora Gonzaga, Duchess of Urbino, sent her a service of Urbino maiolica painted with narrative scenes. The circumstances of the commission are known from a revealing letter sent by Eleonora to her mother on 15 November 1524:

> Thinking of visiting Your Excellency with some of the products of this country, which might please you, and not finding at this time anything which seemed to me to the purpose, I have had made a service ['*credenza*'] of earthenware pottery, which I am sending to Your Excellency by Battista my steward … since the masters of our lands have some reputation for good work. I shall be pleased if your Excellency likes it and if you will make use of it at Porto, since it is something suitable for a villa.[16]

We have no idea if the cultured Isabella indeed liked it, but we can probably recognize it as the most famous of all surviving sets of maiolica, showing Isabella's coat of arms, Gonzaga impaling d'Este, and several of her personal devices. Twenty-three pieces are known, and several plate shapes are represented, including large plates (about 52 cm in diameter), smaller, flattish dishes (around 25 to 30 cm), and one dish of 40 cm. The best painter working in Urbino at that time, Nicola da Urbino, was entrusted with this ambitious commission. The mythological scenes on Isabella's set, derived mainly from Ovid's *Metamorphoses*, would have been appropriate for an informal evening with cultivated guests. A broad-rimmed bowl shows Hippolytus and Phaedra (pl. 148). Some of the figures from the decoration of the bowl are derived from a woodcut illustration in the first illustrated printed edition of the *Metamorphoses* in Italian, published in Venice by Lucantonio Giunta in 1497.

Although Isabella was a widow at this time, she continued to use the joint arms of herself and her late husband, Gianfrancesco Gonzaga. Some of her many devices appear on the bowl. The meaning of Isabella's personal musical device, seen below the central coat of arms, is not entirely clear. The Roman figure 'XXVII' repeated twice stands for *ventisette* (27), sounding like '*vinti sete*', meaning 'you are defeated', or alternatively '*sette vinte*', meaning 'factions overcome'. 'NEC SPE NEC METU' ('without hope or fear'), Isabella's most famous motto, represents indifference to the vicissitudes of fortune.[17]

Eleonora's letter shows that women could be prime movers in the commissioning of sets, as well as being the recipients of such commissions. She suggested that her mother could use the service in her country villa at Porto, near Mantua, a more relaxed setting than the court. The letter quoted above referring to Lorenzo de' Medici receiving *istoriato* maiolica meant for use at his villa in Careggi during the summer (see p.120) confirms the idea that *istoriato* maiolica was a type of tableware seen as appropriate for an informal setting.

Evidence of the appreciation and use at the table of *istoriato* maiolica sets comes from the Medici Pope Clement VII (1523–34). According to a letter of 1528 from Giovanmaria Della Porta, the Duke of Urbino's agent at the papal court, to Isabella's daughter Eleonora, Duchess of Urbino, the Pope used *istoriato* maiolica only when dining with cardinals, while he himself preferred to dine off 'white on white' maiolica:

> Seeing our lord eat off earthenware decorated with white on white, I asked his steward why his Holiness didn't eat from ware painted with figures. He answered me that he ate off nothing else, reserving the other type [*istoriato*] for the use of cardinals, and that its arrival could not be better timed, as he has almost finished [presumably broken through use] one similarly made that came to him from Faenza …

149 Dish with the Abduction of Helen and device of Federico Duke of Mantua
Nicola da Urbino
Urbino, c.1535–8
Diam: 45.5 cm
Salting Bequest V&A: C.2246–1910

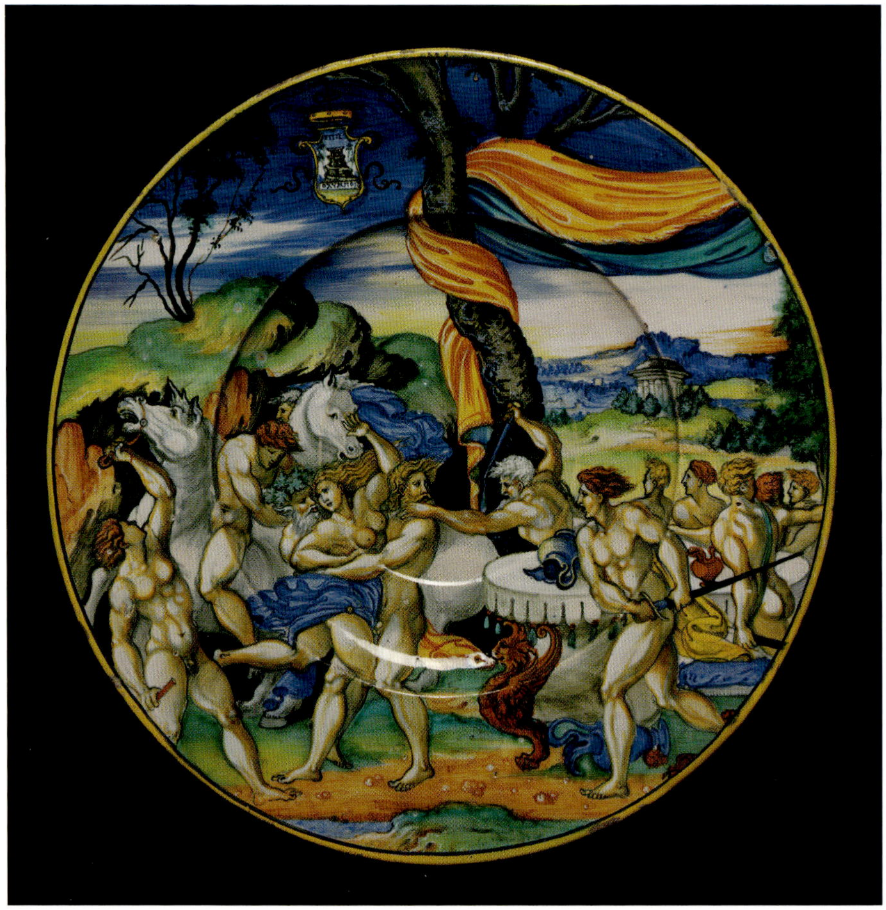

The letter continues with some detail on the type of tableware preferred by the Pope:

> He does not care for large or small bowls nor candlesticks, nor much for flasks. What he really likes is to have lots of plates of this size which I enclose, and of two smaller sizes of the same. Of large dishes not more than two. Two basins and ewers, salt cellars, and other things as seems best to our Genga [Girolamo Genga, the court artist at Urbino], but above all quickly, quickly, because the time is ripe, and to speed things one could entrust the work to two masters who would work simultaneously.[18]

This letter shows the various concerns and the level of detail involved in the commissioning of a dinner service for such an eminent patron. The specificity about the type and number of wares to be ordered is of particular interest, but the letter also reveals how court artists could be involved as intermediaries in the commissioning of maiolica and how large, pressing commissions could be entrusted to more that one workshop or master.

At this time, maiolica from Urbino decorated with narrative scenes was the height of fashion among the nobility. Nicola da Urbino also produced one or more sets for Isabella's son Federico Gonzaga, Duke of Mantua. A large dish decorated with

150 Dish with Hannibal reviewing captured weapons
Probably Fontana (Durantino) workshop
Urbino, c.1545–60
Diam: 24.5 cm
Salting Bequest V&A: C.2275–1910

151 Drawing of *'paesi'* *The Three Books of the Potter's Art*, fol. 69r (detail)
Cipriano Piccolpasso
Castel Durante, 1557
NAL: MSL/1861/7446

the dramatic scene of the Abduction of Helen bears the emblem of Mount Olympus, one of Federico's devices (pl. 149).

In 1530 Federico's secretary enquired about ordering a set from Urbino. A letter written to him by a 'Ioanfrancesco, alias El Poeta', from Pesaro illustrates the high esteem enjoyed by Urbino *istoriati*:

> I have been in Urbino and I have seen really excellent pottery, painted with landscapes, myths, and stories, to my eye of surpassing beauty, and I explained about the service you wrote to me about. The reply was that they cannot tell me the price, if they do not know the quality and quantity … because they are worth more or less according to the amount of work involved.[19]

One of the most ambitious *istoriato* sets in terms of its subject is decorated with episodes from the Second Punic war between the Roman and the Carthaginians (219–217 BC). This so-called 'Hannibal set', produced in Urbino around 1545–60, has the unique feature of sequential numbering (going up to 114), as well as explanatory rhyming couplets painted on the back of the wares.[20] The dish in pl. 150 shows Carthaginian soldiers carrying captured spears. The couplet on the back explains the scene: 'Hannibal inspects the trophies taken by his men.' The subject is taken from Livy's *History of Rome* (Book XXII.6-7). The complex historical sequence and the verses must be the work of an educated person. On some of the plates an oval-shaped area probably intended for a coat of arms is left blank. Perhaps the potters started executing the set while waiting for a design that never arrived?

The only narrative decoration represented in Piccolpasso's drawings of maiolica patterns is a design with landscapes (pl. 151). The only service with landscapes that has survived was probably made in Urbino around the time the manual was written (pl. 152).

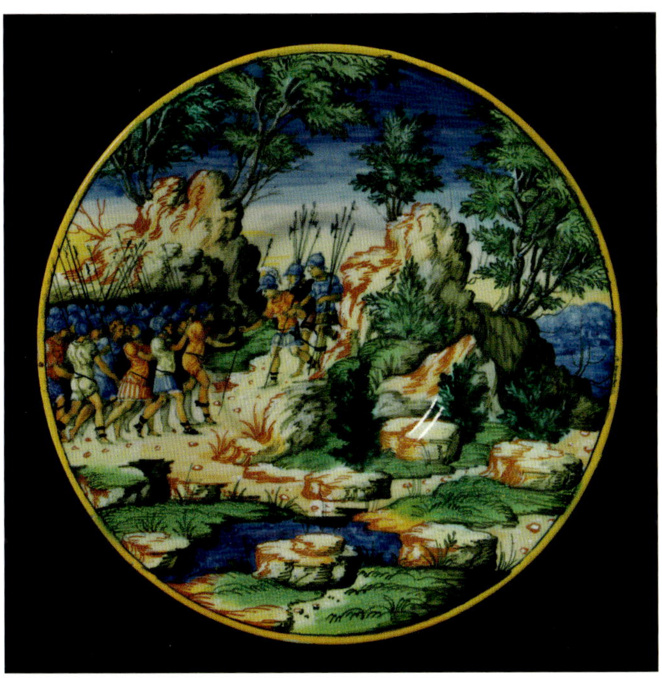

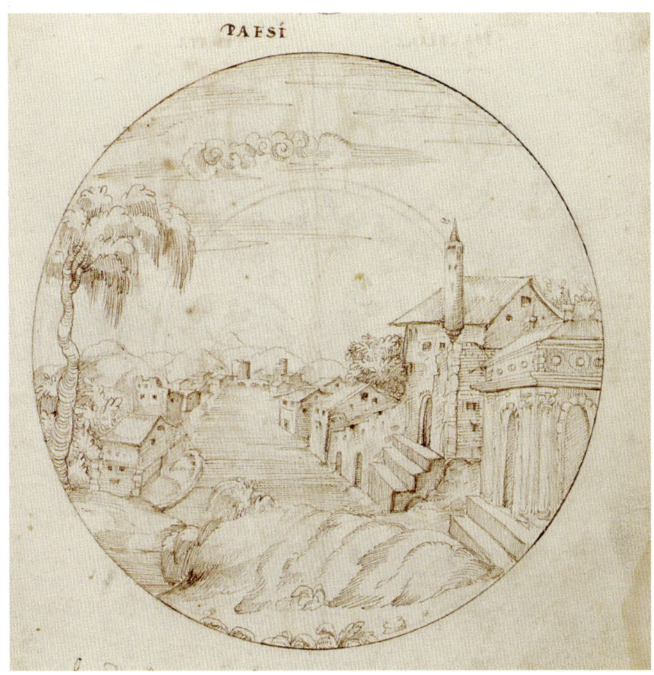

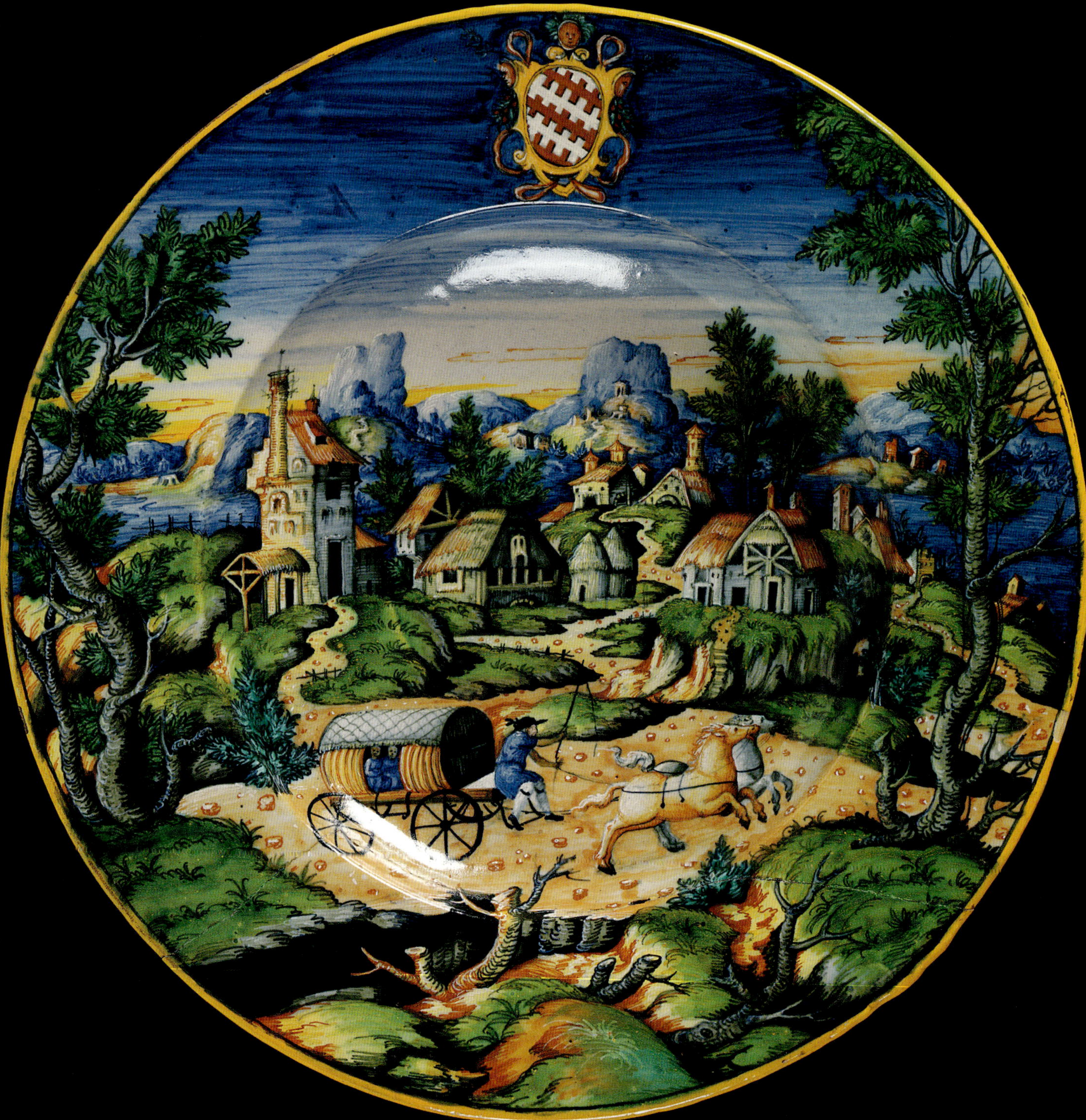

152 Dish with landscape and Salviati arms
Probably Fontana (Durantino) workshop
Urbino, c.1559
Diam: 40.5 cm
V&A: 1784–1855

153 Dish with Mucius Scaevola and arms of Guidobaldus II, Duke of Urbino
Fontana (Durantino) workshop
Urbino, c.1559–70
Diam: 39.5 cm
V&A: 4728–1901

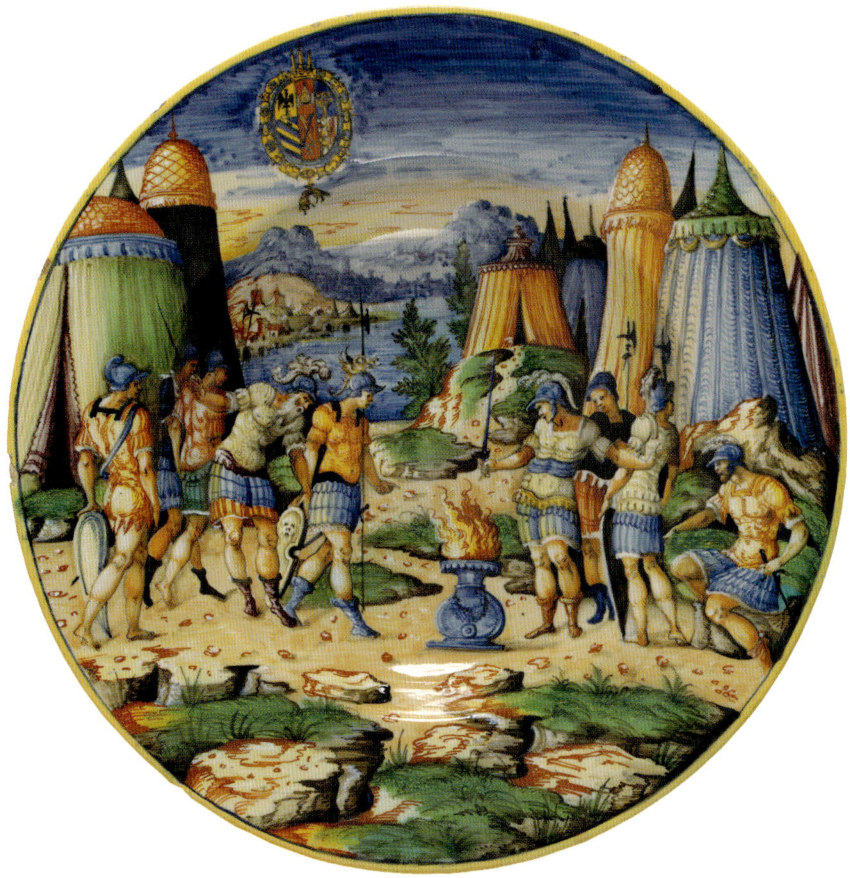

It depicts beautiful alpine scenes. No piece is inscribed but all bear the arms of the Salviati family and the set was probably made for Jacopo di Alamanno, perhaps on the occasion of his marriage to his cousin Isabella Salviati in 1559. Exceptionally the set can be traced in a sixteenth-century inventory, that of the Salviati family palace in via del Corso in Florence of 1583. Even though the inventory was drawn up some years after the service was made, it gives us an idea of its original size. A total of 178 pieces is listed – large jugs, wine coolers, large dishes, ordinary size bowls and deep bowls. The large plate shown in pl. 152 must be one of the *'piatti grandi'*, probably meant to be serving dishes, from the 24 listed in the inventory.[21]

In the second half of the sixteenth century, the Della Rovere Dukes of Urbino commissioned maiolica services to send as diplomatic gifts, to promote their local industry as well as to cement alliances. A service commissioned by Guidobaldo, Duke of Urbino (1538–74) for a priest, Frate Andrea da Volterra, is a rare example of such a prestigious gift. All the plates and dishes from the set have the arms of Guidobaldo on the front; uniquely, the reverses bear his initials 'G.V.V.D.' (Guidus Ubaldus Urbini Dux) accompanied by the word 'Munus' (meaning 'gift') to 'Andrea F. Volterrano' (pls 153, 154).[22]

Maiolica services also reached elites outside Italy. In 1535 the workshop of Guido Durantino, one of the biggest *istoriato* producers in Urbino, received commissions intended for two of the most important and influential men in France: Cardinal Antoine Duprat, Chancellor of France (1463–1535), and Anne de Montmorency,

154 Reverse of pl.153
Inscribed: 'G.V.V.D. given as a gift to Andrea F. Volterrano'

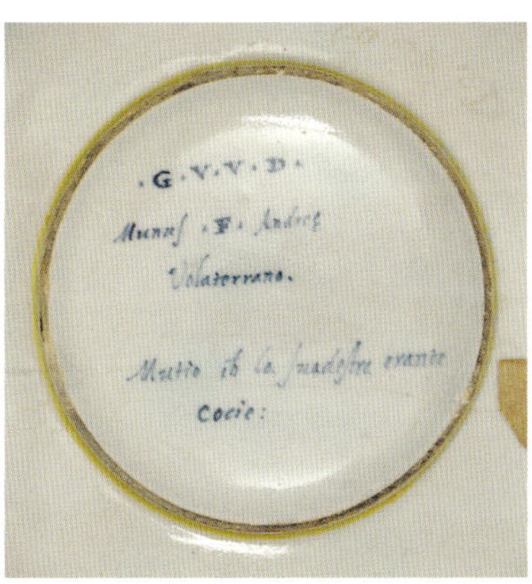

155 Candlestick with Alpheus and Arethusa, dish with Hippolytus and Phaedra and dish with an episode from the Trojan War, all with arms of Anne de Montmorency
Workshop of Guido Durantino
Urbino, 1535
Diam: H: 19 cm; 29.9 cm; 30.5 cm
Salting Bequest V&A C.2244–1910;
V&A: C.2243–1910; R.J. Dyson Bequest
V&A: C.28–1943

Grand-Maître of France (1493–1567). Inscriptions on the reverse of the surviving dishes of both sets, stating that they were made in 1535 in the workshop of Maestro Guido Durantino in Urbino, can be seen as an advertisement for the workshop.

The set made for Cardinal Duprat shows Biblical subjects, appropriate for a Church official, while the scenes from classical mythology on the Montmorency service are suitable for a cultured statesman. There are around 20 known pieces belonging to the widely dispersed Montmorency service: plates of different sizes and shapes, candlesticks and a flask. Three pieces from the set are in the V&A – two plates of the same shape and a candlestick (pl. 155). The candlestick is marked underneath with the number '16' perhaps referring to the size of the set of candlesticks. All the pieces in the set have a slightly inaccurate rendering of the arms, which might indicate that the set was a diplomatic gift rather than a commission directly from the recipient.[23]

Sets of narrative ware in the Urbino style became popular with affluent Germans, especially merchant families of Augsburg and Nuremberg with strong trading interests in Italy. Such families commissioned maiolica services of different types throughout the sixteenth century. A large serving plate, smaller plate and a salt cellar (pl. 156) belong to a set commemorating the union of two Augsburg families. Around 15 pieces are known, showing the arms of Hans Herwart and Helena Schellenberger, who married in 1528. However the set was made much later, probably in the 1540s, and, judging by the style of painting, in the workshop of Guido di Merlino in Urbino. It is also clear that two different painters were involved in depicting an array of classical and Biblical subjects.[24]

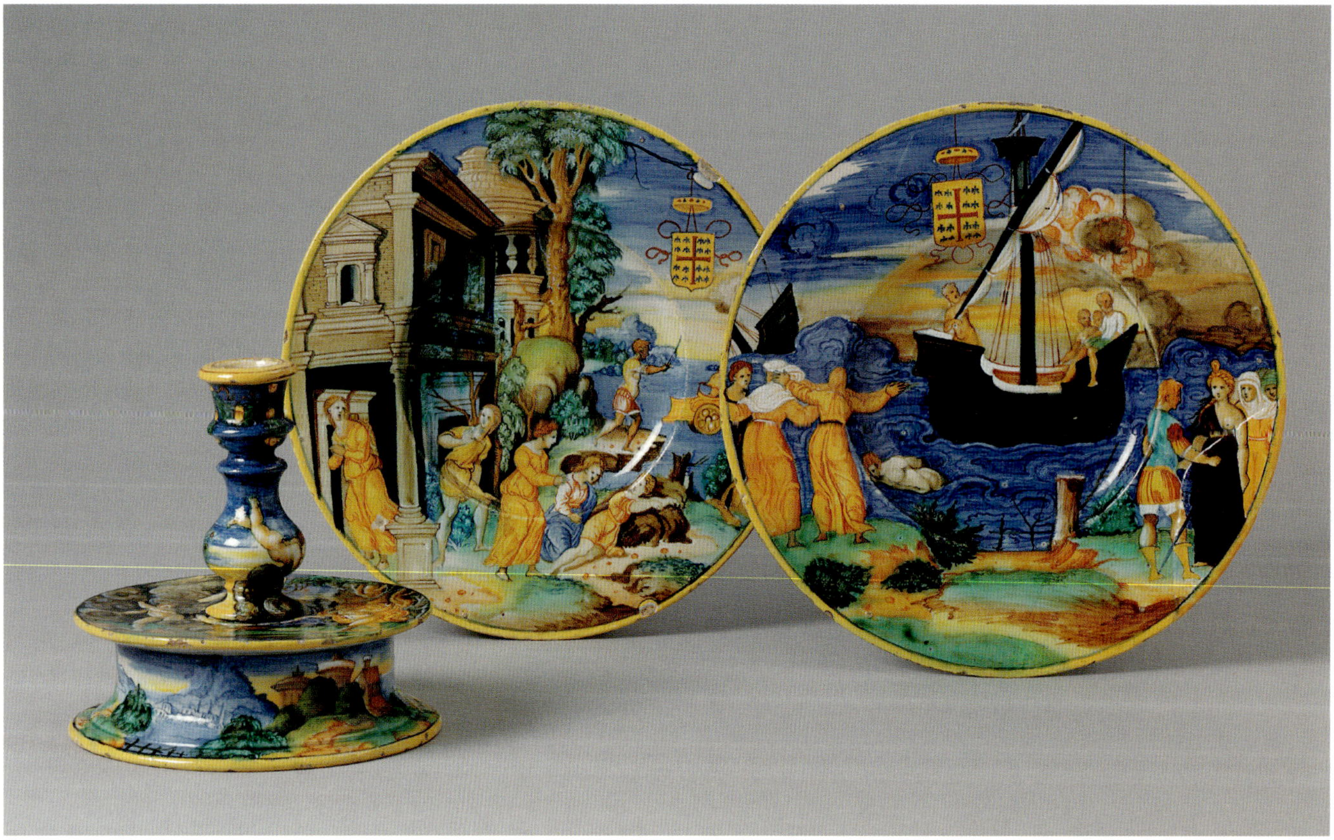

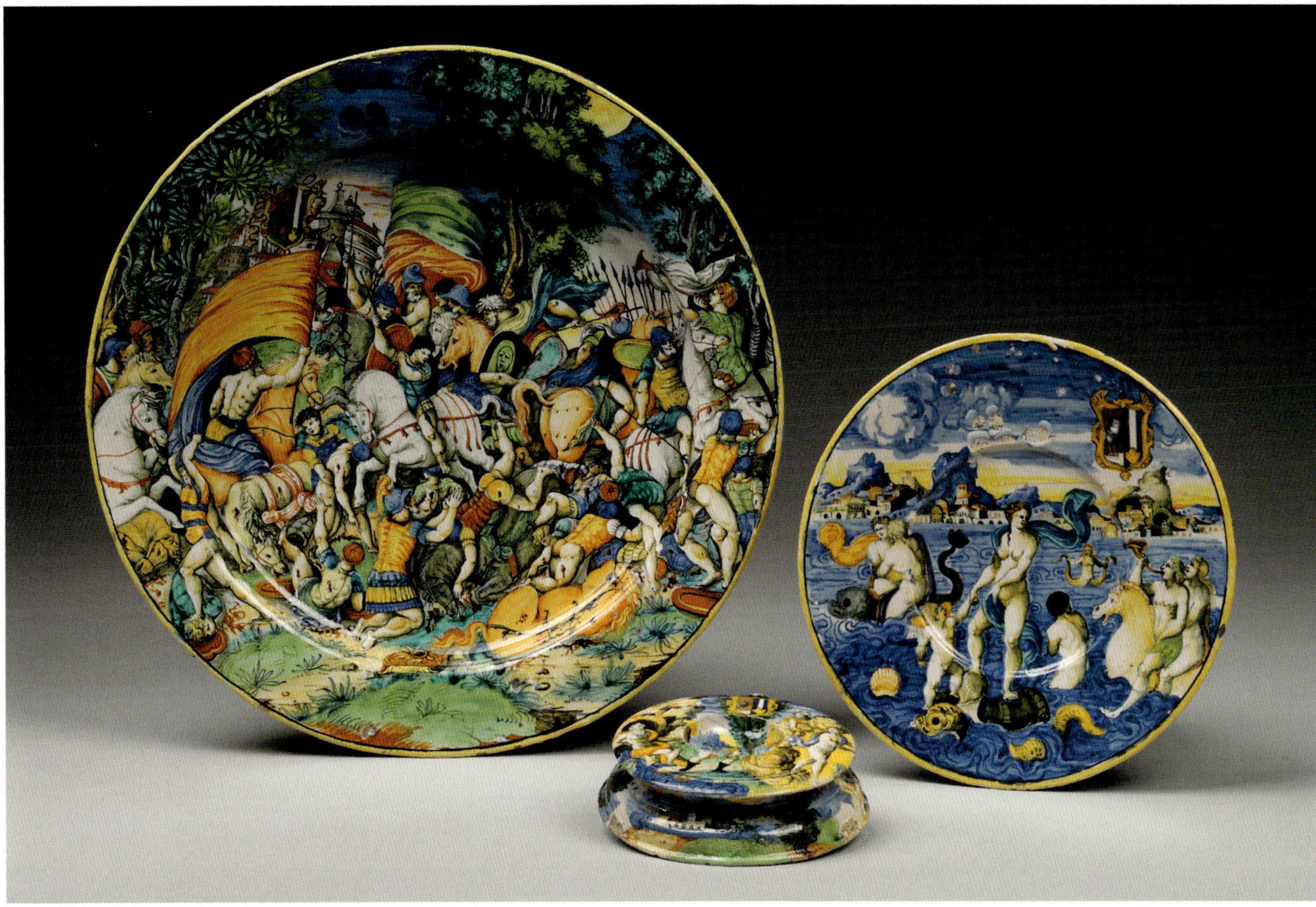

156 Salt cellar with Alpheus chasing Arethusa, dish with the Battle of the Israelites and Amorites and plate with marine deities, all with arms of Herwart impaling Schellenberger
Probably workshop of Guido di Merlino
Urbino, c.1540
Diam: 15.5 cm; 43 cm; 26.5 cm
Salting Bequest V&A: C.2276–1910; V&A: 8924–1863; V&A: 1704–1855

Late sixteenth-century developments

From the 1560s, grotesques on white ground surpassed narrative wares as the decoration of choice for important families commissioning Italian maiolica services. One of the most imposing sets decorated entirely with grotesques was made for Alfonso II d'Este, Duke of Ferrara, and his third wife Margherita Gonzaga. All of the 43 known surviving pieces of this service show a flaming piece of asbestos surrounded by the Latin motto *'ardet aeternum'* ('it burns for ever') painted on a scroll. An identical device, a symbol of undying love, appears on the reverse of a medal with the portraits of the couple facing each other probably made for their wedding in 1579.

The large number of surviving pieces, and their extraordinary variety of shapes, give a good idea of the ambition and scope of a late-sixteenth-century maiolica service of the highest quality. It might have consisted originally of several hundred pieces. There are elaborate vases with scrolling snake handles, oval and triangular dishes, sculptural salts and cruets. Two cruets in the V&A are inscribed *'olio'* and *'aceto'* ('oil' and 'vinegar') respectively (in group image pl. 157). Their differences in shape and painted decoration might imply that they were executed by different hands.[25]

The Medici Grand Dukes of Tuscany shared the taste for Urbino white ground grotesques. A number of exceptional Urbino pieces decorated with grotesques on white ground originally belonging to the Grand Dukes remain in the Bargello Museum in Florence today.[26]

157 Cruets for oil & vinegar with emblem of Alfonso II D'Este, Duke of Ferrara and his wife
Patanazzi family workshop
Urbino, c.1585–1600
H: 17.5cm
V&A: 504–1865; 505–1865

Salt cellar
Patanazzi workshop
Urbino, 1580–1600
H: 14 cm
V&A: 8403–1863

Dish with Biblical scenes and effaced arms of Cardinal Inigo d'Avalos
Perhaps Orazio Fontana
Urbino or Turin, c.1565
Diam: 45 cm
V&A: 8–1864

Bowl on high foot with Caesar and the Menapians
Fontana or Patanazzi workshop
Urbino, c.1560–80
H: 8.5 cm
Salting Bequest V&A: C.2259–1910

Pilgrim flask
Fontana or Patanazzi workshop, c.1560–80
H: 45 cm
V&A: 8409–1863

The first Grand Duke Cosimo and his sons Francesco and Ferdinando were greatly interested in ceramics. Under their patronage, one of the first European attempts to imitate Chinese porcelain led to the creation, around 1575, of the earliest known European soft-paste porcelain, now known as 'Medici porcelain'.[27] Francesco amassed an enormous collection of nearly 4,500 ceramics, including Chinese porcelain, specially kept in the Casino di San Marco.

Two large pilgrim flasks decorated with grotesques show the arms of Ferdinando, Francesco's successor as Grand Duke of Tuscany, and of his wife Cristina of Lorraine, who married in 1589 (pl. 158). A pilgrim flask is an elaborate, flattened type of bottle with a screw top. Loops around the body of the flask are designed to fit a strap, as the shape is derived from water bottles carried by pilgrims. The Medici flasks were probably made in Montelupo, as they are comparable to kiln wasters found there, showing a coarse local version of the fashionable Urbino grotesques on white ground.[28] The flasks are probably two survivors of the nine listed in the 1596 inventory of Ferdinando's Guardaroba: '9 flasks from Montelupo, painted in the Urbino manner, with the coat of arms of his Highness'.[29] The same inventory also lists vessels of *'terra bianca di Faenza'* ('Faenza white'), a type of ware from Faenza which was extremely popular from the middle of the sixteenth century onwards. Both Grand Dukes, Francesco and Ferdinando, ordered large sets from Faenza workshops.[30]

The best Faenza white maiolica was relatively expensive because of its thick layer of tin-rich glaze. Thick white glaze was most effective on elaborate shapes, often inspired by silver ware. A salt cellar with dolphins, shells and grotesque masks is covered in a thick, smooth white glaze, giving it an almost 'melted' appearance (pl. 159).

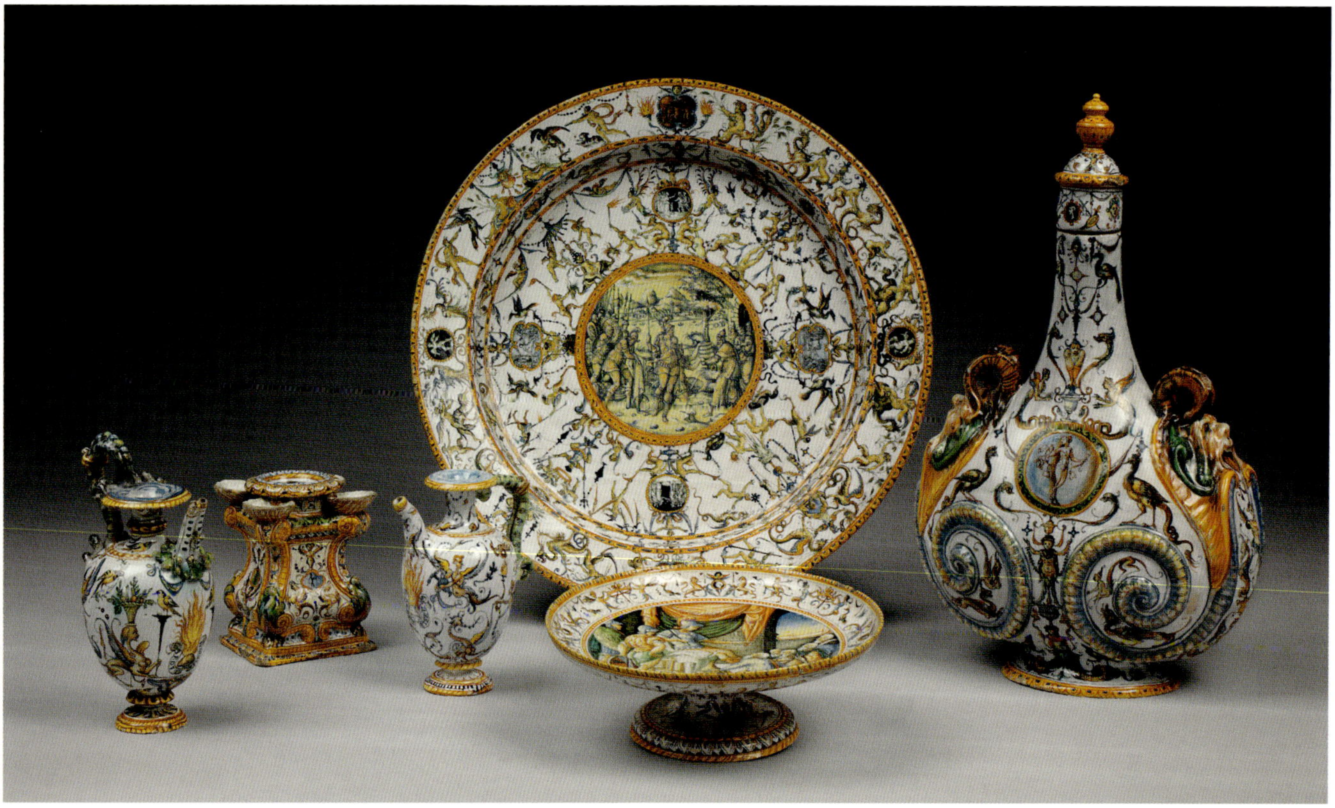

158 Pilgrim flasks with the arms of Ferdinando de Medici Grand Duke of Tuscany and his wife Cristina of Lorraine
Montelupo, c.1590
H: 40.5 cm; 38.5 cm
V&A: 322–1854; 323–1854

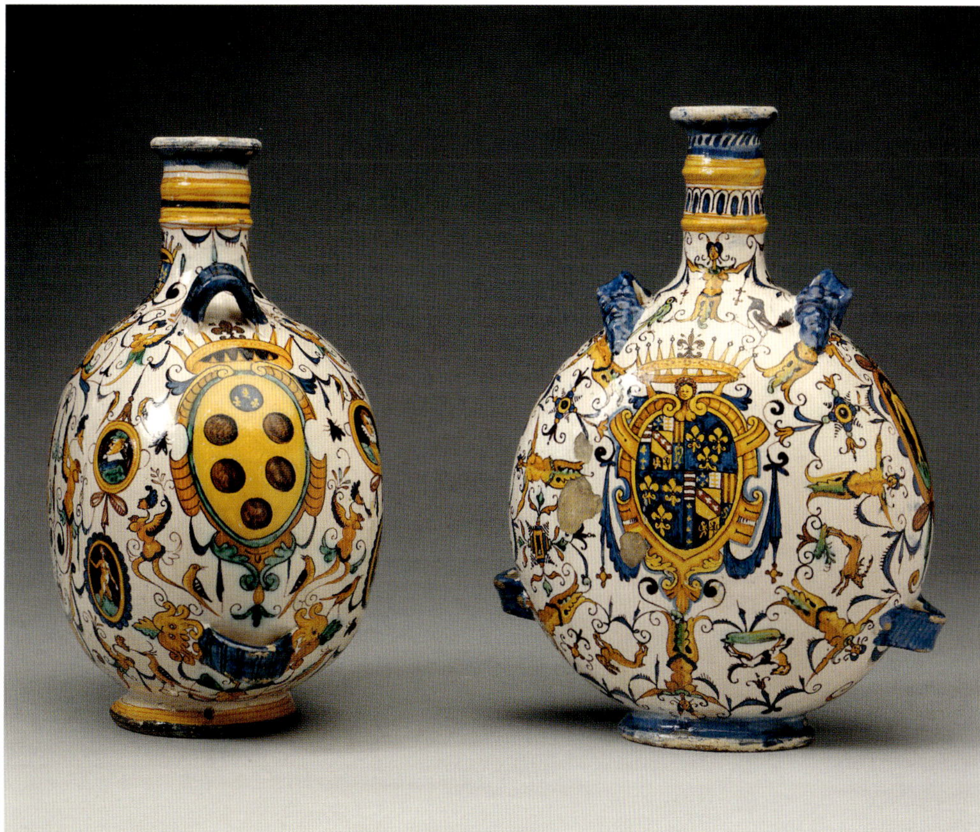

159 Moulded salt cellar
Virgiliotto Calamelli
Faenza, c.1550–75
H: 18 cm
V&A: C.27–1923

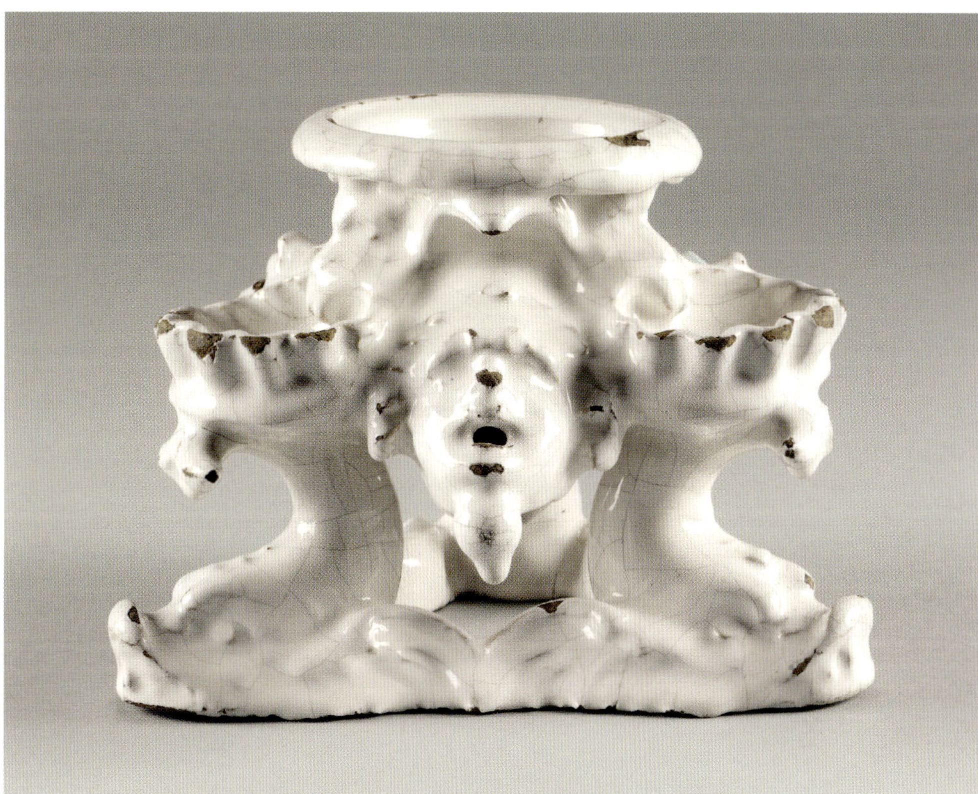

160 Aquamanile with Sforza family emblem
Probably Pesaro, c.1490–1500
L: 36 cm
V&A: 669–1884

Salt cellars are often listed in inventories. Salt was highly valued and taxed (its taxation was a significant issue in Italy, notoriously leading to wars) and was thought to have special properties: consequently salt cellars were often made of gold and silver. Salts and containers for other spices were essential components of maiolica table services.

The largest sets of Faenza whiteware might consist of hundreds of pieces. An invoice issued by the workshop of a famous Faenza white producer 'Don Pino' (Leonardo Bettisi) details wares from the 610-piece service of Count Camillo Gonzaga of Novellara in 1590 and lists tableware intended for specific types of meat including peacocks, pheasants and hares.[31]

Towards the end of the sixteenth century white maiolica became more widely available and was popular for tableware. The French statesman and writer Michel de Montaigne admired it on his journey through Italy in 1581:

> Considering the cleanness of these earthenware vessels, which are so white and neat that they seem like porcelain, and are so cheap, they really seem more pleasant for eating than the pewter of France, especially when that is dirty, as you find in the hostelries ...[32]

Playful dining

In his treatise on social virtues, the Neapolitan humanist Giovanni Pontano discusses dining as one of the most important communal activities. He calls this virtue 'conviviality', the civility of being in the company of others at table.[33] The importance of entertaining and dining in Renaissance Italy is reflected in the growing demand for innovative and playful tableware in maiolica.

Extraordinary sculptural ewers and pouring vessels were created from the second half of the fifteenth century onwards. Perhaps the most daring known to us is a large *aquamanile*, a pouring vessel with a handle shaped as a female figure kneeling to grasp with both hands an animal's head, which forms the spout (pl. 160). Despite its sculptural and playful appearance the object remains functional. It was filled through the hole at the top of the barrel, and water or wine poured out from the animal's head. At the bottom there is a hole for emptying the barrel. Such zoomorphic pouring vessels are descendants of medieval metal and ceramic *aquamanili* from Europe and the Middle East and they would have been a source of amusement for guests at a banquet.[34] The prominent decoration on the front of the barrel, a flower within a diamond ring interlaced by two wavy leaves, is a well-known device of the Sforza family, rulers of Pesaro, and the object might well have been produced locally.

Around 1500, an unknown workshop, perhaps active in the Marches or in Faenza, produced unique sculptural groups including fountains and pouring vessels. Shown in pl. 161 is a group representing the scene preceding the Judgment of Paris: Mercury holds the golden apple, about to wake Paris who lies asleep. Despite its strong sculptural appearance the object is actually a functioning fountain. It could be filled through an opening in the top of the turret on the left, and the contents would then flow out from the hole by Paris's right hand, which might have been fitted with a metal tap or spout.

Playful table fountains were also produced for noble households in the second half of the sixteenth century. Among the many products of the Patanazzi workshop of Urbino during the last quarter of the sixteenth century were figural fountains, such as the extraordinary example shaped as a drunken Bacchus leaning on a barrel

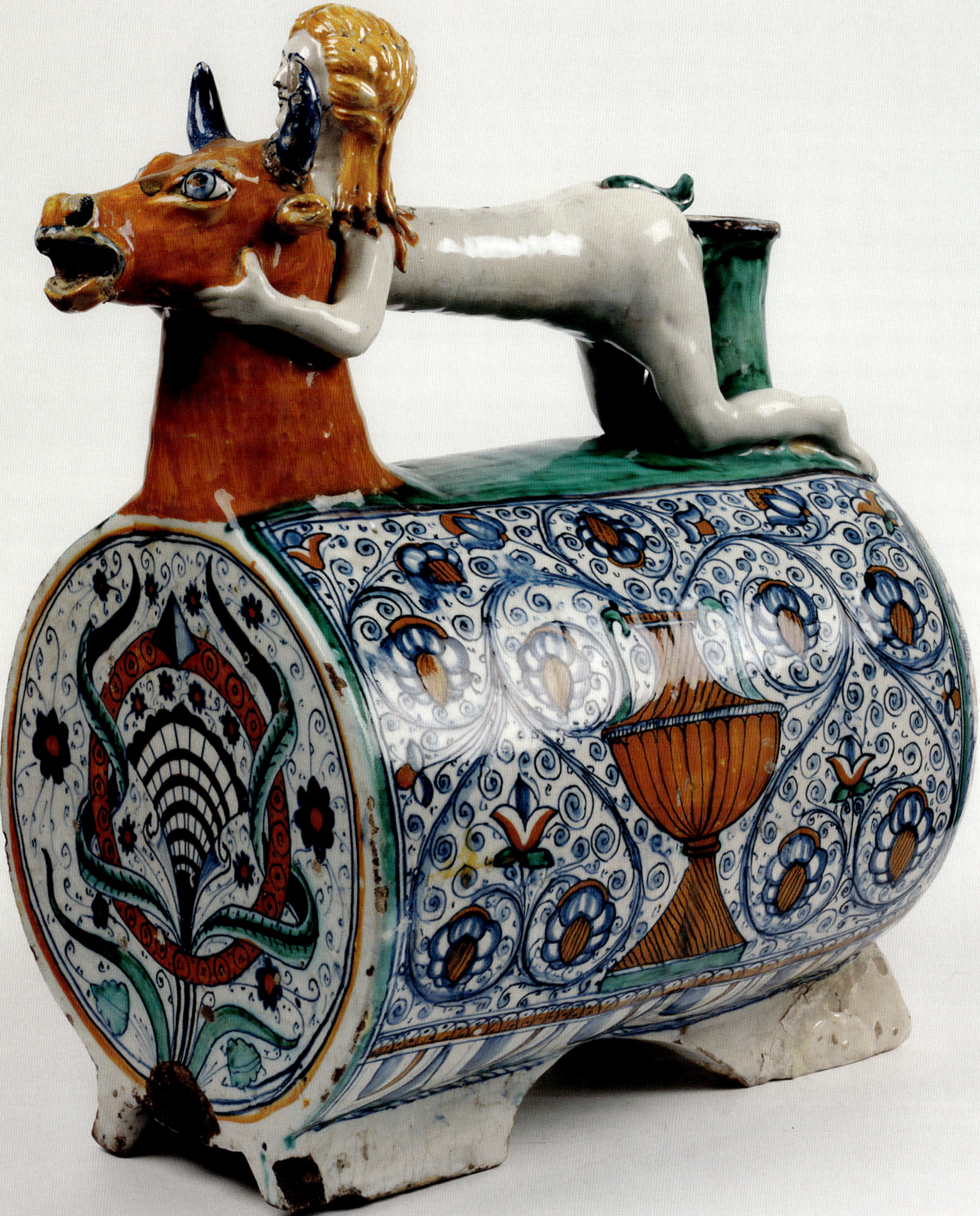

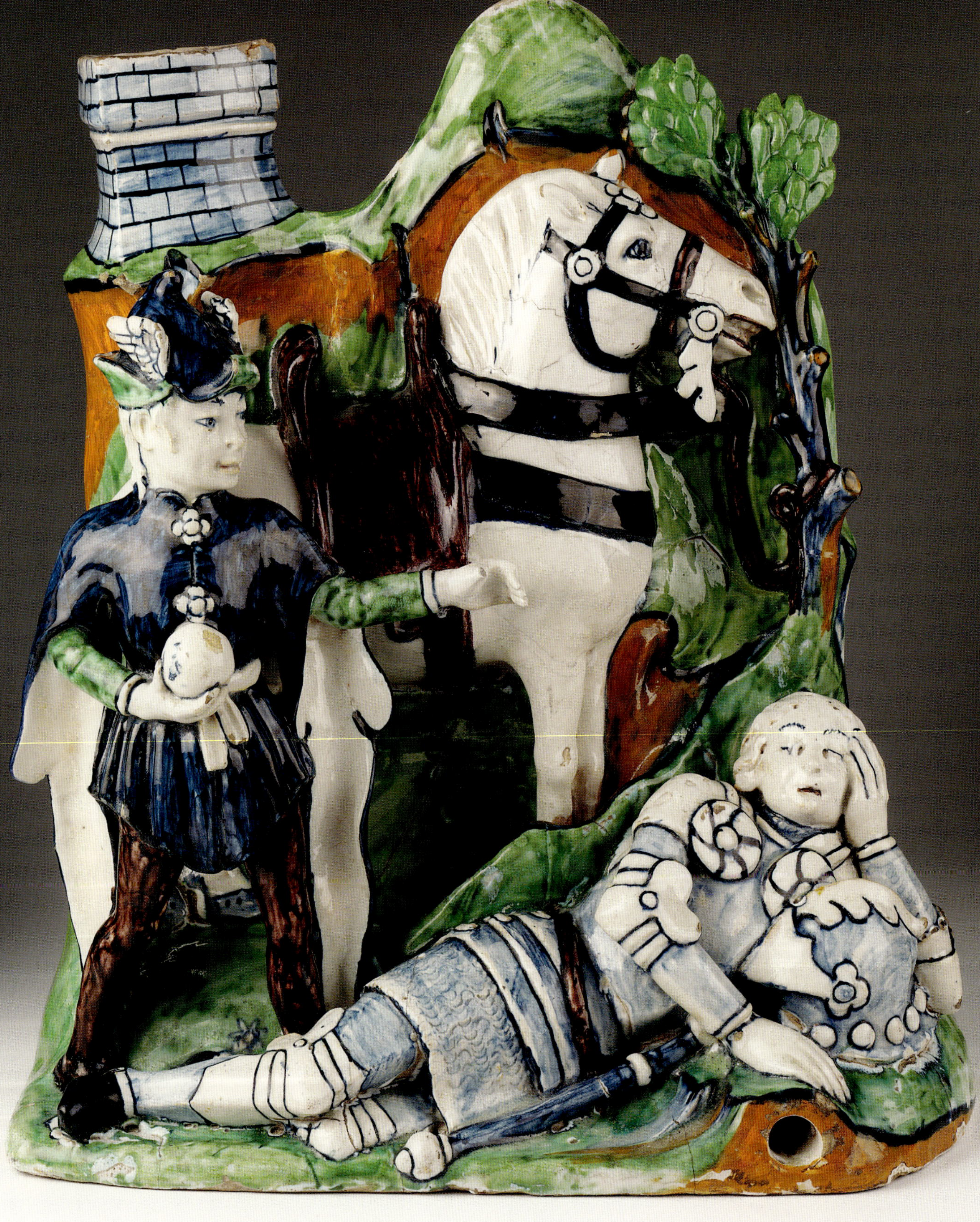

161 Fountain with Mercury giving the golden apple to Paris (The Judgment of Paris)
Possibly Faenza, c.1500
H: 46 cm
V&A: 551–1864

162 Lustred puzzle cup
Deruta, c.1520
Diam: 23.2 cm
Salting Bequest V&A: C.2195–1910

(pl. 136). The 1596 inventory of the Ducal palace in Urbino lists several types of fanciful maiolica fountains including one comparable to the V&A example: 'A figure of Bacchus seated on a barrel holding a cup to his lip with a satyr and a goat'.[35] These figures are stylistically similar to those on inkstands and other types of small sculptures produced by the workshop.

Drinking games were an important part of dining rituals. Maiolica 'puzzle jugs' and 'puzzle cups' or, as Piccolpasso calls them, *'tazze da inganno'*, are vessels created solely for the purpose of entertaining. Puzzle cups have several spouts and the user can only drink from them without spilling by blocking up specific holes. The lustred example in pl. 162 must have been a much-admired possession. Cups of this type were made from the fifteenth century and are listed in inventories of noble households.[36] These playful objects give us a rare insight into the less formal aspects of dining while conveying all the splendour of the Renaissance table.

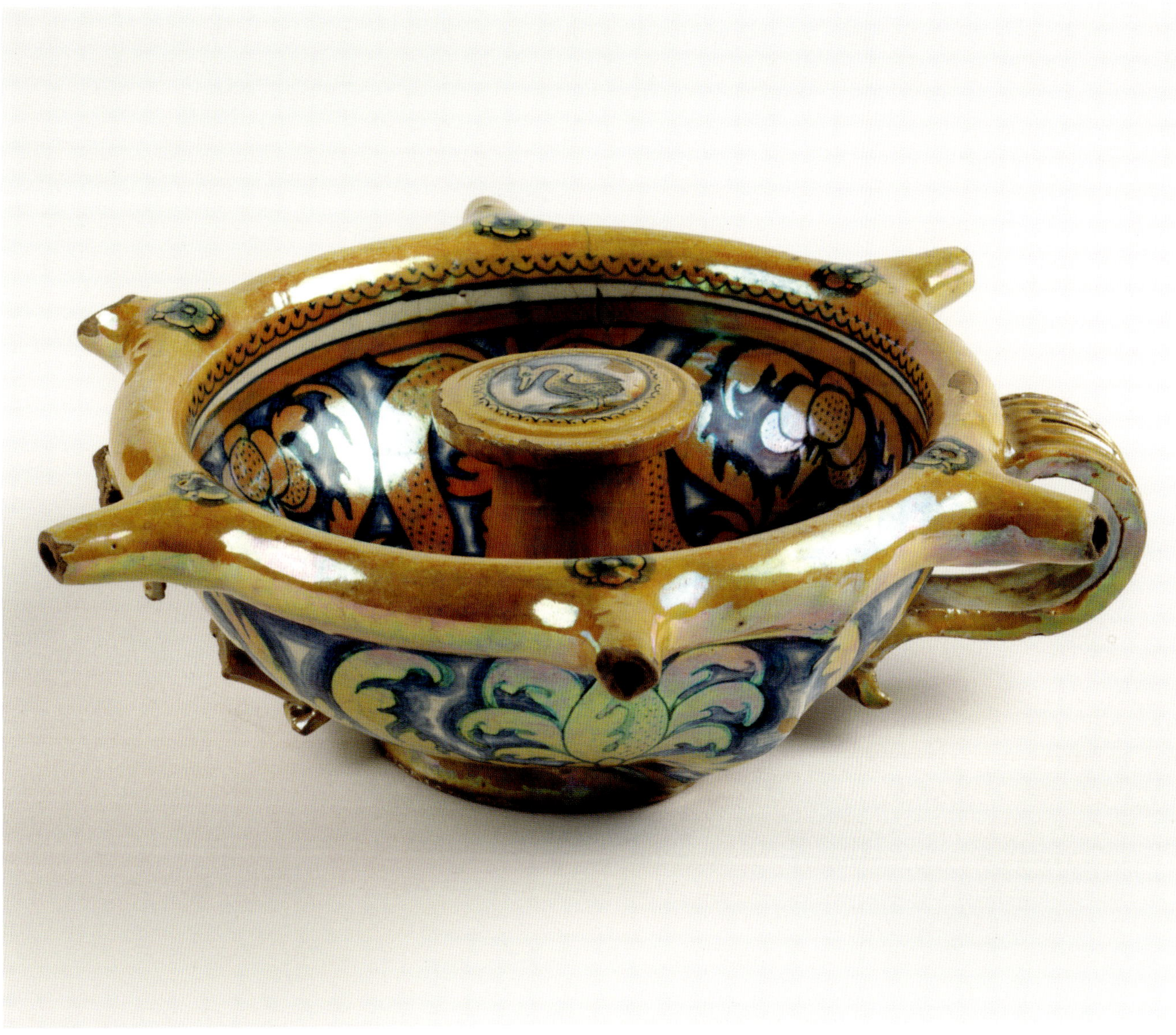

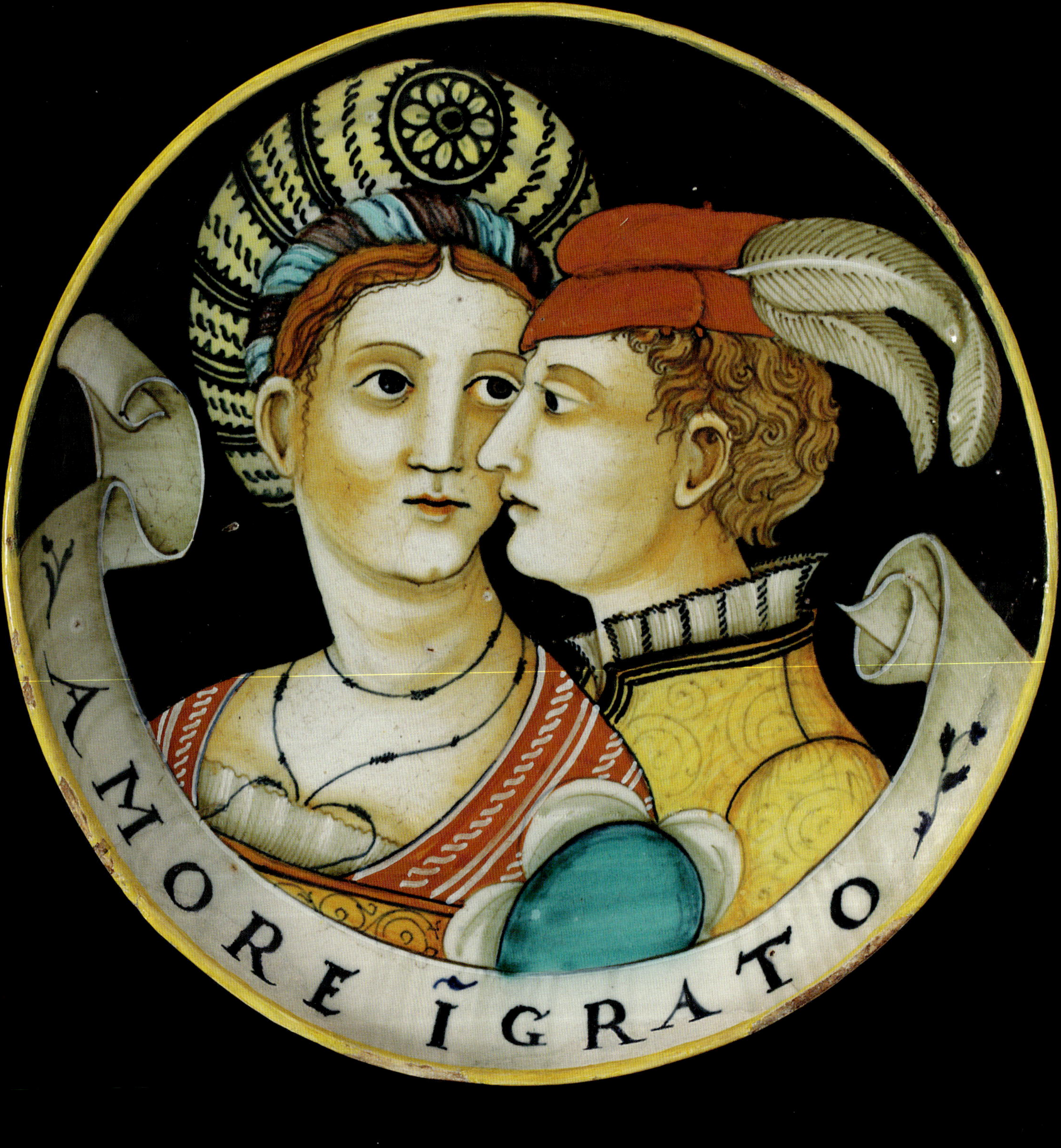
AMORE ĨGRATO

Maiolica of Love and Marriage

163 Bowl on low foot with a couple
Inscribed: 'Ungrateful love'
Urbino district, c.1530–40
Diam: 24.5 cm
Salting Bequest V&A: C.2222–1910

Subjects related to love were popular during the Renaissance in different media and especially so on maiolica.[37] From the second half of the fifteenth century, paired female and male busts, pierced hearts, rabbits and stags symbolizing fertility and amorous inscriptions are prominent in the late Gothic repertoire of maiolica from Faenza, Deruta, Pesaro and other pottery centres.

Allegories related to the cruelty of love, such as images of bleeding hearts or women about to pierce the lover's heart, were favoured themes in medieval and Renaissance literature and frequently occur on maiolica. A large dish probably made in Deruta around 1470–80 showing a young woman holding a cup with a crowned, pierced heart is inscribed 'My heart is wounded by you' (pl. 164), language influenced by Renaissance love poetry, especially that of Petrarch. The dish has holes pierced through the foot rim so that it can be suspended from a piece of string and is one of the earliest examples known of a *'piatto da pompa'* (display plate), a typical product of Deruta potteries: once on the wall, the dish would have been a strong testament to love.[38]

Belle donne (beautiful women) constitute one of the most fascinating of all types of maiolica. These are wares with standardized bust portraits of attractive women in elegant dress.[39] These ideal beauties are often accompanied by scrolls inscribed with female names followed normally by *'bella'* or the letter B, but also, less frequently by *'pulita'* (pure) or *'diva'* (divine). *'Galante'* (gracious) and *'pia'* (devout) also appear occasionally. A tradition dating back to the eighteenth century considers these wares *'coppe amatorie'* (loving cups), presents given by young men to the object of their affections.[40] Examples with personal inscriptions such as 'Silvia my beautiful goddess' might indeed have been part of the ritual exchange of gifts between lovers, which was an important part of courtship etiquette in the Renaissance.[41]

Potters from Deruta were celebrated for their depictions of beautiful women to the extent that in 1557 the poet Andreano da Concole of Todi (near Deruta) wrote a poem 'To a potter from Deruta', encouraging him to depict the most beautiful local women if he wants to sell his wares fast, and including a list of such beauties.[42] *Belle donne* made in Deruta are profile or three-quarter bust portraits appearing in

164 Dish with woman holding cup with a pierced heart
Inscribed: 'My heart is wounded by you'
Deruta, c.1470–80
Diam: 38.5 cm
V&A: 2558–1856

165 Lustred dish with woman in profile
Deruta, c.1520
Diam: 40.5 cm
Salting Bequest V&A: C.2172–1910

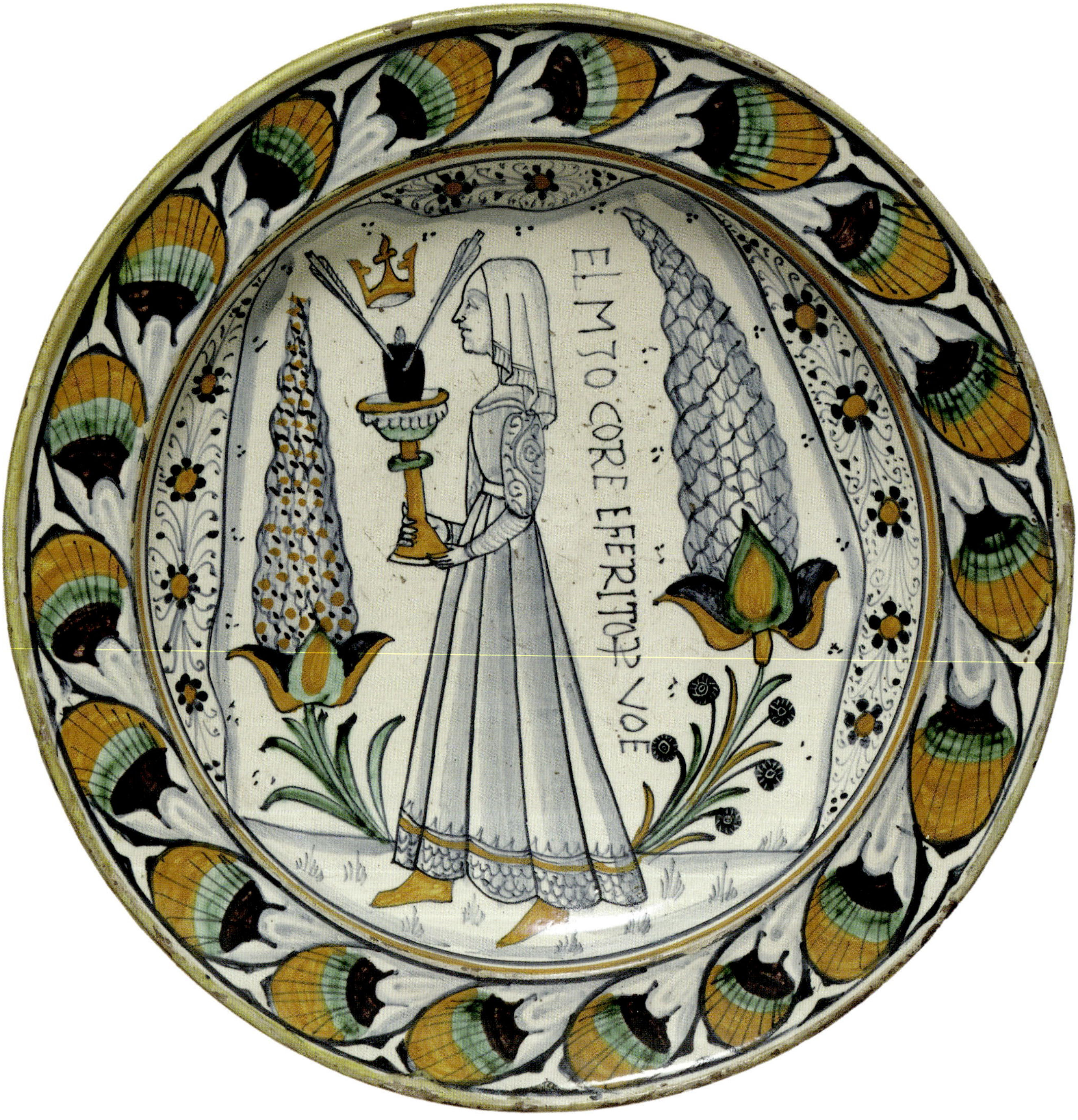

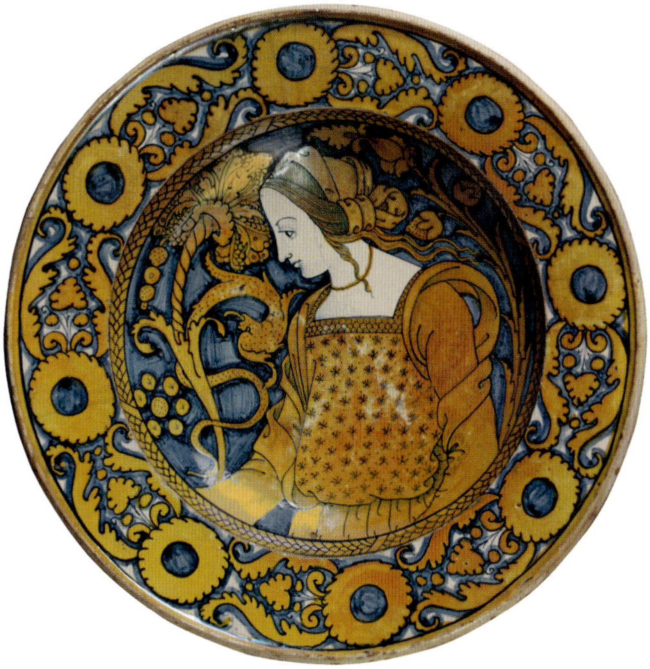

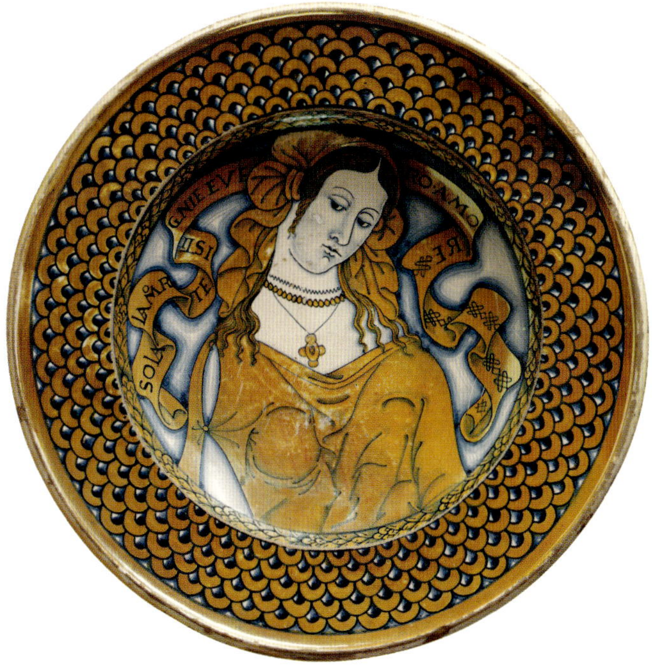

166 Lustred dish with woman and scroll
Inscribed: 'Solo la morte esaurisce il vero amore' ('Only death extinguishes true love')
Deruta, c.1520–40
Diam: 45.5 cm
Salting Bequest V&A: C.2161–1910

167 Delphic Sybil, Hall of the Sybils, detail of ceiling
Bernardino Pinturicchio
Fresco
Borgia apartments, Vatican, 1492–4
© 2012. Photo Scala, Florence

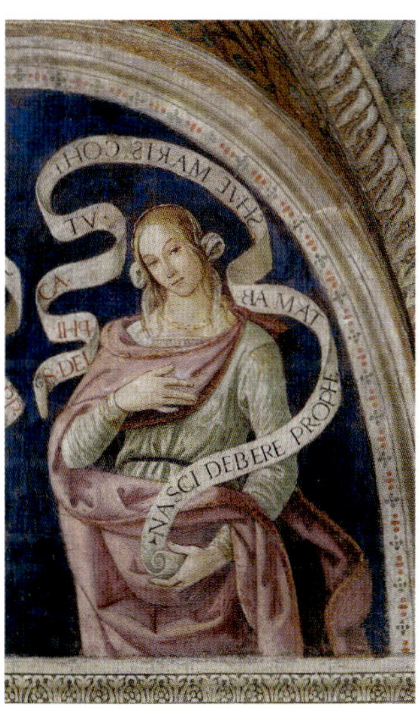

the well of large display dishes, many of them lustred (pl. 165). The Deruta stock includes about five basic types of beauties, examples of which have survived in large numbers. The elegantly dressed women with elaborate head-dresses and jewellery bear a close resemblance to the paintings of the local and celebrated artists Perugino and Pinturicchio (pl. 167).[43] The outlines of the figures were probably transferred to the plate with the aid of stencils, a technique employed by Perugino, who famously used his compositions again and again. The images are accompanied by long, curving scrolls bearing female names or, more frequently, inscriptions, which are often proverbs such as 'Only death extinguishes true love' (pl. 166).

Potteries in the Urbino district also produced large numbers of bowls decorated with busts of women but also, occasionally, of men, from the early 1520s to the 1560s. Their typical iconography features female bust portraits (profile, three-quarter or frontal) accompanied by scrolls with the name followed by *'bella'*, often painted on a blue background (pls 171, 172). An unusual and late example is a dish on low foot of 1559 showing a portrait of 'Francesco di Lorenzo', an elegant man holding in his hand a bunch of wild flowers, perhaps meant as a symbolic gift to a woman (pl. 168).

Paired bust portraits of young men and women, appearing either on the opposite sides of a vase, facing each other, or side by side on dishes, are also known. While the portraits are often standard designs, names were probably added on request. Examples survive of plates with portraits accompanied by scrolls left empty so that the purchaser could have the names added at a later stage (pl. 169).

During a betrothal ceremony in Renaissance Italy, the couple would exchange vows accompanied by a ritual handclasp as a symbol of faith (*'fede'*).[44] The *'fede'* motif of two clasped hands, often found in conjunction with the word 'faith', appears frequently on maiolica plates from the early fifteenth century onwards (pl. 170). It is one of the earliest of all love symbols, dating back to the Roman period, and is also found in the form of Renaissance rings, which were presented during the exchange of vows.[45]

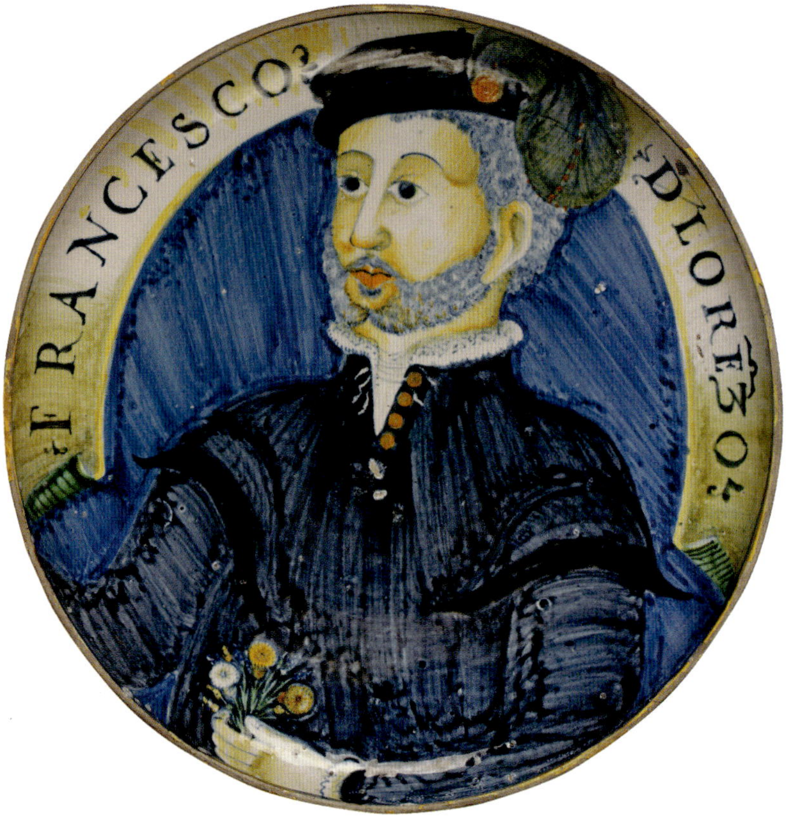

168 Bowl with bust of young man
Urbino, 1559
Diam: 25.5 cm
Salting Bequest V&A: C.2220–1910

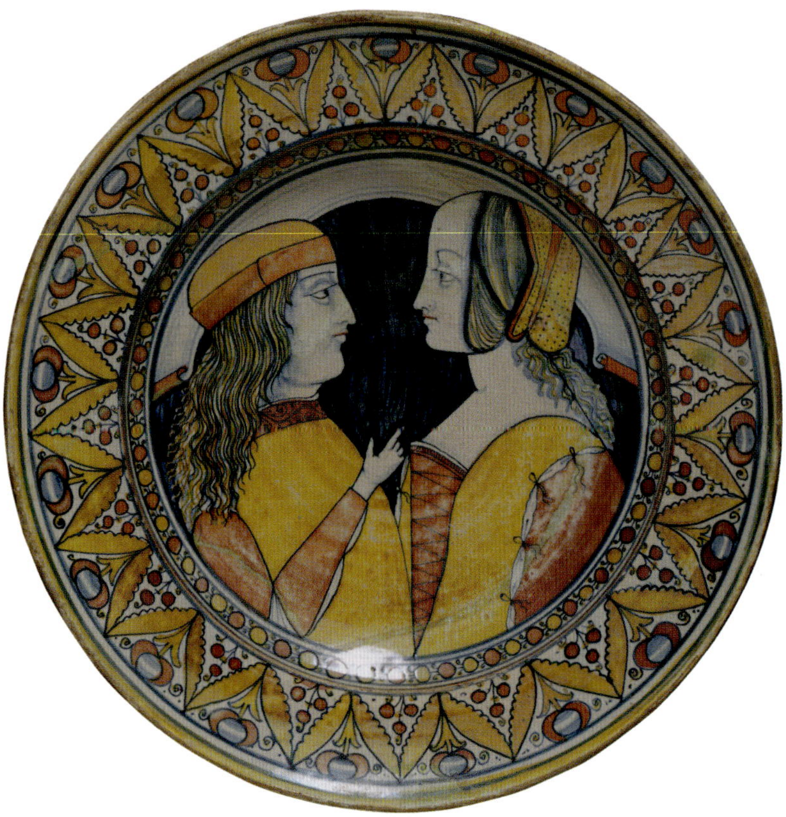

169 Lustred dish with couple facing each other and empty scroll
Probably Gubbio, c.1510
Diam: 37 cm
Salting Bequest V&A: C.2186–1910

170 Lustred dish with clasped hands under a pierced heart
Gubbio or Deruta, c.1510–15
Diam: 29 cm
V&A: 8900–1863

171 (overleaf) Bowl on low foot with bust of Armaciotto Ramazzotti
Urbino district, c.1525
Diam: 22 cm
Salting Bequest V&A: C.2214–1910

172 (overleaf) Bowl on low foot with the bust of a young woman and scroll with 'Silvia Bella' ('Beautiful Silvia')
Urbino district, c.1525
Diam: 23 cm
V&A: 8923–1863

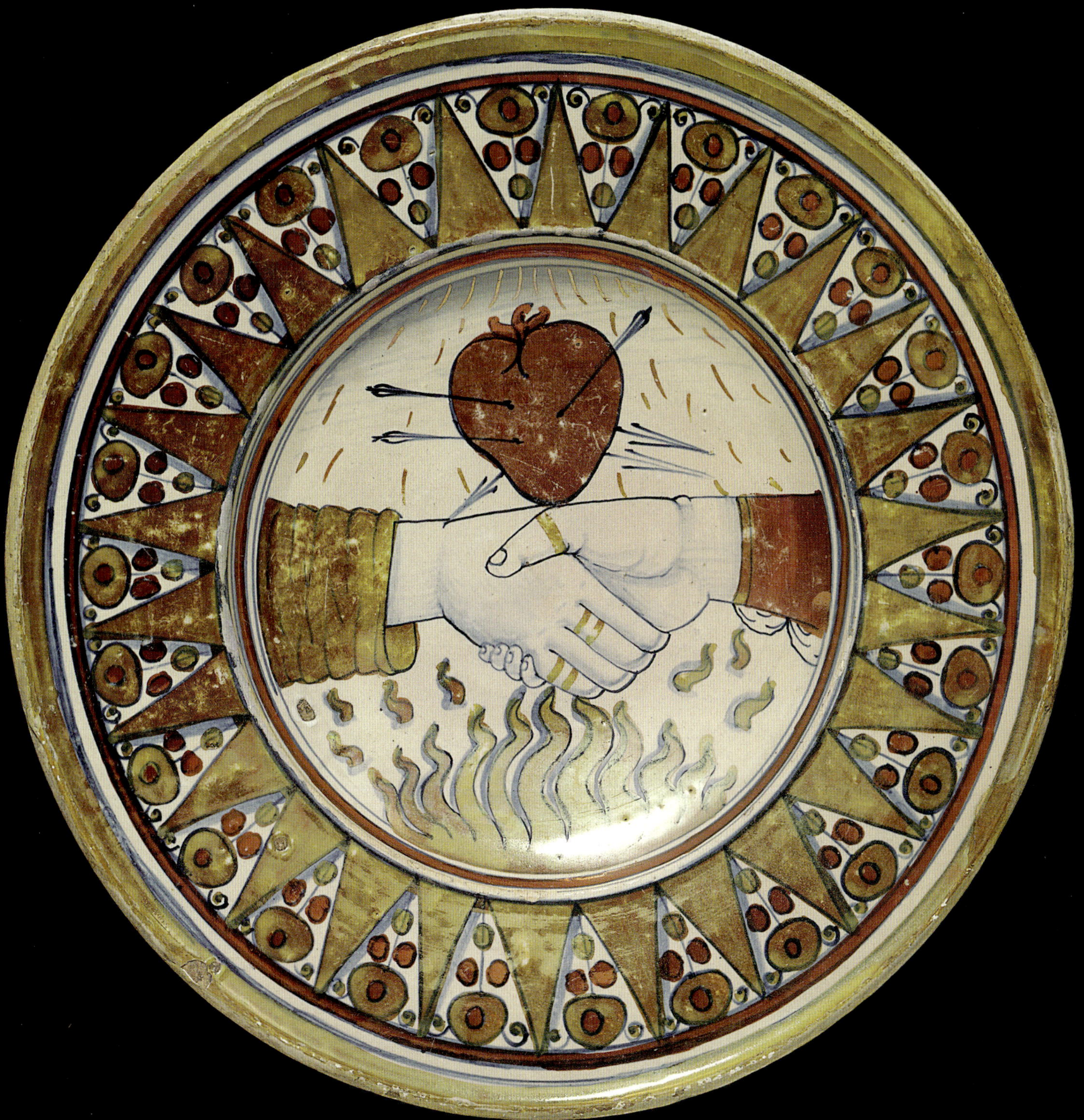

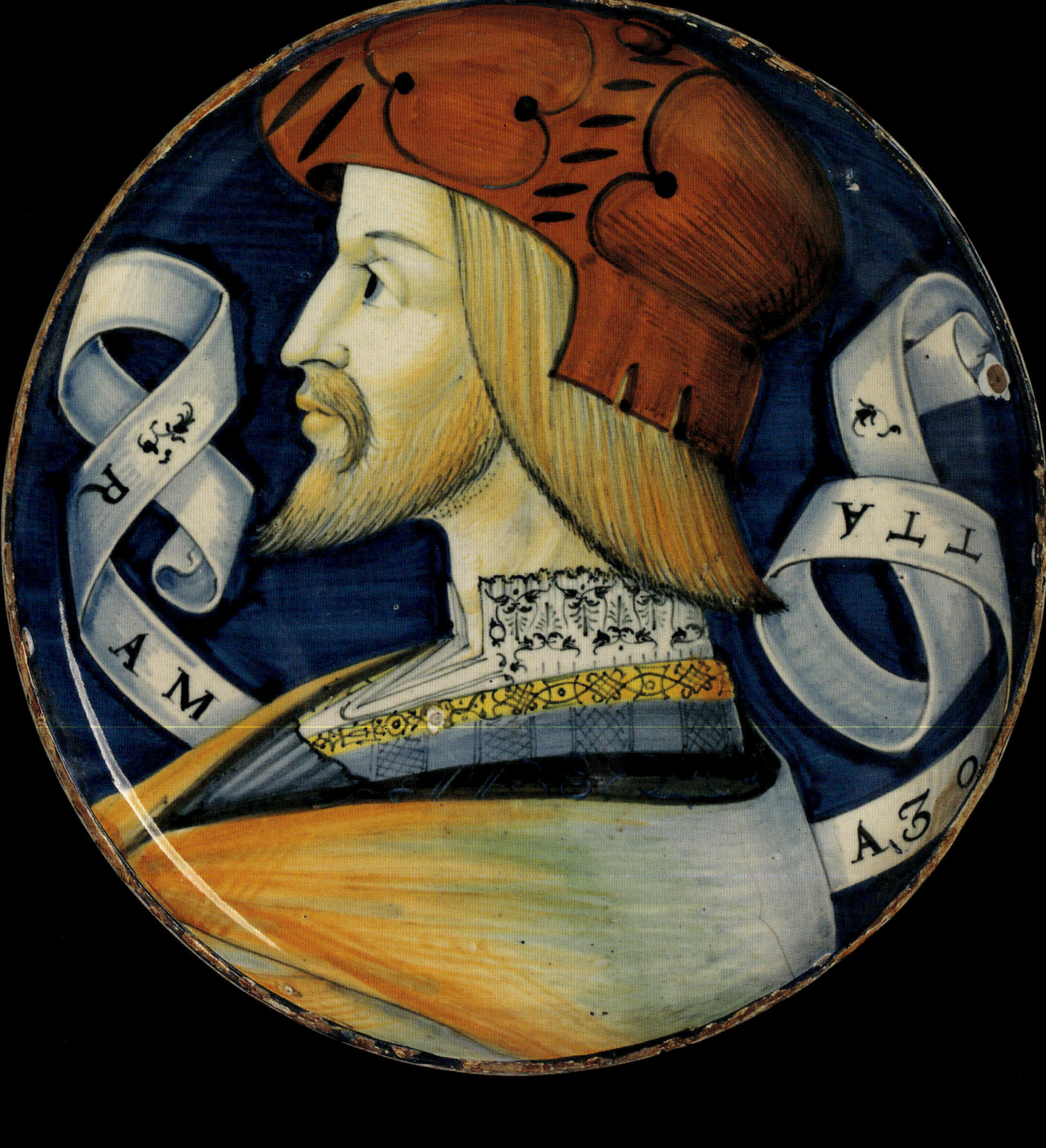
R
AM

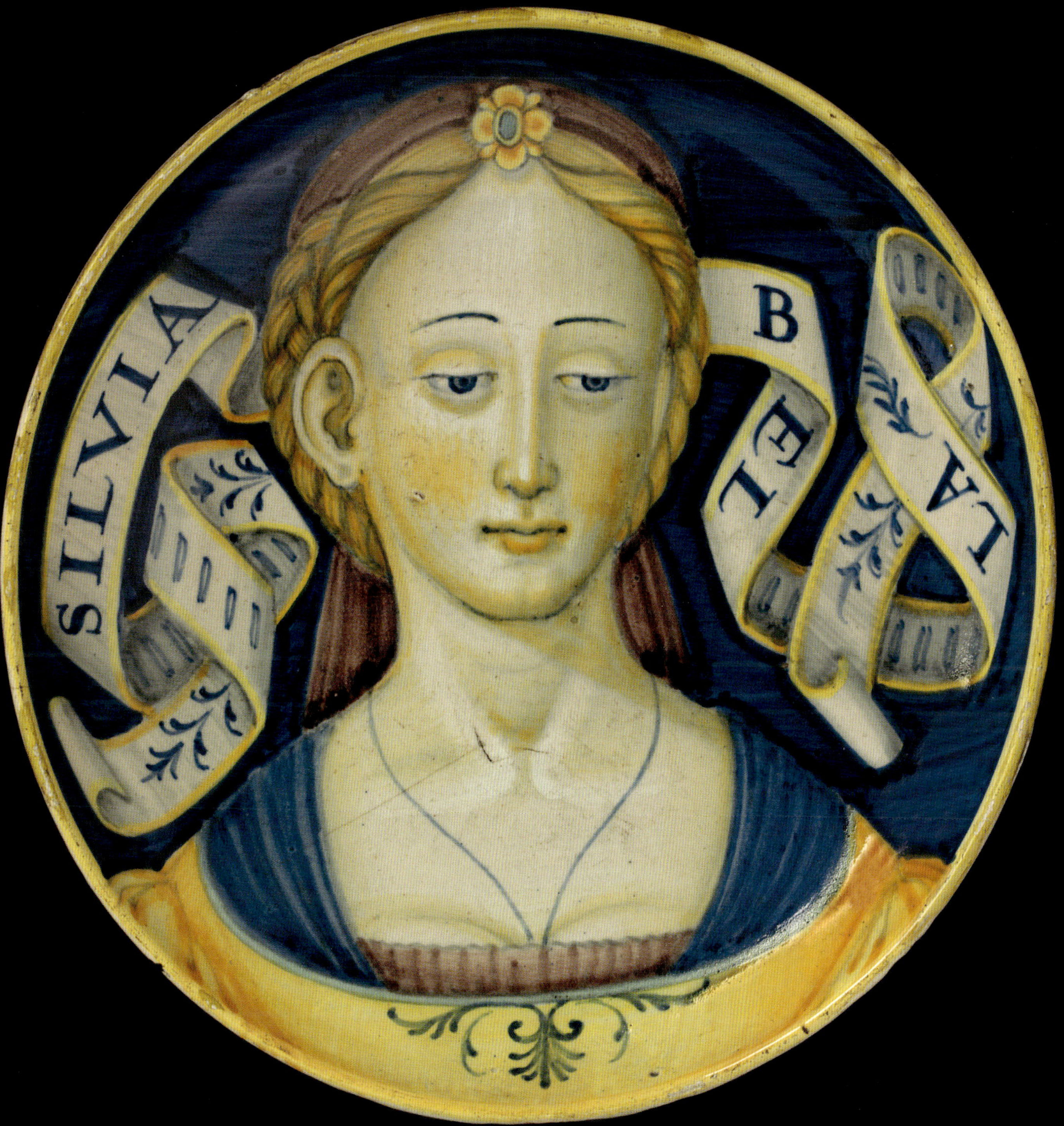
SILVIA
BELLA

173 Two-handled cup with Cupid holding a cup with a pierced heart
Deruta, c.1470–80
H: 24.5 cm
V&A: 525–1865

174 Jug with the Triumph of Cupid
Florence, c.1480
H: 38.5 cm
V&A: 1568–1855

Maiolica vessels with amorous subjects might have been used at banquets celebrating a betrothal or a newly wedded couple. Newly betrothed couples would drink from the same cup and share a celebratory meal with their families. A cup with two handles depicting Cupid holding a chalice with a pierced heart, has an inscription on each side referring to the symbolic giving of the cup as a token of love: 'I give you this, beautiful one' and 'For the love I bear thee in this fine cup' (pl. 173).[46] An extraordinary late fifteenth-century Florentine jug featuring the Triumph of Cupid was probably used in connection with a celebration for a new couple (pl. 174). The flowers painted on the body of the jug are carnations, often associated with love and courtship, while the large size suggests a celebratory function, rather than everyday use.

Among the less common items manufactured in maiolica are some dedicated to women's use, often explicitly made as gifts. A rare moulded maiolica frame made in Montelupo around 1510 would have originally held a small convex mirror of glass or polished steel (pl. 175). It bears a portrait of an ideal beauty and a woman's name, 'Isoretta', followed by 'galante' (gracious). The frame might have had a symbolic meaning: the reflected image of the user will mirror the ideal beauty and virtue depicted on the frame. During the Renaissance beauty was seen as a divine gift and a woman's face was considered a reflection of her virtues, hence the proliferation of mirrors. Objects were invested with particular meanings and mirrors might have played a role in the ritual gift-giving between couples.[47]

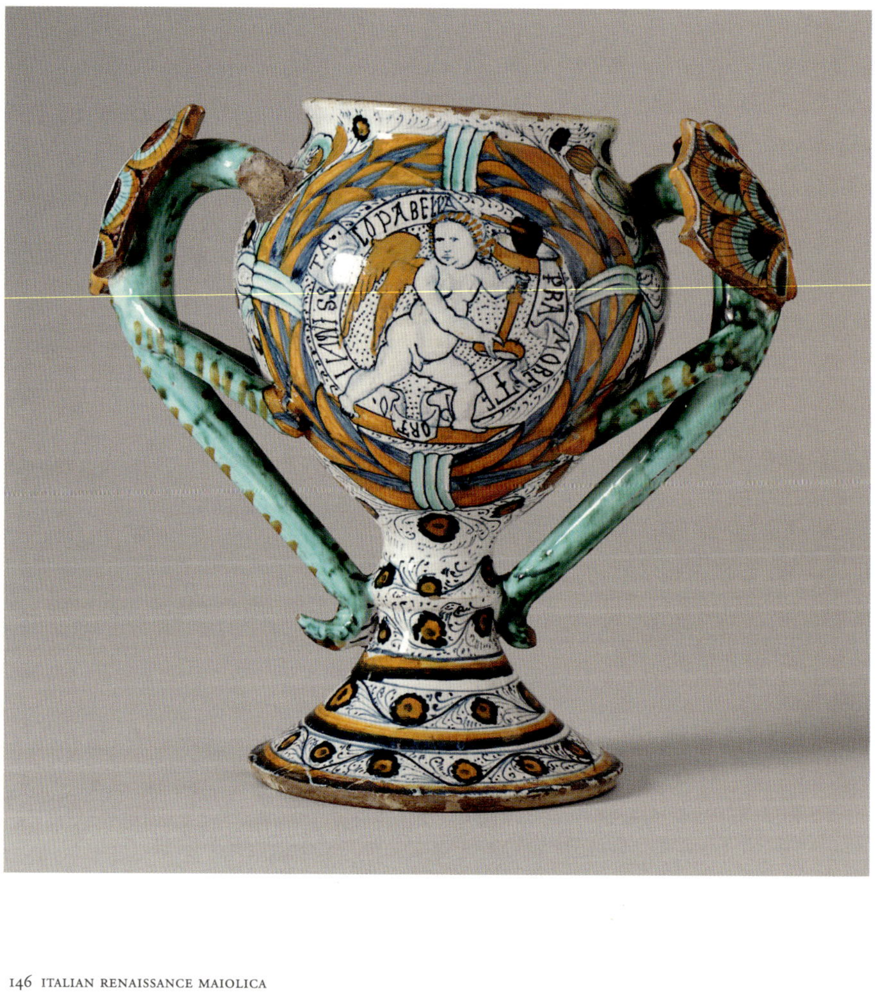

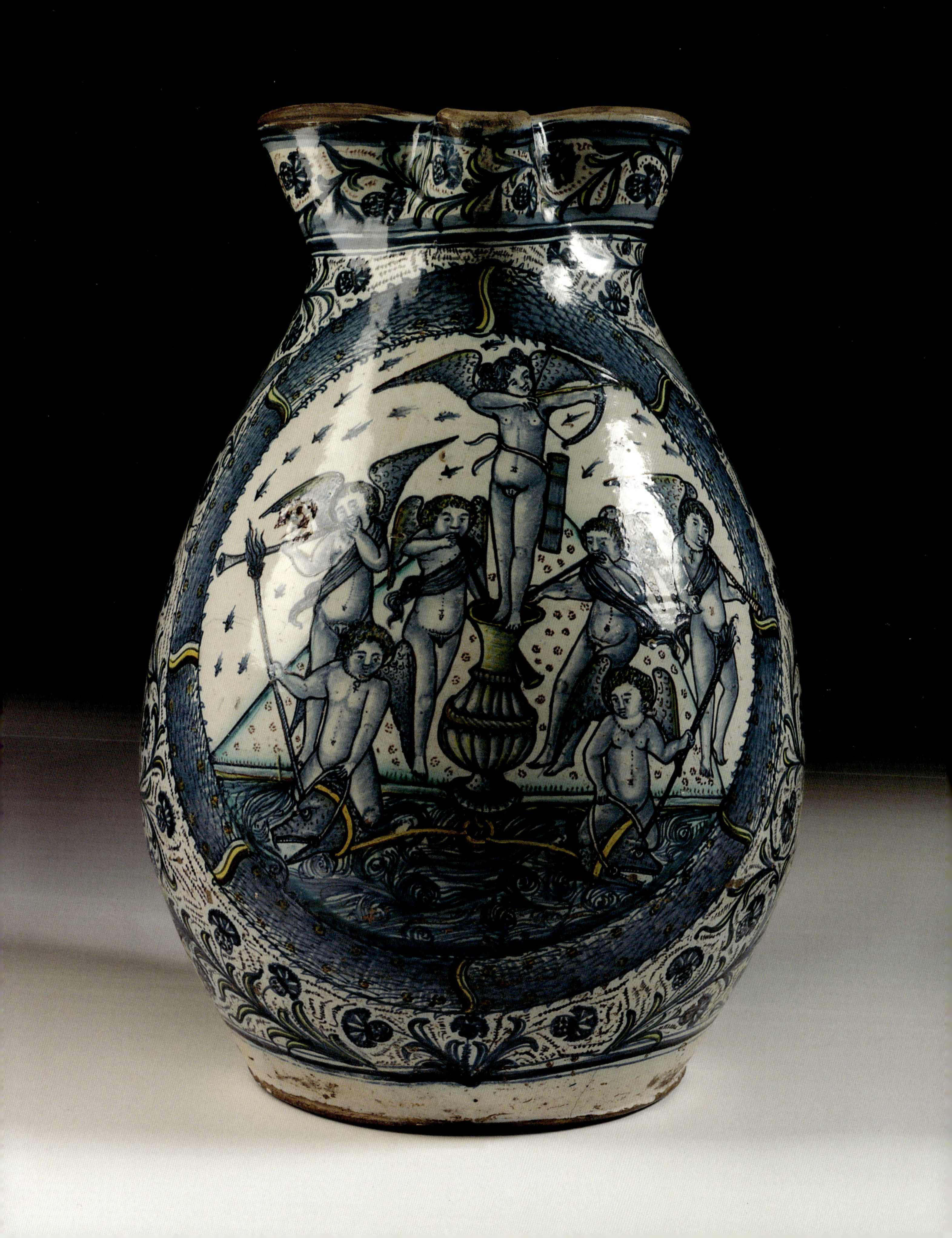

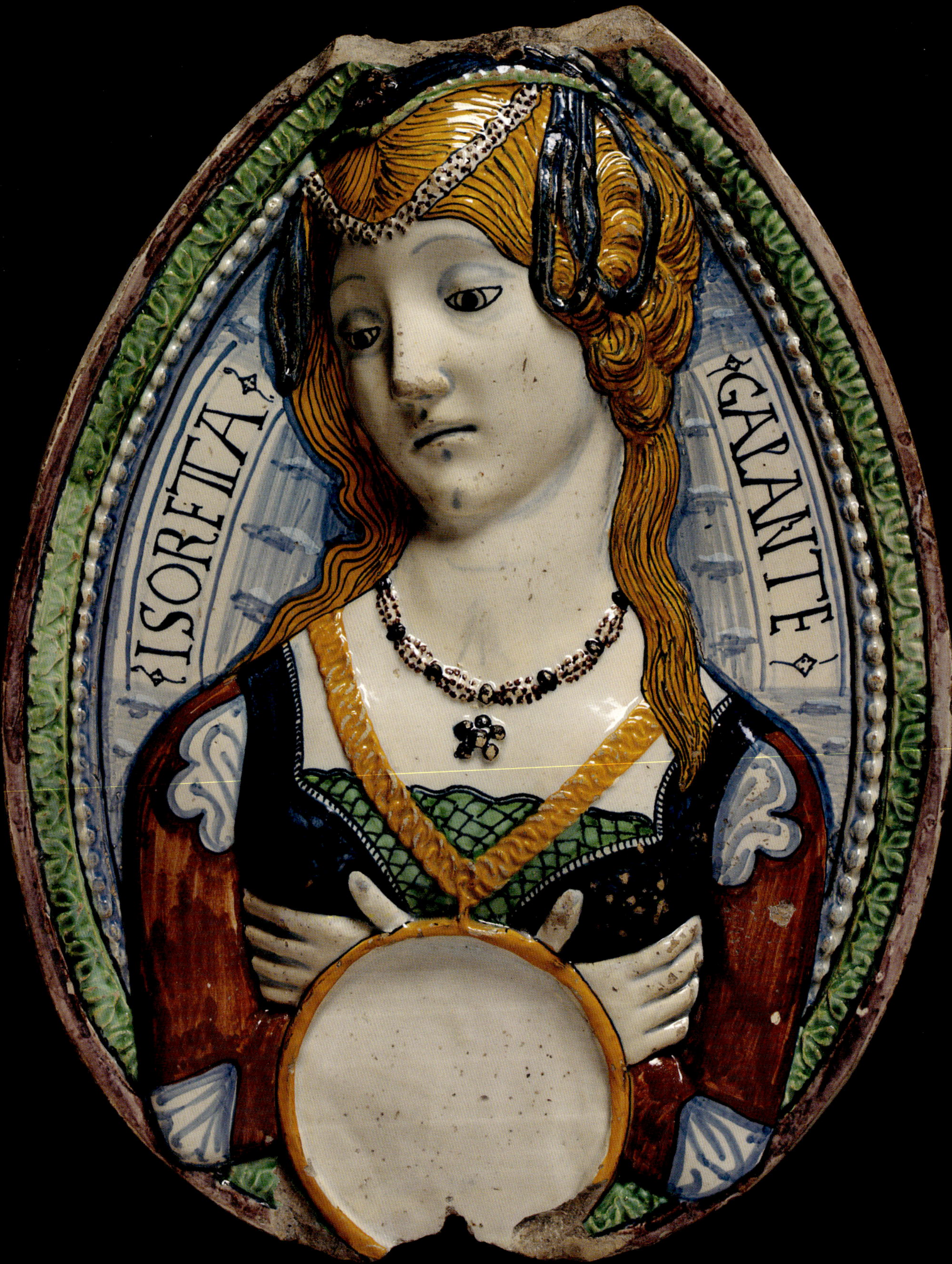
ISORETTA
GALANTE

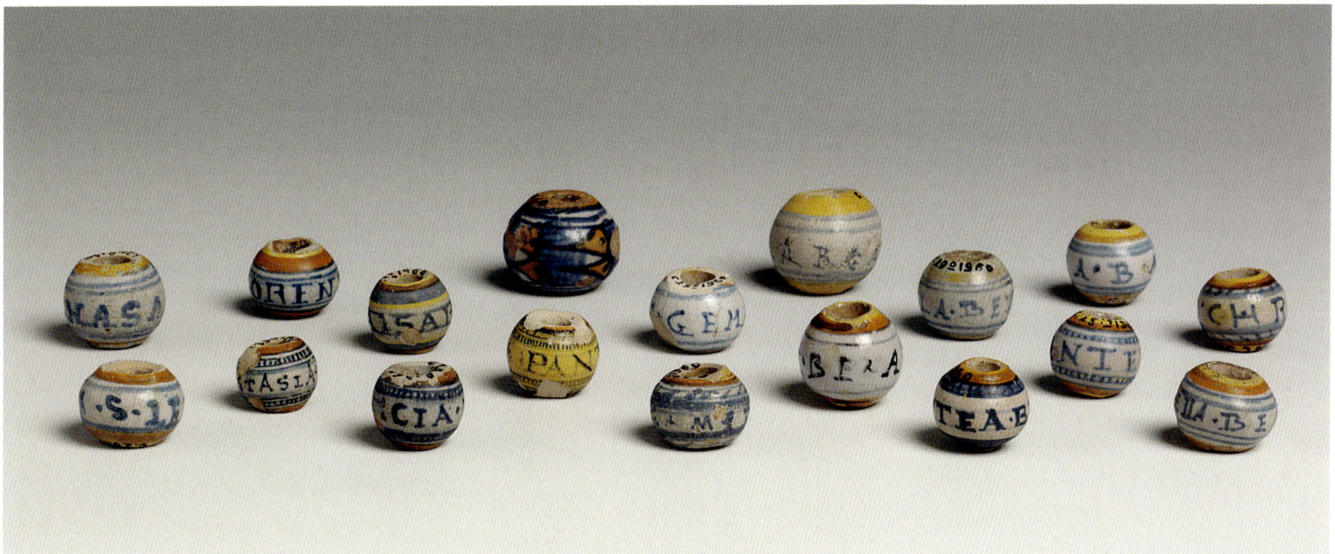

175 Moulded mirror frame with bust of a lady
Inscribed: 'Isoretta Galante' ('gracious Isoretta')
Montelupo, c.1510
H: 37.5 cm, W: 29 cm
Salting Bequest V&A: C.2111–1910

176 Spindle-whorls with women's names
Possibly Deruta, c.1520–60, one dated 1564
Diam: c.2 cm
V&A: C.29–1960

Other little known maiolica objects likely to have been given as love gifts are spindle-whorls. These colourful round beads pierced through the middle, were used as fly-wheels on the lower end of a distaff spindle to help it rotate evenly. Spinning was one of the major domestic activities of women and strongly associated with female virtue. Whorls are found in a wide variety of media from classical antiquity onwards.[48] The majority of the maiolica spindle-whorls which have survived are painted with female names or nick-names followed or preceded by the word *'bella'*. Names were probably inscribed by potters on commission and these whorls might have been presented to women as betrothal or marriage gifts.[49]

Maiolica spindle-whorls were produced in most major pottery centres such as Deruta, Montelupo and Faenza. The V&A has a number of such whorls, including the only known dated example, of 1564. Some carry popular Renaissance names like Margarita and Antonia, others have more unusual names such as Violante and Cassandra, likely to belong to women from the elite (pl. 176).

One of the most remarkable types of maiolica was specifically made for the new mother. So-called accouchement sets, consisting of a footed bowl, a cover/trencher, a smaller bowl and a salt with its lid, would stack together to form one complex object. The purpose of such a set was to serve a nutritious meal (chicken and chicken broth) for the recovering mother while she remained in bed after giving birth. A complete childbirth set, *'scudelle de impagliate'* (bowls for new mothers), of five pieces is illustrated and described by Piccolpasso *c.*1557 (pl. 177):

> You must know then that as to the five pieces of which the *scudella* for a woman in childbed is made up, all five have their function and all five are put together to make a vessel … and the method of making a complete vessel from them is this: the trencher-plate [1] is turned upside down on the footed bowl [1] … the hollow of the bowl (*ongaresca*) [3] goes turned up on the foot of the trencher; the salt-cellar [4] is placed thus upright on the foot of the *ongaresca*, and on it goes the lid [5], as will be seen here. See how all together they make a single vessel like the present one, a thing of no little ingenuity.[50]

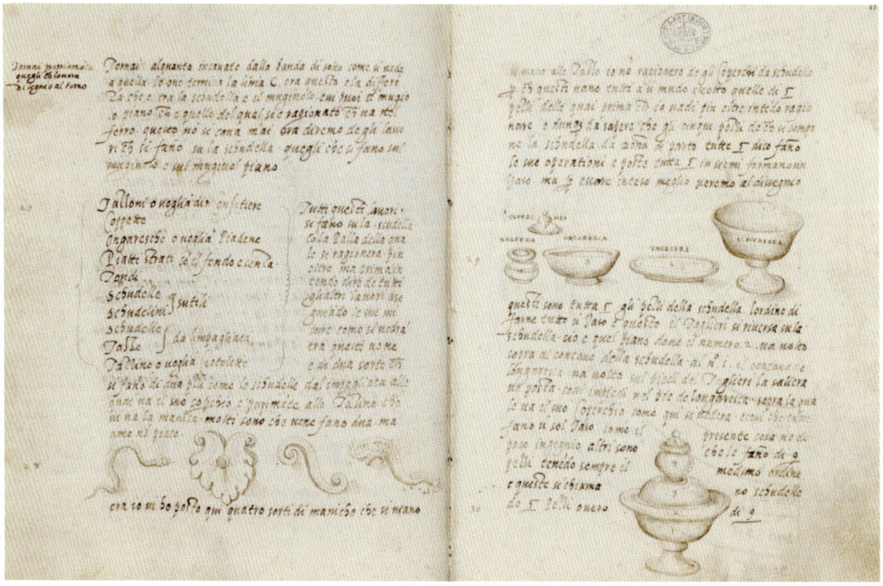

177 Drawing of childbirth set
***The Three Books of the Potter's Art*, fol.13**
Cipriano Piccolpasso
Pen and ink
Castel Durante, 1557
NAL: MSL/1861/7446

These sets were often listed in Renaissance inventories as *'credentini di donne da parto'* or *'scodelle da parto'* (accouchement sets or bowls). The first known reference to childbirth wares dates from 1457, but it is unclear when exactly the custom started.[51] Such early documentary evidence, including the *'scodelle da maiolicha di donne da parto'* listed in the kitchen of a Florentine household in 1482, probably refers to Spanish lustreware imports.[52] At least one known example bears the name of the woman meant to receive it.[53]

No complete set is known, but two or three pieces from different sets have survived together. These are decorated with realistic scenes of childbirth, with the woman giving birth surrounded by midwives and other female attendants. Other scenes show the new mother in bed being served a broth, while the newborn child is washed or swaddled. At a time when procreation was seen as one of the most important duties of women and when childbirth was a very risky event, such scenes of successful birth in a comfortable setting were deemed particularly appropriate for contemplation by expectant mothers, and there is evidence that accouchement sets were actually acquired some time before the birth of a child.[54] After the birth these sets were used by the mother and subsequently kept, probably as a treasured memento, but also to be used again for future births and new generations of mothers. An accouchement bowl, decorated with narrative scenes and grotesques, is listed in the inventories of the Urbino dukes, while some surviving examples show armorials, including those of German nobility.[55]

Istoriato examples were made from the 1520s, some decorated by well-known pottery painters. A fine matching childbirth bowl and trencher plate in the V&A, painted by Nicola da Urbino, are all that is left of what must have been a prized set. The cover shows a women giving birth, supported by a midwife and two female helpers, while an astrologer is casting the horoscope of the child (pl. 179).

The fragmentary cover of another childbirth bowl shows the birth of Hercules, as described in Ovid's *Metamorphoses* (pl. 178). Here this mythological subject is depicted as a contemporary scene, illustrating the actual moment of birth and giving us a glimpse into this most intimate aspect of Renaissance life.[56]

178 Trencher from an accouchement set with the Birth of Hercules
Probably Urbino, c.1525
Diam: 28 cm
V&A: C.755–1925

179 Broth bowl and trencher from an accouchement set with a mother giving birth and an astrologer
Nicola da Urbino
Urbino, 1533–8
H: 9.8 cm, Diam: 17.9 cm
Salting Bequest V&A: C.2258–1910

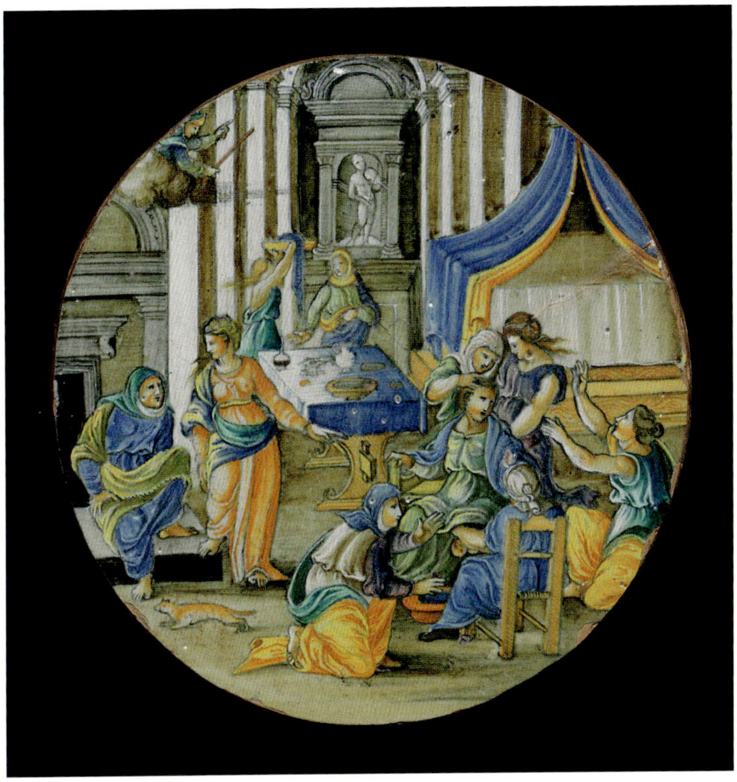

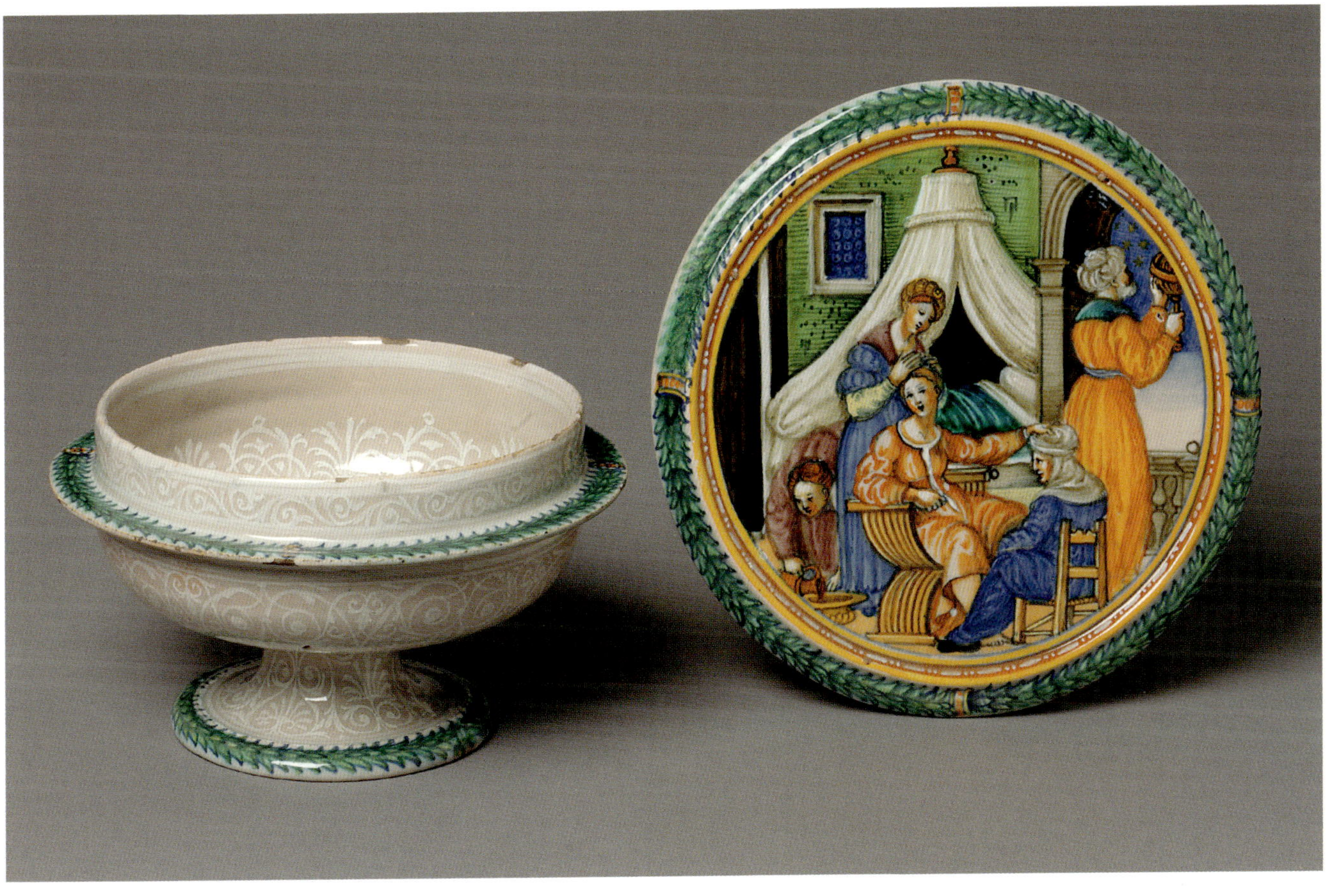

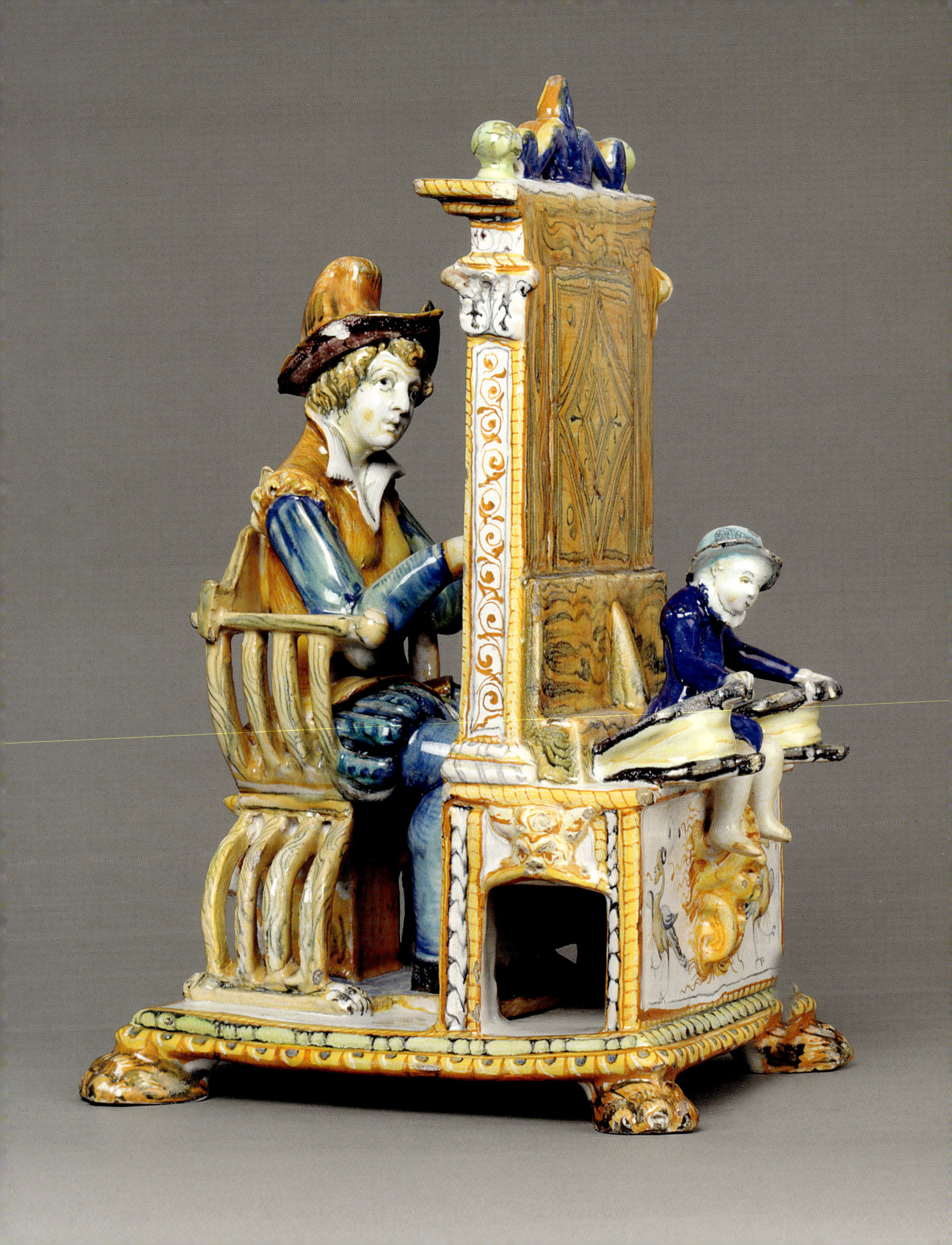

Inkstands

180 Inkstand with man playing an organ
Patanazzi family workshop
Urbino, c.1580
H: 38 cm
V&A: 8400–1863

Renaissance paintings showing scholars and collectors in their studies often include beautiful inkstands, essential adjuncts of the art of writing (pl. 181). Inkstands, usually comprising a container for ink and a compartment for quill pens and other writing equipment, were used by scholars, businessmen and those in charge of household accounts. They were essentially functional objects, but, in a society where only a minority of the population could read or write, they were also a sign of the owner's literacy and erudition.

Decorative inkstands that went beyond the merely utilitarian were created to respond to the demand of urban elites for small domestic art objects to use and display in the Renaissance home. Inkstands were made of many different metals including iron, lead, pewter and copper. Bronze inkstands imitating classical sculptures were created by Renaissance sculptors such as Riccio and Severo da Ravenna, while art patrons such as Isabella d'Este or the Cardinal Francesco Gonzaga also enjoyed silver inkstands in their studies.[57] These metal shapes were also copied in relatively inexpensive materials such as glass and maiolica.

The first maiolica inkstands recorded in Italy were those imported from Spain for the use of Florentine families in the first half of the fifteenth century, and were probably lustred.[58] Italian potters started producing inkstands probably from the second half of the fifteenth century. From contemporary inventories, we know that maiolica inkstands were usually kept in the *scrittoio* or *studiolo* (study). During the Renaissance the study was an important space for demonstrating the owner's sophistication and education. Reflecting their position in this prestigious part of the house, maiolica inkstands could in some instances constitute extraordinary three-dimensional figural compositions, effectively desktop sculptures.

The earliest known maiolica inkstands often comprised a rectangular base with a round receptacle for ink, other containers for writing tools and a socket for a candle – handy for writing by candlelight during the hours of darkness but also useful for sealing letters with wax. The base was often surmounted by sculptural figures. Among the earliest examples known are some made in northern Italy in lead-glazed earthenware

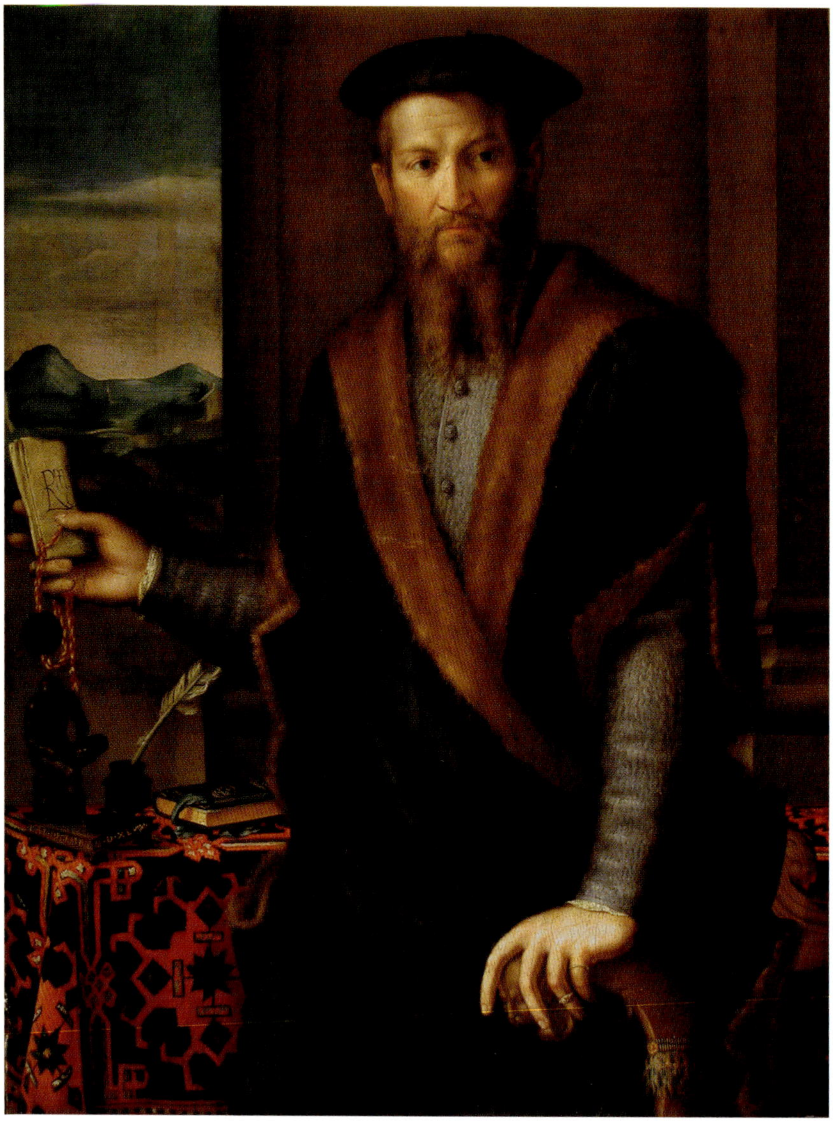

181 Cardinal Antonio Pucci
Pierfrancesco Foschi
Oil on canvas
Florence, 1540
Galleria Corsini, Florence
Courtesy of Galleria Corsini

182 Inkstand with St George killing the dragon
Ferrara, c.1480
H: 38.5 cm
V&A: 1207–1864

with incised and stamped decoration. The inkstand shown in pl. 182 features St George killing the dragon and was made around 1480. The shape imitates small bronze sculptures, which enjoyed high status as a revival of a classical shape. The inkstand is covered with a shiny purple manganese glaze to evoke metal prototypes. Other examples survive, all slightly different. Demand for this kind of sophisticated art object, partly functional, partly decorative, must have been high.[59] Inkstands such as this one were built up from moulded parts, hence the existence of similar or almost identical models.[60]

The Nativity is the subject of the largest surviving group of inkstands, known from more than 20 examples. All have a large, circular container surrounded or surmounted by the Virgin and St Joseph, the baby Jesus and animals in the stable (pl. 183). Around the container is an inscription celebrating the birth of Jesus: 'And the Word was made Flesh from the Virgin Mary'. The figures are supported by dogs, as in this example, or more usually by lions. A few Nativity examples bear the name of the maker, Giovanni

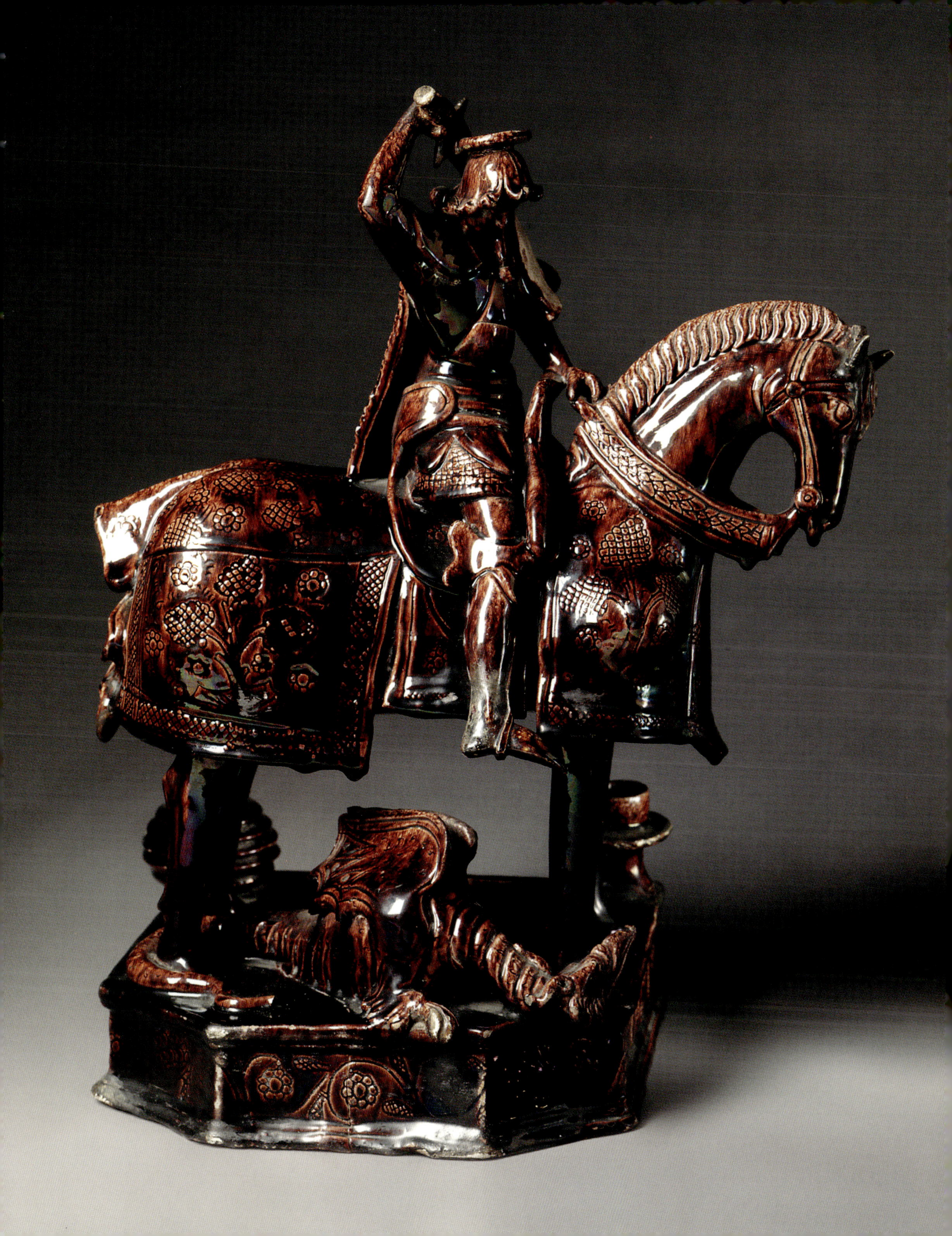

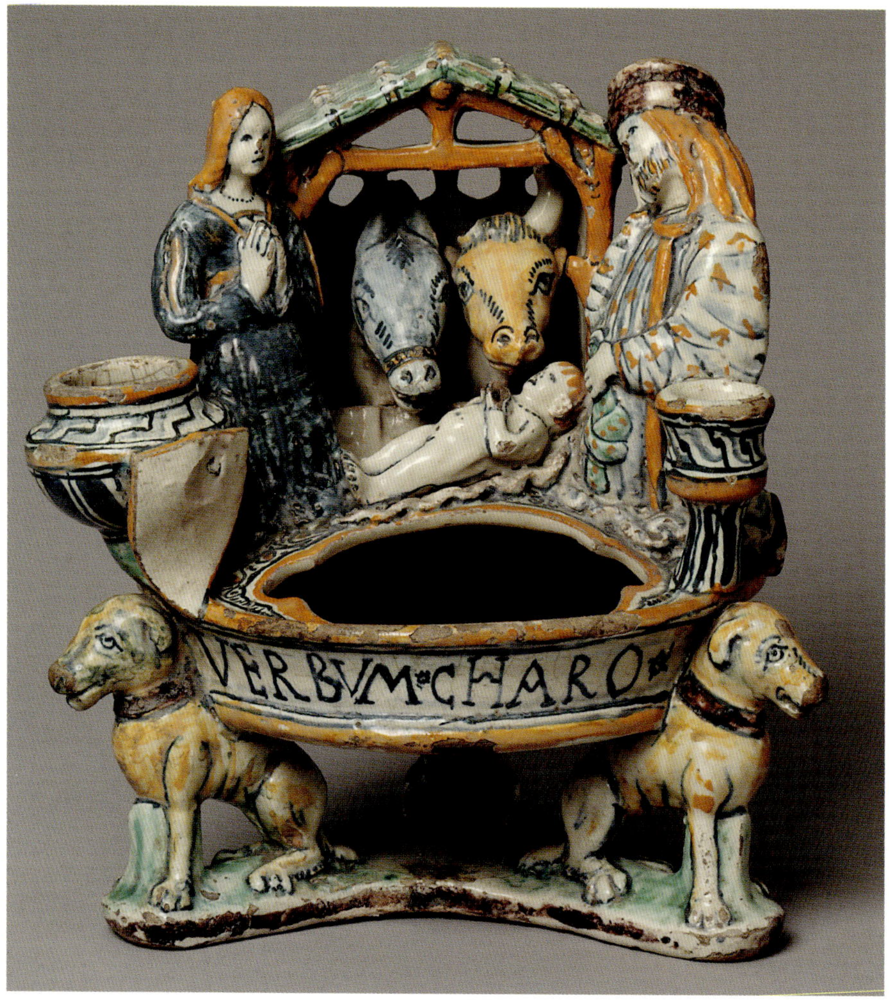

183 Inkstand with nativity scene
Giovanni di Nicola Manzoni
Colle Val d'Elsa, c.1510
H: 24.5 cm
V&A: 396–1889

di Nicola Manzoni, now thought to have been active in Colle Val d'Elsa, near Siena.[61] These inkstands are usually dated between 1509 and 1516.

The frequency of dates on inkstands might mean that they were often produced to mark special occasions or given as gifts.[62] They were certainly treasured possessions. Just like their metal prototypes, maiolica inkstands often bear coats of arms or have space for a coat of arms left blank: this would allow a client to choose a particular inkstand from those in stock and have the arms added, painted in non-fired colours to order.

During the second half of the sixteenth century Faenza potteries produced fashionable inkstands decorated solely in white. The inventory of the leading Faenza potter Virgiliotto Calamelli in 1556 lists several inkstands, including some in the shape of animals (lions and asses) as well as some *'calamari bianchi'* (white inkstands).[63]

In the last quarter of the sixteenth century, extraordinary sculptural inkstands decorated with grotesques were one of the specialities of Urbino workshops. The Patanazzi family was probably the main producer.[64] Such inkstands were made of several parts. In an example dated 1584 the base sits on lion's paws (now metal replacements of the ceramic originals) and there are several drawers and compartments (pl. 184). One of these is circular to contain an inkwell, others have painted on the base the items that they are meant to contain: quill pens, penknives, set-squares, scissors, compasses and signet rings. Originally, a detachable sculptural cover would have hidden the compartments below. With writing implements stowed in drawers the inkstand would appear purely sculptural. The base is painted with the four Evangelists busy writing their Gospels, an appropriate theme for an inkstand which might have belonged to a cleric. The upper part was probably formed of a sculptural group with a religious subject.

There is certainly evidence for the use of such maiolica inkstands by eminent religious figures. The inventory of Cardinal Ferdinando de' Medici made between 1571 and 1587 lists around 20 ceramic inkstands of different shapes and decoration, including some formed of seven pieces. In 1575 he presented a fellow cleric with a maiolica inkwell made in Urbino by Flaminio Fontana in the form of a casket in seven sections.[65]

Religious institutions might order inkstands on occasion. The workshop of Maestro Giorgio of Gubbio is documented to have supplied inkstands to monasteries.[66] Urbino-made inkstands were not always of religious subjects: surviving examples include musicians playing to diners, Leda and the Swan and fishermen on a boat. Tastes might run to both types of subject. The inventory of the dukes of Urbino of 1609 lists numerous inkstands decorated with religious or secular figures including a Dead Christ with Angels, a shepherd with sheep and Orpheus surrounded by animals.[67]

A delightful sculptural group featuring a young man playing an organ marked 'Urbino' was most likely originally intended as an inkstand (pl. 180). The now empty compartment below the organ, which is missing a drawer, was probably where the inkwell and writing instruments were stored.[68]

Elaborate architectural and sculptural inkstands were one of the most ambitious products of Renaissance potteries and show an inventiveness of design rarely matched. They continued in fashion, as dated examples show, into the seventeenth century.

184 Inkstand with drawer and lion's feet
Patanazzi family workshop
Urbino, 1584
H: 16.5 cm
V&A: 1681–1855

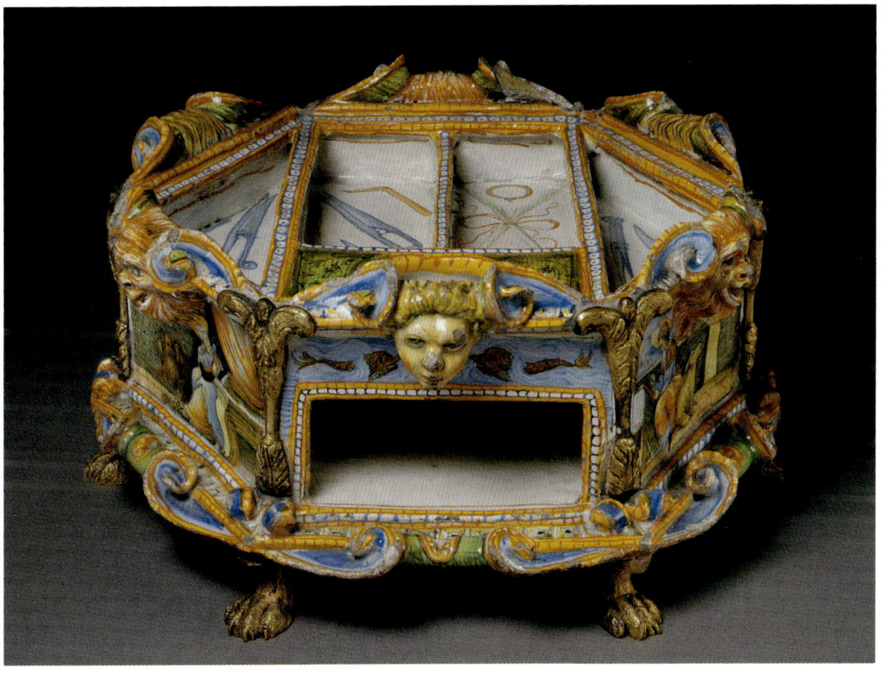

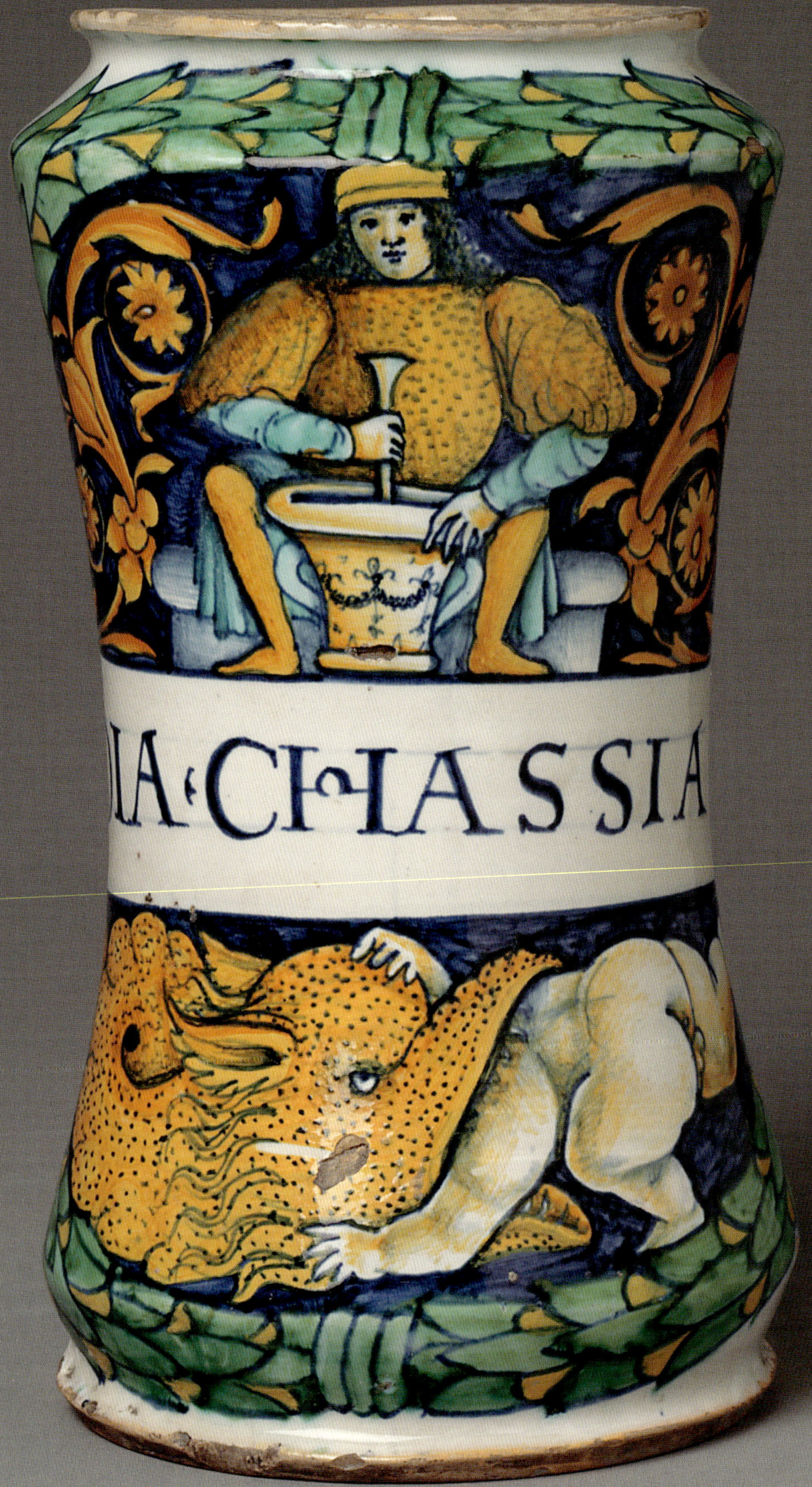
DIA·CHASSIA

Maiolica for Pharmacies

185 Drug jar (*albarello*) for electuary of Cassia with apothecary
Probably Deruta, c.1510
H: 22.4 cm
Salting Bequest
V&A: C.2093–1910

The emergence of pharmacies in Italy was driven by the establishment of apothecaries' guilds in the middle of the thirteenth century and, later, by the growing number and importance of hospitals.[69] Pharmacies required a large number of containers to store an ever-growing number of remedies. These needed to be impermeable to liquids, and easy to clean as well as decorative: maiolica proved an ideal material for such containers.

Drug jar production was a major source of income for potters and was a significant factor in the development of the pottery industry in Italy.[70] Records of large maiolica orders from court or institutional pharmacies and the dispensaries of monastic orders show that sets often comprised several hundred jars; however, have only rarely significant numbers of Renaissance drug jars from the same series remained together. Examples are series from the pharmacy of Roccavaldina in Sicily, the Marian sanctuary at Loreto in the Marches, and the Jesuit pharmacy at Novellara in Emilia Romagna.[71]

Contemporary images of Renaissance pharmacies always show drug jars prominently displayed on the shelves. The beautiful containers highlighted the importance and value of the remedies sold, and their uniformity promoted the brand reputation of the particular pharmacy. Pharmacies were centres of social and cultural importance, places for social interaction, and their richly furnished interiors and eye-catching rows of jars contributed to their economic success. Mid-fifteenth-century 'oak-leaf' drug jars can be seen on the shelves of an apothecary's shop in an illustration in a copy of *The Canon of Medicine* by the eleventh-century Persian polymath Avicenna, dated around 1440 (pl. 186). The *Canon* was an important medical text during the Middle Ages and the Renaissance, used widely at universities throughout Europe.

The shape of drug jars varied, but the essential distinction was between containers designed to hold solids and those intended for liquids. The development of shapes of drug jars also varied according to locality. For instance, spherical jars, '*bocce*', were predominantly a Venetian speciality.

The earliest and most common type of vessel for solids was a cylindrical jar with a large mouth to facilitate the extraction of its contents with a spoon or other utensil,

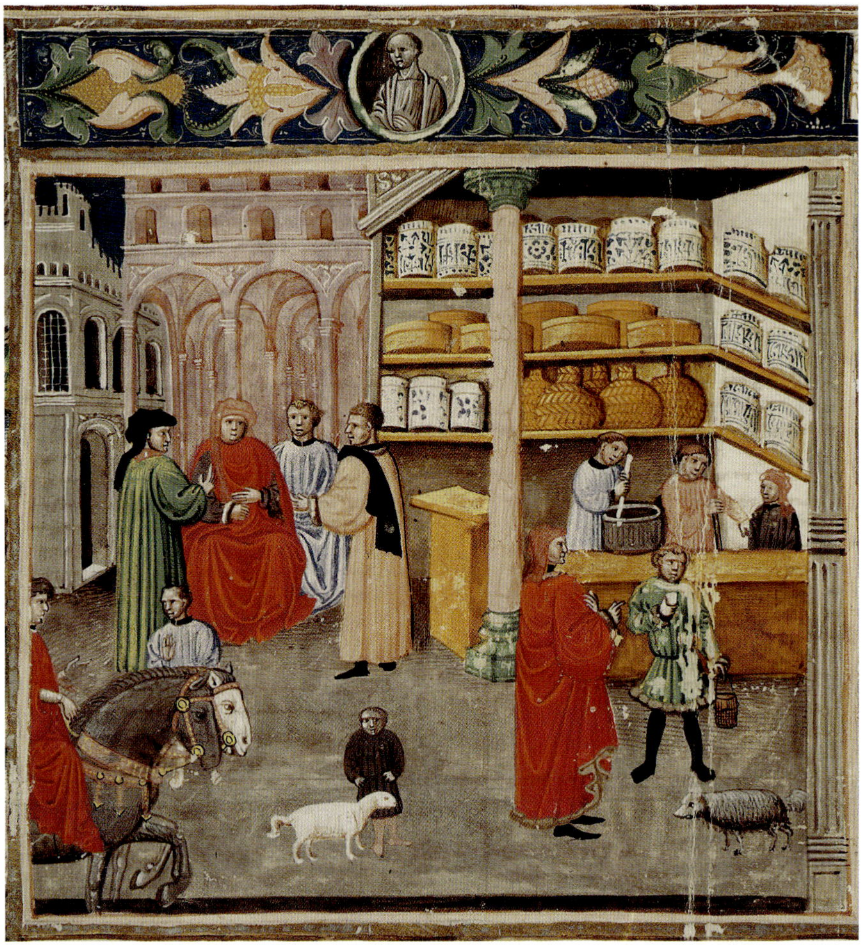

186 Apothecary's shop
***The Canon of Medicine* (detail)**
Avicenna
c.1440
Bologna University Library.
© 2012. Photo Scala, Florence

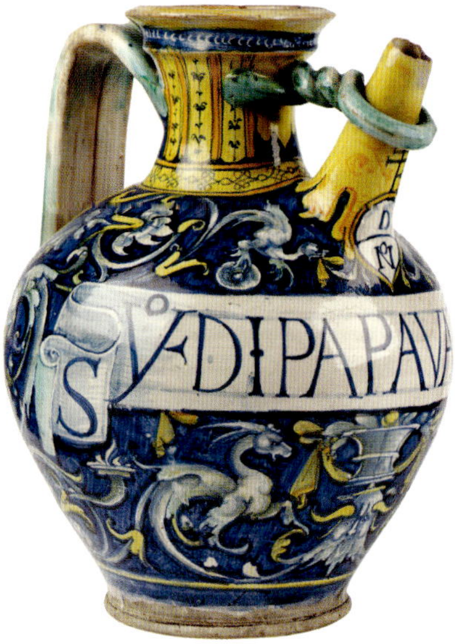

187 Spouted jar for poppy syrup
Siena, 1500–15
H: 24 cm
Salting Bequest V&A: C.2287–1910

widely known in Italy as an *'albarello'* (pl. 185). Around 1557 Piccolpasso illustrates an *albarello* and comments:

> I don't find myself that this vessel goes by any other name among the Italian master potters than that of *albarello*, nor is it called differently in apothecaries' shops. It is regularly made all in a single piece and has various sizes.

This type of vessel originated in the Middle East. Syrian *albarelli* were imported into Europe before European versions were produced in Spain and Italy. Spanish lustreware versions were popular in Italy and appear in Tuscan paintings of the fifteenth century. Italian orders for small, medium and large *alberelli da speziali* (apothecary jars) from Valencia are recorded as early as 1394.[72] Italian potters produced similar jars in quantities from the last few decades of the fifteenth century onwards.

A flanged rim allowed a parchment or similar cover to be secured with a string. During the sixteenth century *albarelli* were sometimes made with matching ceramic lids. Some *albarelli* have slightly waisted bodies to assist taking the jars off the shelf when they were lined up in close-packed rows.

Apothecaries' *albarelli* would contain a wide variety of medical remedies including ointments, electuaries, lozenges and pills. They were also widely used for domestic

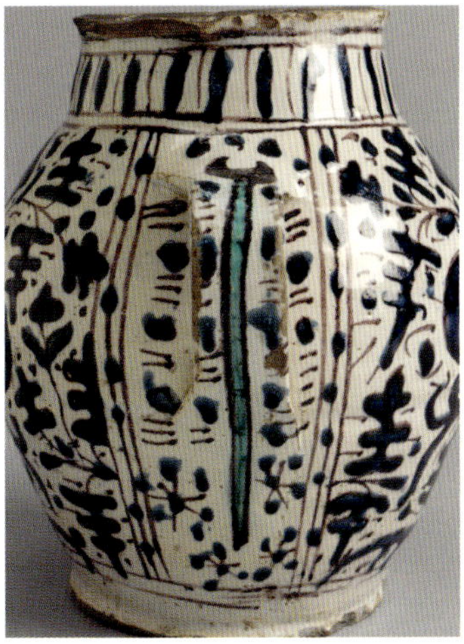

188 Drug jar (detail)
The crutch was the emblem of the Hospital of Santa Maria Nuova, Florence
Salting Bequest V&A: C.2063–1910

189 Group of drug jars
Workshop of Maso and Miniato di Domenico or Giunta di Tugio
Florence, 1420s
H: 12.5 cm; 21 cm; 21 cm; 13 cm
V&A: 1124–1904; 386–1889; Salting Bequest: C.2063–1910; 1139–1904

purposes, to store a variety of foods such as dried fruit and herbs, roots, seeds and even dried bones. They were essentially multipurpose containers and, as we can see from fifteenth-century paintings, also used as flower vases.

Liquid drugs such as medicinal waters, oils or syrups were stored in jars or bottles. Wet-drug jars had a handle, a small cylindrical neck and a narrow spout for controlling the quantity of liquid poured. Globular bottles, often quite large, would be handled by their long, narrow neck. On some of the wet-drug jars from the fifteenth and early sixteenth century, the potter has added a strip of clay joining the spout to the body of the jar, probably to provide additional support for this vulnerable area (pl. 187).

Hospitals commissioned very large quantities of ware for their pharmacies. One of the earliest as well as largest documented commissions was for the main Florentine hospital, Santa Maria Nuova. Fitting out a new pharmacy in the 1420s it ordered thousands of drug jars from the workshops of Maso and Miniato di Domenico and Giunta di Tugio, both in Florence.[73] Drug jars of different sizes with 'oak-leaf' decoration are thought to be part of these commissions as they bear the emblem of the hospital, a crutch, under the handles (pl. 188). Most of these jars are two-handled globular vases (pl. 189). Records show that the hospital ordered replacement jars frequently during the sixteenth century.[74] Examples of the same type of jar bearing a ladder (*scala*) surmounted by a cross, the badge of the Hospital of Santa Maria della Scala in Siena, are also known.[75] The hospital had branches outside Siena, including one in Florence, and it is not certain for which city the jars were produced.[76]

None of the 'oak-leaf' jars bears an inscription of its contents. The custom of inscribing a drug's name on a jar only became established in the last quarter of the fifteenth century. An early exception from the beginning of the fifteenth century is a fragmentary wet-drug jar intended to contain syrup of amber.[77] Where jars did carry the name of their intended contents it was painted on a white horizontal band imitating the labels made of paper or parchment that apothecaries probably glued

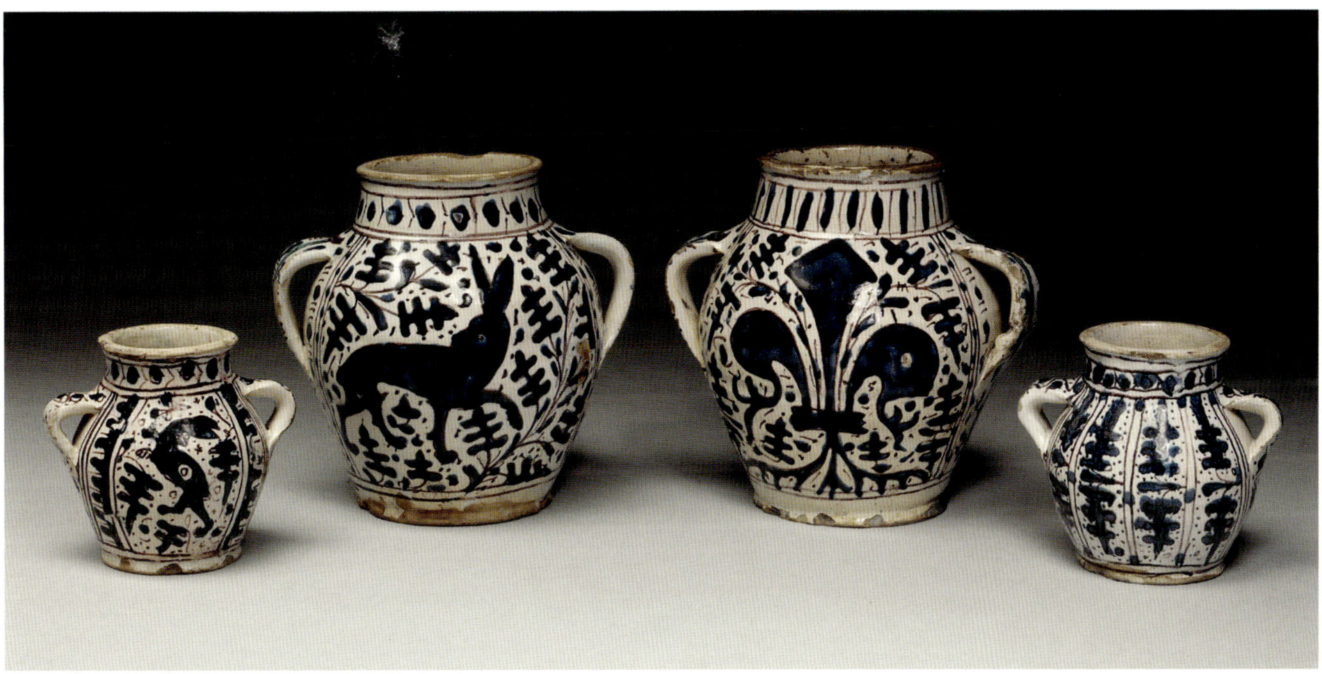

190 Drug jar for ammonium chloride from Moor's head set
Deruta, 1501
H: 32 cm
V&A: C.132–1931

onto their vessels. Inscriptions on the jars were often written in Latin in bold capitals or Gothic script. Names of drugs are often abbreviated and almost incomprehensible to any but an apothecary; errors in spelling also sometimes occur. It is likely that apothecaries specified the drug names to the potters, perhaps through written lists of remedies (*ricettari*).[78]

From the beginning of the sixteenth century, the name of the contents, and the emblem of the pharmacy owning the jar, often a religious institution, became standard elements of drug jar decoration throughout Italy. Symbols of pharmacies normally comprised an emblem, a coat of arms or other image in combination with a monogram. The names of the pharmacies never appear and the cryptic emblems and monograms are unfortunately often difficult to identify.

A large *albarello* of 1501 is one of the earliest known dated examples of a pharmacy jar (pl. 190). Around the front of the body a cartouche displays in capital letters the name of the drug: *sal ammoniac[um]* (ammonium chloride). Just below, the device of the pharmacy, a moor's head, is prominently displayed in a roundel. A monogram which can be read as 'PAM', 'PAMQ' or 'PAQ' is repeated twice: the double patriarchal cross just above it might indicate an ecclesiastical institution. The jar is part of one of the most impressive early sixteenth-century pharmacy sets known, but the pharmacy it comes from is unfortunately still unidentified. The set was produced in 1501–2 and contains jars of extraordinary quality and variety, among them beautifully painted large *albarelli* and elaborate spouted jars. The inclusion of a single lustred piece supports the theory that the set was made in Deruta.[79]

In general lustre-decorated drug jars are exceedingly rare. This might be due to the fact that the technique of lustre, expensive and highly specialized, was not suitable for the large-scale production necessary for extensive sets of matching drug jars. An exceptional two-handled lustred *albarello* that might have been used as a drug jar was probably made by Maestro Giorgio of Gubbio at the beginning of his career, between 1490 and 1500 (pl. 191).

The prestige of the court pharmacy in the sixteenth century, which became the focus for many noblemen's secret pursuit of an interest in alchemy, gave an additional impetus to the demand for appropriate furnishings, including beautiful drug jars. In 1520 Alfonso d'Este, the Duke of Ferrara, ordered some maiolica jars for his pharmacy from Venice. To ensure their artistic quality, he commissioned the painter Titian to inspect the work. Titian assured him that the jars would be 'of excellent quality'. Five months later large, medium and small jars with their covers were delivered to the duke. Unfortunately, we have no idea of how the jars looked or who was the potter.[80]

Two finely painted jars both bearing the arms of the Montefeltro, dukes of Urbino, might have been part of a set of drug jars made for the court pharmacy of the Ducal Palace in Urbino (pl. 192). In all probability, they show the arms of Guidobaldo, the last Montefeltro duke (1472–1508). The coat of arms, encircled by a wreath, is held by a crowned black eagle, the emblem of the Montefeltro. The elegant decoration incorporates emblems and inscriptions referring to the Roman Empire and one jar represents Mucius Scaevola deliberately burning his hand, an example of Roman fortitude appropriate for a duke.

Both jars have symbols scratched into the base after firing (pl. 193). These symbols, only found on pharmaceutical jars, were probably added by the apothecaries and might be related to the jar's weight, contents, price or capacity. It has been suggested that they

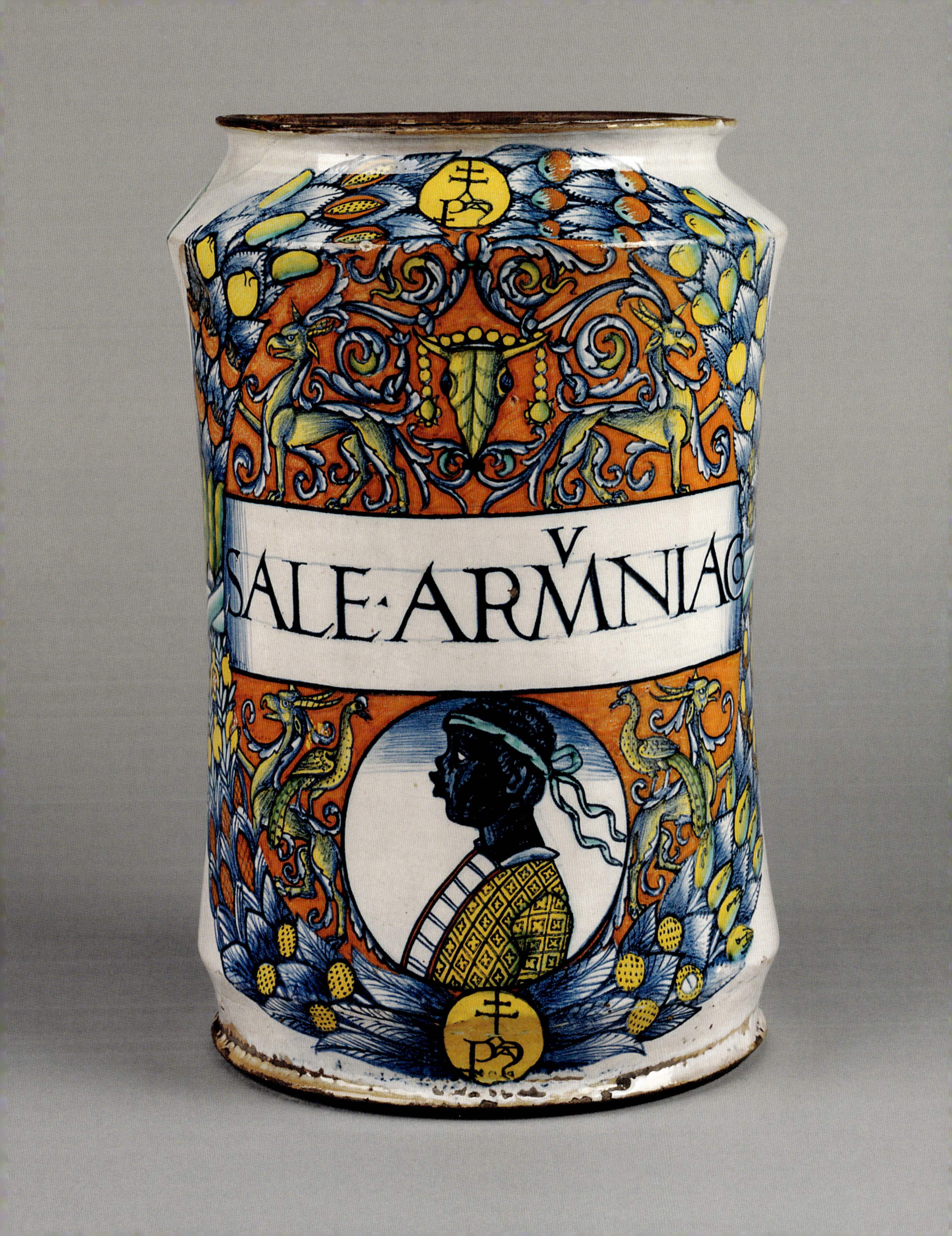
V
SALE·ARMNIAC

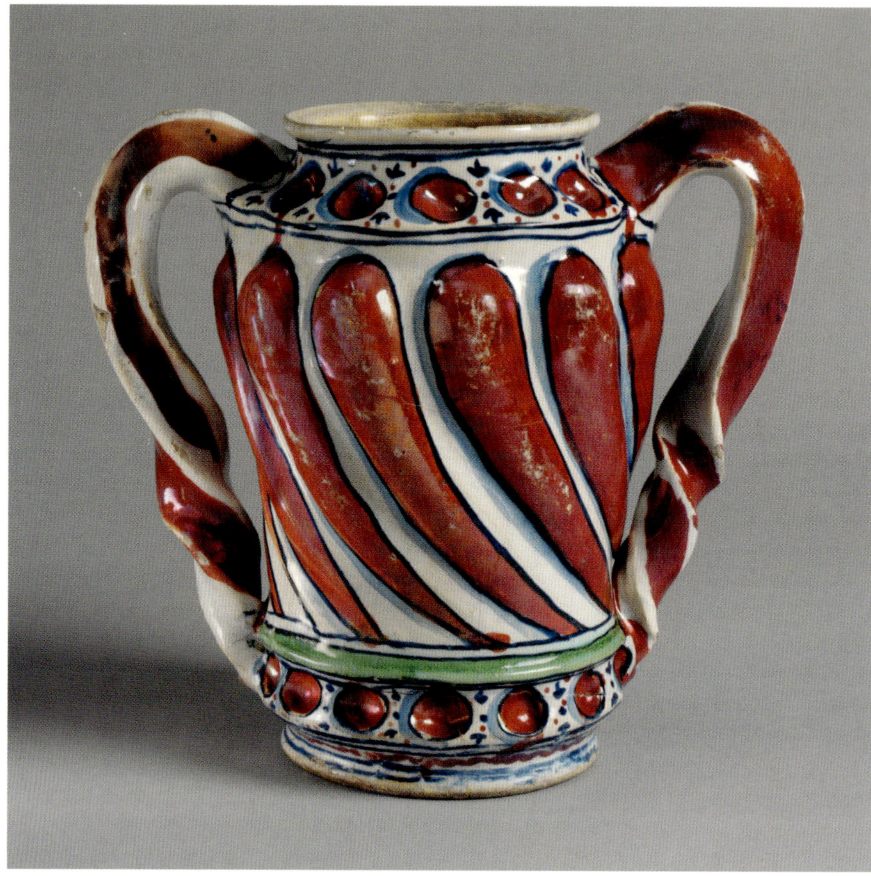

191 Two-handled lustred jar
Probably workshop of Maestro Giorgio Andreoli
Gubbio, 1490–1500
H: 23.5 cm
V&A: 498–1865

indicate the weight of the jar when empty, enabling the apothecary to determine the weight of the contents by subtraction.[81] There is no inscription on these jars referring to specific contents, making them more flexible.

One of the most celebrated types of pharmacy jars has been named 'Orsini-Colonna' after a jar of this type in the British Museum which is painted with the emblems of these two families: a bear (*orso*) embracing a column (*colonna*). Many jars of this type survive and they were clearly produced in large numbers. The jars might have been made over a period of time, perhaps from the 1530s to the 1550s, and it is reasonable to suggest that the main market for them was Rome. It is likely that the jars were produced under the patronage of the Orsini family.[82]

The 'Orsini-Colonna' jars and bottles have very distinctive shapes and decoration. The shapes include very tall bottles, round two-handled jars and jars with a moulded spout in the shape of a dragon's head (pl. 194). They are decorated in bold colours dominated by blue and have inscriptions in a thick Gothic script. Common images on the jars and bottles are paired portraits, often of old men or women, battling horsemen, and satirical or even erotic subjects. Images appear only on the front of the jars while the backs show simple scrolls, painted in blue.

Although it is clear that the jars and bottles of this type have been made over a period of time, and that different painters were involved, it is likely that they all originate from the same workshop. On stylistic grounds, various attributions have been proposed, ranging from Faenza and Siena to Deruta. However comparison with

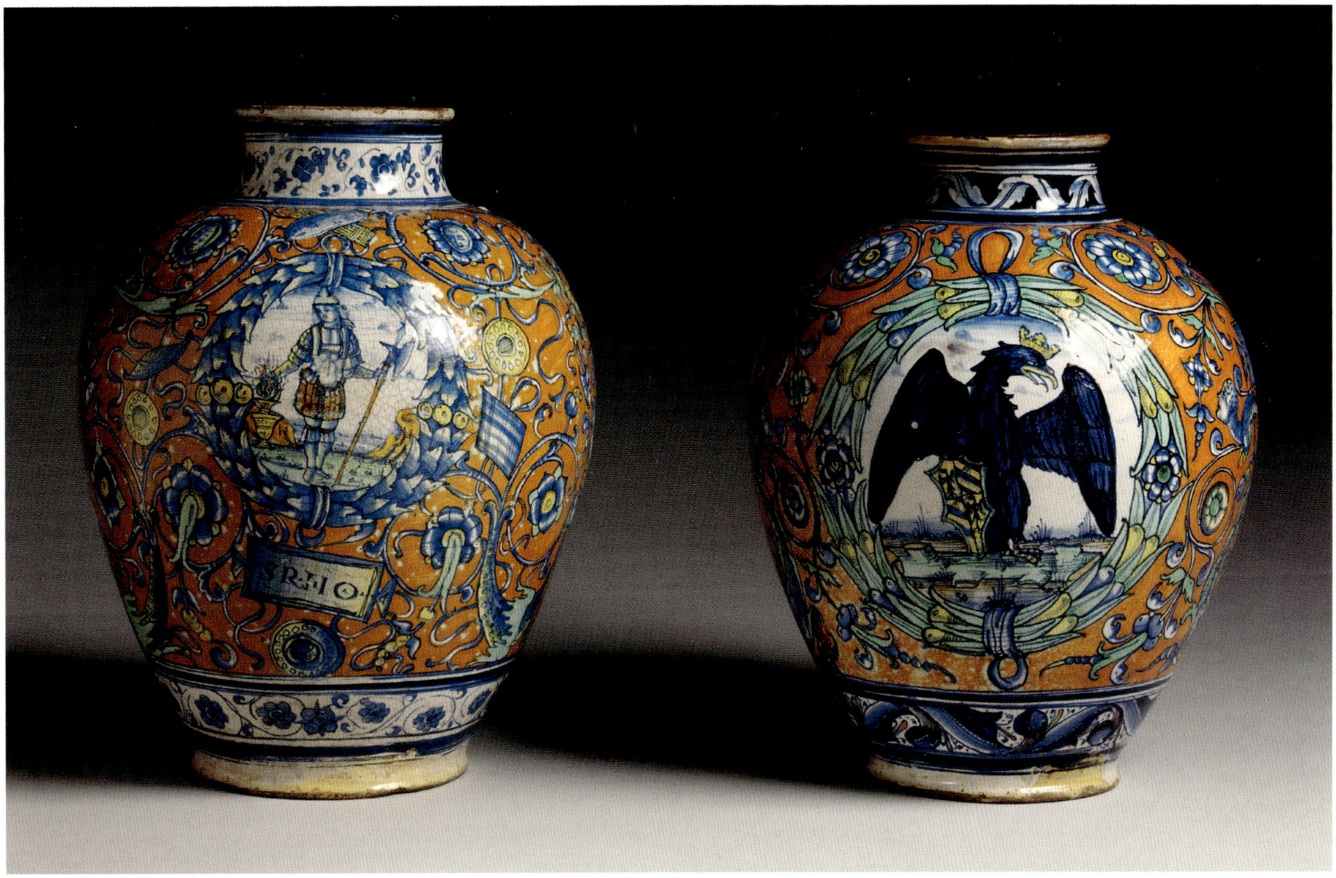

192 Two drug jars with arms of the Montefeltro Dukes of Urbino
Urbino district, c.1500–8
H: 33.5 cm; 32 cm
Salting Bequest V&A: C.2121–1910, C. 2122–1910

193 Scratches on base of V&A: C.2122–1910
(see pl.192)

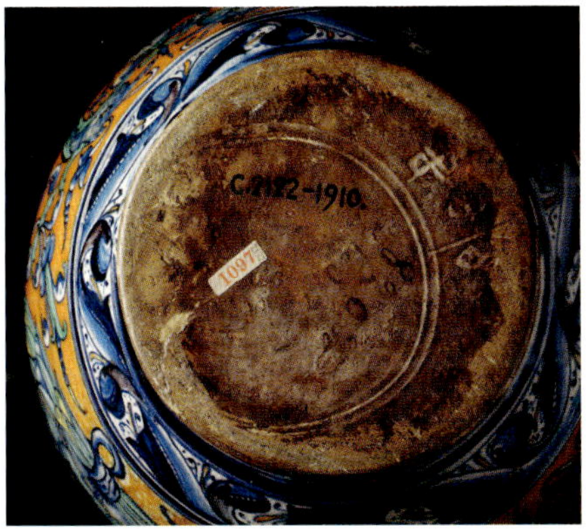

excavated fragments and kiln waste in the remote village of Castelli in Abruzzi, has proved that they were made in the workshop of Orazio Pompei, whose family made their fortune from the manufacture of pottery.[83]

An *albarello* and a small, globular lidded jar in the V&A are decorated with trophies as well as the figure of a seated queen holding a sceptre (pl. 195). The lidded jar was meant to contain 'Hemp agrimony lozenges'. Hemp was considered a good remedy for purifying the blood and as a treatment for influenza. The jar also bears an emblem of a patriarchal cross flanked by the letters 'D O', probably from the unknown monastic pharmacy that commissioned the jars. The same queen figure also appears on other drug jars and vases decorated with narrative painting and must be the emblem of a pharmacy.

Of the several other jars with trophies known from the set, two are dated 1574 and 1575 respectively.[84] Within the set, differences occur in the painting of the queen figure and in the handwriting of the labels. This could be explained by the involvement of different painters working on a large set, but it is also possible that replacements were ordered at a later stage to replace broken jars. The set was probably made in the Duchy of Urbino, where maiolica fragments showing similar trophies have been found.

Series of drug jars with narrative painting, all decorated with different scenes, became a speciality of the potteries of the Duchy of Urbino from the second half of the sixteenth century. An *albarello* depicting a scene from Roman history was probably part of one of the many large pharmacy sets produced in Castel Durante around the 1550s (pl. 196).

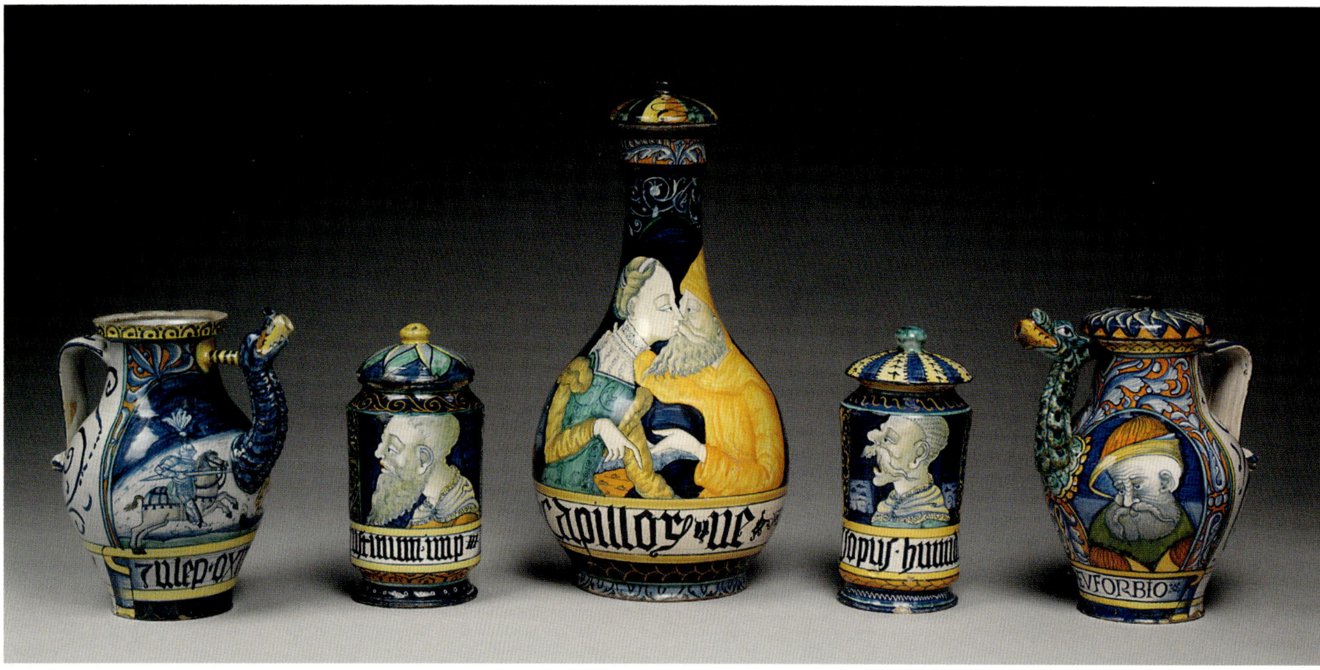
EVFORBIO

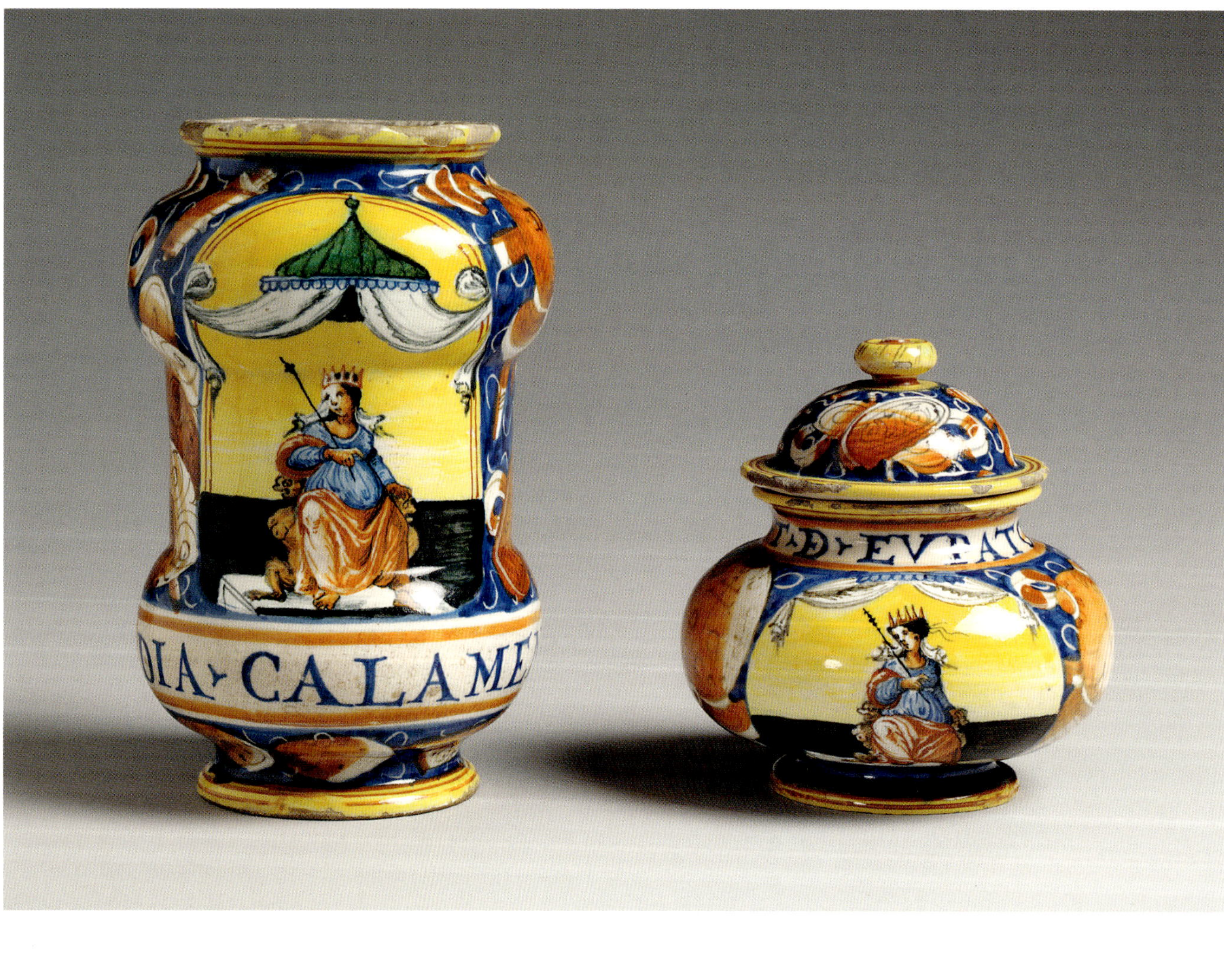
DIA CALAME

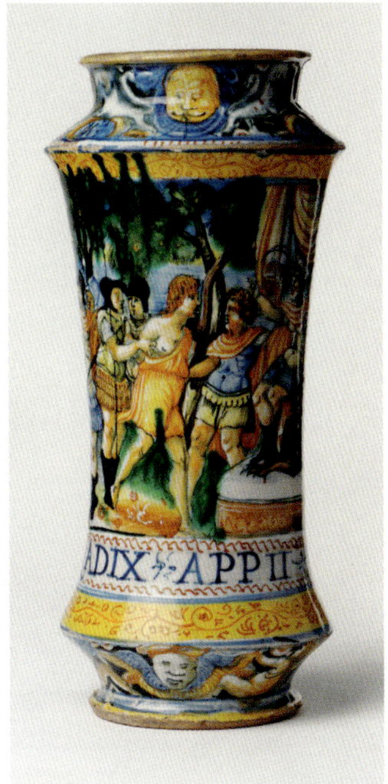

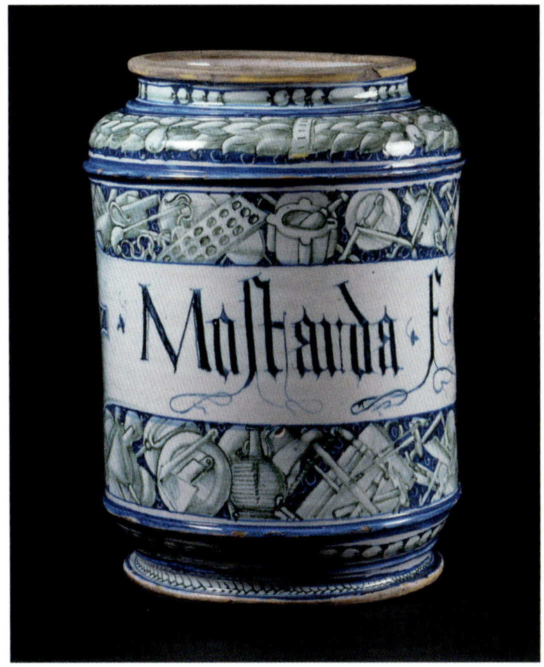

194 'Orsini-Colonna' drug jars
Workshop of Orazio Pompei
Castelli, c.1530s–50s
H: 23.5 cm; 23.5 cm; 44 cm; 25.5 cm; 26 cm
V&A: 1270–1855: 1271–1855; 1798&A–1855; Salting Bequest V&A: C.2286–1910; C.80–1944

195 *Albarello* and pill pot with an emblem of a queen holding a sceptre
Urbino district, c.1575
H: 20.3 cm; 13 cm
V&A: 4389–1857; Salting Bequest C.2268–1910

196 Drug jar for parsley root with a scene from Roman history
Castel Durante, 1550s
H: 32 cm
Salting Bequest V&A: C.2256–1910

197 *Albarello* for mostarda
Venice, 1556
H: 38.5 cm
V&A: 2587–1856

It is stylistically very close to a drug jar marked as made in the workshop of Ludovico Picchi in Castel Durante.[85] Ludovico and his brother Angelo were from a well-established family of potters.[86] Archival documents mention them and other potters from Castel Durante receiving commissions to be sent outside the Duchy of Urbino for hundreds and even thousands of drug jars, from Andrea Boerio, a Genoese merchant residing in Palermo. A formal contract of August 1562 concerns a commission split between the Picchi brothers and other potters for 307 drug jars. These had to be ready by the end of September and their decoration, shape and prices are described in detail:

> 59 large vases, 12 painted *istoriati* and all the others with trophies .... 38 large *albarelli* 7 *scudi* each, 30 *fiole* [phials or flasks], 7 for one *scudo*, 30 bottles, 7 for one *scudo*, 100 medium *albarelli*, 11 for a *scudo*, 50 small *albarelli*, 20 for a *scudo*.[87]

A few months later the brothers were sued for failing to deliver 400 jars in time to the same client.[88]

In addition to medicines, pharmacies sold perfumes, candles, spices and cooking ingredients (such as saffron, pepper, cloves and pine nuts) and sweetmeats like candied fruits and liquorice. Sometimes we encounter drug jars inscribed with the names of sweet confections. Many unusually large drug jars painted with typical Venetian decorations are inscribed *'Mostarda'*. This was not mustard in the modern sense but a type of fruit compote made of quinces with mustard and honey, which was a speciality of Venice and its region. A jar for *'Mostarda Fina'* dated 1556 shows us a cross-section of Renaissance culture and science: alchemical and scientific apparatus including the celestial and terrestrial globes, instruments used by apothecaries to make remedies and items of household equipment (pl. 197). The imagery on the jar can be seen as encapsulating the world of a Renaissance pharmacy, a meeting place between nature and science.

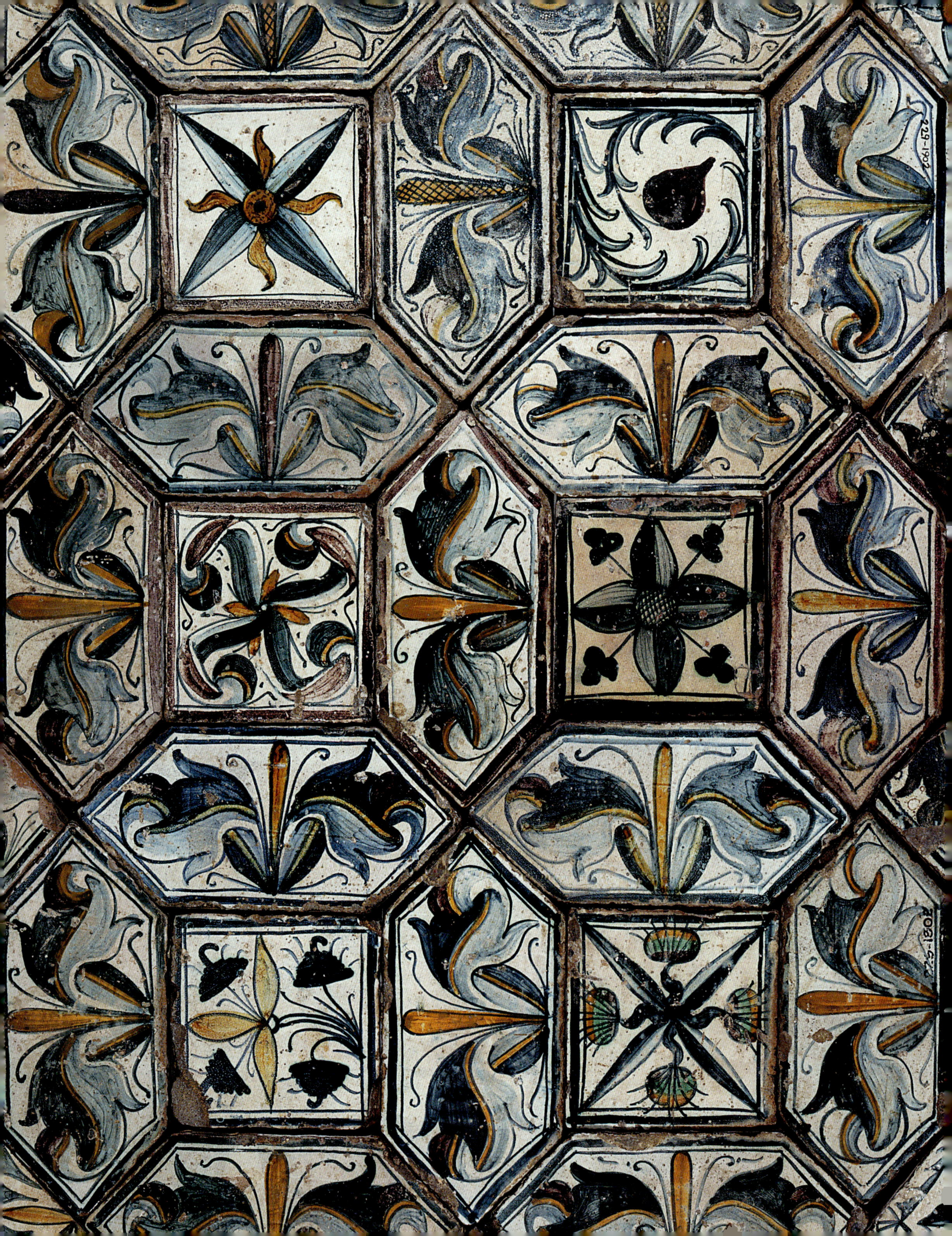

Floors

198 Floor tiles with ornamental decoration from the Mazzatosta Chapel in Santa Maria della Verità
Viterbo, c.1470
V&A: 229–1902

Maiolica floor tiles represent one of the most noteworthy aspects of Renaissance maiolica production. Often many hundreds of tiles were needed for a single maiolica floor, and their overall designs, as well as the execution of many of the individual tiles, show extraordinary inventiveness. A maiolica floor was the perfect complement to a lavish Renaissance interior and often formed part of complex architectural and decorative schemes. Unfortunately almost all of these have been entirely lost.[89]

Maiolica floor tiles for prestigious commissions were imported into Italy from Spain during the fifteenth century. Alfonso I of Aragon, King of Naples, commissioned several floors from Valencian potters. These splendid examples must have prompted local potters to produce similar products and several floors appeared in churches in Naples. One of the earliest datable Italian maiolica floors, from around 1441, was laid in the Caracciolo Chapel of the Church of San Giovanni a Carbonara.[90] Its shape and decoration were inspired by Spanish prototypes. The powerful Borgia family was of Spanish origin and contributed to the taste for maiolica floors tiles in Italy. The Borgia Pope Alexander VI (1492–1503) was particularly influential: his apartments in the Vatican were decorated with both Valencian and Italian pavements.

From the second half of the fifteenth century Italian potters produced floors of outstanding quality and great originality. The floor of the Mazzatosta Chapel in Santa Maria della Verità in Viterbo, made around 1470 and probably of local manufacture, is a good example of maiolica pavement production of the time (pl. 198). The decoration is predominantly ornamental, with stylized Gothic foliage painted onto a white background. Only a few profile or three-quarter views of men and women are incorporated in the design. Few colours are used, the dominant colouring being blue and orange. Floor tiles at this time were square, triangular or hexagonal. The Mazzatosta pavement incorporated both square and hexagonal tiles in an arrangement inspired by Spanish prototypes. The chapel's walls were decorated with frescoes, and here, as elsewhere, the tiled floor was designed to complement the rest of the richly ornamented interior.[91]

199 Floor tile with Gonzaga device, from the study of Isabella d'Este, Mantua
Workshop of Antonio Fedeli
Pesaro, c.1494
H: 23.5 cm, W: 23.5 cm
V&A: 334: 6–1903

200 Floor tiles with Gonzaga arms and devices, from the study of Isabella d'Este, Mantua
Workshop of Antonio Fedeli
Pesaro, c.1494
H: 23.5 cm, W: 23.5 cm
V&A: 334: 1-5–1903

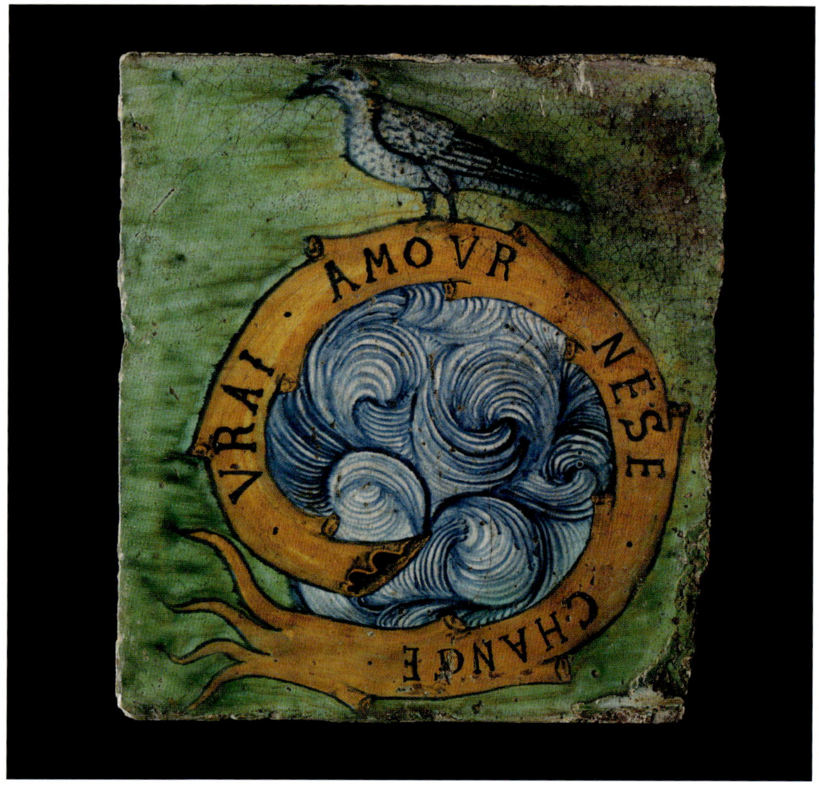

Maiolica floors decorated some of the most splendid Renaissance interiors although the fragility of their soft tin-glaze made them unsuitable for public spaces and more appropriate to small, exclusive rooms such as private chapels and studies. While the primary appeal of the colourful maiolica tiles was decorative, there were also practical reasons for a tiled floor. The Marchioness of Mantua Isabella d'Este used tiles in her *studiolo* (study) in order to combat vermin. The situation in the Castello San Giorgio had become so bad that the old floor had to be ripped up because of the damage done by rats nesting under the floorboards. Cases of tiles arrived in 1494 and were split between Isabella's *studiolo* and the floor of her husband Francesco Gonzaga's villa at Marmirolo. On July 1494 the governess of Isabella's daughter wrote:

> Today your ladyship's *studiolo* was paved with square tiles painted with the devices of our most illustrious Lord, which match each other very well, and in truth it was an excellent bit of foresight and almost necessary since under the floorboards were found many rats nests.[92]

The surviving tiles from Isabella's *studiolo* are large, square and unusually thick (pls 199, 200). There are eight different designs, showing the arms of the Gonzaga family and seven of their devices: each tile bears a single motif perhaps meant to alternate with the Gonzaga arms in a formal arrangement. The V&A collection holds six of the tiles, one depicting the Gonzaga arms and the other five the following devices: a hound muzzled and leashed; a steel gauntlet inscribed in Spanish with the motto 'Good faith is unchanging'; a white doe with a motto in German 'Righteous power'; a craggy mountain surmounted by a diamond with smoking fire-brands and the word

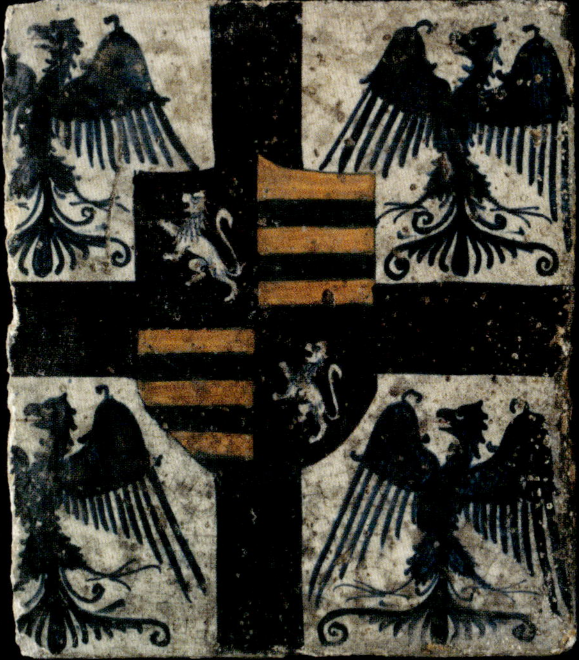

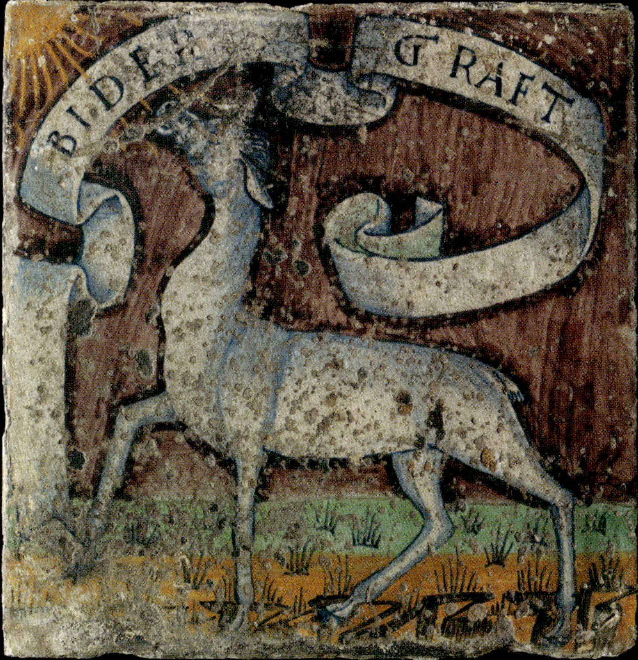

GRAFT

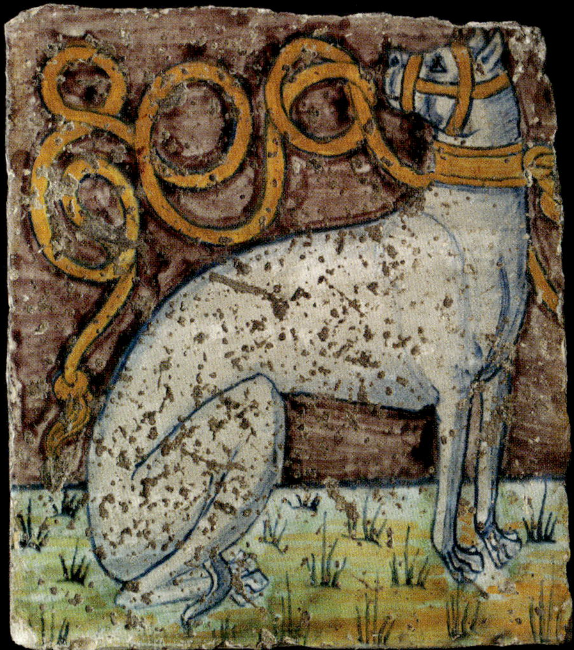

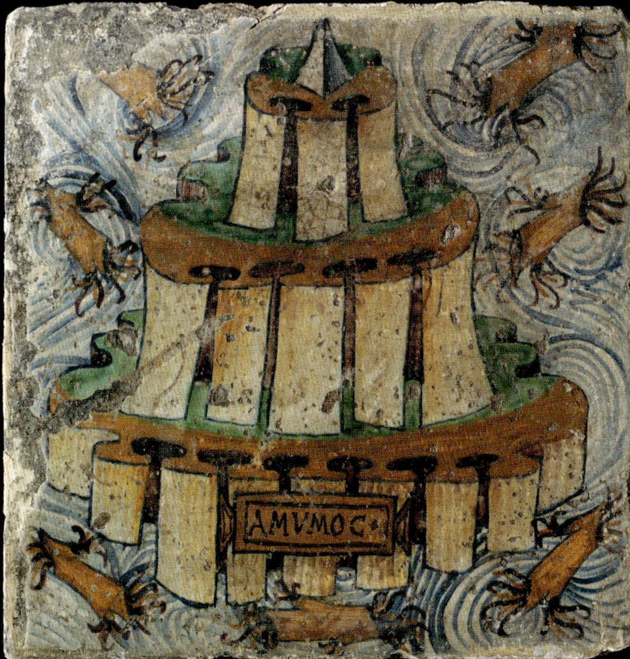

AMVMOC

201 Floor tile with profile of youth, from the Convent of San Paolo, Parma
Probably Pesaro, c.1471–82
H: 21.5 cm, W: 20 cm
V&A: 12–1890

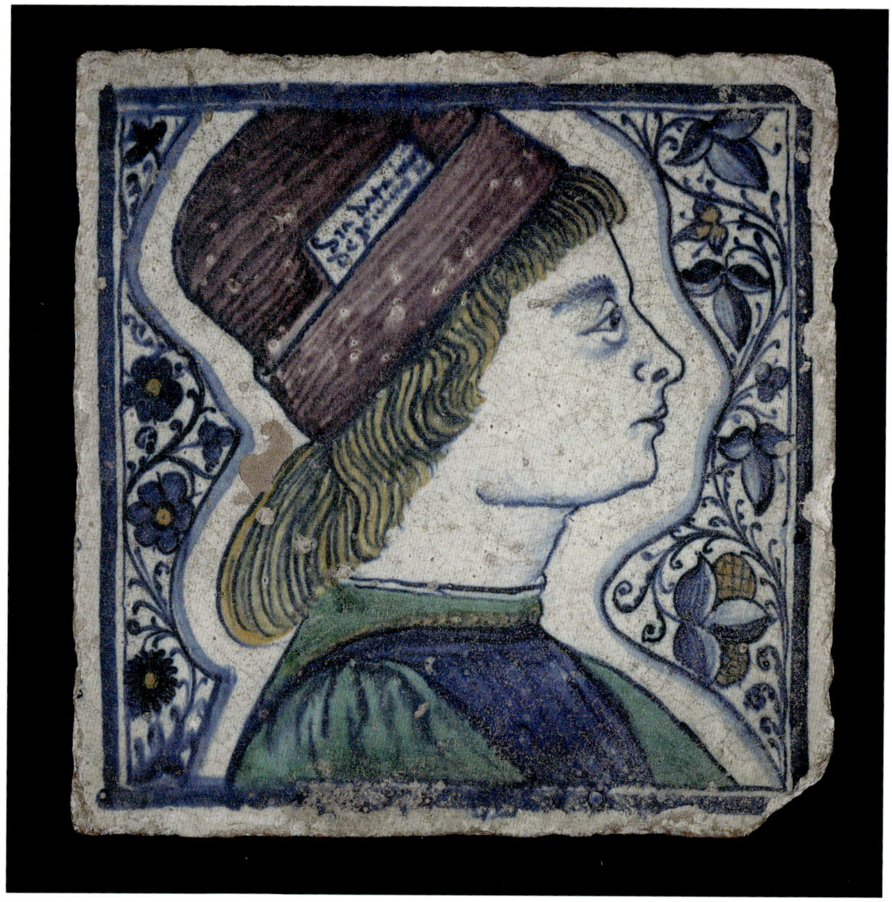

'Blameless' in Greek; and a dove perched on a twisted and smouldering tree-stump inscribed in French with the motto 'True love does not change' (pl. 199). The same emblems were repeated on furnishings and architectural elements.[93]

The sophisticated designs were probably provided by a court artist. Giovanni Sforza (lord of Pesaro and widower of Francesco Gonzaga's sister) mentioned in a letter of 1493 that he was having the tiles made with the devices of the house of Gonzaga according to 'agreed designs'. The tiles were probably made in Pesaro in one of the major workshops of the city, that of Antonio dei Fedeli. Potteries in this city produced some of the most splendid pavements of the time.

Floor tiles offer a fascinating insight into the imagery preferred by Renaissance elites and religious orders in their homes, palaces and chapels. One of the most splendid pavements of the late fifteenth century, made for the Convent of San Paolo in Parma around 1471–82, has again been attributed to Pesaro potters.[94] It features bust portraits of young men and women and other subjects related to courtly love, animals and mythology (pl. 201). Some of the tiles bear the arms and initials of Maria de Benedetti, the Abbess of the convent from 1471–82, who might have commissioned the work.[95] The secular subjects of the tiles seem somewhat inappropriate for the floor of a nunnery, but the motifs were popular at the time and can be found on other late fifteenth- or early sixteenth-century floors made for chapels or churches.

Animals, trophies and other motifs set into roundels were a fashionable decoration on floor tiles from the period 1470 to 1510. They feature on two of the most important

Renaissance floors known, those of the Vaselli Chapel in Bologna (1487) and the Lando Chapel of the Church of San Sebastiano in Venice (1510).[96] This type of design gained wide popularity and was imitated in France, the Netherlands and England in the sixteenth century. Hounds, rosettes, trophies and a hand grasping a fish with an hourglass beside it, all enclosed by a twisted ribbon circular border, figure on the square tiles that probably once decorated the floor of the Church of Santa Maria del Riposo in Fano. One of the surviving tiles bears the date 1501. The floor must originally have comprised around 1,600 tiles, probably of Pesaro manufacture; 25 of them are in the V&A's collection (pl. 202).[97]

From the early sixteenth century elaborate arrangements of tiles of different shapes developed, and newly fashionable ornaments, such as grotesques and patterns inspired by blue and white Chinese porcelain, began to appear.

The floor commissioned by the physician Bartolomeo Lombardini in 1511 for his chapel in the church of San Francesco Grande in Forlì is probably of local manufacture. Polygonal tiles painted in delicate blue and white resembling Ming porcelain surround highly original octagonal tiles painted in a yellow or a dark orange ground. The circumstances around the commission and design of the pavement are puzzling. The floor bears two dates, 1513 and 1523, and the significance of the prominent arms of Della Rovere and of Cardinal Francesco Alidosi (1455–1511) is unexplained. Lombardini died

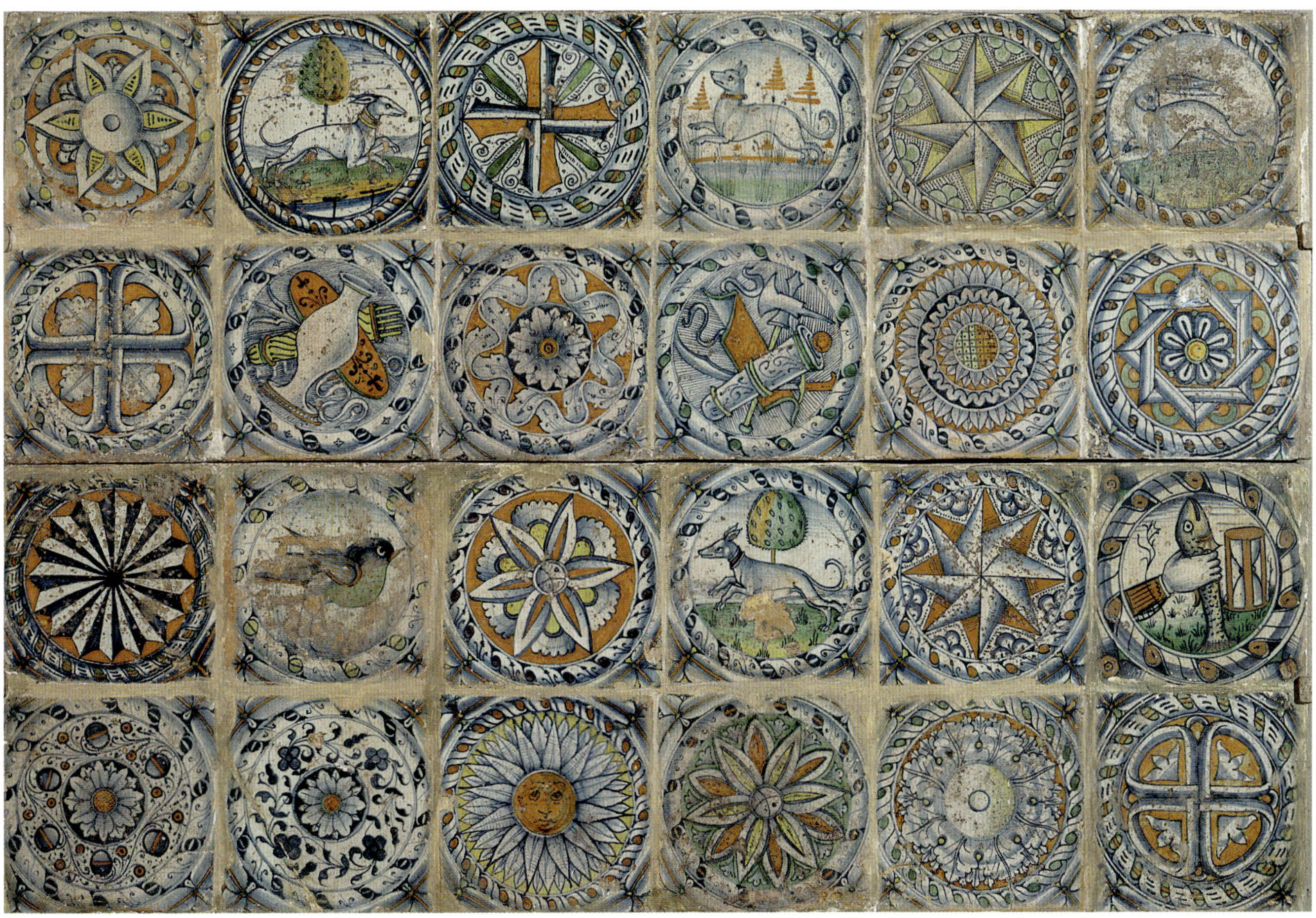

202 Floor tiles with animals and trophies probably from the church of Santa Maria del Riposo in Fano
Probably Pesaro, c.1501
V&A: 333–1903

203 Floor tiles from the Lombardini chapel in the church of San Francesco Grande in Forlì
Painted by 'Petrus'
Probably Forlì, 1513–24
V&A: 30–1866

in 1512 and work on the chapel was continued by his daughter, married to Giovanni Monsignani, and by their sons.[98] The floor was around 40 square metres in size. The chapel was destroyed in 1793 and the tiles were relaid in the Villa Monsignani at Pieve a Quinta, where they remained until 1862. In 1866 the V&A acquired the majority of the floor, over 1,400 tiles (pl. 203).

The original arrangement of the tiles is unknown, but from the large number available for study we can appreciate the inventive design of the work. The octagonal tiles mostly carry elegant bust portraits, including some of contemporary characters, delicately sketched (pl. 204). One tile includes the portrait and name of the maiolica painter responsible for the pavement: 'Petrus' (perhaps Pietro dal Castel). Other octagonal tiles show a wide variety of subjects including *belle donne*, Roman emperors, animals and trophies. All of the images are remarkable for their originality. The high quality of the portraits suggests that the designs might have been provided by an artist. Among the most likely candidates are the painters working on the architecture and decoration of the chapel, Girolamo Genga and Marco Palmezzano.[99]

We can get an idea of the function of a tiled floor within a room decorated *'all'antica'* ('in the antique manner') from the splendid floor tiles with grotesques made for the *Camera Bella* in the palace of the ruler of Siena, Pandolfo Petrucci. The room was part of the apartment prepared for his son Borghese on his marriage to Vittoria Piccolomini in 1509. The walls were decorated with beautiful frescoes painted by some of the most

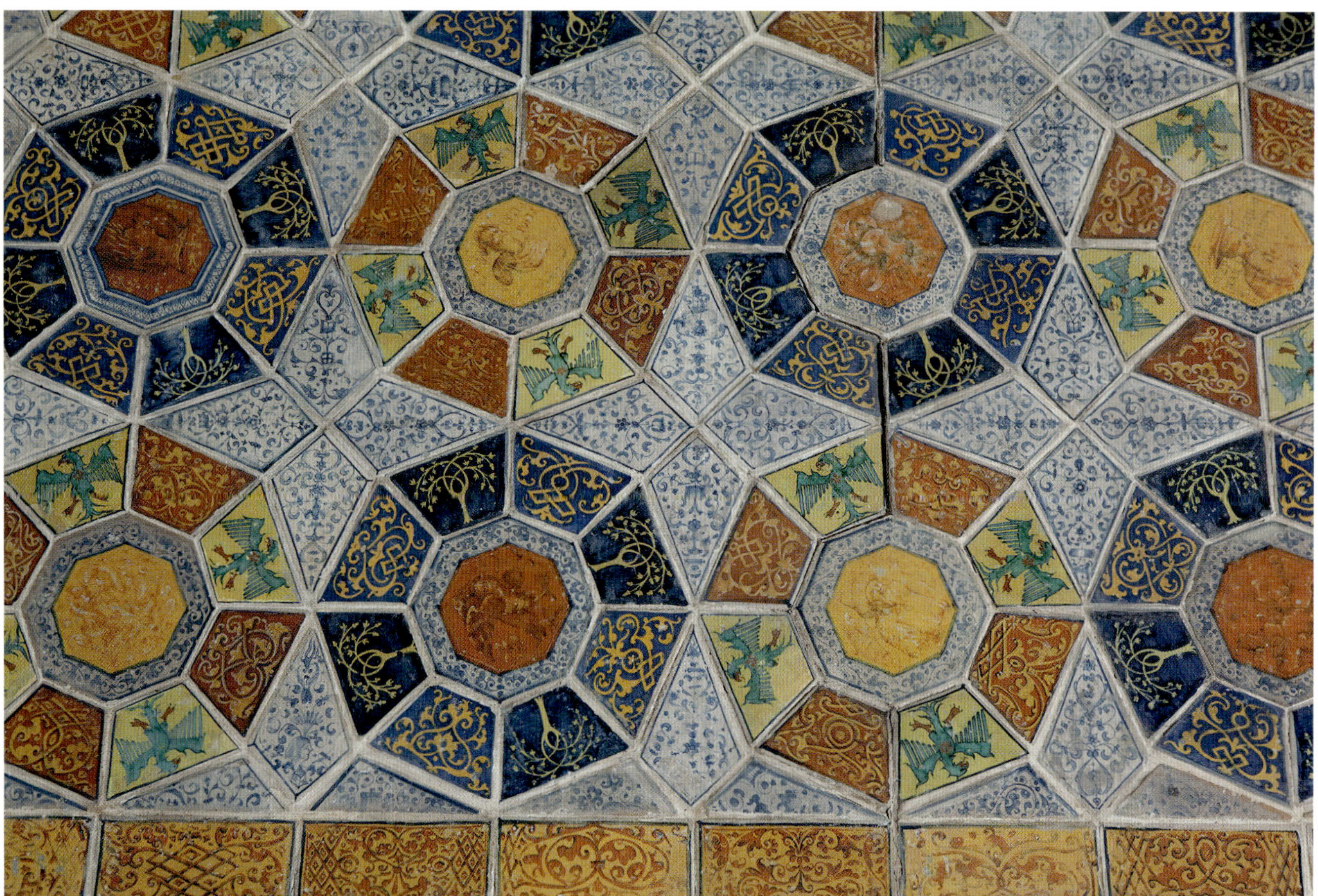

204 Detail of pl.203

205 (overleaf) Floor tiles from the Camera Bella, Palazzo Petrucci, Siena
Siena, c.1509
V&A: 4915–1857

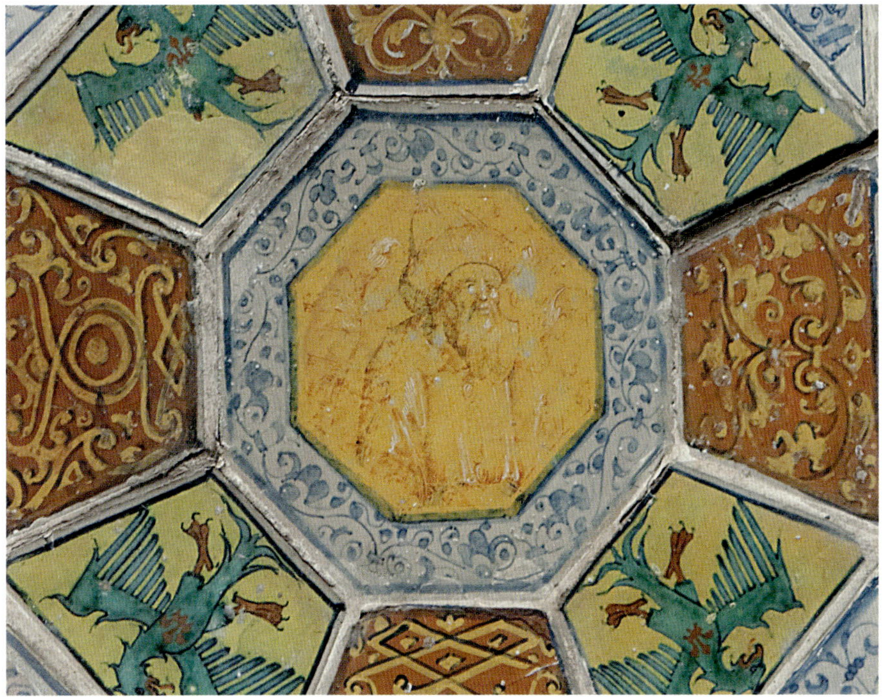

famous artists of the time – Pinturicchio, Luca Signorelli and Gerolamo Genga – and the woodwork was elaborate.[100] While there is no certainty that any of these artists designed the floor tiles, ceiling friezes in the palace resemble the border decoration on the tiles. Experienced *'all'antica'* decorators such as Pinturicchio, Signorelli and their collaborators would have found the task of producing drawings for the floor straightforward.

Over 400 tiles from the floor are held at the V&A (pl. 205). They are of different shape and sizes – triangular, two sizes of square, and two sizes of pentagonal tiles. Most are painted with inventive grotesque and trophy designs on orange, yellow and black backgrounds. Some larger square tiles depict shields with combinations of the arms of the Petrucci and Piccolomini families, while a few others have delicate figures in landscapes. Square tiles with a typically Sienese black background decorated with sphinxes and other grotesques form a continuous border. A recent study has suggested that the likely original arrangement of the tiles formed a star and cross pattern ultimately derived from Islamic tiles dating back to the eleventh century, but also found in the paintings of Pinturicchio.[101] The elaborate decoration, based on both classical and Islamic sources, and the combination of 16 different shapes of tile, make this floor one of the finest and most complex ever executed.

Elaborate grotesques and trophies continue to appear on floors produced up to the middle of the sixteenth century and beyond. However, prestigious commissions for pavements became rarer in this period, and maiolica floors may have gone out of fashion. Prone to damage, many maiolica tiles were replaced with more durable materials.

The worn appearance of most Renaissance pavements today, with pale, matt tiles, makes it difficult to appreciate their original splendour. We can get a glimpse of this where, occasionally, a depression in the tile has protected the glaze in that area from wear. Sadly, the full appearance of a dazzling newly-laid maiolica floor cannot be recaptured.

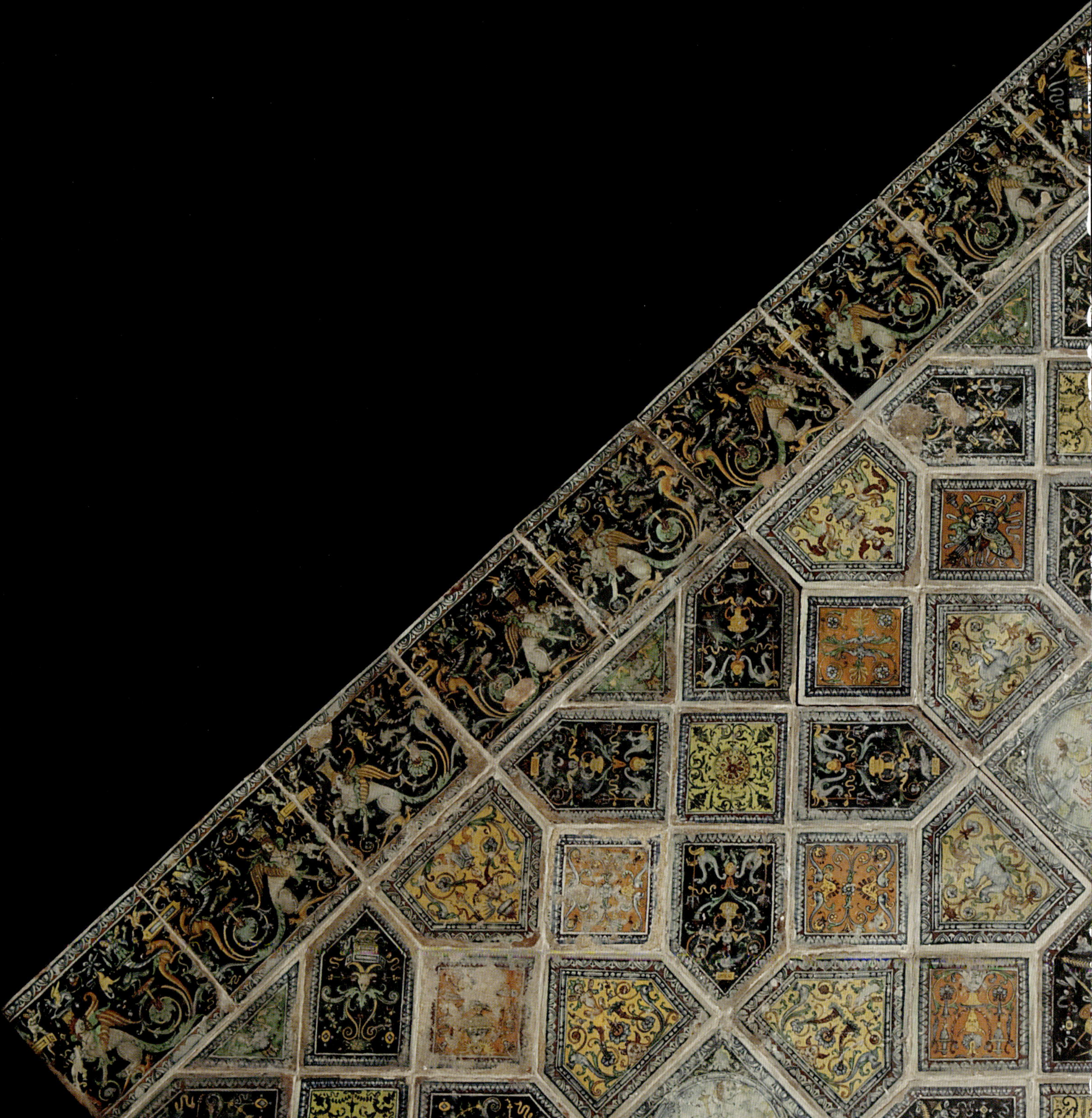

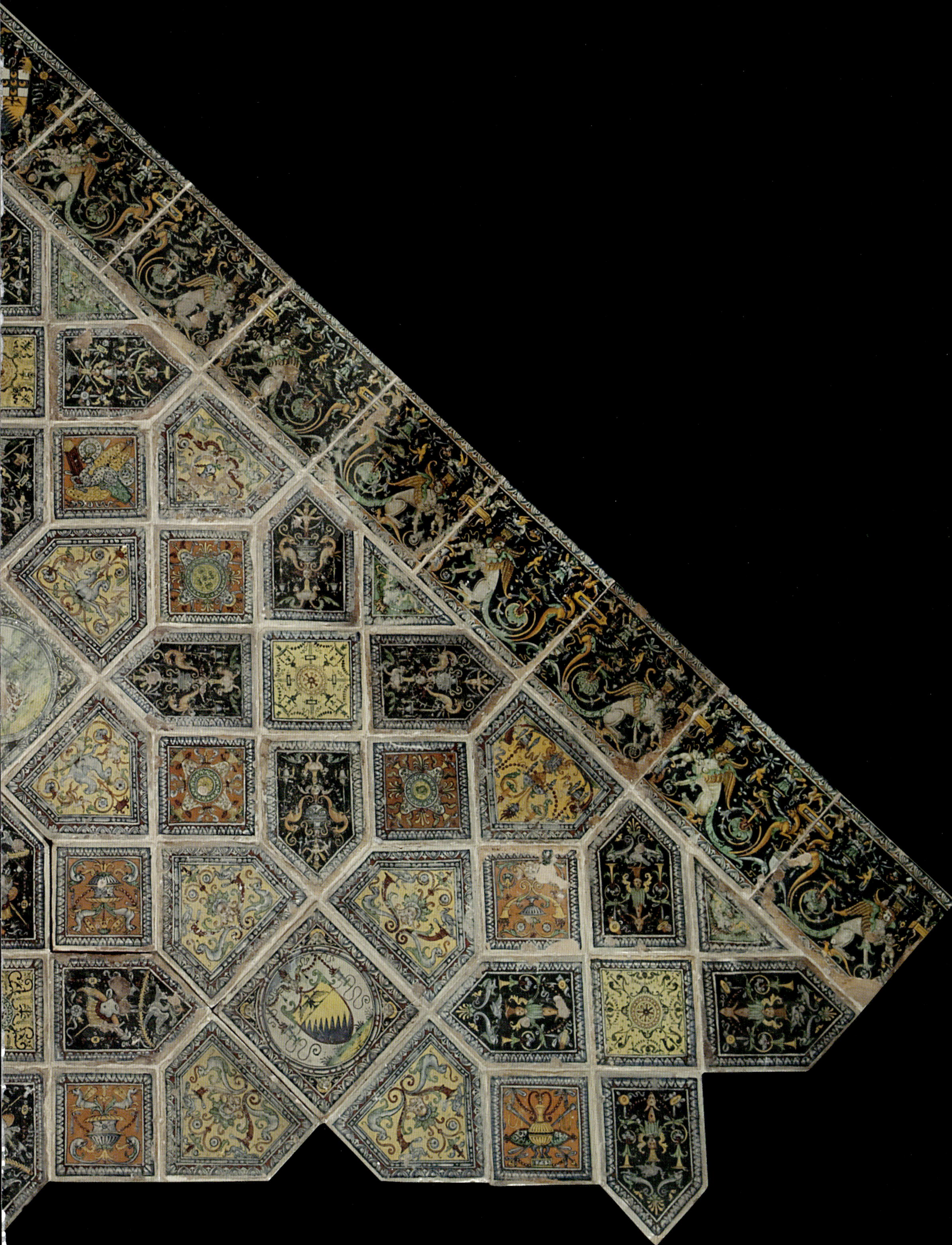

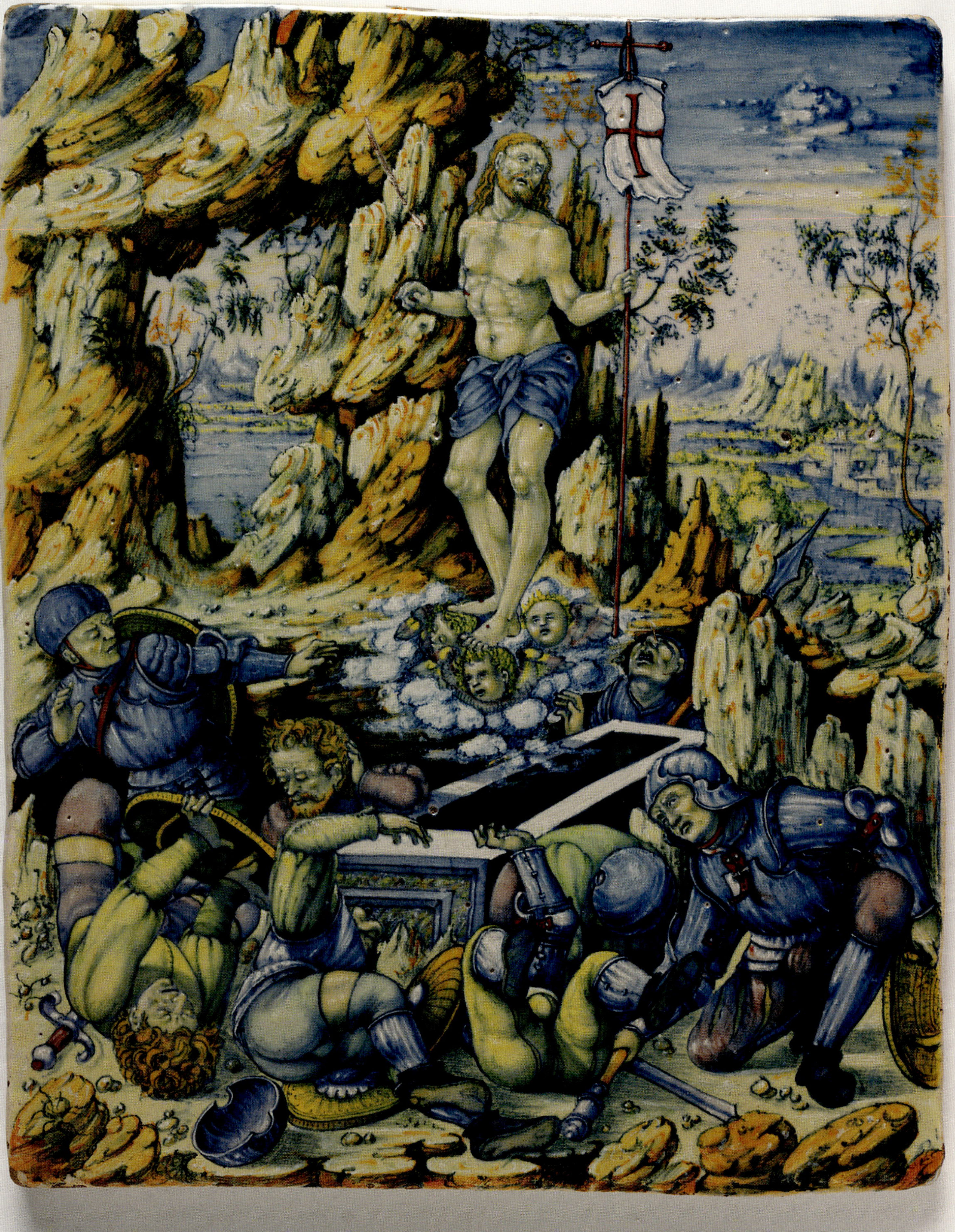

Plaques

206 Plaque with the Resurrection
'TB'
Urbino district or Faenza, c.1510–15
H: 25 cm, W: 20.5 cm
V&A: 69–1865

The relative durability of maiolica compared to other media made it suitable for exterior decoration. The tradition of adding ceramics to the exterior of churches started in Italy in the twelfth and thirteenth centuries when decorative basins (*'bacini'*), often of near-eastern origin, were incorporated into the outer walls of buildings for decoration. Later, during the fifteenth century, the Della Robbia workshop in Florence produced sculptural exterior decorations executed in tin-glazed earthenware of different sizes and forms.

Maiolica workshops followed this example by making colourful tin-glazed plaques, if on a far less ambitious scale. Simple flat plaques could be made by cutting a slab of clay from a large round block with a metal wire, as illustrated by Piccolpasso (see pl. 16). This could then be cut to the desired size or shape, most commonly rectangular, but also circular, square or pentagonal. After biscuit firing and tin-glazing, the maiolica painter could decorate these plaques to form a durable, polychrome picture. Holes pierced through the clay before firing allowed the plaques to be suspended from a wire, while others were framed or incorporated into walls.

Maiolica plaques were made from the second half of the fifteenth century. Among the oldest examples are circular plaques painted with the emblem for Christ, *IHS* (for *Iesus Hominum Salvator*, Jesus Saviour of Mankind), surrounded by rays. Devotion to the Holy Name became very popular in fifteenth-century Italy and plaques bearing the *IHS* trigram were often displayed over the doorways of houses (pl. 209). They were used as *'dischi di censo'* to mark the foundation of a property and are therefore often dated, the earliest ones belonging to the 1470s.

Plaques were also used as signs for hospitals and convents and to mark the ownership of a property. The owner's arms were often painted or moulded on a large scale, to be seen from a distance, and are frequently flanked by initials and the date. The corner panel shown in pl. 208 bears the arms of the Cinquedenti family, five teeth (*cinque denti*), flanked by the initials S and R. Documentary evidence suggests that the initials probably stand for Simone di Roberto Cinquedenti, a potter active in Rimini, who might have executed the plaque himself as a sign for his house or workshop.[102] On the back of the panel there is a year, 1498, and an inscription, only visible when the plaque was removed from the wall: 'He who will turn me over will find a great treasure'.

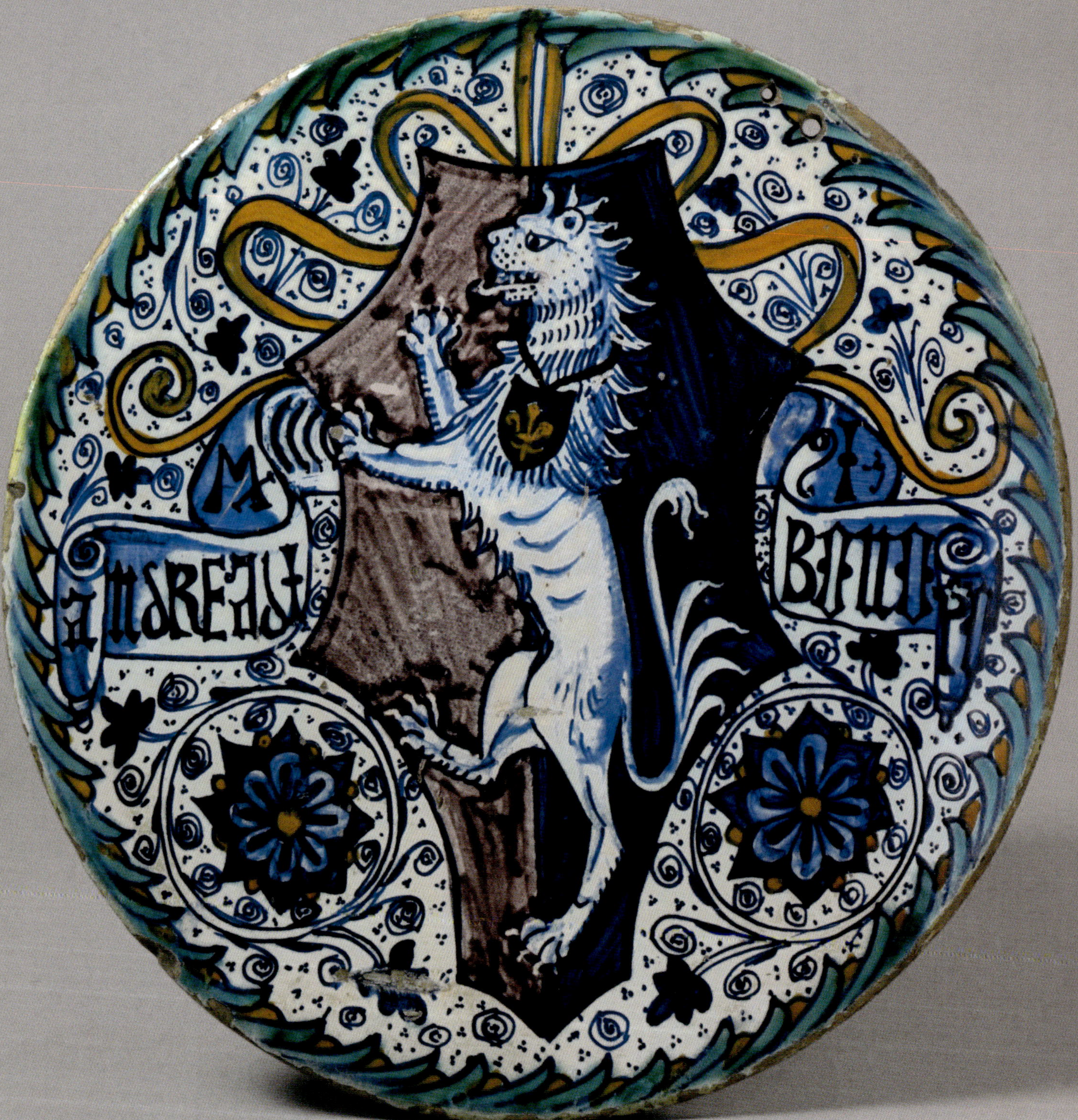

207 Plaque with the arms of Andrea Boni
Florence area, 1491
Diam: 30 cm
V&A: 6655–1860

208 Corner tile with the arms of the Cinquedenti family
Probably Rimini, 1498
H: 37.5 cm, W: 14 cm
V&A: 657–1884

209 Circular plaque with IHS, the trigram for Christ
Northern-central Italy, c.1470
Diam: 34.5 cm
V&A: C.196–1937

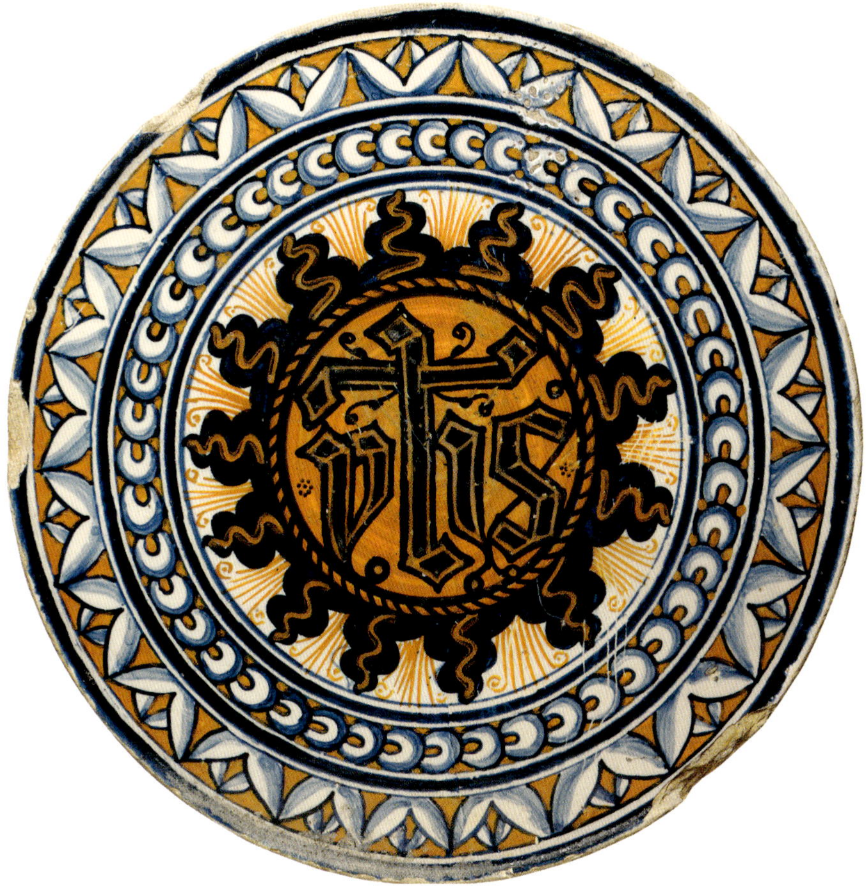

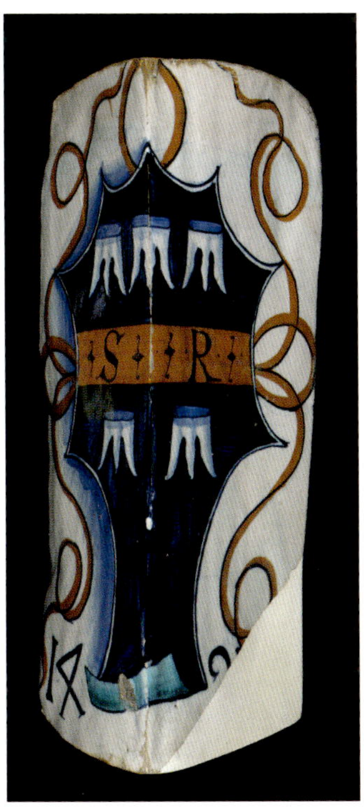

The shape suggests that the plaque was meant to be mounted on the corner of two exterior walls. Panels that were inserted into outer walls as house-signs often show signs of wear and tear. The Cinquedenti tile has a piece missing rendering the date on its front incomplete. Many other plaques now in public and private collections show signs of damage, probably from when they were removed.

A circular plaque bearing the arms of the Florentine Boni family is inscribed 'M ANDREA DI BONO PO 1491' (pl. 207). In 1491 Andrea Boni was elected *'podesta'* (head of town) at Larciano, near Pistoia: it seems likely that the letters 'PO' refer to this new appointment and that the plaque was made to commemorate it.[103] Unlike the Cinquedenti plaque, this piece has little sign of wear around the rim and is in very good condition. Its relatively modest size suggests that it was made for interior use. It might have been framed originally, but two holes drilled through the plaque at some time after firing suggest that it was once simply suspended from a string.

The most common function for maiolica panels was devotional. While historical or mythological subjects are sometimes represented on plaques, the vast majority feature religious images. The V&A's collection contains some of the finest examples of religious plaques (pl. 206).[104] Such panels were made for both institutional and domestic use. In churches they were placed both outside and inside, often above doorways. They were also set in shrines on street corners and sometimes above a doorway. In many regions of Italy they can still be found in situ. In the home, devotional panels were kept in the bedroom or in private chapels.[105]

210 Panel with the Virgin and Child
Probably Pesaro, 1489
H: 47 cm, W: 35 cm
V&A: 490–1864

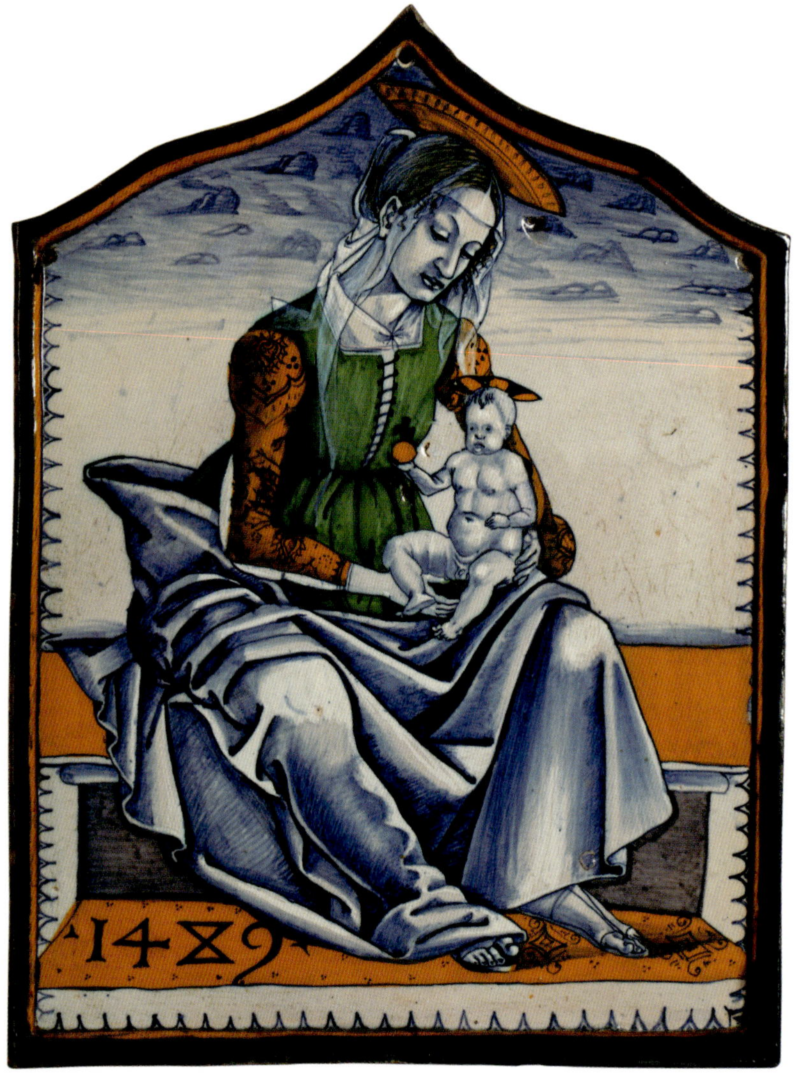

Images of the Virgin and Child are among the most common in Renaissance art. The Virgin was seen as a protector and an exemplar for mothers and mothers to be, and prayers were offered in front of her effigy. A beautiful maiolica plaque dated 1489, perhaps made in Pesaro, is one of the earliest dated figural panels to survive (pl. 210). It shows masterly execution in its figure drawing and in the detailing of the Virgin's robe, although it still lacks proper perspective. The canopy shape of the frame is consistent with other late fifteenth-century Virgin and Child maiolica panels inserted into Gothic-style niches. Devotional maiolica panels with the Virgin and Child were often dated to commemorate events such as the birth of an heir.

Maiolica plaques were an ideal pictorial medium for complex devotional scenes. An exceptional small panel showing the Resurrection is a masterpiece of narrative painting on maiolica (pl. 206). A few other maiolica objects bear the same initials ('TB' was perhaps a workshop or a maker's mark) including a plaque of the same size showing the Martyrdom of St Sebastian (at the Bargello Museum). The two were perhaps meant to be displayed together. The subtle detailing has the quality of a miniature and the small size suggests that it was intended for private devotional use.

Sculptural panels for private devotion were made in different media, from papier-mâché and wood to more precious materials such as marble. Maiolica relief panels were based on sculptural prototypes and they were often mould-pressed to produce multiple copies. Another advantage was the durability of their painted decoration. Well-known fifteenth-century Florentine sculptures often provided the models for these colourful maiolica reliefs, which have additional decorations such as inscriptions, coats of arms and dates.[106]

A moulded and lustred plaque showing St Sebastian, dated 14 July 1501, is the earliest dated example of lustreware produced in Italy and was probably made to commemorate an event (pl. 211). It derives from an anonymous fifteenth-century stone sculpture.[107]

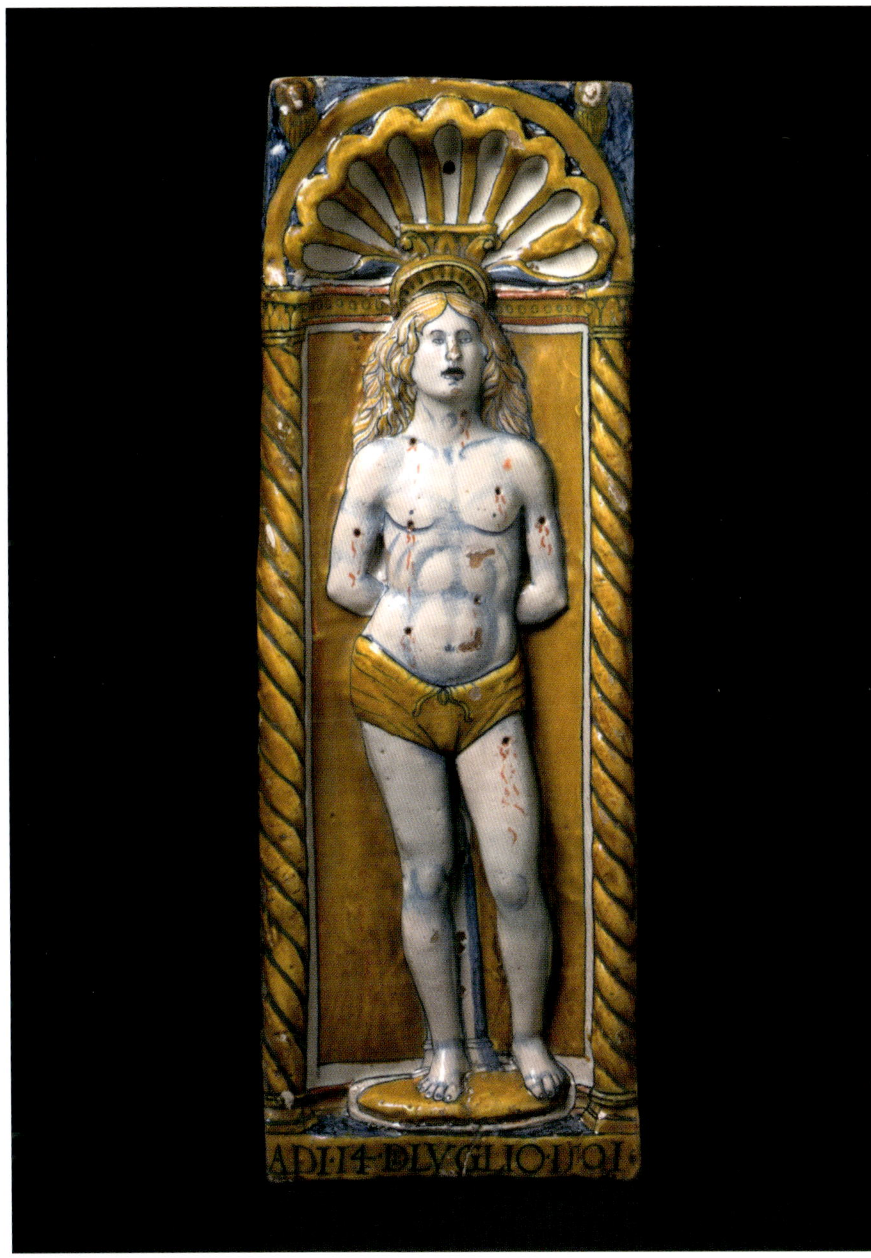

211 Lustred Panel with the Martyrdom of St Sebastian
Deruta, 14 July 1501
H: 51 cm, W: 19 cm
V&A: 2601–1856

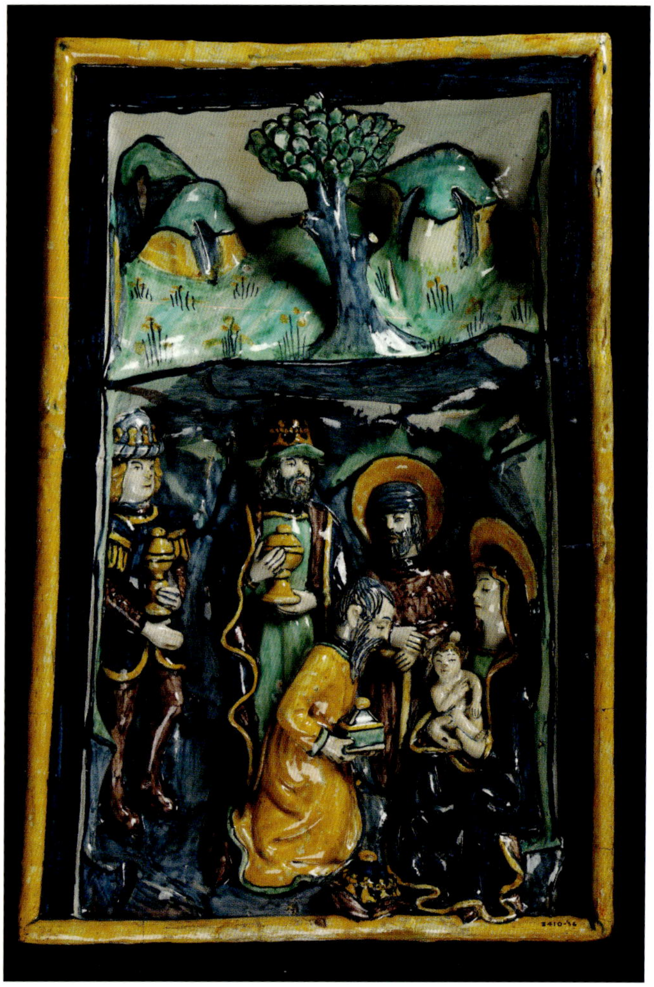

212 Panel with the Adoration of the Magi modelled in high relief
Probably Faenza, c.1500
H: 64 cm, W: 41 cm
V&A: 2410–1856

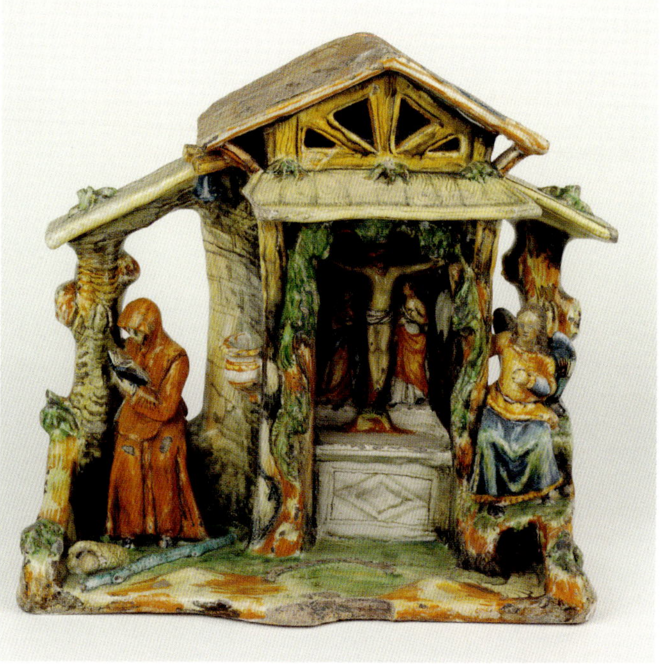

213 Model of a wayside altar
Probably Patanazzi family
Urbino, 1590–1600
H: 36 cm
V&A: C.258–1926

With its delicate lustre decoration, it was probably never meant to be exposed to the elements, and like a number of surviving small-scale plaques in lustre was presumably intended for display indoors. Saints were often depicted on plaques, especially those for private devotion. St Jerome in the Wilderness was particularly popular, but so also were St Sebastian and St Roch, shown together as protectors against the plague.[108]

An extraordinary group of elaborate devotional panels with nativity scenes in high relief within a frame were made around the end of the fifteenth century. These highly sculptural reliefs are attributed to either Emilia Romagna or the Marches.[109] One in the V&A shows the Adoration of the Magi (pl. 212). The elaborate figure group set in a cave with a rocky landscape above shows great three-dimensionality compressed within the limited space of the rectangular niche.

The figures of the kneeling magi and the Christ child in particular are modelled almost completely in the round. This deep relief with its relatively large dimensions and its great weight was clearly intended to be inserted in a wall, perhaps of a small chapel.

Sculptural groups in the form of shrines or outdoor chapels were produced in Urbino in the last part of the sixteenth century. The few surviving examples show a wayside altar, with a crucifix and a saint (often St Jerome, St Francis or Mary Magdalene) in prayer in front of it, while angels surround the scene (pl. 213). All known groups are stylistically similar and were probably produced in the Patanazzi family workshop. The chapels are made as if they were integrated into the landscape, like hermitages. These fascinating and little-known maiolica objects are loosely inspired by prototypes created by the Della Robbia family workshop on a slightly larger scale around the first quarter of the sixteenth century.

Such maiolica shrines are listed in the inventory of the Palazzo Ducale of Urbino of 1596: among them are some akin to the example illustrated here: 'A large painted hermitage in relief with a chapel with St Jerome, a crucifix and one angel'.[110] The presence of such objects in a ducal palace, where they were certainly used for private devotion, gives a fascinating insight into the devotional practices at the court.

Votive offerings to a saint or divinity given in fulfilment of a vow or in gratitude or devotion were made in maiolica from the early sixteenth century. Ex-votos in various materials were (and still are) placed in a church or chapel where the worshipper sought aid or wished to give thanks. Maiolica votive plaques show realistic details of life events, from attacks by bulls to falls from horses to robberies. The plaque shown in pl. 214 shows a couple kneeling in front of the Virgin and Child. The man holds a baby in his arms, and a long inscription explains that the plaque was executed in fulfilment of the couple's vow: 'Alessandro Ricci and his wife Francesca are grateful for the healing of their child Giovanni Angelo from a deformity'. Alessandro was a potter from Deruta who probably painted the plaque himself.[111]

Votive plaques are one of the most widespread maiolica wares in Italy. Deruta, Faenza and other centres produced them in large numbers through the seventeenth century and they are still made today.

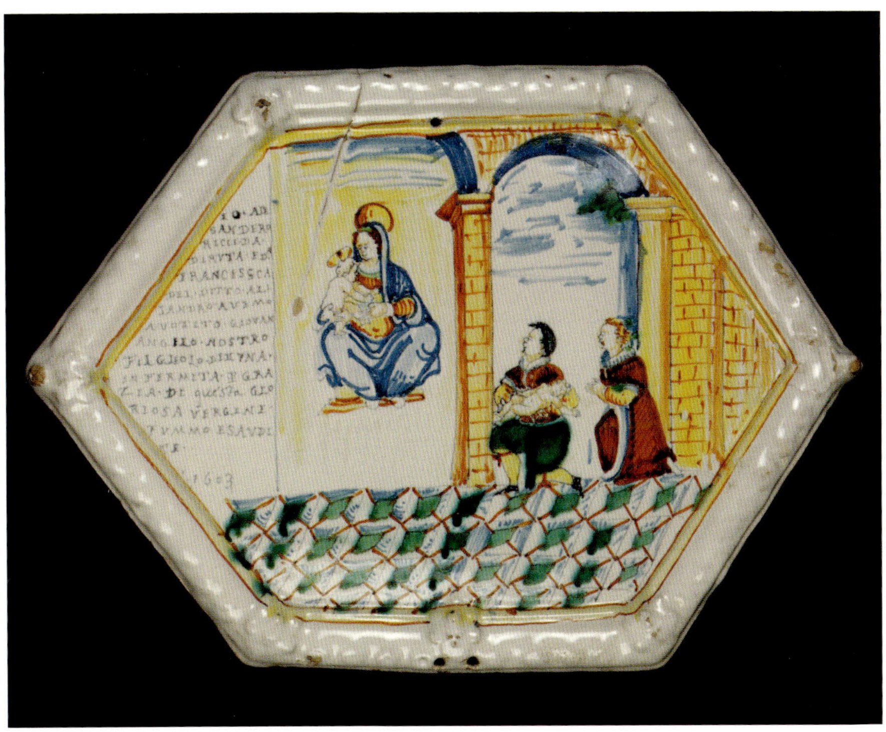

214 Hexagonal votive plaque with a couple holding a baby kneeling before the Virgin and Child
Alessandro Ricci
Deruta, 1603
H: 24 cm, W: 33.4 cm
V&A: 402–1889

Notes

Section 1: The Making of Maiolica

1. Syson & Thornton 2001, p.214.
2. Ray 2000, pp.5–7.
3. Mallet & Dreier 1998, p.12, quotes Dante's *Inferno* XXVIII 82, but Mallet believes that 'maiolica' is derived, in the first place, from *obra de Mallequa*, the term used in Valencia for lustred wares.
4. Wilson 1996, p.36.
5. Piccolpasso 1980, vol.1, pp.xxi–xxiv.
6. Piccolpasso 1980, vol.2, p.xiv.
7. Piccolpasso 1980, vol.2, p.41: for shallow ware, the potter holds the template in his left hand; note that the hands are reversed on the drawing.
8. Piccolpasso 1980, vol.2, p.54; Grigioni 1937, pp.67–8.
9. Piccolpasso does not describe the use of the banding wheel. Grigioni 1937, pp.59–60, lists '2 tornelli per i pittori' in the 1581 inventory of the workshop of Fabio Marchetti and Francesco Dalle Palle in Faenza. Güll 2003, p.412, also lists them in Roman inventories of the 16th century.
10. Piccolpasso 1980, vol.2, p.xvii. Piccolpasso mentions that the wares can also be dipped into the glaze, but Caiger-Smith points out that this could easily damage the layer of tin-glaze.
11. Piccolpasso 1980, vol.2, p.61, calls it the 'White of the most illustrious Duke of Ferrara', but is now more commonly known as Faenza white.
12. Güll 2003, pp.90–1.
13. Grigioni 1937, pp.71–2.
14. Goldthwaite 1989, pp.7–10.
15. For Faenza, Grigioni 1937, p.76; for 16th-century Rome, Güll 2003, pp.92–8, 411–15.
16. Grigioni 1937, p.76.
17. Piccolpasso 1980, vol.2, pp.106–9. Piccolpasso describes how fine wares and ordinary wares are stacked together in the kiln.
18. Mallet 2007, p.31. This document relating to Maestro Giorgio is dated 14 July 1525. There are many other examples of itinerant painters.
19. Fiocco & Gherardi 1994, p.98. During the 15th century, craftsmen were often employed simultaneously in Deruta and Perugia.
20. Mallet 2004, pp.190–1. This practice probably explains why some painters signed their work with their own name as well as the name of the workshop in which it was painted.
21. Mallet 2007, p.13.
22. Goldthwaite 1989, p.20.
23. Ballardini 1915, p.117, quotes 600 or more per month based on the 15th-century account book of Maestro Gentile di Antonia Fornarini.
24. Mallet 1981, p.167.
25. Thornton & Wilson 2009, pp.488–90, cat. 295.
26. Mallet 2007, p.27; Goldthwaite 1989, p.9.
27. Grigioni 1937, p.58.

Section 2: Stylistic Development

1. Conti et al. 1991.
2. Moore Valeri 1984 and 1984B.
3. Spallanzani 2006.
4. Spallanzani 1986, p.166. See Thornton & Wilson 2009, no.27.
5. For Faenza see Ravanelli Guidotti 1998, pp.153–68; for Pesaro, see Ciaroni 2004, pp.37–9, pls on pp.169–70; for Montelupo see Cora 1973, vol.2, pl. 269, fig. 269b; for Siena see Luccarelli 1983.
6. Ravanelli Guidotti 1990.
7. Spallanzani 1994, p.142.
8. Ballardini 1911, p.3, quoting Ranieri's *Bolognese Chronicle*.
9. Bellini & Conti 1964, p.27
10. Dacos 1969, pp.139–50.
11. Rackham 1915.
12. On the problem see Fiocco & Gherardi 2004; on the series see Thornton & Wilson 2009, no. 74.
13. Poke 2001.
14. The group has been traditionally linked with a famous bowl marked as made in the workshop of Zoan Maria in Castel Durante in 1508, though it might have been made elsewhere in the Marches: see Rasmussen 1989, no. 62 and Thornton & Wilson 2009, no. 215.
15. Fiocco & Gherardi 2004, p.10.
16. On the subject of musical instruments and maiolica see Ravanelli Guidotti 2004; see also Chambers & Martineau 1981, cat. 198.
17. Spallanzani 1994.
18. On Benedetto see Luccarelli 1984, Luccarelli 2005.
19. See Rackham 1940, no. 339, for an example with the Cafaggiolo mark perhaps painted by Jacopo.
20. Spallanzani 1994, pp.45–6, 148–9.
21. Ravanelli Guidotti 1996, pp.86–7.
22. Cora & Fanfani 1986, Spallanzani 1994.
23. Alverà Bortolotto 1988, pp.17–30.
24. Tagliente 1529, p.23.
25. On the ornament 'vaghezze e gentilezze' see Ravanelli Guidotti 1998, pp.306–38; on *berettino* glaze, p.306.
26. Wilson 1996, nos 182–3.
27. Grigioni 1937, p.78.
28. On the spread of Faenza white in Italy and abroad see De Pompeis 2010.
29. Shearman 1975.
30. Woodcuts by Jacob of Strasbourg [Jacobus Argentoratensis] to designs by Benedetto Bordon of Padua, published in Venice in 1504.
31. Massing 1990 and Poole 1995, no. 188.
32. Massing in Wilson 1991.
33. On El Frate see Busti & Cocchi 1997, pp.69–70.
34. See *Raphael Invenit* 1985.
35. Ravanelli Guidotti 1990.
36. Syson 2007, no. 81.
37. Vasari 1966–87, vol.5, p.465.
38. Clifford & Mallet 1976, Thornton & Wilson 2009, no. 233.
39. Letter by Paolo Mario, see Gere 1963, p.306, Wilson & Sani 2006–7, vol.2, no. 142.
40. Gere 1963.
41. See for instance Berardi 1984, Mallet 1990, Luccarelli 2002, Wilson 2005.
42. Biganti 2002, pp.58.
43. Mallet 1971.
44. On Nicola see Mallet 2002 and Mallet 2007B.
45. Mallet 2007, pp.27–8, 33–4, Thornton & Wilson 2009, nos 154–5.
46. Mallet 2007.
47. On Xanto see Mallet 2007 with previous bibliography.
48. Triolo 1996, Sani in Mallet 2007.
49. See Bojani 2002, Fiocco & Gherardi 2007.
50. Mallet 2007, pp.39–40.
51. Negroni 1985.
52. Mallet 1979.
53. Wilson in Glaser 2004.
54. Ravanelli Guidotti 1996B
55. Fiocco, Gherardi & Sfeir-Fakhri 2001, no. 1.
56. On Domenego see Wilson 1996, no. 171.

Section 3: Use and Consumption

1. Grigioni 1934.
2. Sangiorgi 1976, pp.48–9, 186–98.
3. Fusco & Corti 2006, doc. 134.
4. Spallanzani 1994, 1997.
5. Messisbugo 1557, see also Grieco in Ajmar-Wollheim & Dennis 2006.
6. On maiolica sets see Mazzucato 1982, Crépin-Leblond & Ennès 1995, Liefkes in Ajmar-Wollheim & Dennis 2006, Brody forthcoming.
7. Goldthwaite 1989.
8. Fusco & Corti 2006, doc. 21.
9. Wilson & Sani 2006–7, p.13; see also Balla & Jékely 2008.
10. Wilson 2004, pp.152–3.
11. Thornton & Wilson 2009, no. 295.
12. Wilson 2003–4.
13. Rackham 1940, no. 285.
14. Ravanelli Guidotti 1990, no. 143, Brody 2000, Ajmar-Wollheim & Dennis 2006, 210–12.
15. Ravanelli Guidotti 1990, no. 147.
16. First published in Palvarini Gobio Casali 1987, pp.111–12, n.29. For a translation of the letter in full and discussion of the set see Thornton & Wilson 2009, nos 143–4.
17. See Mallet in Chambers & Martineau 1981, pp.175–8, Palvarini Gobio Casali 1987,

Thornton & Wilson 2009, nos 143–4.
18. Spallanzani 1994, p.129.
19. Mallet in Chambers & Martineau 1981, p.167.
20. On the set see Drey in Wilson 1991 and Thornton & Wilson 2009, no. 192.
21. Brody 2000.
22. Wilson 2002, in Bojani 2002, pp.125–65.
23. Crépin-Leblond & Ennès 1995, Rasmussen 1989, nos 90–1, Mallet & Dreier 1998, pp.248–9, Thornton & Wilson 2009, no. 174.
24. On the set see Lessmann 1979, pp.178–9, no. 18, Szczepanek 2009, pp.98–9.
25. Ravanelli Guidotti 2000B, Wilson 2000, p.228, Thornton & Wilson 2009, nos 240–1.
26. Spallanzani 1994 and 2010.
27. Cora & Fanfani 1986, Spallanzani 1994.
28. Berti 1997–2003, pp.199–200, 380–4.
29. Spallanzani 1994, p.196.
30. Spallanzani 1994, pp.62, 110–11.
31. Ravanelli Guidotti 1996B, p.164.
32. Montaigne 1946, pp.401–2; see also Goldthwaite 1989, p.20.
33. Giovanni Pontano, *I trattati delle virtù sociali*, Rome, 1965; see also Ajmar in Ajmar Wollheim & Dennis 2006, pp.206–21.
34. See Wilson & Sani 2006–7, cat. 91 for a comparable example.
35. Sangiorgi 1976, pp.188–9.
36. Sangiorgi 1976, p.187 for one mentioned in the Urbino Ducal inventory. On the subject see also Higgott 2004.
37. See Briganti 1903, Fiocco & Gherardi 1981, Ajmar & Thornton 1998, Ravanelli Guidotti 2000, Bayer 2008, pp.68–92, 164–75.
38. Bayer 2008, no. 22b.
39. See Ajmar & Thornton 1998, Ravanelli Guidotti 2000.
40. Passeri 1758.
41. Rackham 1940, no. 554.
42. Busti & Cocchi 2001.
43. On Deruta maiolica and Perugino, see Busti & Cocchi 2004.
44. Bayer 2008, pp.100–2.
45. Ravanelli Guidotti 2000, pp.349–52.
46. Bayer 2008, no. 2.
47. Similar objects were also made in other media: see Syson 2007, no. 52, Ajmar-Wollheim & Dennis 2006, no. 13.6 for an example in the collection made in papier-mâché. Kiln wasters of such maiolica mirror frames have been found in Montelupo: see Berti 1997–2003, vol.3, p.183, figs 324–7.
48. Musacchio in Bayer 2008, nos 42–3, Thornton & Wilson 2009, no. 263, Ajmar-Wollheim & Dennis 2008, p.157, no. 204.
49. On maiolica spindle-whorls see Bellucci 1895, pp.8–14, Briganti 1903.
50. Piccolpasso 1557, 1 fol.10v–11r.
51. Musacchio 1999, p. 92.
52. Spallanzani 2006, doc. 350.
53. 'For Madalena wife of Bartolomeo' at the Louvre, Giacomotti 1974, no. 775; on the subject see Musacchio 1999, pp.91–123.
54. Musacchio 1999, pp. 130.
55. Sangiorgi 1976, p.189, Szczepanek 2009, figs 15–16.
56. Bayer 2008, no. 77.
57. See Thornton 1997, pp.142–67.
58. Spallanzani 2006, docs 127, 153, 244.
59. For other examples of the same prototype see Magnani 2007.
60. Plaster moulds for inkstands have been excavated for example at Montelupo: Berti 1997–2003, vol.3, figs 78–9.
61. Wilson & Sani 2006–7, vol.2, no. 87.
62. Rackham 1940, nos 560, 848, 897, 1042 for examples dated 1524, 1544, 1584 and 1651.
63. Ravanelli Guidotti 1996, pp.86–7; see Rackham 1940, no.1042 for a mid-17th-century example in Faenza white.
64. On the subject see Wilson 1996, p.384; for a signed example of 1584, Poole 1995, nos 435–6.
65. Spallanzani 1994, p.164; see Ravanelli Guidotti 1989, no. 511596 for an example with the cardinal's Baronius arms.
66. See a similarly constructed object also missing drawers at the Bargello, Conti 1971, no. 196.
67. In 1519 and 1522: see Biganti 2002, docs 153, 177.
68. Sangiorgi 1976, pp.186–90.
69. Henderson 2006.
70. On pharmacy jars see Drey 1978, Biscontini Ugolini 1997, Bojani 2005, Berti 2010.
71. For the Loreto jars see Colapinto, Grimaldi & Bettini 1994; for Roccavaldina see Liverani 1991; for Novellara see Ravanelli Guidotti 1994.
72. Spallanzani 2006, doc. 22.
73. Cora 1973, pp.56, 272–5, 288–90; Alinari and Berti in Conti 1991.
74. Wilson & Sani 2006–7, no. 86; Poole 1995, no. 187.
75. Rackham 1940, nos 34, 35, see V&A: 371–1889 and pl. 8
76. Conti et al. 1991, p.108.
77. Rackham 1940, no. 24.
78. See Ravanelli Guidotti 1994, p.36–40 for an example of a 16th-century *ricettario* from the pharmacy at Novellara.
79. Rackham 1915; Thornton & Wilson 2009, nos 248–9, 266.
80. Campori in Vanzolini 1879, vol.2, pp.119–20.
81. Nardelli 2003; see also Mazzucato 2006.
82. Thornton & Wilson 2009, no. 338.
83. Pescara 1989.
84. Wilson 1996, no. 145; Sani 2010, nos 40–1.
85. Biscontini Ugolini 1997, no. 19, Wilson 2002.
86. Leonardi & Moretti 2002.
87. Wilson 2002, appendix 4, doc. 1.
88. Wilson 2002, pp.143, Leonardi & Moretti 2002.
89. On Renaissance maiolica tiles see Lane 1960, ch.5; Graves 2002, ch.3; Mallet 1997; Arbace 1993.
90. See Rackham 1940, no. 184 for an example of this type of tile; on the subject see Donatone 1993, Thornton & Wilson 2009, no. 390.
91. Thornton & Wilson 2009, no. 386.
92. Polverini Gobio Casali 1987, pp.152–70, Thornton 1997, pp.48–9.
93. See Mallet in Chambers & Martineau 1981.
94. Berardi 1984, pp.207–9.
95. Fornari Schianchi 1988, Thornton 1997, p.46.
96. On the Vaselli floor see Ravanelli Guidotti 1988; on the Lando Chapel Alverà Bortolotto 1991.
97. Arbace 1993, Giardini 1996, Thornton & Wilson 2009, no. 382.
98. On the floor see Gardelli 1993, pp.49–55, Fiocco & Gherardi 2004, Thornton & Wilson 2009, no. 375.
99. On the problem see Wilson 1991, Mallet 1997, p.265.
100. Syson 2007, pp.270–84.
101. Miller & Graves 2010.
102. Delucca 1987.
103. Spallanzani 1976.
104. Rackham 1940, nos 149, 156, 168, 263, 267, 275, 277, 278, 628, 799, 995.
105. For Faentine devotional panels see Cecchetti 1984; for Umbrian, Busti & Cocchi 1997, Sani 2005.
106. See Rackham 1940, no. 148 for an example of a popular prototype.
107. On the panel see Busti & Cocchi 2004, no. 15, Sani 2005, pp.70–9.
108. Rackham 1940, no. 628.
109. Ravanelli Guidotti 1998, pp.221–9.
110. 'un eremo grando con un San Girolamo un Christo et un angelo et la Chiesa accima, di rilievo et dipinto': see Sangiorgi 1976, pp.188–9.
111. See Busti in Santantoni Menichelli 2010. I am grateful to Giulio Busti and Clara Menganna for information on the plaque.

Map

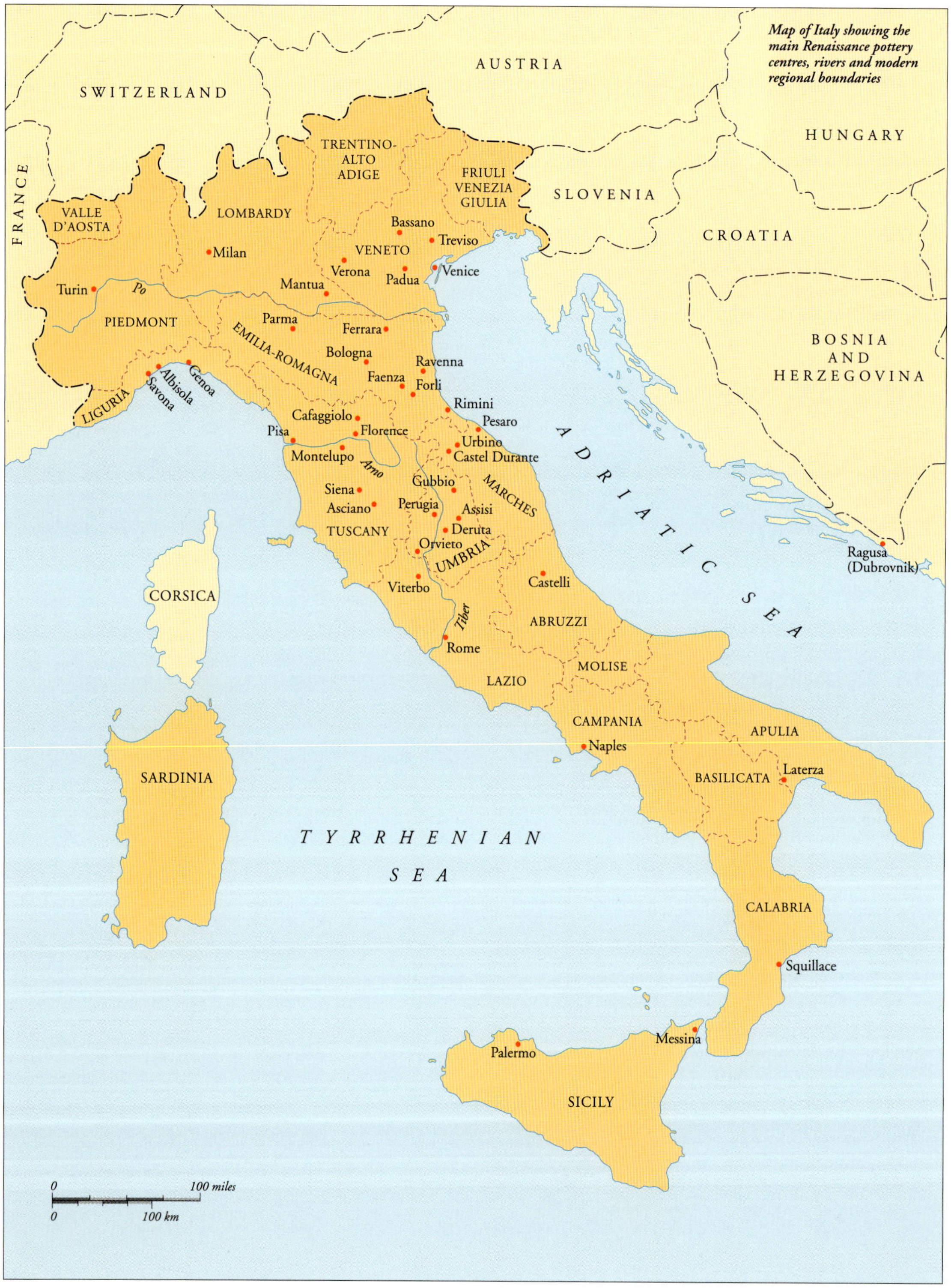
Map of Italy showing the main Renaissance pottery centres, rivers and modern regional boundaries
AUSTRIA
SWITZERLAND
HUNGARY
FRANCE
SLOVENIA
CROATIA
BOSNIA AND HERZEGOVINA
TRENTINO-ALTO ADIGE
FRIULI VENEZIA GIULIA
VALLE D'AOSTA
LOMBARDY
VENETO
PIEDMONT
EMILIA-ROMAGNA
LIGURIA
TUSCANY
MARCHES
UMBRIA
ABRUZZI
MOLISE
LAZIO
CAMPANIA
APULIA
BASILICATA
CALABRIA
CORSICA
SARDINIA
SICILY
ADRIATIC SEA
TYRRHENIAN SEA
Bassano
Treviso
Milan
Verona
Padua
Venice
Turin
Po
Mantua
Parma
Ferrara
Bologna
Ravenna
Faenza
Forlì
Genoa
Albisola
Savona
Rimini
Pesaro
Cafaggiolo
Pisa
Florence
Urbino
Castel Durante
Montelupo
Arno
Gubbio
Siena
Asciano
Perugia
Assisi
Deruta
Orvieto
Viterbo
Castelli
Tiber
Rome
Naples
Laterza
Squillace
Messina
Palermo
Ragusa (Dubrovnik)
0 100 miles
0 100 km

Bibliography

Ajmar, Marta, and Thornton, Dora, 'When is a portrait not a portrait? *Belle Donne* on maiolica and the Renaissance praise of local beauties', in Nicholas Mann and Luke Syson (eds), *The Image of the Individual. Portraits in the Renaissance*, London, 1998, pp.138–53

Ajmar-Wollheim, Marta, and Dennis, Flora (eds), *At Home in Renaissance Italy*, exhib. cat., Victoria and Albert Museum, London, 2006

Alverà Bortolotto, Angelica, *Maiolica a Venezia nel Rinascimento*, Bergamo, 1988

Alverà Bortolotto, Angelica, 'La Cappella Lando e il suo pavimento maiolicato alla luce di ritrovati documenti e di nuove ricerche', *Faenza*, vol.77, 1991, pp.231-6

Ames-Lewis, Francis, 'Nicola da Urbino and Raphael', *Burlington Magazine*, vol.130, 1988, pp.690–2

Antichi documenti sulla ceramica di Castelli: atti del convegno di Castelli, August 1984, Castelli, 1985

Arbace, Luciana, *Il conoscitore di maioliche italiane del rinascimento*, Milan, 1992

Arbace, Luciana, *Maioliche di Castelli: La Raccolta Acerbo*, Ferrara, 1993

Ausenda, Raffaella (ed.), *Musei e Gallerie di Milano, Museo d'Arti Applicate: Le ceramiche*, vol.1, Milan, 2000

Balla, Gabriella and Jèkely, Zsombor, *The Dowry of Beatrice: Italian Maiolica Art and the Court of King Matthias*, exhib. cat., Museum of Applied Arts, Budapest, 2008

Ballardini, Gaetano, 'Per la storia della ceramica', *Il Resto del Carlino*, 13 gennaio 1911

Ballardini, Gaetano, 'La vacchetta dei conti di maestro Gentile di Antonio Fornarini, pittore e maiolicaro faentino della seconda metà del Quattrocento', *Faenza*, vol.3, 1915, pp.113–18, with the text of the book as an appendix to the volume

Balzani, Serena, and Regni, Marina, 'Per la storia della ceramica di Casteldurante: lo stato della ricerca sul fondo *Notarile*', *Faenza*, vol.86, nos 1–3, 2000, pp.154–76

Balzani, Serena, and Regni, Marina, *Vasai e pittori a Casteldurante nei primi due decenni del secolo XVI. Nuovi apporti documentari*, Accademia Raffaello Urbino, Collana di studi e testi 21, Urbino, 2004

Bayer, Andrea (ed.), *Art and Love in Renaissance Italy*, exhib. cat., Metropolitan Museum of Art, New York & Kimbell Art Museum, Fort Worth, 2008

Bellucci, Giuseppe, *Usi nuziali nell'Umbria, nel giorno degli sponsali Taticchi-Meniconi Bracceschi*, Perugia, 1895

Berardi, Paride, *L'antica maiolica di Pesaro*, Florence, 1984

Berti, Fausto, *Storia della ceramica di Montelupo*, Montelupo, 1997–2003

Berti, Fausto, *La farmacia storica fiorentina: I fornimenti in maiolica di Montelupo (secc. XV–XVIII)*, Florence, 2010

Biganti, Tiziana, *Maestro Giorgio Andreoli nei documenti eugubini (Regesti 1488–1575): Un contributo alla storia della ceramica nel Cinquecento*, Florence, 2002

Biscontini Ugolini, Grazia (ed.), *I vasi da farmacia nella collezione Bayer*, Pisa & Milan, 1997

Bojani, Gian Carlo, 'Ceramiche', in Giovanni Mariacher and Gian Carlo Bojani, *Vetri e ceramiche*, Edizioni Museo Civico, Piacenza, 1985

Bojani, Gian Carlo (ed.), *I Della Rovere nell'Italia delle corti. Atti del convegno di Urbania 1999*, vol.4, *Arte della maiolica*, Urbino & Urbania, 2002

Bojani, Gian Carlo (ed.), *La maiolica italiana del Cinquecento. Il lustro eugubino e l'istoriato del ducato di Urbino. Atti del convegno di studi, Gubbio, 21, 22, 23 settembre 1998*, Florence, 2002 [B]

Bojani, Gian Carlo, 'Per un progetto sforzesco pesarese', *CeramicAntica*, vol.15, no.2, February 2005, pp.6–9

Briganti, Francesco, *Le coppe amatorie del sec. XVI nelle maioliche di Deruta*, Perugia, 1903

Brody, Michael, ' "Terra d'Urbino tutta dipinta a paesi con l'armi de' Salviati": the *paesi* service in the 1583 inventory of Jacopo di Alamanno Salviati (1537–1586)', *Faenza*, vol.86, nos 4–6, 2000, pp.30–46

Busti, Giulio, and Cocchi, Franco, *Maestri ceramisti e ceramiche di Deruta*, Deruta, 1997

Busti, Giulio, and Cocchi, Franco, *Museo Regionale della Ceramica di Deruta. Ceramiche policrome, a lustro e terrecotte di Deruta dei secoli XV e XVI*, Perugia & Milan, 1999

Busti, Giulio, and Cocchi, Franco, *Dulce est amare: Ceramiche tradizionali a Deruta a soggetto amoroso*, exhib. cat., Museo Regionale della Ceramica, Deruta, 2001

Busti, Giulio, and Cocchi, Franco (eds), *La ceramica umbra al tempo di Perugino*, exhib. cat., Deruta, 2004

Cecchetti, Maria, *Targhe devozionali dell' Emilia-Romagna*, Catalogo generale del Museo Internazionale delle Ceramiche in Faenza, vol.1, Faenza 1984, 2nd edn 2005

Chambers, David, and Martineau, Jane, *Splendours of the Gonzaga*, exhib. cat., Victoria & Albert Museum, London, 1981

Ciaroni, Andrea (con testi di Massimo Moretti e Paolo Piovaticci), *Maioliche del Quattrocento a Pesaro, Frammenti di Storia dell'arte ceramica dalla bottega dei Fedeli*, Florence, 2004

Cioci, Francesco, 'I Della Rovere di Senigallia e alcune testimonianze ceramiche', *Faenza*, vol.68, 1982, pp.251–60

Clifford, Timothy, and Mallet, J.V.G., 'Battista Franco as a designer for maiolica', *Burlington Magazine*, vol.118, 1976, pp.387–410

Colapinto, Leonardo, Grimaldi, Floriano, and Bettini, Alessandro, *L'antica spezieria della Santa Casa di Loreto: L'arte della ceramica nella farmacia*, Bologna, 1994

Conti, Giovanni, *Museo Nazionale di Firenze. Palazzo del Bargello: Catalogo delle maioliche*, Florence, 1971

Conti, Giovanni et al., *Zaffera et similia nella maiolica italiana*, Viterbo, 1991

Cora, Galeazzo, *Storia della maiolica di Firenze e del contado: Secoli XIV e XV*, Florence, 1973

Cora, Galeazzo, and Fanfani, Angiolo, *La porcellana dei Medici*, Milan, 1986

Crépin-Leblond, Thierry, and Ennès, Pierre, *Le dressoir du prince*, exhib. cat., Musée National de la Renaissance, Ecouen, 1995

Dacos, Nicole, *La découverte de la Domus Aurea et la formation des grotesques à la Renaissance*, Studies of the Warburg Institute 31, London & Leiden, 1969

Delucca, Oreste, *La famiglia riminese Cinquedenti nel Quattrocento, Romagna Arte e Storia*, Romanga, 1987

De Pompeis, Vincenzo (ed.), *La maiolica italiana di stile compendiario: I bianchi*, exhib. cat., Ascoli Piceno, Faenza & Rome, 2010

Donatone, Guido, *La maiolica napoletana del rinascimento*, Naples, 1993

Drey, R.E.A., *Apothecary Jars*, London, 1978

Fiocco, Carola, and Gherardi, Gabriella, 'Vasellame amoroso e neoplatonismo a Faenza', *Romagna arte e storia* vol.1, no.2, 1981, pp. 68–77

Fiocco, Carola, and Gherardi, Gabriella, *Ceramiche umbre dal Medioevo allo Storicismo*, Catalogo generale del Museo Internazionale delle Ceramiche in Faenza, vol.5, 2 parts, Faenza, 1988–9

Fiocco, Carola, and Gherardi, Gabriella, *La ceramica di Deruta dal XIII al XVIII secolo*, Perugia, 1994

Fiocco, Carola, and Gherardi, Gabriella, 'Lustri precoci di Gubbio', *Faenza*, vol.82, 1996, pp.5–11

Fiocco, Carola, and Gherardi, Gabriella, 'Ceramica forlivese della prima metà del '500: 'Petrus'', *Keramos*, vol.186, 2004, pp.9–36

Fiocco, Carola, and Gherardi, Gabriella, 'La bottega di Maestro Giorgio Andreoli e il problema dei lustri a Urbino', *Faenza*, vol.93, 2007, pp.299–308

Fiocco, Carola, Gherardi, Gabriella, and Sfeir-Fakhri, Liliane, *Majoliques italiennes du Musée des Arts Décoratifs de Lyon. Collection Gillet*, Dijon, 2001

Fontana, Maria Vittoria, 'L'influence islamique sur la production de céramique à Venise et Padoue', in *Venise et l'Orient*, exhib. cat., Institut du Monde Arabe, Paris, 2006, pp.281–93

Fornari Schianchi, Lucia, *Ai piedi della Badessa*, Parma, 1988

Fusco, Laurie, and Corti, Gino, *Lorenzo de' Medici collector and antiquarian*, Cambridge, 2006

Gardelli, Giuliana, *Maiolica per l'architettura: Pavimenti e rivestimenti rinascimentali di Urbino e del suo territorio*, Urbino, 1993

Gere, John A., 'Taddeo Zuccaro as a designer for Maiolica', *Burlington Magazine*, vol.105, 1963, pp.306-15

Giacomotti, Jeanne, *Catalogue des majoliques des musées nationaux*, Paris, 1974

Giardini, Claudio, 'Su Nicola da Urbino ed alcune sue maioliche nei Musei Civici di Pesaro', *CeramicAntica*, vol.1, no. 9, October 1991, pp.32–43

Giardini, Claudio (ed.), *Immagini dai Piattelletti*, Archeoclub d'Italia, Sede di Fano, 1996

Glaser, Silvia (ed.), *Italienische Fayencen der Renaissance: Ihre Spuren in internationalen Museumssammlungen*, Wissenschaftliche Beibände zum Anzeiger des germanischen Nationalmuseums, vol.22, Nuremberg, 2004

Goldthwaite, Richard A.,'The economic and social world of Italian renaissance maiolica', *Renaissance Quarterly*, vol.42, 1989, pp.1–32 [translated into Italian in *Faenza*, vol.83, 1997, pp.176–204]

Governale, Antonello, *Rectoverso – La maiolica siciliana*, Palermo, 1986

Graves, Alun, *Tiles and tilework*, London, 2002

Grigioni, Carlo, 'Documenti: serie faentina – I Calamelli maiolicari di Faenza', *Faenza*, vol.22, 1934, pp. 50–4, 88–90, 143–53

Grigioni, Carlo, 'La bottega del vasaio del bel tempo', *Faenza*, vol.25, 1937, pp.51–88 [and separately published in Piccola Biblioteca del Museo delle Ceramiche in Faenza, 4].

Güll, Paolo, *L'industrie du quotidien: production, importations et consommation de la céramique à Rome entre XIVe et XVIe siècle*, Rome: École française de Rome, 2003

Henderson, John, *The Renaissance Hospital*, New Haven & London, 2006

Hess, Catherine, *Maiolica in the Making: The Gentili/Barnabei Archive*, Bibliographies & Dossiers of the Getty Research Institute, Los Angeles, 1999

Higgott, Suzanne, 'Raffraîchissoir à vin, fabriquée dans l'atelier de Flaminio Fontana, Urbino, 1574', *L'Estampille/L'Objet d'Art*, vol.379, April 2003, pp.85–6, fiche no.379B

Holcroft, Alison, 'Francesco Xanto Avelli and Petrarch', *Journal of the Warburg and Courtauld Institutes*, vol.51, 1988, pp.225–34

Lane, Arthur, *Victoria and Albert Museum: A Guide to the Collection of Tiles*, 2nd edn, London, 1960

Leonardi, Corrado, and Moretti, Massimo, *I Picchi maiolicari da Casteldurante a Roma*, Urbania, 2002

Lessmann, Johanna, *Herzog Anton Ulrich-Museum Braunschweig, Italienische Majolika, Katalog der Sammlung*, Brunswick, 1979

Litta, Pompeo et al., *Celebri Famiglie Italiane*, Milan & Turin, 1819–1923

Liverani, Francesco, 'Sei maioliche del rinascimento italiano: preliminari allo studio delle iscrizioni nell'istoriato ceramico', in Wilson 1991, pp.46–50

Luccarelli, Mario, 'Contributo alla conoscenza della maiolica senese, (1) Il pavimento della Cappella Bichi in S. Agostino, (2) Fedele da Urbino', *Faenza*, vol.69, 1983, pp.197–201

Luccarelli, Mario, 'Contributo alla conoscenza della maiolica senese. Il pavimento della cappella Docci nella chiesa di S. Francesco a Siena', *Faenza*, vol.70, 1984, pp.391–7

Luccarelli, Mario, 'Contributo alla conoscenza della maiolica senese', *CeramicAntica* vol.12, no.10, November 2002, pp.32–61

Luccarelli, Mario, 'Inventario dele masarizie dela butiga dele Rede di benedeto da faeza orcolaio', *Faenza*, vol.91, 2005, nos 1–6, pp.193–202

Magnani, Romolo, 'Un San Giorgio 'orientale' da Ferrara ad Hannover', *CeramicAntica*, vol.186, 2007, p.7–13

Mallet, J.V.G., 'Maiolica at Polesden Lacey' (3 parts), *Apollo*, vol.92, 1970, pp.260–5, 340–5; vol.93, 1971, pp.170–83

Mallet, J.V.G., 'Francesco Urbini in Gubbio and Deruta', *Faenza*, vol.65, 1979, pp.279–96

Mallet, J.V.G., 'Mantua and Urbino: Gonzaga Patronage of Maiolica', *Apollo*, vol.14, 1981, pp.398–402

Mallet, J.V.G., ' "In Botega di Maestro Guido Durantino in Urbino"', *Burlington Magazine*, vol.129, 1987, pp.284–98

Mallet, J.V.G., Contribution on 1503 dish to 'Acquisitions in the Victoria and Albert Museum's Department of Ceramics and Glass 1987–89', *Burlington Magazine*, vol.132, 1990, pp.384–5

Mallet, J.V.G., 'Tiled floors and court designers in Mantua and Northern Italy', in Cesare Mozzarelli, Robert Oresko, and Leandro Ventura (eds), *The Court of the Gonzaga in the Age of Mantegna: 1450–1550*, Atti del Convegno London/Mantua,1992, Rome, 1997, pp.253–72

Mallet, J.V.G., 'Considerazioni su Nicola da Urbino e le fonti delle sue composizioni su maiolica', in Bojani 2002, pp.89–99

Mallet, J.V.G., 'Compendiario grotesque: the evidence of two basins at Waddesdon Manor', in Glaser 2004, pp.181–97

Mallet, J.V.G., with contributions by Giovanna Hendel and Elisa Paola Sani, *Xanto: Pottery-painter, Poet, Man of the Italian Renaissance*, exhib. cat., Wallace Collection, London, 2007

Mallet, J.V.G., 'Nicola da Urbino and Francesco Xanto Avelli', *Faenza*, vol.93, 2007, pp.199–250 [B]

Mallet, J.V.G. and Dreier, Franz Adrian, *The Hockemeyer Collection: Maiolica and Glass*, Bremen, 1998

Massing, Jean Michel, *Du texte à l'image: La Calomnie d'Apelle et son iconographie*, Strasbourg, 1990

Mazzucato, Otto, 'Sulla definizione del "servizio da tavola"', *Atti del XV Convegno Internazionale della Ceramica, Albisola 1982*, 1982, pp.19–27.

Mazzucato, Otto, 'Simboli alchemici per indicare in libbre ed once i prodotti della farmacopea', *CeramicAntica*, vol.16, no. 8, September 2006, pp.28–39

Messisbugo, Cristoforo da, *Banchetti, composizioni di vivande e apparecchio generale*, 1557, reprint Neri Pozza, 1992

Miller, Elizabeth, and Graves, Alun, 'Rethinking the Petrucci pavement', in Peta Motture and Michelle O'Malley (eds), *Rethinking Renaissance Objects: Design, Function and Meaning, Renaissance Studies*, vol.24, no.1, 2010, pp.94–118

Montaigne, Michel Eyquem de, *Journal de Voyage en Italie par la Suisse et l'Allemagne en 1580–1581*, ed. C. Dédéyan, Paris, 1946

Moore Valeri, Anna, 'Florentine "Zaffera a rilievo" maiolica: a new look at the "oriental influence"', *Archeologia medievale*, vol.11, 1984, pp.477–500

Moore Valeri, Anna, 'La mezzaluna dentata: le sue origini ed il suo sviluppo', *Faenza*, vol.70, 1984, pp.375–80 [B]

Musacchio, Jacqueline Marie, *The Art and Ritual of Childbirth in Renaissance Italy*, New Haven & London, 1999

Nardelli, Giuseppe Maria, 'L'importanza del peso nei contenitori da spezieria', *CeramicAntica*, vol.13, no.11, December 2003, pp.44–53

Negroni, Franco, 'Nicolò Pellipario: ceramista fantasma', *Notizie da Palazzo Albani* (Urbino), vol.14, no.1, pp.13-20

Norman, A.V.B., 'A note on the so-called Casa Pirota mark', *Burlington Magazine*, vol.111, 1969, pp.447–8

Palvarini Gobio Casali, Mariarosa, *La ceramica a Mantova*, Ferrara,1987

Passeri, Giambattista, *Histoire des peintures sur majoliques faites à Pesaro*, 1st edn 1758, republished Paris 1853 [also in Vanzolini 1879, vol.1]

Pescara 1989. Various authors, *Le maioliche cinquecentesche di Castelli. Una grande stagione artistica ritrovata*, Pescara, 1989

Pescara 1990. *Castelli e la maiolica cinquecentesca italiana*. Atti del convegno in Pescara, 22–25 April 1989, Pescara, 1990

Piccolpasso, Cipriano, *The Three Books of the Potter's Art*, ed. Ronald Lightbown and Alan Caiger-Smith, London, 1980

Poke, Christopher, 'Jacques Androuet Ducerceau's "Petites Grotesques" as a source for Urbino maiolica decoration', *Burlington Magazine*, vol.143, 2001, pp.332–44

Poole, Julia, *Italian maiolica and incised slipware in the Fitzwilliam Museum, Cambridge*, Cambridge, 1995

Rackham, Bernard, 'A new chapter in the history of Italian maiolica', *Burlington Magazine*, vol.27, 1915, pp.28–35, 49–55

Rackham, Bernard, *Victoria and Albert Museum: Catalogue of Italian Maiolica*, London, 1940 [re-issued with additions by J.V.G. Mallet, 1977]

Raphael Invenit. Stampe da Raffaello nelle collezioni dell'Istituto Nazionale per la Grafica (catalogo di Grazia Bernini Pezzini, Stefania Massari, and Simonetta Prosperi Valenti Rodinò), exhib. cat., Istituto Nazionale per la Grafica, Rome, 1985

Rasmussen, Jörg, *The Robert Lehman Collection. 10: Italian Majolica*, Metropolitan Museum of Art, New York, 1989

Ravanelli Guidotti, Carmen, *Il pavimento della Cappella Vaselli in San Petronio a Bologna*, Bologna, 1988

Ravanelli Guidotti, Carmen, 'Maioliche', in *Arti del Medioevo e del Rinascimento. Omaggio ai Carrand*, exhib. cat., Museo Nazionale del Bargello, Florence, 1989, pp.294–303

Ravanelli Guidotti, Carmen, 'La ceramica a Faenza nell'età dei Manfredi: botteghe, produzione comune e vasellame celebrativo', in various authors, *Faenza nell'età dei Manfredi*, Faenza, 1990, pp.149–203

Ravanelli Guidotti, Carmen, *La farmacia dei Gesuiti di Novellara*, Faenza, 1994

Ravanelli Guidotti, Carmen, 'Le *Metamorfosi* 'vulgari' d'Ovidio sulla maiolica italiana', in Hermann Walter and Hans-Jürgen Horn (eds), *Die Rezeption der Metamorphosen des Ovid in der Neuzeit: der antike Mythos in Text und Bild*, Proceedings of the International Symposium, Bad Homburg 1991, Berlin, 1996, pp.85–97

Ravanelli Guidotti, Carmen, *Baldassarre Manara faentino Pittore di maioliche nel Cinquecento*, Ferrara, 1996 [B]

Ravanelli Guidotti, Carmen, *Thesaurus di opere della tradizione di Faenza*, Faenza, 1998

Ravanelli Guidotti, Carmen, *Delle gentili donne di Faenza. Studio del 'ritratto' sulla ceramica faentina del Rinascimento*, Ferrara, 2000

Ravanelli Guidotti, Carmen, 'Le 'credenze' nuziali di Alfonso II d'Este', in Trevisani 2000, pp.30–53 [B]

Ravanelli Guidotti, Carmen, *Musica di smalto. Maioliche fra XVI e XVIII secolo del Museo Internazionale delle Ceramiche in Faenza*, exhib. cat., Galleria degli Uffizi, Florence 2004 [also a new edition, Parma, 2006]

Ray, Anthony, *Spanish Pottery 1249–1898 with a catalogue of the collection in the Victoria and Albert Museum*, London, 2000

Sangiorgi, Fert, *Documenti urbinati: inventari del Palazzo Ducale (1582–1631)*, Accademia Raffaello, Collana di Studi e Testi 4, Urbino, 1976

Sani, Elisa Paola, *La maiolica rinascimentale in Umbria. Le targhe devozionali fra arti figurative e ceramica*, Tesi di Specializzazione in Storia delle Arti Minori, Università degli Studi di Siena, 2005

Sani, Elisa Paola, '"Not in Rackham": Italian Renaissance maiolica in the Victoria and Albert Museum, Part 1', *Keramos*, vol.210, October 2010, pp.51–96

Sannipoli, Ettore,'Sulle tecniche di foggiatura delle 'coppe abborchiate'', *L'Eugubino*, no.4, 1999, pp.19–21

Santantoni Menichelli, Antonio, *Ex Voto: Arte e Fede nel Santuario della Madonna del Bagno in Casalina*, Perugia, 2010

Satolli, Alberto, 'Le fabbriche orvietane di ceramica nel '400 e nel '500', in Pescara 1990, pp.235

Shearman, John, 'The Florentine entrata of Leo X', *Journal of the Warburg and Courtauld Institutes*, vol.38, 1975, pp.136–54

Spallanzani, Marco, 'Sull'iscrizione del tondo di Andrea di Bono Boni', *Faenza*, vol.62, 1976, pp.86–9

Spallanzani, Marco, *Ceramiche alla Corte dei Medici nel Cinquecento*, Modena, 1994

Spallanzani, Marco, 'Maioliche di Valenza e di Montezupo' in *Una Casa Pisana del 1480*, Faenza, 1986, pp.164–70

Spallanzani, Marco, *Maioliche ispano-moresche a Firenze nel Rinascimento*, Florence, 2006

Spallanzani, Marco, 'The myth of "Guidobaldo's service" at the Bargello Museum', *Keramos*, vol.210, October 2010, pp.81–96

Syson, Luke, and Thornton, Dora, *Objects of Virtue: Art in Renaissance Italy*, London, 2001

Syson, Luke et al. (eds), *Renaissance Siena: Art for a City*, exhib. cat., National Gallery London, 2007

Szczepanek, Gudrun, *Fürstliche Majolika: Das Majolika-Service für Herzog Albrecht V. von Bayern*, Schriftenreihe der Gesellschaft der Keramikfreunde e. V., vol.3, Munich, 2009

Tagliente, Giovanni Antonio, *Esemplario nuovo che insegna a le donne a cuscire, a raccamare et a disegnare a ciascuno, et anchora e di grande utilità ad ogni artista, per esser il disegno a ogniuno necessario*, 1529

Thornton, Dora, *The Scholar in his Study*, New Haven & London, 1997

Thornton, Dora, and Wilson, Timothy, *Italian Renaissance Ceramics: A catalogue of the British Museum collection*, London, 2009

Trevisani, Filippo (ed.), *Le ceramiche dei Duchi d'Este. Dalla Guardaroba al Collezionismo*, exhib. cat., Palazzo Ducale, Sassuolo 2000

Triolo, Julia, *The Armorial Maiolica of Francesco Xanto Avelli*, PhD thesis, Pennsylvania State University (University Microfilms, Michigan, no. 9628192), 1996

Vanzolini, Giuliano (ed.), *Istorie delle fabbriche di majoliche metaurensi*, Pesaro, 1879

Vasari, Giorgio, *Le vite de' più eccellenti pittori scultori e architetti nelle redazioni del 1550 e 1568*, ed. Rosanna Bettarini and Paola Barocchi, Florence, 1966–87

Watson, Wendy, *Italian Renaissance Maiolica from the William A. Clark Collection*, exhib. cat., Corcoran Gallery of Art, Washington, D.C., and Mount Holyoke College Art Museum, 1986

Wilson, Timothy, 'Maiolica in Renaissance Venice', *Apollo*, vol.125, 1987, pp.184–9

Wilson, Timothy (ed.), *Italian Renaissance Pottery. Papers written in association with a colloquium at the British Museum*, London, 1991

Wilson, Timothy, *Italian Maiolica of the Renaissance*, Milan, 1996

Wilson, Timothy, Catalogue entries on Urbino maiolica in Ausenda 2000, pp.182–97, 210–39

Wilson, Timothy, 'La maiolica a Castel Durante e ad Urbino fra il 1535 e il 1565: alcuni corredi stemmati', in Bojani 2002, pp.125–65

Wilson, Timothy, 'Il servizio siglato 'S' eseguito nella bottega di Maestro Giorgio negli anni 1524–25', in Bojani 2002B, pp.113–24 [B]

Wilson Timothy, 'Faenza maiolica services of the 1520s for the Florentine nobility', in Alan Chong, Donatella Pegazzano, and Dimitrios Zikos (eds), *Raphael, Cellini & a Renaissance Banker: The Patronage of Bindo Altoviti*, exhib. cat., Isabella Stewart Gardner Museum, Boston, and Museo Nazionale del Bargello Florence, 2003–4, pp.174–86, 393–4

Wilson, Timothy, 'Il ruolo di Deruta nello sviluppo della maiolica istoriata', in Busti & Cocchi 2004, pp.38–49

Wilson, Timothy, 'The Maiolica-Painter Francesco Durantino: Mobility and Collaboration in Urbino "istoriato"', in Glaser 2004, pp.111–45

Wilson, Timothy, 'Some *incunabula* of *istoriato*-painting from Pesaro', *Faenza*, vol.91, 2005, nos 1–6, pp.8–24

Wilson, Timothy, and Sani, Elisa Paola (with the collaboration for vol.2 of Carola Fiocco, Gabriella Gherardi, Marino Marini, and Claudio Paolinelli), *Le maioliche rinascimentali nelle collezioni della Fondazione Cassa di Risparmio di Perugia*, 2 vols, Perugia, 2006–7

Index